Alfred Pletsch (Hrsg.): Ethnicity in Canada

Gedruckt bei Wenzel

MARBURGER GEOGRAPHISCHE SCHRIFTEN

Herausgeber: C. Schott
Schriftleiter: A. Pletsch

Heft 96

Alfred Pletsch (Hrsg.)

Ethnicity in Canada
– International Examples and Perspectives –
(Kanada Projekt III)

Marburg/Lahn 1985

Im Selbstverlag des Geographischen Instituts der Universität Marburg

ISSN 0341-9290
ISBN 3-88353-020-4

Inhalt

Seite

Alfred Hecht/Ludger Müller-Wille/Alfred Pletsch:
Ethnic Aspects of Central Canada - an Introduction 1

René König:
Cultural Interplay and Political Anthropology: The Navajo Case 15

Tom G. Svensson:
Basic Anthropological Perspectives in the Study of Ethnicity 30

William C. Wonders:
Native Ethnicity in the Canadian North - a Geographer's
Perspective 51

Edward M. Bennett:
Indian and Federal Government Relationship in Canada: The Constitution and the Mental Well-Being of Indian People in Northwestern Ontario 66

Peter R. Gerber:
Canada's Indians: from "bands" to "First Nations" 80

Claudia Notzke:
Development Problems of Southern Albertan Indian Reserves 90

Ludger Müller-Wille:
Changing Inuit Ethnicity in Canada 102

Hansjürgen Müller-Beck:
Das Problem der archäologischen und historischen Kontinuität
im Gebiet der Kupfer-Inuit 108

Marjut and Pekka Aikio:
Sami and Ethnicity Problems in Finland............................. 121

Robert Omnès:
L'Ethnie Bretonne en France et ses problèmes d'aujourd'hui 134

Jean-Michel Lacroix:
Recent Trends in Immigration Policy in Canada: Some Remarks on
the 1981 Census 147

Eric Waddell:
Les Québécois et le continent, ou la transformation progressive
d'une identité construite en identité réelle 155

Alfred Pletsch:
French and English Settlement in the Eastern Townships (Québec) -
Conflict or Coexistence 164

Martin Schulte:
L'espace social des francophones et des anglophones dans une
communauté rurale des Cantons de l'Est (Québec) 184

Alfred Hecht:
Ethnic Groups as Charter Groups in Ontario, Canada 199

Bradley H. Baltensperger:
Germans on the Great Plains: Environment and Acculturation 220

Inge Vestweber:
Les Allemands à Montréal - intégration ou ségrégation d'une
minorité ethnique 233

Martti Grönfors:
Gypsies as a Visible Minority in Finland. The Proactive
Policing of an Ethnic Minority 246

Robert G. Sharpe:
Visible Ethnic Minorities in Ontario and Toronto 256

Roland Vogelsang:
Visible Minorities in Canada: Problems in the Investigation and
Analysis of Non-White Immigrants 268

Peter Wolff:
Haitians and Anglophone West Indians in the Ethnic and Socio-
Economic Structure of Montreal 286

Vorwort

In der Zeit vom 11. bis 16. Dezember 1984 fand am Fachbereich Geographie der Philipps-Universität Marburg ein Symposium unter dem Titel: "Ethnicity in Canada: Socio-Economic and Spatial Perspectives and Comparisons with other Northern Nations" statt. Die Veranstaltung, an der rund 40 Teilnehmer aus acht Nationen teilnahmen, stellte offiziell den Abschluß eines Forschungsprojektes dar, das, mit Unterstützung der STIFTUNG VOLKSWAGENWERK, gemeinsam mit den beiden kanadischen Kollegen Alfred Hecht, Wilfrid Laurier University Waterloo/Ont. und Ludger Müller-Wille, McGill University Montreal in den Jahren 1981 bis 1984 von Marburg aus durchgeführt wurde. Über die Ergebnisse der Arbeitsgruppe Montreal wurde in den MARBURGER GEOGRAPHISCHEN SCHRIFTEN Heft 89, über die der Arbeitsgruppe Waterloo in der gleichen Reihe in Heft 92 ausführlich berichtet. Weitere Ergebnisse werden in diesem Band vorgestellt, wobei in einem einleitenden Beitrag die Breite des Forschungsprojektes noch einmal skizziert, und in einer Literaturübersicht auf die zahlreichen Veröffentlichungen, die im Zusammenhang mit dem Projekt erschienen sind, hingewiesen wird. Obwohl noch nicht alle begonnenen Untersuchungen des Projektes abgeschlossen sind, konnten im Rahmen des Marburger Symposiums doch wichtige Teile der erarbeiteten Ergebnisse einem breiten wissenschaftlichen Forum zur Diskussion gestellt werden. Da die Ethnizitäts-Forschung als Forschungsgegenstand der Geographie noch sehr jung ist, war es das Bestreben der Veranstalter, eine interdisziplinäre Arbeitsgruppe zusammenzuführen. Dieses Bestreben war zweifellos sinnvoll und nützlich, wie die intensiven Diskussionen während und am Rande des Symposiums zeigten. Daß die verschiedenen Beiträge in Methode und Sichtweisen sehr heterogen sein würden, war zu erwarten und lag in der Absicht der Veranstalter. Diese Heterogenität spiegelt sich auch in diesem Band wider, in dem, mit einer drucktechnisch begründeten Ausnahme, alle Vorträge aufgenommen werden konnten. Um die Gliederung des Bandes verständlicher zu machen, sei hier kurz der Ablauf der Veranstaltung skizziert. Das Symposium untergliederte sich in folgende Arbeitsabschnitte:

Section 1: Key-Notes on General Aspects of Ethnicity Research (Leiter: Karl Lenz, Berlin)
Referenten:
René König, Soziologe, Köln
Tom G. Svensson, Anthropologe, Oslo
William C. Wonders, Geograph, Edmonton

Section 2: Indigenous Peoples (Leiter: Hansjürgen Müller-Beck, Tübingen)
Referenten:
Edward M. Bennett, Psychologe, Waterloo/Ont.
Peter R. Gerber, Ethnologe, Zürich
Claudia Notzke, Geographin, Düsseldorf/Lethbridge
Ludger Müller-Wille, Ethnologe und Geograph, Montreal
Hansjürgen Müller-Beck, Frühgeschichte und Jägerische Archäologie, Tübingen

Section 3: Ethnicity and Power Relations (Leiter: W. v. Bredow, Marburg)
Referenten:
Marjut Aikio, Ethnologin und Journalistin, Rovaniemi
Horst Bronny, Geograph, Bochum
Robert Omnès, Hispanologe und Historiker, Brest
Jean-Michel Lacroix, Kanadist, Bordeaux

Section 4: Ethnicity and Power Relations (Leiter: Alfred Pletsch, Marburg)
Referenten:
Eric Waddell, Geograph, Québec
Alfred Pletsch, Geograph, Marburg
Martin Schulte, Geograph, Marburg
Alfred Hecht, Geograph, Waterloo/Ont.
Bradley H. Baltensperger, Social Sciences, Houghton/Michigan
Inge Vestweber, Geographin, Marburg

Section 5: Visible Minorities (Leiter: Eckart Ehlers, Marburg)
           Referenten:
           Martti Grönfors, Soziologe, Helsinki
           Robert G. Sharpe, Geograph, Toronto
           Roland Vogelsang, Geograph, Paderborn
           Peter Wolff, Geograph, Marburg

Es ist mir ein aufrichtiges Bedürfnis, allen zu danken, die zum Gelingen des Symposiums - sei es durch wissenschaftliche Beiträge, durch Hilfe bei der Organisation und Durchführung oder bei der Betreuung der Gäste - beigetragen haben. Den Referenten danke ich für die Bereitwilligkeit, ihre Manuskripte für eine Veröffentlichung in den MARBURGER GEOGRAPHISCHEN SCHRIFTEN zur Verfügung zu stellen und Frau Helene Fett für deren Reinschrift und Herstellung der Druckvorlagen.

Besonderer Dank gebührt aber auch denjenigen, die durch ideelle und materielle Hilfe die Durchführung des Symposiums und die Drucklegung dieses Bandes ermöglicht haben. Diesbezüglich sind insbesondere zu nennen:

   STIFTUNG VOLKSWAGENWERK
   GESELLSCHAFT FÜR KANADA STUDIEN
   KANADISCHE BOTSCHAFT (Bonn)
   PHILIPPS-UNIVERSITÄT MARBURG

Die Unterstützung, die wir durch diese und andere Institutionen und Personen erfahren haben, werte ich als Anerkennung unserer Forschungsbemühungen im Rahmen des Projektes, aber auch als Verpflichtung und Aufforderung, im Sinne der bisherigen Arbeit fortzufahren.

Schließlich richte ich einen privaten Dank an zwei Personen, die während der Durchführung der Forschungsarbeiten nicht nur zu außerordentlich geschätzten Kollegen, sondern zu sehr persönlichen Freunden geworden sind: Alfred Hecht und Ludger Müller-Wille. Dies schließt auch die betroffenen Familien ein. Ich halte es für ein gutes Omen, wenn wissenschaftliche Kooperation auch zu einem persönlichen, menschlichen Zusammenrücken der Beteiligten führt. Gerade die Erforschung des Ethnizitätsproblems hat sehr deutlich gezeigt, daß ein solches Näherrücken der Menschen, die durch Grenzen gleich welcher Art voneinander getrennt sind, heute notwendiger denn je geworden ist. Dieser Wert scheint mir sogar oft wichtiger zu sein als die rein wissenschaftlichen Ergebnisse unserer Arbeit.

                                                        Alfred Pletsch

Marburg/Lahn, Mai 1985

Ethnic Aspects of Central Canada
An Introduction

by
Alfred Hecht, Ludger Müller-Wille and Alfred Pletsch

Studies on ethnicity seem to be primarily the field of sociologists, anthropologists or historians and less the interest of geographers. However, the traditional understanding of geographical research, strongly influenced by its German forefathers, has always focussed on the premise that any human influence on the physical or cultural landscape provokes - and must provoke - the geographer's interest, however without intending to compete with other social sciences. Not "competition", but "collaboration" and "interdisciplinary research" are the appropriate terms if we look at ethnic studies and the problems related to ethnicity. This should also hold true for any other kind of scientific research.

The idea to conduct a study on ethnicity problems in Canada could not be more logical. A country with 82 different ethnic groups apart from the indigenous peoples, where 72 different non-native "mother tongues" and more than 50 indigenous languages are spoken can legitimately be called a cultural mosaic. The Canadian state is constantly confronted - politically, economically, socially and geographically - with problems based in ethnicity.

Studies on ethnicity, neglected for a long time, have fortunately been intensified in Canada since the 1960s. Research on this topic has not only been undertaken by Canadians but has become lately a sphere of interest for Canadianists worldwide. Ethnicity was not only a concern to the "classical" social sciences but, at the same time, other disciplines have focussed on different aspects of human influence on nature and society (cf. Clarke et al. 1984; Ley 1984).

It was in this spirit that, in 1980, the idea was born to start a research project on "Ethnicity Problems in Québec and Ontario", which centered around (1): geographical aspects of ethnicity problems and (2): Central Canada, where ethnic conflicts have a history almost 400 years, where the two "founding peoples" of Canada - English and French - are strongly involved in the conflicts, and where the actuality of the discussion is undeniable if one looks at the broad range of the conflict's visible and invisible features. Northern Québec, for example, has been severely disturbed by large scale development projects not only in ecological, but also very strongly in ethnic dimensions. Central Québec has experienced what was termed the "Quiet Revolution" during the last 25 years, a revolution which was the result of a more than 200 year old cultural conflict, which began with the Treaty of Paris in 1763, but which had its roots far beyond that event. Central Ontario became one of those parts of Canada where the British predominance was constantly challenged by an increasingly multicultural society, overlapped by the spatial aspects of "core" and "periphery" structures within the province.

It is evident that this enumeration does not cover the whole range of possible ethnic conflicts. But Central Canada takes part in the most severe aspects of ethnicity problems that concern the country as a whole, aspects such as indigenous ethnicity and minority (visible and invisible) immigrant ethnicity and their influence on the Canadian landscape and society. The research projects undertaken were aimed at an integration into a broader scientific discussion currently conducted in Canada and elsewhere. The aspects dealt with are not only characteristic of the Canadian scene but can be observed all over the world. The results elaborated through our research might not be appropriate for solving problems but we hope they can contribute to a better understanding of issues surrounding ethnicity. The following paragraphs are a brief summary of the main research thrust and results obtained between 1981 and 1985. They are followed by an appendix containing a complete bibliography of publications, reports and theses based on and related to the research project.

Indigenous Ethnicity in Nouveau-Québec
(Ludger Müller-Wille)

The study of indigenous ethnicity in northern Québec or generally in northern circumpolar regions is often approached under the assumption of an expanding spatial and socio-economic integration process emanating from southern political and economic centers, which expand their interests into their perceived "northern periphery". In fact, the studies carried out under this project looked at the spatial and institutional integration of the Inuit population living in the Kativik Region into the Province of Québec with its aspiring drive towards sovereignty and territoriality. Although the results indicated a considerable degree of integration of Québec's northernmost region into the mainstream of its economic and politico-administrative institutions, it became very much apparent that a pronounced cultural difference continues to exist between Euro-Canadian and Inuit society supported by the resurgence and affirmation of Inuit ethnicity within the context of a strong relationship between the people and their land and their reluctance to assimilate into Canadian society. Therefore, ethnicity will remain a key issue in the future of the North notwithstanding the ever increasing influences from the southern regions. The major phases in the history of relations between indigenous and immigrant peoples in the North gives an indication of the adaptability of Inuit society to new political and socio-economic conditions.

The indigenous peoples of the northern circumpolar regions, be it in northern Eurasia or northern North America, have utilized the environment as the mainstay for their livelihood and cultural survival since time immemorial, i.e. since their first arrival in these regions. In adapting to the particular natural environmental conditions, various types of social organizations and economic systems have evolved. It is apparent that these indigenous populations did not develop their societies in isolation but rather continued contact and mixing with neighbouring cultures, although at times intermittent, contributed to change by innovations of ideas and material items. These contacts between northern peoples and expanding southern populations have taken on different regional forms during the last centuries. Today, the external parties represent stronger political and economic organizations and assert a more prominent and demanding role in the affairs and development of northern regions. This spatially and institutionally expanding process has meant that the already, albeit locally and regionally, established sovereignty and territoriality of the indigenous peoples or Urbevölkerung have been undermined, superimposed and/or even displaced by political and economic structures introduced into the North.

In the case of the Inuit of northern Québec the development of integration has been rather recent. The Inuit system of land use and occupancy throughout the Canadian arctic and its effective control over land and accessible renewable resources have been intact until quite recently. Although the Inuit had experienced European contact since the 18th century, only the decades since the early 1950s have brought rapid changes and transitions. With the increasing demands for access to non-renewable resources by the southern industrial core, the Inuit lands have almost fully been coopted into the national system of Québec and Canada. Still today, the Inuit are a majority in their home region, Kativik Region in northern Québec. They outnumber the several hundred, mainly transient Euro-Canadians with their population of more than 6,000. However, the transient Euro-Canadians have obtained a crucial and decisive position in the externally based control of the political, socio-economic and cultural development of the region. This position can only be differentiated if the Inuit can assert more control over their own aspirations and the implementation thereof. Therefore the key issues for the continuation of cultural difference and thus the acceptance of the equality of cultures center around three topics:

(1) political control and regulation of territory and land use patterns and practices;
(2) accessibility and utilization of renewable and non-renewable resources to allow returns to be kept in the North;
(3) positive development in the cultural and educational fields with direct control by the people concerned.

For the Inuit this means that, historically, developments by now have almost gone full cycle from the locally controlled conditions of pre-European contact, to a gradually de-localized or displaced control under the ever increasing contact with Euro-Canadian society and government and, finally, to the contemporary stage of indigenous claims and rights over self-determination within the existing framework of the Canadian state.

It is this last phase which is of interest because it is related to the revitalization of local interests and resources to obtain political control and support a dynamic ethnic identification among the Inuit in order to manage the relations with external factors such as government authorities. This is the phase whose origins go back only some decades and which is clearly the outcome of a broadening horizon for indigenous peoples, imputed by continuing contact with the outside, that has enabled as well as forced them to project their concerns beyond their immediate local boundaries. This evolving ethnic and political awareness, supported from within their culture, could only have happened as a reflection on the aims of integration and assimilation expressed by Euro-Canadian society. There is every indication that the assimilation of indigenous peoples in Canada has failed and that indigenous ethnicity will remain a viable and necessary aspect of the multicultural structure of modern Canadian society.

On the other hand, the support for the increasing demands by indigenous peoples for control over land, economic base, culture and language had to be obtained by legal recourse and negotiations with the government. In the case of the Inuit as for other indigenous peoples, the increased control over one's own fate is the key issue in future development. However, it is quite apparent that the overall sovereignty of the Canadian state is not immediately threatened although developments such as in Greenland are a sign of changing political constellations in the North.

Still the question arises why, after all, should indigenous peoples in modern states strive towards regaining control over their destiny? Is sovereignty not solved? Have indigenous peoples not benefited from contact with modern societies? In the north, indigenous peoples make up only a few per cent of the national populations of polar nations. Is national security and welfare a more pressing priority than the political and cultural aspirations of small populations which, today, are ethnic minorities within state societies? Northern peoples, it is said, cannot live in their homeland without help and support by the South under the existing conditions of modern technology and its amenities.

To the Inuit the answer is obvious. They propose the use of their own and externally acquired resources to achieve, extract and maintain the maximum acceptance and participation in decision-making concerning their living conditions in the North. They know as well that the continuation of cultural difference or ethnicity is a crucial aspect to stake one's boundaries without closing them to a fair and just participation by others and to the equal distribution of well-being between indigenous and immigrant peoples alike.

Ethnicity Aspects of Québec
(Alfred Pletsch)

The history of French and British neighbourhood in Canada is marked by ethnic confrontation among other matters. Today's discussion of self-identification and self-awareness among the French Canadians has many roots going far back. Ever since the two founding nations of the "new continent" began to conquer the new land, there was spatial and economic competition without being necessarily, at the very beginning, an ethnic conflict. French people started to settle in the St. Lawrence Valley shortly after the founding of Québec in 1608. One year earlier, the British had founded Jamestown farther south on the eastern Seabord where they did not yet interfere spatially with the first French settlers. Both had similar trouble in defending their settlements against the indigenous peoples living in the area, but this conflict also was not necessarily an ethnic one, although it was the beginning of a gradual loss of ethnic identity to some of the Indians.

In 1610, Henry Hudson sailed into Hudson Bay and, despite his dramatic end, his discovery resulted in a foothold for the British north of the French settlements, but again too far away to be reason for an immediate conflict. Yet, the geopolitical situation of La Nouvelle France was already desperate, two years after the colonization process had begun; the French colony was sandwiched between British lands and, as history showed later, was thus bound to run into unavoidable conflicts. The chance to escape from that strategically unfortunate position was involuntarily missed when Louis XIV rejected Radisson's and Groseiller's suggestions of founding trading posts on the coast of Hudson Bay. The two disappointed Frenchmen went to Charles II, King of England, who did not hesitate to encourage the foundation of the Hudson's Bay Company, the trading company which, under British flag, became one of the most powerful institutions in Canada, both politically and economically. That was undoubtedly one of the greatest misjudgements made by the French Regime. The century following that event was constantly marked by competition between French and British explorers in the furtrade, activities which prevented the French from giving more emphasis to the settlement process in La Nouvelle France. That neglect became, as history should demonstrate later, the second mistake, because, when the British took over the French colony, only about 70.000 people of French descent lived on the banks of the St. Lawrence River.

After the takeover of the French colony by the British, it was up to them to make the mistakes. Comparable in its consequences, if not worse than that made by Louis XIV, mentioned earlier, was the mistake made by the British government in 1774 in its Quebec Act, in which a great number of privileges were accorded to the French settlers. These measures were meant mainly to "buy" their loyalty in time to counteract the American independence movement in the not so distant New England colonies. A loyal French population would be one less danger in case of an open conflict, and if this held true in the beginning for the French people it still did not prevent England from losing its New England colony in 1776. The guaranteed rights and privileges in the Quebec Act, however, continued to protect French people and French identity in a superimposed britainized environment. The people of French descent, not wishing to lose either these privileges or their land, decided to protect themselves against all British influence and to preserve their identity. In this they were strongly influenced and supported by the Roman Catholic Church. At that time the economic and spatial conflict received an ethnic dimension which has continued into the present.

The impact of two different nations conquering a continent has been immense. This is apparent in the actual conflicts between francophone Québec and the rest of anglophone Canada. In historical terms, e.g., the shaping of the cultural landscape has created very visible differences in settlement patterns, house forms, etc. the differences in demographic and social behavior of the two peoples have also left their mark. These were, among others, questions asked in our project. Much interest was directed towards the aspect of mutual influence between the two peoples. In Canada German Geographers have focussed their research especially on these aspects since the 1930s. Carl Schott (1936) gave one of the most detailed analyses of · the settlement process in British settled southern Ontario. Fritz Bartz (1955) looked at the French influence in the cultural landscape in North America. No one examined in detail the aspects of mutual influence of one group on the other, be it in respect to field patterns or land tenancy, or any other dimension. Canadian Geographers, too, seem to have neglected these aspects at times. It should be added that the historical dimensions of the settlement process in Canada have frequently not been attacked at all by Canadian geographers. R. C. HARRIS' and John WARKENTIN's works (1966, 1974), and naturally those of L. E. HAMELIN (1971) are outstanding, but they seem to be isolated highlights among the great number of geographers who prefer to examine contemporary features.

The question of whether there has been an influence of the French settlement system on the British field pattern (or vice versa) had to be examined in a historical dimension. One of the important political events arount 1763 was that French jurisdiction was abolished and English Law substituted. Along with other events, this had a decisive influence on the field survey, characterized during the French period by the seigneurial system. After the British conquest, the lands were exclusively surveyed in the township system, but, unlike the pattern in the United States, the layout of the early surveys followed a strip system, very similar to the pattern in French settled areas. This phenomenon becomes explicable only if one considers that, already in 1771, French jurisdiction was reintroduced under the pressure from the French settlers. Also the land survey by the British did not start before 1781 in the so-called Western Townships. The French influence went so far that, even within townships, land was given to the non-French settlers on the feudal loan basis, for which the French term "fief" was used in English. The townships were referred to as "Seigneurie". The Constitution Act of 1791 altered the situation and reintroduced English jurisdiction in Upper Canada, while, in Lower Canada, parts of the French jurisdiction were maintained. The consequence was that land surveys within the Eastern Townships of Québec continued to follow the strip division system, while Upper Canada was surveyed with the square grid pattern, which would later become the standard in all of Canada except Québec.

Other aspects of the project concerned especially the Eastern Townships of Québec, an area which was initially supposed to be reserved for English settlers. Land speculation and the isolated situation between the French settled St. Lawrence Lowlands and the United States were the main reasons for the relatively small success of the English settlement initiatives in this area.

After 1849, when the Eastern Townships were opened for French Canadian settlement, a real invasion took place. The fascinating process, often described as the "Spring Tide of the French Canadians", was examined in several case studies based on archives in the registrar's offices. In almost all cases the same strategy can be observed; Francophones started to settle in little nuclei, from which they spread spatially during the next years, thus pressuring the non-French settlers to move elsewhere. This occupation tactic continued in waves until, finally, the whole Township was settled and owned by French Canadians.

To understand the contemporary position of the two main ethnic groups within Québec society, attention was given to the spatial dimension in the dynamics of land abandonment in the Eastern Townships. In addition, farm activities, land-use and modernization tendencies were observed. This was always done with a special focus on the different behaviour of the francophone and anglophone populations. Final results are not presented because the 1981 Census data is not yet completely accessible. Specially requested excerpts from the data base allowed comparisons between the two groups (and others) for 1971 and 1981. Preliminary results seem to confirm partly the hypothesis that the influence of ethnic identity on the behaviour of the rural population is still important today, but probably less so than historically (Schulte, in this vol.). Among farmers, i.e., economic determinants seem to be more important than ethnic or cultural ones. Nevertheless, there seems to be more spatial and economic flexibility in the non-French population.

Population movements, altering the traditional patterns at different moments of Québec history, were also studied during the project. For a long time, this aspect has been the main interest of demographers, sociologists and, at times, geographers. Those studies, dealing with the spatial location of the two groups and its evolution need to be complemented by the analysis of the spatial structure of their social relations, i.e., their respective social spaces, considering the ethnic constellation (intra-ethnic or inter-ethnic) of those relations in particular.

The Eastern Townships of Québec, as one of the rural zones of transition between English speaking and French speaking populations, are a promising area to study those questions. There both groups have lived together for several generations and have shared the territory of many ethnicity mixed small communities. One hypothesis of the project was that the francophone and anglophone groups in those communities live in social spaces distinct from each other, each having its own characteristics. Furthermore, is was assumed that both of these social spaces were altered considerably, due to the social changes in Québec society since the 1940s.

Three rural communities - Sawyerville (Compton County), Durham-Sud (Drummond County) and Stanbridge East (Missisquoi County) - were chosen as case studies. A variety of methods were used to gather information on the spatial structure of basic social links in both intra- and inter-ethnic constellation (relations with the provincial and federal government and other municipal und local institutions at work and in the family). The research includes the analysis of census data and municipal population lists completed by informants as well as searches in church, school and other archives. A series of interviews was augmented by personal observations and participation in the local social life of each of the three communities during many weeks of personal presence.

Much of the collected material has already been analysed. It allows a first insight into the complex spatial identity of the two ethnic groups. The most striking results have been the social space of the anglophones, who are a regional ethnic minority with a continuously shrinking population. In contrast to the francophones, their social relations in the political, economic and private domains very often reach beyond the province of Québec. They are oriented towards Anglo-Canada, especially the province of Ontario. The importance of interethnic relations has grown in recent years (work relations with francophone companies, mixed marriages), but it has remained limited in extent and local in character unless imposed from "the outside" (for instance by provincial institutions functioning more and more in French). Having had the choice of either leaving the province, increased (intra-ethnic) isolation in the region or further (inter-ethnic) integration into the dominant Québécois (francophone) society, many rural English speaking Townshippers have done the first. Their options, consequently, affected the spatial structure of many social relations of those who stayed in their home communities. Thus, in a way, they have "gone with them". The social space of the anglophone sector in mixed rural communities, like the ones that were studied, indicates the degree of their alienation from francophone Québec society, although they remain residents in that territory.

Finally, the special case of Montreal was examined during our project. The focus was not on the traditional conflict of the anglophones and the francophones, but on visible and invisible immigrant minority groups. As examples of visible minorities, the Haitians and the anglophone West Indians were chosen. Since the late 1960s, when Canada changed her immigration policy, the number of immigrants from Third World countries has increased sharply. Today well above 50% of the annual influx of immigrants to Canada belong to this group. Thus, Montreal, only next to Toronto in the number of immigrants it receives, saw the emergence of a number of sizeable visible minorities during the 1970. The two most important ones, Haitians and anglophone West Indians, were compared in a study focussing on their residential pattern with respect to each other and some of the city's other major ethnic groups. It is particularly interesting to compare these visible minorities in the context of Montreal. Due to their linguistic affinities they integrate into the two different sectors of the city. This creates an intriguing setting for comparisons, not only between those two groups, but also for possible impacts of the different environments of the respective charter groups on the socio-economic integration of the immigrant groups.

The main source of information of the project are special tabulations created by Statistics Canada for 24 areas in the C.M.A. of Montreal giving 1981 census results. First of all, these statistics provide a much needed general information about the most important ethnic groups in Montreal. They permit a comparison for characteristics such as age, sex, marital, status, language, religion, mobility, education, income etc. But, perhaps most importantly, these cross-tabulations give a spatially differentiated picture of these characteristics. That makes it neccessary to correlate the distribution of a particular group with characteristics of the total population to obtain an idea of the spatial distribution of those characteristics for that peculiar group. The type of information enables us to pursue the following questions:
(1) How do socio-economic and other characteristics correlate with the spatial pattern of the Haitian and the anglophone West Indian group?
(2) How do spatial pattern and socio-economic status of these two groups compare with that of other groups, in particular that of the charter groups?
(3) Are there significant differences in the spatial distribution and the socio-economic status of those groups that settle in the predominantly French east

of Montreal as compared to those that live in the west of the city?

The selected invisible minority group in Montreal was the German population, which represents only 0,5% of the total population in Québec, far below the Canadian average. A number of questions arise from this almost insignificant percentage, such as the residential pattern of Germans in Montreal, segregational behaviour of the group, maintenance of mother tongue use, assimilation trends with other ethnic groups, socio-cultural integration, economic integration and many others. An important question also was to examine the reactions of the Germans to the francisizing policy since the latest language law (Bill 101) was passed in 1977 (Vestweber, in this volume). The empirical enquiry of this part of the research is not yet finished, thus, only a few preliminary results can be mentioned here. Looking at different aspects, it appears, that the Germans in Montreal have many similarities with the traditional "charter group", the British, at least in socio-linguistic, socio-cultural and economic fields. Politically, Germans have never taken active part in the decision making process, either in Montreal or in the Province of Québec as a whole. Although not apolitical, Germans seem to be more involved in economic than in political discussion. The Germans cannot be seen as being a charter group in Montreal, but neither are they a peripheral ethnic minority, if their economic integration is disregarded, which is generally successfully accomplished within several years of immigration. There was one very clear tendency observed: Germans integrate much easier into the anglophone milieu, even in a francophone surrounding. Their integration process is accomplished very quickly, and thus German ethnic identity will have a challenge to maintain itself in Canada in the future.

Ethnicity in Ontario
(Alfred Hecht)

As is indicated in other sections of this monograph, our research in ethnicity in central Canada has dealt with the socio-economic integration of ethnic groups into Ontario's society. Secondly, it dealt with spatial distribution of ethnic groups in Ontario, using Ontario's ethnic charter group as a reference. The term <u>charter group</u> comes from sociology and refers to the group of people in a society that established the norms for that society. For Ontario, this has meant the people of British Isle descent that first settled Ontario in the beginning of the 19th century. One of their characteristics was a strong loyalty to the British crown and a strong preference for the British way of life. As a result, Upper Canada, or as it is now known, Ontario, in large part was modelled after British political, settlement and socio-economic norms.

But people of British Isle descent are not the only ones who have settled in Ontario, and are not the only ones who are now molding the present society of Ontario. Other ethnic groups are also involved. The large number of ethnic groups from all over the world present in Ontario makes this imperative. From Table 1 one can see that the British Isle ethnic group makes up now only some 52% of the total population. Nearly 50% of the people of Ontario have a different ethnic background or may even have a multiple ethnic background. Some of the strong groups are the Germans, French, Ukrainians, Italians and Native Indians. But people from Third World countries are increasing rapidly. If the present Third World immigration trend continues, Canadian society, as well as Ontario society, will have its strong European ethnic component drastically decreased (Table 2).

Over the last few years, our ethnic research in Ontario has focussed mainly on (1) determining the socio-economic status of ethnic groups within the general Ontario society and (2) exploring the geographic locations of ethnic groups in relation to the charter group. These two fundamental questions were modelled initially by Hecht, Sharpe and Wong (1983). In this model it was hypothesized that ethnic groups entering Ontario would enter at the bottom of the socio-economic scale and would work their way up. Also, it was hypothesized that ethnic groups as a whole would enter proportionately more into Ontario's geographic peripheral region, the poorer region, and with time would move to the core geographical region of Ontario, mainly the metropolitan area of Toronto. In order to do this, however, it was also

Table 1: Major Ethnic Groups in Ontario, 1981

	British	French	Italian	German	Dutch	Ukrainian	Jewish	Native People	Province Total
Single Origin	4,487,800	652,900	487,310	373,390	191,125	133,995	131,320	83,880	8,534,265
			British/ French	British/ Other	French/ Other	British/ French/ Other	European Other	Native/ Other	Province Total
Multiple Origin			201,415	375,800	45,145	50,110	83,985	26,200	782,650

Source: Statistics Canada, Advanced Ethnic Data Sheet, 1983

⇔⇔⇔⇔⇔⇔⇔⇔⇔⇔⇔⇔⇔⇔⇔⇔⇔⇔⇔⇔⇔⇔⇔⇔⇔⇔

Table 2: Ten Leading Countries of Birth of Immigrants for Each Period of Immigration, Canada, 1981

Before 1961 Country of birth	Number	% of total	1961-1970 Country of birth	Number	% of total	1971-1981 Country of birth	Number	% of total
Great Britain	524,900	29.8	Great Britain	195,300	21.2	Great Britain	158,800	13.8
Italy	214,700	12.2	Italy	141,000	15.2	United States	97,600	8.5
United States	136,900	7.8	United States	67,000	7.2	India	75,100	6.5
Poland	118,000	6.7	Portugal	57,300	6.2	Portugal	66,400	5.8
U.S.S.R.	112,600	6.4	Greece	40,700	4.4	Philippines	55,300	4.8
Netherlands	112,400	6.4	Yugoslavia	33,200	3.6	Jamaica	49,900	4.3
Fed.Rep.Germany	107,200	6.1	Fed.Rep.Germany	31,400	3.4	Soc.Rep.Vietnam	49,400	4.3
Yugoslavia	39,100	2.2	India	28,200	3.0	Hong Kong	42,200	3.7
German Dem.Rep.	28,400	1.6	Jamaica	23,600	2.5	Italy	29,100	2.5
Austria	28,300	1.6	France	19,100	2.1	Guyana	27,500	2.4
Ten leading countries as a percentage of all immigrants who arrived before 1961		80.8	Ten leading countries as a percentage of all immigrants who arrived during the 1961-1970 period		68.7	Ten leading countries as a percentage of all immigrants who arrived during the 1971-1981 period		56.6

Source: Statistics Canada, Canada's Immigrants, 1982, Table 2

hypothesized that ethnic groups would have to accept and practice the traditional behavioural norms of the British charter group. These major questions were explored in a number of research papers and publications.

A thorough examination of the spatial location pattern of ethnic groups and the charter group in Ontario up to 1971 and in Toronto up to 1976, showed that the initial hypothesis was true. Over time ethnic groups tended to concentrate more and more in southern Ontario (Hecht, Sharpe and Wong, 1983). This concentration in the core, especially in Toronto, seemed to be the norm for most ethnic groups, even for the Native Indians. The latter, however, did not display the same strong movement towards southern Ontario as the white ethnic groups did. Secondly, people of French ethnic background seemed to stay proportionately more on the periphery than other ethnic groups. Within the metropolitan area of Toronto, it was shown that over time most of the ethnic groups also had a similar location pattern to that of the British. The only real exceptions occurred with people of Jewish and Italian backgrounds. These groups tended to remain geographically separate from the charter group. It was surprising that in Metropolitan Toronto even visible minority ethnic groups, such as Native Indians, Chinese and Blacks, tended to have a location pattern that very much corresponded with those of the charter group. It may be a reflection of the large number of ethnic people in the city. For instance, in 1981, 38% of all Metro residents were immigrants. This high percentage also shows the tremendous pull that Toronto has had on recent immigrants. Whereas old immigrants, those who came before World War II, tended to go into the geographical peripheries of Ontario and only with time migrated to the core, new immigrants tend to go directly to the metropolitan areas. Within the major cities they also do not concentrate in the central area of the city anymore, but disperse within the city. Part of the explanation for this behaviour is that newer immigrants are highly educated and qualified individuals, some even with capital. Consequently, they have a far easier time adjusting to the new society's norms than the traditional immigrants who lacked both language and technical skills and rarely had capital.

From the above discussion one can see that the hypothesis that immigrants would come into the central city of Toronto and only with time move up the socio-economic ladder as well as decentralize, was not completely borne out in our research. The immigrant model of spatial and socio-economic adjustment which was true for immigrants at the end of the 19th century and in the first half of the 20th century will have to be revised for immigrants to Canadian cities in the last quarter of the 20th century.

But how have immigrants into Ontario fared over time in the socio-economic realm? A number of papers focussed on this question. In our study of the German ethnic population in Ontario, we found that in a number of socio-economic characteristics very little distinguished them from the British Isle charter group. Even in the area of language, the difference is disappearing. Of the approximately 373,000 people of German ethnic background in Ontario in 1981, only about 177,000 had German as their mother tongue and only about 58,000 were using the German language in their homes. Linguistically, one can therefore conclude that they have lost their identity. They have adopted the language of the charter group, namely English, and in that sense have become part and parcel of the charter group. Similar behaviour was found to be the case for the Polish, Jewish, Greek, Italian, Ukrainian, Portuguese and Yugoslav peoples (Kramarich 1983). Only the French seem to have been able to retain their language more fully than other ethnic groups in Ontario. In large part, this may be due to their high concentration in some peripheral areas of Northern Ontario where they form a majority and hence are able to retain their language easier (Hecht 1984; Yeo 1984).

On the educational front, ethnic groups, especially the older ones, now have educational achievements similar to the British and in some instances even higher, for example the Jewish people. Also as was mentioned earlier, many recent immigrants are highly educated. In their adjustment to Canadian society they do not have to go through this educational upgrading process before they are able to participate in the general society. Their problem seems to be a different one. Since many are non-white, racial problems have emerged as a hindrance. In terms of their settlement patterns, they are found proportionately more in the core region of Ontario, namely in Toronto, than in the peripheries.

But what is the situation of the ethnic groups in Ontario in terms of income and job types? If one does not take into account the skill level or the age level of individuals, the average income of most European ethnic groups is very similar to that of the British. Visible minorities, especially the Native Indians, on the other hand, are substantially lower (Hecht, Wesol, Sharpe, 1983). Also, income variation in the different parts of Ontario are explained by different socio-economic characteristics of ethnic groups than those of the charter group. For instance, an additional amount of higher education does not give the same additional income to an ethnic person as it does to a charter person. Secondly, age also played an important role in income variation. The older the person, the bigger was the difference between the ethnic groups and the charter group, holding constant education. Most younger people had similar income and education characteristics in 1981. Should this similarity continue as they grow older, they may together form a new charter group in Ontario.

Ethnic intermarriage is frequently described as the final stage in the integration and assimilation process of ethnic groups. In Ontario as a whole, most ethnic groups of European origin now have high intermarriage rates with the British charter group. In Toronto, however, where more recent immigrants live, this rate is lower than the provincial average. Part of the slower rate of marital integration in Toronto, the core of Ontario, may not only be due to recent immigrants, but also due to the fact that here each ethnic group is large enough to form a critical mass of its own.

Although the research on ethnicity in Ontario proved to be very interesting and very satisfying, it is by no means complete. In Ontario different ethnic groups seem to follow a different assimilation or integration process. Hence our model was not applicable in all instances; a new one may have to be developed. In such a model the religion of a person should be considered. The Jewish ethnic group has retained a large measure of its identity despite the fact that it has been in Ontario a long time, is highly educated, has a good income, is geographically located in the core of Ontario, namely Toronto, and has adopted the English language completely. It seems that if ethnicity and religion are one, a double bond of cohesiveness seems to exist. Other ethnic groups may experience some similar bonds, e.g., the Mennonites. Secondly, the concept of critical mass which allows an ethnic group to retain its identity has to be explored further. From the ethnic geographical location pattern in Toronto, it would seem that the Italians, for instance, are of sufficient size so that in their location pattern they can be independent of the British charter group. On the other hand, smaller ethnic groups such as the Yugoslavians, the Dutch, and the Ukrainians, etc., are very susceptible to a rapid integration into Ontario's British-dominated society. Visible minorities seem to have a special problem of integrating. Some of the older ones, such as the Chinese and Japanese, have achieved the linguistic, economic and educational norm of the general society, but have not intermarried. More recent visible minority immigrants such as Blacks and East Asians seem to experience a new barrier to integration: the colour of their skin. Even though Canadian society as a whole is not known for its racial tendencies, they nevertheless do exist (Ramcharan 1982). These recent immigrants therefore present a whole new set of questions to the researcher.

References

Bartz, Fritz, 1955: Französische Einflüsse im Bilde der Kulturlandschaft Nordamerikas. Erdkunde. 9, pp. 286-305.

Clarke, Colin and David Ley, Ceri Peach (eds.), 1984: Geography and Ethnic Pluralism. London: G. Allen and Unwin. 294 pp.

Hamelin, Louis-Edmond, 1971: Histoire Economique du Québec, 1851-1896. - Montréal.

Harris, R. C., 1966: The Seigneurial System in Early Canada: A Geographical Study. - Madison (Wisconsin).

Harris, R. C. & Warkentin, 1974: Canada before Confederation. - New York, London, Toronto.

Hecht, Alfred, 1984 (see Appendix).

Hecht, Alfred an R. G. Sharpe, A. C. Y. Wong, 1983 (see Appendix).

Hecht, Alfred and C. Wesol, R. G. Sharpe, 1983 (see Appendix).

Kramerich, Mary-Ann, 1983 (see Appendix).

Ley, David, 1984: Pluralism and the Canadian State, in: Clarke et al. 1984: 87-110.

Ramcharan, S., 1982: Racism: Non-Whites in Canada. Toronto: Butterworth.

Schott, Carl, 1936: Landnahme und Kolonisation in Canada - am Beispiel Südontarios. - Kiel. Schriften des Geogr. Inst. Kiel. 6.

Schulte, Martin (see Appendix).

Statistics Canada 1983. Advanced Ethnic Data Sheet. 1984. Canada's Immigrants.

Vestweber, Inge (see Appendix).

Wolff, Peter (see Appendix).

Yeo, Jenny P. H., 1984 (see Appendix).

Appendix

Publications based on research conducted under or in relation with the project 'Ethnicity Problems in Québec and Ontario' funded by the Foundation Volkswagenwerk (Hannover, Federal Republic of Germany) and carried out at Philipps University Marburg, McGill University Montreal and Wilfrid Laurier University Waterloo/Ont. between 1981 and 1985.

Dufour, Carole, 1983: Exploration minière dans la région de Kativik (Québec), in: Müller-Wille (ed.) 1983: 13-48.

Hastings, Clifford D., 1983: The Canadian State and the North: The Creation of Nouveau-Québec, in: Müller-Wille (ed.) 1983: 67-84.

— 1985: Mercantilism and Laissez-Faire Capitalism in the Ungava Peninsula, 1670-1940: The Economic Geography of the Fur Trade. M. A. Thesis in Geography, McGill University. VI, 165 pp.

Hecht, Alfred, 1983: The Germans and the Anglo-Saxon Milieu in Central Canada, in: German-Canadian Studies in the 1980's. Ed. by M. S. Batts, W. Riedel, and R. Symington. Annals of the Canadian Association of University Teachers of German (CAUTG) 9: 110-142.

— 1985: Ethnic Groups and Charter Groups in Ontario, in: Pletsch (ed.) 1985 (in this volume).

Hecht, Alfred and Ludger Müller-Wille, Alfred Pletsch, 1985: Ethnic Aspects of Central Canada. An Introduction (L. Müller-Wille, Indigenous Ethnicity in Nouveau-Québec; A. Pletsch, Ethnicity Aspects of Québec; A. Hecht, Ethnicity in Ontario), in: Pletsch (ed.) 1985 (in this volume).

— and Robert G. Sharpe, Amy C. Y. Wong, 1983: Ethnicity and Well-Being in Central Canada: The Case of Ontario and Toronto (Kanada-Projekt 2). Marburger Geographische Schriften 92. Marburg: Geographisches Institut. XIV, 192 pp.

— and Catherine M. Wesol, Robert G. Sharpe, 1983: Peripheral Location of Indian People in Ontario, in: Regional Development in the Peripheries of Canada and Europe. Ed. by Alfred Hecht. Manitoba Geographical Studies 8: 52-86.

Koch, Andrea: The Germans in Western Canada. PhD thesis Marburg (in preparation).

Kramarich, Mary-Ann, 1983: Southern Europeans in Ontario's Periphery and Core: A Socio-economic Analysis Based on the Core-Periphery Model. B. A. Honours Thesis in Geography, Wilfrid Laurier University. 115 pp.

Mason, Christine and Linna Weber, 1985 (in press): From Survey to Legal Status: Processing Indigenous Names, in: Müller-Wille (ed.) 1985 (in press).

Müller-Wille, Ludger, 1982: Forschungsbericht - Inuit und Euro-Québecer in der Kativik-Region, in: Zeitschrift der Gesellschaft für Kanada-Studien 2 (1): 137-139.

— 1983 a: Nouveau-Québec - Entwicklungskonflikt in der polaren Ökumene Kanadas, in: Müller-Wille (ed.) 1983: 1-12.

— 1983 b: Inuit Toponymy and Cultural Sovereignty, in: Müller-Wille (ed.) 1983: 131-150.

— 1984 a: The Legacy of Native Toponyms. Towards the Establishing of the Inuit Place Name Inventory of the Kativik Region (Québec), in: Onomastica Canadiana 65: 2-19.

— 1984 b: The Heritage of Inuit Place Names, in: The Northern Raven 4 (2): 1.

— 1985: Changing Inuit Ethnicity in Canada, in: Pletsch (ed.) 1985 (in this volume).

— and Alfred Pletsch, 1981: Ethnizitätskonflikt, sozio-ökonomischer Wandel und Territorialentwicklung in Québec/Kanada, in: Die Erde 112 (1): 61-89.

— and Linna Weber, 1983: Inuit Place Name Inventory of Northeastern Québec-Labrador, in: Müller-Wille (ed.) 1983: 151-222.

— and Linna Weber, 1985 (in press): Inuit Place Name Inventory of the Kativik Region and Off-Shore Areas in Northern Québec-Labrador. Inukjuak: Avataq Cultural Institute.

Müller-Wille, Ludger (ed.), 1983: Beiträge zum Entwicklungskonflikt in Nouveau-Québec / Conflict in Development in Nouveau-Québec. Marburger Geographische Schriften 89 / McGill Subarctic Research Paper 37. Marburg: Geographisches Institut. VII. 222 pp.

Müller-Wille, Ludger (ed.), 1985 (in press): Dynamics of Cultural Development: Indigenous Place Names in the North. Proceedings of a Symposium Held on March 22, 1985. McGill University: Indigenous Names Surveys and Department of Geography.

Orzechowska, Monika H., 1981: Energy Resources in Canada's Arctic: Developments, Issues and Concerns in the 1980's. B. A. Honours Thesis in Geography, McGill University. 68 pp.

Palliser, Johnny, 1984: An Inuit Experience With Place Names, in: The Northern Raven 4 (2): 2-33.

Pletsch, Alfred, 1980: Kolonisationsphasen und Kulturlandschaftswandel im Südosten der Provinz Québec (Kanada), in: Erdkunde 34: 61-73.

— 1981 a: Kanada - Land zwischen Arktis und Prärie, in: Natur und Museum. Bericht der Senckenbergischen Naturforschenden Gesellschaft 111: 426-439.

— 1981 b: Urbanisierung und ihre Auswirkungen auf die Landwirtschaft im Umland von Montréal, in: Zeitschrift der Gesellschaft für Kanada-Studien 1: 76-93.

— 1982 a: Kanada - Schmelztiegel von Völkern und Kulturen am Rande der Ökumene, in: Natur und Museum. Bericht der Senckenbergischen Naturforschenden Gesellschaft 112: 65-76.

— 1982 b: Les Cantons de l'Est - Colonisation et abandon d'une région marginale, in: Norois 114: 185-204.

— 1983: Kanada am Wendepunkt seiner Bevölkerungs- und Wirtschaftsentwicklung, in: Geographische Rundschau 35: 370-380.

— 1984: 'Rang' and 'Township' - Some Deliberations on Their Origin and Mutual Influence, in: Trent University Occasional Papers 10: 347-357.

— 1985 a: French and English Settlement in the Eastern Townships (Québec) - Conflict or Coexistence, in: Pletsch (ed.) 1985 (in this volume).

— 1985 b: Ethnizitätsprobleme in Kanada. Ein Forschungs- und Konferenzbericht, in: Zeitschrift der Gesellschaft für Kanada-Studien 8 (1) (in press).

— and Andrea Koch, Inge Vestweber, 1984: Deutsche in Kanada - eine verschwindende Minorität, in: Zeitschrift der Gesellschaft für Kanada-Studien 4 (1): 123-132.

— and Ludger Müller-Wille, 1983: Kanada - Konfliktraum am Rande der Arktis, in: Alma Mater Philippina 2 /1983: 18-22.

— and Inge Vestweber, 1983: Die Deutschen in Québec - Aspekte der sozialen und wirtschaftlichen Integration, in: German-Canadian Studies in the 1980's. Ed. by M. S. Batts, W. Riedel and R. Symington. Annals of the Canadian Association for University Teachers of German (CAUTG) 9: 42-72.

— 1984. The Germans in Montreal - Problems of Economic Integration and Social Assimilation, in: Trent University Occasional Papers 10: 39-67.

— (ed.), 1985: Ethnicity in Canada - International Examples and Perspectives (Kanada-Projekt 3). Marburger Geographische Schriften 96. Marburg (this volume).

Schulte, Martin, 1985: L'espace social des francophones et des anglophones dans une communauté rurale des Cantons de l'Est (Québec), in: Pletsch (ed.) 1985 (in this volume).

— Ethnische Strukturen und Sozialräume in den Eastern Townships von Québec. PhD thesis Marburg (in preparation).

Sharpe, Robert G., 1983: Regional Variation Among Ethnic Groups in Ontario: A Core-Periphery Model. M.A. Thesis in Geography, Wilfrid Laurier University. 236 pp.

— 1985: Visible Ethnic Minorities in Ontario and Toronto, in: Pletsch (ed.) 1985 (in this volume).

Vestweber, Inge, 1984: Les Allemands à Montréal - Intégration ou ségrégation d'une minorité ethnique, Staatsexamensarbeit, Fachbereich Geographie, Philipps-Universität Marburg.

— 1985: Les Allemands à Montréal - Intégration ou ségrégation d'une minorité ethnique, in: Pletsch (ed.) 1985 (in this volume).

— Die Deutschen in Montreal. PhD thesis Marburg (in preparation).

Warburton, Lynn M., 1985: Comparative Well-Being of Native Indians in Ontario and Quebec. B. Sc. Honours Thesis in Geography, Wilfrid Laurier University. 65 pp.

Weber, Linna, 1984: Franz Boas' Inuit Geographical Survey, in: The Northern Raven 4 (2): 2.

Wesol, Catherine M., 1982: Ontario's Indians in the Periphery: An Examination of the Economic, Political and Cultural Situation. B. A. Honours Thesis in Geography, Wilfrid Laurier University. 94 pp.

Wolff, Peter, 1985: Haitians and Anglophone West Indians in the Ethnic and Socio-Economic Structure of Montreal, in: Pletsch (ed.) 1985 (in this volume).

— Ethnische Randgruppen in Montreal. PhD thesis Marburg (in preparation).

Wong, Amy C. Y., 1982: An Examination of the Geographic and Socio-economic Spaces of Ethnic Groups in Toronto: A Core-Periphery Perspective. M.A. Thesis in Geography, Wilfrid Laurier University. 188 pp.

Yeo, Jenny P. H., 1984: The Conditions of British, French and Italian Ethnic-Groups in the Cores and Peripheries of Ontario. B.A. Honours Thesis in Geography, Wilfrid Laurier University. 115 pp.

Addresses of the authors:

Alfred Hecht	Ludger Müller-Wille	Alfred Pletsch
Dept. of Geography	Dept. of Geography	Geographisches Institut
Wilfrid Laurier University	McGill University	Philipps-Universität
Waterloo/Ontario	805 Sherbrooke W.	Deutschhausstraße 10
Canada N2L 3C5	Montreal PQ	D 3550 Marburg
	Canada H3A 2 K6	Fed.Rep. Germany

Cultural Interplay and Political Anthropology:
The Navajo Case*

René König

Abstract: This article presents some of the findings of my last field work on the Navajo Reservation in Northern Arizona in 1981, and emphasizes critical aspects of contemporary cultural and social anthropology and the necessity of a general reorientation. While anthropologists ascribed a general dynamic caracter to industrial societies, they defined the simpler societies as rather conservative, traditionalistic and afraid of innovation. Such a theory underestimates the political ressources awakened by the cultural choc produced by the economic life of American society and modernization. The analysis of these ressources shows unexpected internal conflicts of these simpler societies who begin to look for a new way of life without, however, loosing their identity, and this the more so after the Indian "tribes" have declared themselves, in 1973, as "national enclaves" within the Euro-American society.

Résumé: L'article suivant est le résultat d'une dernière étude sur le champ en 1981 chez les Indiens Navajos au Nord de l'Arizona, et signale la nécessité de critiquer et de réorienter certaines vues acceptées en anthropologie culturelle et sociale. En attribuant aux sociétés industrielles un caractère essentiellement dynamique, on a cru pouvoir définir les sociétés simples comme plutôt conservatrices, traditionnalistes et redoutant toute action innovatrice. Une théorie pareille sous-estime les ressources politiques éveillées par le choc subi avec la réalité économique des Etats Unis et la vie "moderne". L'analyse de ces ressources rend visibles des conflits intérieures inattendus dans ces sociétés qui cherchent à développer un forme nouvelle de vie sans cependant mettre en jeu leur identité, et ceci particulièrement après que les "tribus" indigènes du continent Américain se sont déclarées, en 1973, comme "enclaves nationales" à l'intérieur de la société euro-américaine.

Zusammenfassung: Aufgrund einer letzten Feldbegehung im Jahre 1981 auf dem Reservat der Navajos in Arizona werden im folgenden Artikel einige Kritiken und Neuorientierungen in der Kultur- und Sozialanthropologie entwickelt. Wenn man den Industriegesellschaften einen dynamischen Charakter zusprach, glaubte man, die einfachen Gesellschaften als konservativ, traditionalistisch und jeder Innovation abgeneigt einstufen zu können. Eine solche Betrachtungsweise unterschätzt jedoch die politischen Ressourcen, die in diesen Gesellschaften durch den Zusammenstoß speziell mit neuen Wirtschaftsformen geweckt worden sind. Auch werden dabei interne Konflikte sichtbar, die nach neuen Reaktionsweisen zum Schutze der Identität rufen, speziell, nachdem sich die "Stämme" der Ureinwohner des Kontinents im Jahre 1973 als "nationale Enklaven" in der euroamerikanischen Gesellschaft erklärt haben.

I.

This paper grows out of a gnawing sense of uneasiness which troubles me more and more as I pursue my research on Native Americans of the Southwest, among them especially the Navajos. Whereas traditional cultural anthropology has been mostly concerned with problems of cultural contact, enculturation, personality development, acculturation and social assimilation among these peoples, I became increasingly confronted with a different set of questions. These were essentially problems relating to intersocietal conflict and to personality disintegration such as alcoholism, on the one hand. On the other hand, there appeared to be clear indications that I should

---

*) This paper has grown out of a more comprehensive study. I gladly acknowledge that the Fritz Thyssen Foundation in Cologne has contributed to the travel expenses during my field work in October/November 1981. David Baker was very helpful in the final editing of this paper.

address problems of counter-acculturation, of withdrawal in search for a lost identity. In view of the powerful revivalist social movements that I saw afoot, I felt that the signals among the Native Americans pointed away from continuity and toward radical discontinuity with the dominant society.

Years ago, in 1970, when on the way to the Pueblo of Santa Clara in New Mexico, I suddenly noticed a sign on a roadside post: "Visitors are not welcome!" This appeared despite the fact that the pueblo was doing a brisk business with its excellent and very beautiful pottery. Clearly, the sign worked against the interests of the people in the pueblo who made a living of throwing and selling pottery. But seemingly, they did not care about the loss of business. Rather, it appeared that they wanted to be left alone as their chances for success in a rapidly changing world were not all that good anyway. During my long and repeated residences on the Navajo reservation since 1953 I also noticed that the people had taken a defensive posture that was far reaching. Indeed, their resistance to change as well as to acculturation was aggravated by a revolting indifference on the part of the wider public in the future of Native Americans. This set of circumstances was obviously serious and was heading in the direction of an acute crisis. The decade between 1970 and 1980 has in fact been full of unrest and conflict as everyone knows (although the history of this development has never been written, neither by the Indians themselves, nor by the Anglos, nor by any other White scholar). As for myself, I have tried to create a special term to define a situation that I viewed as an attempt on the part of the Indians at a "defensive culture", by which the big revival would commence. As I conceived of it, the "defensive culture" was to give rise to another situation which I called "counter-assimilation" at the time (KÖNIG, 1969: 28 ff).

This is not the place to discuss any further the usage of these terms. May it suffice to say that they have been constructed by analogy to and as a consequence of cultural defense mechanisms, as the psychoanalysts call them. This influence in turn becomes responsible for the building of a defensive culture, the essential component of counter-acculturation in which both the particular and the uncommon characteristics of highly complex situations are spontaneously melted together in an inextricably new and original unity (cultural syncretism). Defensive cultures, in other words, tend to have their origins in moments of extreme distress. This condition has been aptly expressed by the former chairman of the Navajo Nation, Peter MacDonald, when in 1979 be stated: "I wonder if this is a new beginning or the beginning of the end?" Thus, defensive cultures originate spontaneously in extreme situations where the circumstances are such that no perceivable outlet presents itself. In other words, a defensive culture emerges at the moment when a decision must be made favoring either destruction or redemption.

That these problems have been rather neglected in modern cultural anthropology demonstrates a remarkable tendency in the discipline to overemphasize concerns of stability and of social harmony when discussing the life chances of Indian cultures and of other cultures in the Third World as well. However, we may reasonably assume that things are changing in the field today. For example, at least one of the great representatives of the Third World, Frantz Fanon, looked at these problems not only as a professional revolutionary, but also as a medical doctor, and in particular as a psychoanalyst in the tradition of Alfred Adler. Following Adler, he introduced the concept of inferiority complex in the description and analysis of the means by which colonizers from a superior nation develop the technical means for oppressing the so-called "underdeveloped" cultures. The false claim on the part of cultural superordinates that Third World cultures were underdeveloped thus became the rationale for their subjugation. The cultures of the Third World responded to this state of affairs with neurotic abandon, the threshold to alienation and its beginning. However, one still has to bear in mind that the neurosis of abandonment also nourishes the obstinacy as well as the hope for eventual acceptance. Although abandoned, people in fact know that this situation is by no means natural. It simply cannot be the state of nature. Rather, things are as they are due to extreme historical developments which eventually change one day into quite opposite conditions. It may be added that this formula has often been expressed in the case of Cargo cults where typically a "messiah" is called to free his people, "Let my people go!"

Although this process is a rather important aspect of contemporary cultural anthropology, I shall not give it adequate treatment here. Instead, I will focus on a few of its neglected consequences and take as my empirical data base the development of the Navajo Nation. The neglected consequences I want to pursue in the following sections of this paper find their locus in the search of other essential components of cultural contact out of which emerge the problems of a defensive culture. Cultural contact and cultural interplay are not limited only to cultural and psychological consequences. We have to keep in mind that the recourse to reaction has grown out of political conflagrations. Even after a period of pacification (which would follow from the establishment and development of a so-called "neutral" administration like the Bureau of Indian Affairs) the situation cannot be adequately grasped unless we introduce political categories. After all, "cultural interplay is essentially a political problem" (D. C. BRAITHWAITE, 1973).

II.

We can immediately add that this political problem is often implied in processes of acculturation. Moreover, it is essentially and unavoidably of a highly destructive nature. In fact, acculturation always means the final loss of a traditional culture and its replacement by another set of ideas. Indeed, enforced acculturation all too often means annihilation. Consequently, an Indian policy that adopts the idea of enforced acculturation as its most fundamental principle necessarily faces the annihilation of the culture or cultures in question. Sociologists often refer to this process as "proletarization". The thing that most disturbs me in all of this is the fact that neither party to the ongoing chain of events, whether bureaucrat or anthropologist, ever openly admitted this inherent danger in their developmental policies. In other words, if our intent is to protect Indian cultures (and likewise those of all underdeveloped people) then we have to replace the policy of "destructive acculturation" by "intercultural communication" (KÖNIG, 1972: 38). In so doing we can obtain the necessary information about the needs and desires of a culture different from our own. Only one assumption is made here, namely that the preservation of existing ethnic groups requires that we dispense with the notion of "one world" and replace it by the term "cultural pluralism".

Such are the ideas I discussed with several Navajos in the field in the fall of 1981. For obvious reasons I cannot disclose their names here. It must therefore suffice to say that they were between thirty and thirty-five years of age, college educated, and part of that generation that has assumed power in the Navajo government since the elections of November 10, 1982. In addition, these same persons were probably part of that group which had been promoting Peterson Zah, the new chairman of the Navajo Nation.

Obviously, the preceeding discussion provides an explicit criticism of many accepted concepts in traditional cultural anthropology and ethnosociology. To find a foothold in this complex field of theory and of politics, we have to take notice of a strange reserve in professional anthropology. Looking back in the history of the discipline, we initially of course meet the name of John Collier. Collier was the first Indian commissioner to develop a unique style in Indian policymaking during the New Deal period. It is certainly correct to say that general policy changed considerably during the New Deal, but these changes have not brought about my essential changes in the overall orientation of present day Indian policy. Although Collier understood, it is true, that the Indians "cannot be destroyed and (that) they are now advancing into the world" (J. COLLIER, 1947: 187), he first paid very little attention to the <u>results</u> of cultural anthropology. Secondly, he developed for himself a rather strange approach. The facts related to Collier's involvement in Indian affairs have only recently come to my attention since my last field trip. This is especially so as I have just completed reading Kenneth R. Philp's work on Collier. Moreover, I have had the opportunity in the last year to discuss Collier's activities with a personal friend who had met Collier while he was still running the BIA (K. R. PHILP, 1977). At the same time I happened to read David H. Lawrence's memoirs about his stay in Santa Fé in the early Twenties. Lawrence met Collier in 1920 or 1921 long before the latter became the Indian commissioner in 1934, but still at the time when he was preparing himself for a leading position in the Indian administration (D. H. LAWRENCE, 1927). According to Lawrence, Collier viewed the administration's activities as an attempt at "crushing" Indian cultures, whereas he "wanted to preserve Indian heritage". Philp writes that "Collier assumed that Indians such as the Pueblos represented not an inferior but simply a different world holding the secrets of communal life" (K. R. PHILP, 1977: 55 ff). All that is, of course, very acceptable. Quite useful too was Collier's fight against the ridiculous prejudices of so many people about Indian culture. But this was only one aspect of his activities. We have to ask ourselves what he wanted to promote in place of these simplified misconceptions. It is precisely at this point that we find Lawrence making another insightful comment (a comment, it should be added, that in my opinion does him great credit as a penetrating observer of sociocultural phenomena). Lawrence pointed out that Collier might unintentionally destroy Indian culture and identity by "setting the claws of his own benevolent volition in them" (quoted in K. R. PHILP 24, 257, note 112). This interpretation refutes the notion that Collier planned to reform Indian policy by respecting the wishes of the people involved. Still more, it is an amazing documentation of that principle of anthropological hybris which states the scientist knows better than the Indians what is good for them. As a matter of fact, Collier had not really ever left behind the ward-like mentality that makes one decide about Indian problems without taking into consideration their own wishes. This also explains the only too frequent dictatorial aspects of his Indian policy especially in matters of sheep reduction generally, and in the matter of the Fruitland irrigation project specifically (KÖNIG, 1983: part IV, 3).

Intercultural communication is always a risky affair and this seems especially so in the case of American anthropology. The problem is that it is very difficult to overcome the process whereby an observer projects his own personal concerns onto a presumed collective Native American mentality. The best example of this kind of shortcoming is seen in the case of Collier himself. It was never quite clear whether he was interested more in reforming Indian policy or more in criticising the exasperated individualism of White Americans of his time. Again as Philp puts it (1978: 3), "He concluded that pueblo culture offered a model for the redemption of American society because it concerned itself very little with the material aspects of life; its goals were beauty, adventure, joy, comradeship, and the connection of man with God." This point of view rather suits the attitude of a disappointed middle class social worker or adult educator of New York. It is emphatically not the orientation one ought to adopt for a profitable and realistic approach to Indian communities. In any case, this conviction made him get caught up in the idea of pueblo unanimity, and generally he became trapped in a belief in the unanimity of all Indian people. Clearly, Collier had no appreciation of pueblo factionalism, of the Navajo and Apache tendency to split off from the larger tribe.

It is known that Collier attached groups of professional anthropologists to his administration, but it is interesting to note that he also typically rejected their advice with the comment that it was not "practicable" (K. R. PHILP, 1978: 207). This persuasion necessarily gave preference to "political" solutions instead of solutions suggested by anthropologists and by my own concept of intercultural communication. In this sense he swerved more and more away from his original attempt at "Indian Reform" and left behind the group of anthropologists he had assembled in Chicago to study the Indian personality under the guidance of W. Lloyd Warner. It was this fundamental difference in outlook that separated the Collier administration from the anthropologists. It was not, as some have suggested, a mere spatial separation brought on either by the onset of World War Two or by the alienating influence of the Washington administration at the Bureau. So it happened that some years later another liberal Indian commissioner under the Kennedy administration, Philleo Nash, came to the following disastrous conclusion: "I did not see, in my five years in the Bureau, any changes in attitudes on the part of the Bureau personnel, or any direct one-to-one relationship between this high quality research and the end product of improved or changed administration" (P. NASH in: Anthropology and the American Indian 1973: 27). In his eyes, there had been no exchange between the existing research results and administrative action whatsoever. To me this conclusion sounds the deathknell for a rationally conducted Indian policy and leaves it to the vicissitudes of day to day politics. On the other hand, Philleo Nash emphasizes that the suggestions of the tribal leaders had often proved much more practicable in contrast to the planning of the Bureau. In the full realization of this fact he tried to develop an action orientation against the research orientation based on a "partnership relation" through "guided acculturation" (eodem loco: 30). Nash was probably the first scholar to use this term and perhaps the first to try to apply the concept in practice, specifically in developmental aid programs. His fresh approach to these problems clearly opens up new frontiers and new perspectives that we are compelled to explore further. One decisive step has already been taken to erase the old exclusionist policy of forced acculturation. In fact, Indian policy simply cannot proceed along the lines of "termination policy" with equal treatment for everybody. It most definitely has to proceed to create a system of justice that is "compensatory", in order to produce a system that somehow trys to overcome the innumerable injustices of the past (Steve TALBOT, 1977: 43). Unfortunately, after the death of President Kennedy, Philleo Nash was immediately removed from office by the presidential successor, Lyndon Baines Johnson.

III.

The most disturbing question is to know why the professional anthropologists adopted so passive or so indifferent an attitude at a time when the Indians needed protection against administrative abuse and chicanery. Vine Deloria, Jr., a Sioux from Standing Rock in South Dakota and today at the Law School of the University of Arizona in Tucson, puts it this way when describing the attitude of anthropologists during the so-called period of "Termination Policy": "Why did no social scientist, particularly anthropologist, raise his voice in our behalf?" (in: Anthropology and the American Indian, 1973: 93 ff). The same could be said of the lack of any response on the part of the government when big energy firms robbed the reservations of their mineral resources (coal, oil, gas, uranium) without adequate compensation (P. IVERSON, 1981: 104-110; R. KÖNIG, 1983, Part IV). The Indian service should have foreseen that, given the circumstances, an alternative to out and out highway robbery should have been found (to replace the selling to discount prices in contracting with Indian tribes). The point is that, methodologically speaking, traditional cultural anthropology was simply unaware of these problems. The old school took them as unforeseen and uncontrollable accidents which were of course deplorable, but inevitable. My last point refers to the fact that the single most important American contribution to Indian economic development (I refer here to that encyclopedic fund of knowledge produced by Sam Steven and his associates) has been passed over in complete silence. So, although pregnant with valuable information, the American intellectual contribution has remained inefficient and sterile (S. STEVEN (ed.), 1978; R. KÖNIG, 1979). In my opinion, all that this really indicates is an embarassing avowal of ignorance and incompetence. Such a mess can be overcome only by rethinking the assumptions under which cultural anthropology has worked in the past.

One of the most disturbing points here is that this deplorable lack of activism on the part of professional social and cultural anthropologists has had serious consequences for the understanding of native societies. I am rather inclined to say that their obvious inactivism is felt in a typical prejudicial topos that depicts native societies as static, immovable, traditionalistic, keeping to the past. In fact, of course, they are clearly in flux as is any other society, though at a different rhythm, at a different velocity, and in a different direction. The static condition of native societies is by no means their "normal" condition but rather a highly critical state, the cause of which must be further explored. Even the most primitive societies move on in time, they change continuously so long as they are viable. Indeed, to renounce or to dispense with change may be lethal for any society. Therefore cultural anthropology has sometimes behaved as a moral grave digger for these societies by looking at them as highly integrated and immobile systems. Their immobility only too often has been taken for granted, all possible change being reduced to the external impact of other "more" developed societies. In some way they are looked upon as mummified relics of an unknown past rather than as part of a continuously changing contemporary reality. Yet strangely enough, this orientation is to be found among both the more conservative anthropologists of the past and contemporary alternative anthropologists alike. We shall have to shift away from both groups in order to find our way out of this very unsatisfactory situation.

Deloria made another remark, often emphasized by many red man - and my native experts all agreed on this point - that it is surely not the anthropologist who influences native life but rather it is the BIA, in other words: an organization developed by white people that follows white policy standards in thinking and evaluation. A more or less unspoken, but nevertheless agreed upon principle among members of this organization, suggests that everybody would be far better off if the red man could suddenly turn white. Then all the problems would be solved. This is precisely what Robert A. Roessel, Jr., a deserving white educator married to a Navajo woman who has become a prominent representative of college educated Navajos, has in mind when he says that the reservation schools have so far only tried to scrub the Indian white (1979: 209-210). The problem they ought to be concerned with is how to transfer to the Navajo an education that simultaneously preserves his identity as an Indian and increases his chances of survivability in a white dominant culture. For Roessel and a few of his colleagues (R. KÖNIG, 1981), especially the most important Navajo educators Samuel Billison and Dillon Platero, this could only be achieved by founding schools under Indian administration that are independent and that have a special curriculum appropriate to Indian needs. Elsewhere, I have described this most ingenious attempt at fundamental change on the reservation and so I will not dwell any further on it here (R. KÖNIG 1980 and 1983; 1981). A "do it yourself" approach was surely indicated as the first step toward overcoming the guardianship of the BIA. But such self-reliance was only achievable by developing a "contracting" system with the BIA over financing, competence, curricula, infrastructures (buildings and road construction), and other administrative chores. Incidentally, the term "Contract School" has often been used inappropriately to refer to these schools. At its inception, the contracting system may have meant, and may still mean, that dependence has only been redirected and not abolished altogether. Still, according to Deloria, the current situation could lead to a system of "checks and balances" by which the Indians might protect their interests, follow up on what seems useful to them, and avert harmful influences (V. DELORIA in: Anthropology and the American Indian, 1973: 97). Deloria's reference here to "checks and balances" seems to me to have an important, if unexpected, consequence for anthropology. Namely, that by reference to one of the most essential categories of political science, Deloria has opened a new dimension for anthropology; a dimension that sorely needs exploration and one that provides anthropology with the chance to take the place it deserves among the social sciences. In other words, the scandalous lack of intellectual awareness and political involvement on the part of cultural anthropologists will only be overcome when the field is accessed by political anthropology. So influenced, cultural anthropology would become better grounded in applied anthropology in the sense that its practice would become an "enlightened" practice, one protected from routine-like and bureaucratized activity as has been the case so far with the Indian policy of the BIA.

The occasion for this new development was of course President Nixon's address of July 8, 1970 entitled, "Self-Determination Without Termination", in which he attempted to erase scathing Indian criticism of traditional government policy (for the text, see A. M. JOSEPHY Jr. (ed.), 1971). Realistically considered however, this statement was nothing more than a declaration of purpose since its implementation would have required an additional corpus of specific regulations. As a matter of fact, these were never promulgated. Therefore the whole thing remained sequestered and inconsequential, passing on into one of those "Chinese shades" so typical of this man's presidency. So when the Indians took his speech literally and turned in about thirty formal requests before December 1970 for the promised self-determination nothing happened in Washington because the stage had not yet been set for real action. The result was the rapid growth of rebellion in the early seventies among all Indians in the United States, climaxing in November 1972 in the occupation of the BIA in Washington and in 1973 with the formal declaration of "Indian Nations" within the country (V. DELORIA, 1974).

The most important point in these developments, as I have described elsewhere (R. KÖNIG, 1980, 1983), is that none of the anthropologists dealing with Indian problems sought to push Nixon's initiative toward a realistic end. Not a single one raised his voice in favor of promoting autonomous Indian developments. On the other hand, the Nixon address combined with Washington's inconsiderate attitude simply had to break up the field for the heavy swelling of the political factor in Indian affairs, that factor that anthropologists and ethnosociologists have thus far so irresponsibly neglected. If anthropologists became aware at all of this change then, at the very most, they felt taken aback. Their fleeting consternation has produced only irrelevant conclusions instead of a full methodological overhaul of the anthropological approach to these new problems. More or less the same series of events took place with reference to the main culprit under indictment here, the Bureau of Indian Affairs. After the first alarm and after a period of dodging and ducking, the BIA returned reinvigorated and smugly indifferent to its previous posture of authoritarian guardianship. But once a process of collective consciousness formation has begun, it cannot be simply retrieved. This is exactly the situation we have to face today. Several important steps toward maturity have already been taken so that the Indian movement can no longer be arbitrarily cancelled. The stage is set for a new beginning, a beginning that must inevitably force cultural anthropology into rethinking its most fundamental premises.

Several factors have conspired to urge a new approach to our problem. First of all, I would like to say that over the last forty years a series of important Navajo leaders have appeared each of whom in concert with the others contributed equally to the considerable furthering of self-consciousness among the people of the Navajo Nation. If we consider the succession of chairmen like Chee Dodge (1942-1946), Sam Akeah (1947-1954), Paul Jones (1955-1962), Raymond Nakai (1963-1970), Peter MacDonald (1971-1982), and Peterson Zah (1983-), we can see without explanation that to an equal degree each represents Navajo culture, Navajo character, and an evergrowing Navajo self-consciousness that cannot be repealed. The nation has matured, a maturity that persists due to the take over by the young Indians, especially in the person of Peterson Zah. My comments here are not meant in a figurative sense, but in a literal one insofar as the new generation has entered this stage of development, one that the young Indians have had plenty of time to prepare for. In 1970 Peterson Zah early epitomized these events as he was already involved in a piece of "action research" against the institution of the reservation trading posts (on Peterson Zah's activities in 1970 see R. KÖNIG, 1973; ch. VI). In contrast to his predecessor, Peter MacDonald, Zah represents the grass-roots Navajos who have kept their distance from Window Rock. Now, even if my expectations are not shortly realized, we still have to remember that the new Navajo Nation has definitely come to life. Its new genesis will force cultural anthropology to adopt an approach, to take a stand, against what has so far hampered Indian development. This too is a highly political problem, one that summons a political anthropology into action.

Step number one in this matter is naturally a basic and detailed critique of the Bureau of Indian Affairs as an institution. After all, this is the most central development on the Navajo reservation, indeed on all Indian reservations, that has deeply influenced the course cultural anthropology has taken (this was also the main focus of my last field trip in the fall of 1981). Cultural anthropology simply cannot afford to ignore the power of the BIA over scientific work when there is such widespread agreement with public statements made by native individuals such as the Assiniboine, Ken Martin. For example, four months after the Nixon declaration on self-determination, in November, 1970, Martin affirmed that, "everything is allowed which they, the BIA, allows ... I say the BIA has only one eye, and this is on itself" (Anthropology and the American Indian,

1973: 44 f; same statement by Alfonso ORTIZ: 89, and others). Under these circumstances, and this is what Ken Martin had in mind when he made these statements, there simply cannot be any kind of Indian self-determination. On the contrary, this is most definitely colonialism of the first order. There will not be, there cannot be, any change in this ossified condition until fundamental change takes place, until Indian dependence on the BIA is permanently abolished. Here exactly incipit political anthropology.

The same point of view is taken by Alfonso Ortiz of San Juan Pueblo in New Mexico when he says that the BIA plays a more important role in Indian life than does cultural anthropology (eodem loco: 85-92). I would like to add to his remarks by saying that this essential institutional misemphasis is probably also responsible for the distortions in anthropologists' pictures of Indian life in general. A kind of cultural lag enters their representations and forces them to emphasize the archaic features of Indian life. Of course, they should instead attend to the current features of these civilizations, civilizations that are our contemporaries and that have to find their way in contemporary civilization without losing their identities. Obviously, the Indians can only achieve independence from all the remnants of forced acculturation through active pursuit of full political emancipation. Obviously too, the future of cultural anthropology and ethnosociology is intimately and irretrievably bound up with a critical reform of the BIA. As these problems are political in nature, cultural anthropology can only survive as a discipline when it becomes a political anthropology. It will otherwise become useless. Cognition as an important aspect of cultural interplay thus becomes itself a political problem, insofar as it develops new approaches in anthropology and ethnosociology that have so far been rather neglected.

V.

In two other publications dealing with protecting Navajo identity in a rapidly changing world, I have made it very clear that an emphasis on the political aspects of these problems should by no means imply personal attacks. As a matter of fact, I have known many BIA officials who were devoted to the Indians, and I have quoted them by name with warmest gratitude (R. KÖNIG, 1973, 1980, 1983). In general the development of a political anthropology is in itself by no means a political action, but rather a shift in alignment with a new conceptual emphasis as new segments of the research topic emerge - segments which have so far been neglected by cultural anthropologists. These aspects are, first of all, characterized by conflict. But, when the old style of cultural anthropology called special attention to apparent unanimity and harmony of Indian cultures, a very peculiar picture of them arose. John Collier puts it this way, "All the dichotomies are melted away: joy requires sorrow, and sorrow, joy; man and society and the world are one; fantasy and the old, hard wisdom of experience join in the rituals, the moralizing tales, the songs, the myths; idealism and ideality are joined with searching and undeviating practicality. And the child is joined with the man" (J. COLLIER, 1949: 99). Lines with the same meaning could be quoted by the hundreds out of recent literature. I only wonder with this kind of interpretation, what is made of those well known instances of pueblo factionalism which have for generations been the cause for bitter feuds, for secessions, and for separations among and within Indian groups? Indeed, the same kind of segmentation seems already to have occured even in precolombian times as we may cautiously conclude from the presence of several "kiwas" in the old pueblos. In contemporary experience, the kiwas are sometimes the locus of cleavages in the Pueblo and can cause factions to develop. Similar symptoms of this tendency to form factions can be found among the Navajos of both past and present, and in general among Apache cultures with their remarkable propensity to split off in bands from the main group. Finally, how does this model of universalism and harmony help us to explain gossiping, disputes, sorcery and witchcraft when each are the instruments of, or the results of cleavages, tensions, or separations in seemingly closed communities (L. LAMPHERE, 1977: 44 f)? I will not follow up on this line of discourse any further here. My intent in limiting myself to these few remarks, is to prevent the untrained observer from getting bewitched or charmed by the externalities of Indian cultures. The historian knows only too well that these superficial structures are quite often torn to pieces and internally dismembered by enduring feuds. They differ from the processes we are acquainted with in as much as the in-fighting and self-dismemberment that Indian groups experience occur under a very different system of reasoning. Our conception of "indivisibility" or of "unanimity" is nothing but an ethnocentric illusion, the quixotic expression of a bunch of mental fugitives from Western civilization. When so many well informed observers have so fundamentally misunderstood acculturation, by regarding it as a form of integrative assimilation or by classifying it without reference to "antagonistic acculturation", they have then underrated in a most unpardonable way the sometimes highly critical stages of disorganization that Navajos and other Indians have been forced to endure through centuries of European contact (G. DEVEREUX and E. M. LOEB, 1943; J. ADAIR and E. Z. VOGT, 1949). The Indians have put up with the European push since the Spanish conquest of what is today the American Southwest. After World War Two returning Zuni veterans had to endure a form of reinitiation rite (a kind of rite of reintegration) according to E. Vogt (E. Z. VOGT, 1961 and A. W. WILLIAMS Jr., 1970), because they were not supposed to return directly to their lands after service but had to go through a lengthy and agonizing ceremonial of "reintegration" during which they were assailed with restlessness and feelings of anxiety. This was by no means a happy return to the good old style of life they had known. On the contrary, as the ritual assumed the character of a sacrifice with heavy ceremonial obligations, it resulted in a heavy increase in alcoholism among the participants.

In saying this, I want to underline the fact that we have to liberate ourselves from a static conception of Indian life, especially as concerns the grass-root Navajo. Anthropological observers have all too often underestimated the traumatic consequences certain events like sheep reduction (recently at issue again in the fight between Hopi and Navajo over the "joint use area") can have on the Indians. The same holds true in regard to the painful memories many still have of the "long walk" of the Navajos to Bosque Redondo in 1864 (R. ROESSEL (ed.), 1973; R. JOHNSON and R. ROESSEL (eds.), 1974; R. KÖNIG, 1982). These events are real crises with consequences so incisive and far reaching that they will be remembered far into the future and again spoil the political climate. Conflicts and competitions yet to take place may determine the actions of any unit in the society whether individual, family, clan, chapter, or tribe. Indeed, these opposing forces will create an inevitable succession of continuous and rapid changes, changes that have been overlooked by anthropologists in the past because they could not understand and appreciate their importance. Nor could anthropologists comprehend the Indians' motives for fighting and striving - again the consequence of ethnocentrism.

Vine Deloria Jr. (1979: 28) speaks quite correctly of a "process of growth and awareness that characterizes a group of people working toward achieving maturity". During this process, appropriately termed "formation of a nation", traditional Navajo ways become receptive to new methods of political activism and to new political goals, specifically ones aimed at sovereignty. Moreover, the reservation system now becomes outdated and a framework for dialogue comes into existence. Implied here is a "checks and balances" model for social interaction by which unilateral dependency is finally abolished. With the proclamation of the Navajo Nation, the new model becomes fully operational and a new dimension appears in relations between the Navajos and the United States. From this moment, the Navajo Nation is a "national enclave" within the boundaries of the United States as Edward H. Spicer has seen very early (E. H. SPICER 1966; see also G. P. CASTILE and G. KUSHNER (eds.) 1981), and, perhaps under their influence Vine Deloria, Jr. connected with a similar concept developed by a 17th century Spanish philosopher, Francisco de Vittoria (1974, VII and VIII). In addition to their efforts at cultural self-evaluation, the Indians have become more educated. They have also had plenty of opportunity to learn the rules of the game in politics. Deloria (1973: 94) for example, notes that in cases where it does not agree with BIA regulations, the tribal council can simply make a reservation on the next flight to Washington, show up the next morning in the Department of the Interior, and "raise all kinds of hell" in order to force the Interior to surrender to Indian demands. And if still nothing happens, the delegates will make an appointment with one of the local editors of the Washington Post and begin a campaign in the mass media in order to put the government under pressure (R. KÖNIG, 1982: 354). The Navajos and Indians from other tribes have not only succeeded in occupying the BIA in November, 1972 but they have also learned to manipulate the lobby system in the Nation's capitol. Today they are quite aware of the various means by which they can make their voices heard and get action on important issues. They have learned to meet with their senators and congressmen in Arizona and in New Mexico. After all, the Anglo politicians are slightly more inclined to listen to groups such as the Navajo that are composed of 160,000 individuals and whose vote may be quite decisive in the next election. Finally, highly specialized lobbies have emerged to protect the Navajo Arts and Crafts Guild from Anglo competition and Japanese imports of "genuine" Indian jewelry. These same guilds also promote the use of special feathers of protected birds in the fabrication of Kachina dolls, appealing to the freedom of religious cults (R. KÖNIG, 1983: part IV, 5; also see Navajo Times, Vol. 23, No. 42, Oct. 14, 1981: 9). It seems that most of the anthropologists, and especially the BIA, have not yet become aware of the upsurge of newly gained intellectuality on many Indian reservations. Significantly, many Indians have master degrees and a number have earned doctorates, while most of the "college educated" BIA officials have remained at the Bachelor level. Only a handful have taken the Masters degree. In a word, today's Indian intellectual is by far superior to his white counterpart in the BIA. He is able to play on the keyboard of the mass media so that his needs will be made known to the Nation at large.

VI.

An understanding of the development of Indian policy requires that we distinguish between "variable factors" and "constant factors". William T. Hagan (1961: 121) proposes that only the latter factors yield insight into the structural causes of success or failure of a given policy. In other words, the variable factors refer to history, the constant factors to structural constellations of a more lasting character. Practically speaking, Hagan's point would seem to lead inevitably to a reformulation of the organizational structure of the BIA; but as soon as the issue is put forward, it becomes immediately obvious that in fact very little has been accomplished in the way of changing the organizational structure of this important agency. In fact, just as little has been done, by way of academic influence, in the fields of cultural anthropology and ethnosociology. I mentioned above the poor reception the extremely important volume by Sam Steven and his associates had in 1978. This work should have awakened discussion but it has instead remained practically unnoticed. The result has been that no one has so far realized that both approaches - the pragmatic policy making of the BIA and the analytic approach taken by cultural anthropology - will have to make similar changes. The vacuum has meanwhile been filled with heaps of parapolitical literature more representative of a pervasive feeling of uneasiness than of a real attempt at a new beginning. Under these conditions it becomes rather meaningless to discuss single features of routine administrative action without any reference to much needed changes in the methodology of cultural anthropology. It goes almost without saying that the converse also holds true, that changes in cultural anthropology imply corresponding changes in policy.

We have already seen how cultural anthropology has lagged behind developments by not recognizing fundamental changes in the general character of Indian political life. We now have to level the same criticism against the organizational framework of Indian policy, the Bureau of Indian Affairs. This institution was established in order to help Native Americans make a living under rapidly changing social conditions and also to protect their heritage of land, water, and other resources from economic exploitation. Now quite in contrast to these goals, it turns out that the BIA could not keep pace with the new level of awareness experienced by its companion institution, the Native Americans. Clearly the Navajos were developing at a much faster rate than their bureaucratic coordinators. Medically speaking, one must conclude that the influence of the BIA is counterindicated in the presence of Indian policy making. As an administrative body, the Bureau is essentially unable to grasp what in the Navajos' eyes is fundamental for survival.

The political scientist, Paul Stuart (1978: 159) takes up this argument with reference to Philip Selznick's 1949 study of the Tennessee Valley Authority. Selznick spoke of an organization suffering from itself because of its lack of flexibility and its exaggerated rigidity. With respect to the BIA, not even John Collier was able to change basic inflexibilities that from the beginning "in the first fifteen years after the Civil War made it possible for external organizations to influence personnel selection, to control subordinates, and to define organizational goals" (1978: 151). Later on the BIA turnes in on itself, literally lost touch with the changing Native American reality, and thus exposed the Indians to uncontrollable external influences. Three basic issues calling for special treatment arise at this point in our discussion of the BIA as an organization:

1. If we now investigate the organizational goals of the BIA we can easily see that the Nixon proclamation on self-determination has not had any sizeable effect on the BIA. Expert testimony given by both Indians and Anglos alike at the 1970 meeting of the American Anthropological Association in San Diego, California revealed that the BIA still clung to the definition of "termination policy" surviving from the Eisenhower administration and that none of its administrators ever uttered a word against the disastrous Public Law 280 presented in 1953 by Dillon Myer (P. IVERSON, 1981: 50, 74-75). In fact, one could say that since no explicit declaration of purpose had ever been put forward, the old ideas were still alive in Congress (Anthropology and the American Indian, 1973: 31, 48), and this has remained unchanged ever since. This becomes more informative when we compare the arguments at that time of the "budget conscious Republicans (who) predictably feared that too many federal dollars were being lavished on the Indians" (IVERSON: 50) during a period of prosperity, with the same arguments proffered by Reaganomics in 1982, a year of severe recession (R. KÖNIG, 1982, part. IV, 1). The drummers have changed, but the beat remains the same.

2. When organizational goals remain insufficiently defined and essentially unclear, the selection of suitable personnel at all levels in both rank and file, becomes rather precarious. Given the relatively low status of the Indian Service in Federal bureaucracy, the position of Indian Commissioner is either not in great demand or else it is assumed by political carreerists who have little real interest in Indian problems. With few exceptions (John COLLIER, Oliver LaFARGE, Philleo NASH), the responsible men in Washington have typically taken great care to avoid appointing an expert. Here one has to again ask why none of the representative cultural anthropologists has ever run for this key office in Indian affairs? This pattern of inactivism is surely as reprehensible as the ones mentioned above. The same is true of the local representatives of the BIA, although in the case of the Navajos I have had the satisfaction of meeting a few highly qualified experts. However, I must immediately add that they seemed to me to be the exception rather than the rule.

Since the massive offensive on the Southwest by big energy firms during the Seventies, local agents have been instrumental in exploiting the Indians through unfair contract agreements. Instead of being sufficiently informed about the consequences of certain decisions, and instead of receiving protection from fast-talking energy representatives, the Indians were intentionally mislead, especially with regard to ecological problems. In the present as in the past, intercultural communication continues to be hampered by corrupt go-betweens. Jerry Kammer (1981) has recently written about this problem in his treatise on the fateful role played by Harrison Loesch in the Black Mesa scandal (R. KÖNIG, 1982). But he is really only the last in a long line of crooks (R. KÖNIG, 1983, part IV). I have personally listed many of the same kinds of cases in the past in order to show that these deplorable crimes are by no means isolated exceptions to the everyday state of affairs on the reservation. On the contrary, they are the rule due to the inadequacies and inefficiency of the BIA as an organization.

3. This leads us to the last point concerning the reasons for these continuing dysfunctions. In order to avoid corruption and incompetence, organizations must develop procedures to achieve optimal coordination of activities and departments. Unfortunately, this very important third factor, as outlined by Paul Stuart (1978: 150), has been sadly disregarded in organizations for the promotion of Indian policy from the very beginning. When the Indian Service was transferred from the War Department to the Department of the Interior the first in a series of conflicts arose between the two organizations. The battle seriously damaged Indian political activity and policy formation before, during, and after the Civil War. The reason for this failure is easy to understand; the army had no insight into Indian problems to begin with, and the Interior was unable to impose its policy, especially on newly arrived immigrants from Europe, due to insufficient police and military support. Another more incisive conflict arose between different sections in the Department of the Interior, specifically between the office of Public Land and the Indian Service. Whereas the Indian Service was charged with the responsibility to protect Indian land, it nevertheless often promoted the sale of land to European immigrants, robbing these properties from the Indians from 1840 to the present. The same scenario was repeated in the case of that agency responsible for, among other things, water rights and usage, the Bureau of Reclamation. When, for example, the BIA undertook development of the Navajo Indian Irrigation Project (NIIP) to irrigate 110.630 acres in the Shiprock area by taking the water in the San Juan River, the termination of the work was delayed again and again (with the excuse of lack of funds) due to the intervention of the Bureau of Reclamation (P. IVERSON 1981: 107-114). Here big U.S. energy interests interfered with Indian concerns and forced the Navajos to capitulate in the face of the massive political corruption and financial power of these giant industries. Together with Indian dependence these events hatched a general state of corruption that received very little public attention given the helpless situation of the Indians. Negotiations with the energy firms were kept top secret, as Jerry Kammer has noted (1980: 87). However, since the dismissal of Richard Nixon people have become more sensitive to these dark policies. As a result, cultural anthropology has also had to rethink its theoretical position. In a book published in 1973, the fieldwork for which was completed in 1970, I had already discussed the unfair methods of persuasion used against the Navajos in contract negotiations (R. KÖNIG, 1973: 100-105; see also, R. KÖNIG, 1983: 129 f). Among contemporary anthropologists concerned with the Navajos, only Peter Iverson (1981) and Jerry Kammer (1981) have taken a few essential steps in this direction. They asked how could the Navajos be expected to make a well informed decision about stripmining when "officials from Southwestern states, industrial concerns, the Bureau of Indian Affairs, and Navajo technical advisors, advised Diné that they should proceed" (P. IVERSON, 1981: 105). These authors further note that the Black Mesa Power Plant affair "also showed that the Navajos were still getting insufficient technical advice". Thus they concluded that "whether viewed from a colonial, metropolis-satellite, or other model, the situation represents the dilemma faced by Native American people across the country: how to best utilize their resources in the face of external pressure and internal needs" (eodom loco: 105; R. KÖNIG 1983, IV). This approach to the problem puts us squarely in the center of a political anthropology, properly speaking.

Before coming to an end, I would like to make one last remark. As a rule, the main concern of political anthropology has centered around questions dealing with the origins of the state and other political organizations in "stateless" societies. In the case of the Navajos, the establishment of the "chapter organization" has certainly had a tremendous influence on the political development of these people (A. W. WILLIAMS Jr., 1970; R. KÖNIG, 1983: part IV, 5). Under the direction of the new chairman of the Navajo Nation, Peterson Zah, the grass-roots Navajos will undoubtedly continue to make progress, perhaps in spite of the neglect of this group by Zah's predecessor, Peter MacDonald. This of course is a most important topic but it is by no means identical to the interests I am pursuing here. What I have been in search of here is the configuration of political responses a given culture, with the special characteristics of a tribal society, has to external challenge and influence from a dominant political and cultural complex. The kind of cultural interplay we have dealt with so far, is of a very peculiar character, since it is typical of interplay between a fullfledged state system on the one hand and a stateless society on the other. But "stateless" in this context by no means implies an inactive society only capable of acculturation or assimilation as the cultural anthropologists were inclined to believe. That appreciation of Navajo society could only have led to its annihilation. On the contrary, these societies have shown their ability to resist the onslaught of the great American melting pot by learning how to deal with internal conflicts imposed from the outside. Indeed, the Navajo have learned not only how to react after a long and painful learning process, they have made practical use of those political strategies developed by their oppressors and the dominant culture. Today these people have learned their lesson well. They have proved their ability to defend themselves against a heavyweight opponent. Their defense will hold so long as the opponent respects the democratic rules of bargaining and of fair play.

References

The bibliography is strictly limited to the publications quoted in the article. Two much larger bibliographies, referring to the background of the problems discussed, have been compiled by the author. See R. König 1973 (appr. 120 entries) and 1983 (appr. 300 entries). The most important bibliographical work on the Navajos by L. Lee Correll, Editha L. Watson, and David M. Brugge, Navajo bibliography, revised ed. Window Rock 1969 has been discontinued in 1973 after the premature death of two of the editors.

Adair, John and Evon Z. Vogt, 1949: Navajo and Zuni veterans: A study of contrasting modes of culture change. In: American Anthropologist, Vol. 51.

American Anthropological Association, 1973: Anthropology and the American Indian. San Francisco, The Indian Historian Press.

Braithwaite, Douglas C., 1973: Developing political power in two southern Paiute communities. In: Ruth M. Houghton, ed., Native American politics: Power relationships in the Western Great Basin to-day. Bureau of Governmental Research. University of Nevada Press, Reno, Nevada.

Collier, John, 1947: Indians of the Americas. New York, Mentor Books 1961.

— 1963: From every zenith. A memoir and some essais on life and thought. Denver, Colo. Sage Books.

Deloria, Jr., Vine, 1973: Some criticisms and a number of suggestions. In: American Anthropological Association.

— 1974: Behind the trail of broken treaties. An Indian declaration of independence. New York, 4th ed., Dell 1978.

— 1979: Self-determination and the concept of sovereignty. In: Roxanne Dunbar Ortiz, ed., Economic development on American Indian reservations. Albuquerque, Institute for Native American development. Native American Studies Center, Vol. 1.

Devereux, George and E. M. Loeb, 1943: Antagonistic acculturation. In: American Sociological Review, Vol. 8.

Hagan, Willian Thomas, 1961: American Indians, rev. ed. Chicago, The University of Chicago Press.

Iverson, Peter, 1981: The Navajo Nation. Westpoint, Conn. and London, England. Greenwood Press.

Johnson, Broderick H. and Ruth Roessel, eds., 1973: Navajo stories of the long Walk period. Tsaile, Arizona, The Navajo Community College Press.

Josephy, Alvin M., 1971: Red Power. The American Indian's fight for freedom. New York, McGraw Hill.

Kammer, Jerry, 1980: The second long walk. The Navajo-Hopi land dispute. Albuquerque, N.M., The University of New Mexico Press.

König, René, 1969: Über einige offene Fragen und ungelöste Probleme der Entwicklungsforschung. In: R. König, ed., Aspekte der Entwicklungssoziologie. Special issue number 13 to the Kölner Zeitschrift für Soziologie und Sozialpsychologie. Opladen, Westdeutscher Verlag.

— 1972: Über einige Grundlagen der empirischen Kulturanthropologie. In: R. König und A. Schmalfuss, ed., Kulturanthropologie. Düsseldorf - Wien, Econ Verlag.

— 1973: Indianer Wohin? Alternativen in Arizona. Opladen, Westdeutscher Verlag.

— 1979: Neue Linien in der Entwicklungspolitik für Indianer in den Vereinigten Staaten. In: Die Dritte Welt, Vol. 7.

— 1981: The role of bilingual education in safeguarding the identity of the grass-roots Navajos. In: Pieter T. Hovens, ed., North American Indian studies. European contributions. Göttingen, Edition Herodot.

— 1982: Kampf um Raum? Über einige Hintergründe des Konflikts zwischen Navajos und Hopis. In: Kölner Zeitschrift für Soziologie und Sozialpsychologie, Vol. 34.

— 1983: Navajo Report 1970-1980. Von der Kolonie zur Nation. Second considerably enlarged edition. Berlin, Dietrich Reimer Verlag (first ed. 1980).

Lamphere, Louise, 1977: To run after them. Tucson, Arizona. The University of Arizona Press.

Lawrence, David H., 1927: Mornings in Mexico. Etruscan Places. New York, Pinguin Books (1977).

Nash, Philleo, 1973: Applied anthropology and the concept of guided acculturation. In: Anthropology and the American Indian. San Francisco, The Indian Historian Press.

Nixon, Richard, 1971: Self-determination without termination. In: A. M. Josephy, Jr.

Ortiz, Alfonso, 1973: An Indian anthropologist's perspective on anthropology. In: Anthropology and the American Indian. San Francisco, The Indian Historian Press.

Philp, Kenneth R., 1977: John Collier's crusade for Indian reform, 1920-1954. Tucson, Arizona, The University of Arizona Press.

Roessel, Robert A., Jr., 1979: History of Navajo Education 1948-1978. Rough Rock, Arizona.

Roessel, Ruth, ed., 1971: Navajo stories of the Long Walk period. Tsaile. Navajo Community College Press.

Selznick, Philip, 1949: TVA and the grass-roots. A study in sociology of formal organisations. Berkeley, University of California Press.

Steven, Sam, ed., 1978: American Indian economic development. The Hague-Paris-Chicago, Mouton.

Stuart, Paul, 1978: The Indian office. Growth and development of an American Institution (1865-1900). Reno, Nevada, University Research Press.

Talbot, Steve, 1977: The Myth of Indian economic and political incompetence. In: South West Economy and Society, Vol. 2.

Williams, Aubrey W., Jr., 1970: Navajo political process. Washington, D.C., Smithonian Institution Press.

Address of the Author:
Prof. Dr. René König
Marienstraße 9
5000 Köln 40 (Widdersdorf)
Fed.Rep. of Germany

Basic Anthropological Perspectives in the Study of Ethnicity

Tom G. Svensson

Abstract: The article begins with a brief orientation on the background to the development of anthropological research regarding ethnicity as well as of current trends in the theory of this particular field of study. In order to make an appropriate account of the predominant perspectives in the study of ethnicity certain basic concepts, such as ethnic boundary, ethnic identity, interethnic relation, ethnopolitics, and ethnic art, all of which refer to theoretical framework most researchers would adhere to are being discussed in some detail. Ethnographic illustrations are taken mostly from Arctic/subarctic regions. The problems connected to ethnopolitics and ethnic art are illustrated more thoroughly by means of own research among the Sámi. The article ends with some personal reflections about the quality and usefulness of ethnicity studies presently and also about possible directions those may take in the near future.

Résumé: Cet article commence par une orientation brève sur le développement de la recherche anthropologique quant à non seulement l'ethnicité mais encore aux directions de développement actuelles de ce domaine d'étude particulier. Pour faire un compte approprié des perspectives prédominées de l'étude d'ethnicité, certaines notions fondamentales sont discutées en détail, par exemple "les bornes éthniques", "l'identité éthnique", "les relations interéthniques","l'éthnopolitique" et "l'art éthnique", qui tous appartiennent à un cadre théorique accepté par la majorité des savants. La plupart des exemples ethnographiques est dérivée des régions arctiques/subarctiques. Des problèmes appartenant à l'éthnopolitique et l'art éthnique sont présentés plus en détail à cause des recherches personnelles sur les Sámi. L'article termine par des reflections personnelles sur la qualité et l'utilité des études d'éthnicité actuelles et aussi sur la question quelles directions de développement ces études vont prendre dans l'avenir.

Zusammenfassung: Der Beitrag beginnt mit einem kurzen Überblick über die Hintergründe der Entwicklung anthropologischer Forschung bezüglich der Ethnizitätsprobleme sowie der gegenwärtigen theoretischen Trends in dieser Fragestellung. Um einen angemessenen Einstieg zu den vorherrschenden Zielsetzungen der Ethnizitätsforschung zu ermöglichen, werden etwas ausführlicher grundlegende Konzepte diskutiert, z.B. bezüglich "ethnischer Grenzziehungen", "ethnischer Identitäten", "interethnischer Beziehungen", "Ethnopolitik" und "ethnischer Kunst", die alle auf einen von den meisten Forschern akzeptierten theoretischen Rahmen bezogen sind. Die vorgestellten Beispiele betreffen überwiegend die arktischen/subarktischen Gebiete. Probleme der "Ethnopolitik" und "ethnischer Kunst" werden etwas ausführlicher auf der Grundlage eigener Forschungen über die Sami vorgestellt. Einige persönliche Erwägungen über die Qualität und den Nutzen von Ethnizitätsstudien sowie über mögliche Entwicklungstendenzen für die Zukunft stehen am Ende des Beitrages.

↔↔↔↔↔↔↔↔↔↔↔

Introduction

The focus on problems relating to ethnicity is of a rather late date in anthropological research. Without question sociology is the forerunner in developing an interest for the ethnic aspect of social life. Since ethnicity connects to culture in a broad sense, it comes as no surprise that anthropology both follows up and takes a lead in building and refining its own theory. The theoretical preconditions for such headway, however, derive from specific anthropological research dealing with 1) processes of retribalism being observed in many African urban settings (see e.g. Mitchell, 1956, and Epstein, 1958) and 2) plural society studies (Smith, 1965). There is no reason here to give a full account of this significant development in anthropological research. Such reviews have already been carried out by several scholars in the field. It should suffice to mention here the excellent review article by Ronald Cohen (1978) and the programatic statement by Leo Despres (1975). For our purpose I consider it far more valuable to go straight into existing theories and elucidate certain essential parts thereof.

Let us take a statement by Ronald Cohen as a starting point. To him "ethnicity represents a shift to new theoretical and empirical concerns in anthropology" (Cohen, 1978: 384). This assertion has been questioned by quite a few anthropologists who maintain that the general aspect of ethnicity was studied long before it was given such explicit form and content as it has at present. Classical works concerning the Nuer and the Tallensi by Evans-Pritchard and Meyer Fortes respectively are frequently referred to as early thematic predecessors (Evans-Pritchard, 1940, Fortes, 1945). Edmund Leach's study from Highland Burma remains the most important prerequisite for the development of more explicit theories about ethnicity (Leach, 1954). In comparison with recent developments in anthropology these studies deal only implicitly with ethnicity. Despite the justification of arguing for a connecting link between classical social anthropology, as it developed in the early 1940's onwards, and the fairly recent advancement of ethnicity theory, I agree with Ronald Cohen that this shift of concerns is both dramatic and real. For, after all, new concepts have been developed and the emphasis on inter-ethnic relations takes up perspectives of social organization, certainly adding new insights both to culture and society.

There was very little research explicitly devoted to problems of ethnicity in the 1960's and even less before that decade. For that reason it is appropriate to conceive of Fredrik Barth as the most efficient "break-water"; his book of 1969, Ethnic groups and boundaries, makes unquestionable headway in this field. One of Barth's most ardent critics, Leo Despres, goes so far as to draw a line regarding the era of ethnicity studies, i.e. B.B. (before Barth) and A.B. (after Barth) (Despres, 1975: 187). What was new with Barth and his associates was the emphasis on the boundary between different ethnic groups and how it was developed and maintained. Moreover, Barth also introduced a new perception of ethnic identity. According to him ethnic identity is based on the dual concerns of self-ascription and ascription by others. In order to function in organized interethnic relations, the ethnic identity, as an expression of self-identification, must be paired with a recognition of the same identity by others with whom one interacts (Barth, 1969). Any interethnic relation is dependent on such congruence between articulation and recognition of identity, otherwise interaction in this form will break down. This notion of ethnic identity stresses the interactional aspect of identity, i.e. how the role is played in a given context, rather than the subjective feelings and emotions embedded in individual persons.

This point may lead us to other problems under debate, e.g. that of unit for analysis. In ethnicity studies, is it the ethnic identity that should be given primary attention, or is it the ethnic group consisting of a number of people with shared ethnic identity mobilized for a special purpose? No matter how one looks at it, there can be full agreement on at least one point; both these concepts are analytical constructs (Mitchell, 1974: 1). So is the concept of ethnic boundary.

If our main objective is to increase our understanding of interethnic relations, the three concepts mentioned here appear to be equally important, however, they should be viewed as analytical tools rather than units for analysis. In the first place, ethnicity deals with interethnic relations, otherwise it makes little sense talking about ethnicity. In analyzing interethnic relations we are also able to depict in general some of the dynamics of social organization, explained in cultural terms. As I regard it, the emphasis on ethnicity uncovers and identifies in real life many cultural traits otherwise concealed. In this way the study of ethnicity contributes to a more complete and accurate understanding of culture. This makes ethnicity a very significant perspective in anthropological research.

The differences of opinion about the unit problem have caused a rather futile and quite unnecessary debate. Examination of the context in which interethnic relations occur may lead us out of this predicament. Context points to situational ethnicity, and from an anthropological point of view it is the mobilization based on ethnicity in situations of interethnic contact that is our main concern. In a recent article, theoretically well-founded and elaborate, Jonathan Okamura has argued for situational ethnicity. By laying stress on the situational approach to ethnicity it is possible to delineate how ethnicity may differ in reference to varying social contexts as well as different levels of social organization (Okamura, 1981: 452). In my opinion, all forms of ethnicity ought to be considered situational social phenomena. This assumption does not include every aspect of ethnic identity per se.

Ethnicity also implies dichotomization, i.e. there is a diversity between "we" and "they" explicitly spelled out in interaction. Furthermore, it is the process of dichotomization between different ethnic groups that underlies the conception of an ethnic boundary. As Fredrik Barth so clearly stated, this boundary is a social boundary; similarly, ethnic identity is a social identity. The emphasis on the assumption that everything is perceived as social supports the position advocated earlier, i.e. the relational aspect. Approaching ethnicity by means of situational analysis may add, first of all, specification and ethnographic accuracy as to the form and content of interethnic relations. (For the problem of situational ethnicity see also J. Nagata, 1974.)

It has been asserted by some of Barth's critics that his approach is too subjective, leaving out the crucial element of power (Despres, 1975, van den Berghe, 1975). Without recapitulating the issue of a subjective/objective stand on ethnicity, which appears as the most far-reaching controvery in the field so far, I fully admit that power forms an essential part of most interethnic relations. However, one should not be misled into believing that one approach is less scientifically founded than the other; and, in all fairness, Barth does not disregard the political aspect of ethnicity. To him, political groups are ethnic groups, and political movements represent new ways to make cultural differences organizationally relevant (Barth, 1969: 34). On the other hand, the element of power is not given a principal place in Barth's theorizing on ethnicity. This shortcoming deserves special attention. Let me, therefore, sum up this brief orientation concerning the theory building on ethnicity by incorporating the concept of power.

The connection between ethnicity and politics has been stressed by several anthropologists. Abner Cohen, one of the leading advocates for the political dimension of ethnicity, views ethnicity primarily as the dialectic relation between power relations and symbolic actions. To him ethnicity is essentially a political phenomenon; similarly, in formal terms, ethnic groups are non-political groupings that are gradually politicized during the course of interacting with another ethnic group. The process of politicization reflects the fact that these groupings are purposive, aiming at various valued goals (Cohen, 1969 and 1974).

In her brief but theoretically constructive note, Joan Vincent has argued that the political dimension of polyethnicity should be given more attention, accentuating encounters dealing with confrontation in one way or the other. Or, as she so aptly phrases it, "ethnicity is a mask of confrontation" (Vincent, 1974: 377).

For Leo Depres and his colleagues the ecological aspect added to politics represent basic features in understanding ethnicity. Culture maintenance is dependent on the access to and development of certain types of resources. As resources usually are scarce, competition between different groups emerges. For that reason it is necessary to have full control of the access to resource development rather than of environmental resources per se. The distinction is clear enough. For an ethnic minority group, for instance, it is not so much a question of direct competition for the same natural resources; alternative or quite different resource exploitation in a region may render it more difficult, or make it impossible, to continue developing resources in a traditional manner, i.e. resource development required to sustain a distinct way of life. Consequently when ethnic groups confront one another, such encounters deal very much with competition, both directly and in a more indirect fashion. Finally, political power is an indispensable factor to the exercise of control of the access to resource development. Despres considers resource competition as the most impelling force behind the maintenance of ethnic boundaries. Even if such a position may seem rather extreme, I like to point out that both the aspect of relative power and the competitive feature represent valuable theoretical concerns in exploring ethnicity.

In a recent volume about Canadian Ethnopolitics Adrian Tanner (1983) has introduced the distinction between "real competition" and "symbolic competition", the latter being primarily rhetorical or ideological. Ethnic minorities may enter many forms of confrontation with the white dominant society in which competition for scarce resources, be it environmental resources or power, certainly turns out to be more symbolic than real. This has to do with relative power relations between the parties confronting each other, suggesting that the encounter has to take place on an arena under the premises determined entirely by one of the opponents, i.e. the majority. Nevertheless, it is extremely important to initiate and carry through such symbolic power games. As a reminder to the outside world, the minority demonstrates in this way that it is actively engaged in its own affairs, in addition such activities have a bearing on the on-going process of cultural revitalization.

Before discussing in greater detail some of the basic concepts, the current status of ethnicity research could be summed up as follows. There seems to be full agreement on the social emphasis, ethnicity deals predominantly with inter-ethnic relations. In modern theory two distinct approaches prevail; both stress the ethnic boundary, although they are different in analytical focus. To Barth and those following his lead the ethnic boundary is instrumental in understanding interethnic relations. These relations are organized; the superordinate problem to explore refers to the generation and maintenance of this particular form of social organization. Leo Despres, on the other hand, concentrates on resource competition. The ethnic boundary can only be identified as an essential social feature in cases of interethnic competition. Following the notion of competition any interethnic relationship must be politicized. This framework for analysis points to a more materialistic viewpoint. With all their variations expressed in concrete research as well as in theoretical contributions, these main schools of thought may appear complementary rather than irreconcilably opposed to each other.

Basic Concepts

In order to give an account of the predominant perspectives in the study of ethnicity a few basic concepts should be explored in greater detail. In this way I hope to be able to demonstrate the analytical potential of these concepts.

a)   Ethnic Boundary

The imprint of interethnic relations is the boundary between culturally distinct groups. This boundary is conceived by members of a group in the course of interaction and, following Barth, defines the ethnic group (Barth, 1969: 15). The ethnic boundary is maintained through the continuous process of dichotomization between members of a specific group and outsiders. Signs and external signals as well as fundamental value orientations, all of which are expressed in interaction, form the cultural contents of ethnic dichotomization. It is not the sum total of distinctive criteria that constitutes the cultural contents of the boundary, but only those items which the actors consider meaningful in a given situation. The main concern here is the question of relevance. To carry through an interethnic interaction the actors tend to emphasize those factors they deem significant; factors which could make such interaction more difficult, or even render it impossible, are regarded as irrelevant and, accordingly, are played down. Regardless of how important these latter elements may appear in internal cultural contexts, such strategic considerations form a necessary part of adaptation in all interethnic relations. Interethnic relation is a matter of social adaptation as well as of strategy; certain values and norms are modified for purposes of interaction, while at the same time cultural traits appropriate to the occasion are given extra stress in order to mark the difference between we and they. Such selection of cultural traits to establish and maintain dichotomization refers to what Sandra Wallman calls 'the social meaning of difference' (Wallman, 1978: 208).

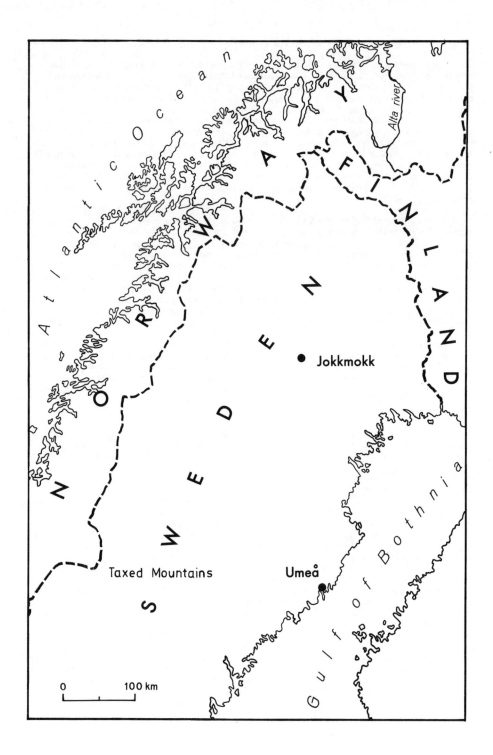

To take this argument one step further, change in the ethnic group is reflected by change of the ethnic boundary, i.e. those factors having an impact on boundary marking (Barth, 1969: 14). In other words, focusing on ethnicity provides a new way of approaching the general problem of social and cultural change. Since we are preoccupied with a notion of cultural diversity between various groups, the ethnic boundary is our main concern. Sandra Wallman has argued for a twofold approach in studying ethnicity. To her ethnicity is a social boundary system which should be ascertained both from a level of action and a level of meaning (Wallman, 1978: 205). In consequence the ethnic boundary ought to include both an actual difference and the meaning actors from different groups impose on cultural distinctiveness. We are interested not only in the establishment of an ethnic boundary, but also in how people themselves perceive the cultural diversity it defines.

Ethnicity can also be viewed as a process of communication. In order to lay the basis for interethnic relation the cultural differentiae being articulated across the ethnic boundary must be mutually comprehensible between the diverse groups involved. How the ethnic boundary is marked in specific interaction is crucial to our understanding of ethnicity. However, we must keep in mind that the social boundaries we are talking of are symbolic rather than real, even if there are real things symbolizing them (Wallman, 1978: 205).

Especially accentuated will be the problem of communication in relationships between a majority society and an ethnic minority group. The framework for interaction between the two parties differs considerably. The majority society is provided with a mobilizing strength consisting of a great variety of statuses derived from a set of institutions on different organizational levels. For example, the Sámi are confronted by many important state institutions such as the cabinet, the parliament, the regional administration and the municipal government; moreover there are a special administrative body regarding the Sámi and finally the courts. The Sámi minority can in no way match such structural resources. Its framework for action is restricted to statuses derived from a limited number of relevant Sámi institutions, such as the Sámi Community, the National Union of Sámi, and the Nordic Sámi Council. These institutions, however, form no basis for acting interethnically, as the Sámi are unable to define an arena appropriate for their aims. Any arena in which interethnic confrontation takes place is defined and governed by their opponent. Besides, the only institution remaining which is culturally genuine, the sii'da, contains no relevant statuses whatever for this form of interaction.

In keeping interaction possible and functioning under appreciable restraints, the minority is bound to experience institutional assimilation (Gregory, 1976). Through this experience the minority can adopt ideas about institutional models from the dominant society and create its own institutions; alternatively, institutions; may be founded for the minority, as, for example, the Sámi community, which is formally a local unit of reindeer Sámi defined in administrative categories by the authorities. The National Union of Sámi, as well as the Nordic Sámi Council, represent such institutional forms of adaptation that facilitate continuous communication with the larger society. On the other hand, institutional assimilation does not necessarily lead to ethnic assimilation, i.e. that the idea of cultural diversity should be blurred. The case is rather the reverse; institutional assimilation may promote resistance to ethnic assimilation. As a result of such adaptation the minority, gaining in organizational strength, will be able to mark more clearly the ethnic boundary; in addition ethnic identity may be reinforced.

Institutional assimilation also implies academic training and scholarly research. The training in disciplines most appropriate for minority-political actions, for instance Sámi linguistics, Sámi history, history of Sámi religion and various social sciences as well as law, will form a basis for recruitment of a new and more articulate leadership. Research projects governed and administered by Sámi scholars have already produced important works in Sámi legal history, traditional Sámi beliefs, contemporary Sámi history and Sámi linguistics. This last is extremely important, for the vitality and creativity of the Sámi language have an enormous value which is both real and symbolic. This research activity presents the Sámi with new and more refined devices for reconstructing and reinforcing their ethnic identity. The increased proficiency in articulation may also aid communication across the ethnic boundary, both in marking ethnic distinctiveness and in modifying the message to make it comprehensible to the opponent; they are now speaking the "same language", although cultura diversity is the primary message to be conveyed in the course of communication. It takes a great deal of skill and versatility to master such tasks, and the process of institutional assimilation is one important means by which the ethnic minority can gain sufficient expertise. This type of interethnic relation, extremely unequal between the parties both as regards political power and economic strength, places great demands on the weaker part. Thus, it is decisive for an ethnic minority to maintain cultural diversity and to articulate it very distinctly. The dominant society must be constantly reminded of the cultural distinctiveness inherent in minority groups. In this way the basic claims qua ethnic minority, or indigenous people, become legitimate and justified.

The marking of the ethnic boundary by different expressive means has a definite impact on the organization of the interethnic relation. Morover, it appears as the most efficient factor in withstanding ethnic assimilation. In order to obtain social strength the process of marking culture difference must be repeated frequently. Thereby the idea of cultural uniqueness ist kept alive, creating a potential force in various ethnopolitical confrontations. These kinds of boundaries are dynamic features on the social map in polyethnic societies and are continually being reconsidered and redefined. As a result of decisions by the political authorities situations may occur that generate new ethnic or sub-ethnic boundaries. A case in point is the enforced relocation of large numbers of Sámi from northernmost Swedish Lapland to central and south Sámi regions which occurred in the 1920's due to overpopulation. Involuntarily, the North Sámi from Karesuando were forced to adapt to a way of life characteristic for other Sámi groups, including a different way of reindeer herding and management, a quite different Sámi language, and other foreign elements. Furthermore, these people found themselves in a new situation marked by contacts with Swedish speaking sedentary people; earlier the Sámi maintained certain relations with Finnish speaking small scale farmers. This transposition caused tremendous readjustment difficulties both for the migrant Sámi and the original group, a problem that remains to this day.

The incoming group of North Sámi maintains a clearly marked dichotomization vis-a-vis the Swedish speaking sedentary population, particularly in Jokkmokk, but also a kind of pseudo-dichotomization in relation to the original Sámi. In the latter instance the relation is often marked by conflict, and the sub-ethnic boundary thus established has become a social reality the local Sámi invariably have to cope with in their daily life. Neither have the migrant Sámi abandoned any of their old customs. Even in the second and third generation they still speak their own Sámi language, they continue to wear their native costumes from Karesuando, and their handicrafts bear clear signs of their provincial origin both in form and decorative elements. If they are large enough the two groups tend to live separately for long periods and mix rather infrequently. Apparently such a sub-ethnic boundary must convey a definite meaning to these people.

A similar case can be found in Labrador. Following a political decision in 1959 an Inuit population from the north was relocated to the small coastal community Makkovik, which was previously inhabited only by settlers. The two ethnic groups maintain a social boundary that keeps them apart in most spheres of life. The very fact that they have been forced to live in the same community in close proximity to each other forms an incentive for more elaborate boundary marking than before. The importance of expressing ethnic identity has increased in the new setting; at the same time social avoidance in spontaneous interaction seems to be a highly cultivated value for both groups. They are, as John C. Kennedy so tellingly states, "holding the line". Nevertheless, in relation to the larger society they join forces because they can both benefit from such mobilization. In this kind of opportunity situation they may redefine themselves as a marginal minority having some basic interests in common and mainly articulating their points by means of Inuit symbols and emblems. The way of articulating is conditioned by strategic consideration. In order to acquire political and economic gains from relations with the dominant society cultural diversity is believed to be an asset; consequently it must be expressed distinctly and in unequivocal terms (Kennedy, 1982).

As we have seen, in Jokkmokk as well as in Makkovik a new situation was developed in which local people had no influence and which generated a new need to establish and maintain two social boundaries marking cultural distinctiveness. Without the effort of denoting cultural difference many ethnic groups would eventually cease to be viable culture units. By focusing on the ethnic boundary, therefore, we will strike at the very core of ethnicity viewed as a socio-cultural process.

b) Ethnic Identity

Following from the position that ethnicity in the main relates to interethnic relations, ethnic identity is viewed as a social status (Barth, 1969: 17). In situations where members of two different cultures confront each other, an identity based on a set of norms and values shared by the members is manifested in interaction. In order to function in an interethnic context the identity adopted must be acknowledged by others (Moerman, 1965). Self-ascription of identity must correspond to the ascription by others, and this is a mutual process in establishing interethnic relations. If the two groups fail to obtain such consistency interaction in this form will terminate. The way of acting and the form and content of verbal articulation convey information about ethnic identity which embodies the notion of cultural distinctiveness. But this is only part of the total message being communicated; far mor important is that dealing with the attainment of predetermined goals which occasioned the interethnic confrontation in the first place. Ethnic identity will be an asset in external confrontations only if it is cultivated continuously. It cannot remain dormant as a latent factor to be mobilized exclusively for specific but infrequent situations. Ethnic identity is conceived as a social status equally on the two levels.

In addition Fredrik Barth considers ethnic identity an imperative status similar to sex and rank in that it constrains the actors in all activities. Once decided, the ethnic identity cannot be disregarded by simply changing definition of the situation (Barth, 1969: 31). The question of the status being imperative can only pertain to situations where the ethnic identity is chosen, for that kind of identity is relevant only in interethnic interaction. If a group of Sámi, for instance, choose to play down or completely deny their identity qua Sámi, they do not enter an interethnic relation.

This leads us to another issue actualized by Barth, that of stigmatization. Most minorities and pariah groups may be subject to derogatory attitudes and prejudices expressed by members of the dominant society. Analogous with the social stigma that is imprinted on many non-normal and largely disabled people in society at large (Goffman, 1963), the ethnic identity may in certain situations be afflicted with a social stigma. In referring to the large group of sedentary Sámi in Northern Norway, Eidheim (1969) claims that many Sámi switch identity as they alternate between a public and an exclusively Sámi sphere of interaction. Due to an apprehension that the Sámi identity is underestimated and irrelevant in the public arena, the Sámi often reserve "use" of this identity for intimate and fairly secure situations where only Sámi participate.

One should not, however, be led to believe that the Sámi experience their identity as stigmatized. It is only in certain critical situations that a feeling of stigmatization may emerge. A minority group marked by stigma must adapt to this constraint to optimalize interethnic interaction, it cannot disregard it entirely. For the latter to occur, the distribution of relative power must change.

Stigmatization of identity does not only strike negatively; in special situations it may be converted to a positive asset. In the Scottish fishing village Ferryden, along the east coast of Scotland, the fisherman status was traditionally a stigmatized identity. Instead of attempting to conceal this identity in contacts with a fairly numerous incoming population in modern times, people have chosen to emphasize it. In that way they are able to manifest a strong feeling of community and togetherness vis-a-vis the newcomers. Upholding the idea of fishing as not only a livelihood, but a way of life, even long after active fishing had ceased, contributed toward marking an ethnic, or a sub-ethnic, boundary that proves to be socially meaningful. Currently, the fisherman identity turns out to be highly valued and most essential to all real Ferrydeners, and the original perception of stigmatization has little significance (Nadel, 1984). Similarly, the conception "black is beautiful" and all that this phrase embraces has also turned a negative designation into something positive, strengthening the selfesteem and awareness of black Americans.

In adherence to the emphasis on ethnic identity being social, this sort of identity is neither given nor innate; it is always generated by a psychosocial process (A. L. Epstein, 1978). In his book Ethos and Identity (1978) A. L. Epstein has made some important advances in specifying the notion of ethnic identity. According to him ethnic identity results from an interchange between internal perception and external response. The former relates to values and attitudes, traditional customs and emotional components, whereas the latter aspect stresses ethnic identity as a social fact which deals with the realization of political interests, ritual and economic goals, etc. Thus, ethnic identity is both a socially defined role and perception of self, and it often emerges in response to particular circumstances. To Epstein the principal questions concern how ethnic identity is generated and transmitted, how it persists and how it is transformed or disappears (Epstein, 1978: 96). This problem of the formation of ethnic identity is determined both by what is called 'affect' and 'circumstance'. This implies the interplay between the internal and the external, the subjective and the objective, and the psychological and the sociological elements (Epstein, 1978: 112).

The ethnic identity being formed must be based on fundamental diacritics, which makes the distinction between "we" and "they" deeply felt and highly valued (R. Cohen, 1978: 397). Not just any emblematic criterion can be used in this formation, since peripheral items are devoid of adequate power to carry on interethnic interaction. Ethnic identity is not something static; instead it is subject to dynamic change, always depending on varying situations. In a recent volume on identity in general, edited by Anita Jacobson-Widding (1983), ethnic identity is viewed, accordingly, as a cultural construction which can be reconstructed and amended, as the particular situation may demand.

Recently there have been many examples illustrating the expansive force in ethnic identity formation. This change is mainly due to changing circumstances. As a result of decolonization in Greenland, for instance, a new Greenlander identity has evolved; i.e. all Inuit are organized ethnically in order to express common values which mark a clear boundary between themselves and the Danish population (Kleivan, 1970). The struggle for and the realization of Greenlandic home rule is the most decisive outcome of this mobilization based on ethnicity. In comparison, the migration of many aborigines of diverse ethnic origin into urban areas in Australia and adaptation to an urban setting on a fairly permanent basis has brought about a new ethnic identity. Identification with tribal origins is set aside in the adjustment to new conditions, where aboriginality is transformed into a form of generalized ethnicity (Pierson, 1981). The realization of aborigine identity proves to be the most efficient means to mark culture distinctiveness towards the Australian mainstream population. Aboriginality as a force makes urban life more endurable. Consequently, in response to new and more demanding circumstances, Inuit from many separate small communities and aborigines from a vast number of distinct tribes similarly redefine their identity for purpose of ethnopolitical mobilization.

The attempt to separate the 8 districts in the Northwest corner of the huge Indian state Uttar Pradesh, an area named Uttarakhand, is also based on ethnic diversity. The great majority of people living in Uttarakhand are Hindus speaking Pahari, a language distinct from the Indo-Iranian languages spoken further south on the Indian plains. Furthermore, Uttarakhand is part of the holy land of Hinduism, the sacred river, the Ganga, has its sourcespring there, for instance.

People nourish the idea of protecting nature and its precious values, considering both resources developed in a traditional way and the beauty of the landscape; these are values which eventually will come into collision with other interestes involving an expansive exploitation of resources. To meet pressure from the Indian dominant society, mobilization of the group ethnically identified as Uttarakhands must be based on a strong sense of community and shared value orientations. The Chipko movement, which emerged in 1972 and is still in force, is the first spontaneous expression of this new ethnicity in which the difference in views toward land use patterns between locals and the government officials involved in forestry development is clearly spelled out. Besides inhibiting uncontrolled forestry and putting some counter pressure on the authorities, the Pahari culture was reinforced by the Chipko movement; regional and cultural awareness and self esteem increased noticeably because of such a dramatic and recurring event (Berreman, 1983). However, for the Uttarakhands the boundary marking is primarily cultural; separation from Uttar Pradesh and creation of their own state is an entirely different matter. The emerging elite, on the other hand, believes statehood is a prerequisite for an efficient realization of its ultimate goals, i.e. long term protection and assurance of natural values in this region most vulnerable to industrial encroachments.

The lesson we can draw from these cases is that various conditions may call for ethnic mobilization on different levels. The ethnic identity people assume reflects the type of interethnic relation at hand. Provided external circumstances change drastically the ethnic identity must be restructured; it does not, however, become less ethnic because of that. For it is the process that lies behind the mobilization of ethnic identity that makes it ethnic, not a notion of being connected to an original culture defined once and for all.

c) Ethnopolitics

The concept of ethnopolitics refers to the aspect of interethnic relations aiming at the realization of specific goals by means of politicized behaviour and articulation, which occur between groups defined and mobilized according to ethnic criteria. In minority/majority contexts the ethnic minority acts ethnopolitically in response to a situation of forced dependency. The activity is persistently constrained by the power relations that prevail between the two parties, the ultimate goal of the ethnopolitical action, therefore, is to change actual power relations in favour of the minority, or to emancipate oneself from and to redefine the minority situation into a purely polyethnic relation (Paine, 1977). The social as well as the physical distance between an encapsulated minority group and the Nation State and its administrative apparatus is usually so great that the interethnic relation must be carried out through an intermediate agent. Due to the minority's lack of real power and the majority's inadequate insight of the minority and its particular way of life, permanent relations between the two units and the flow of communication are severely restricted. This relational predicament creates a niche for career choises for various persons aspiring to a middleman position, be it broker, patron, or some other status variation.

Referring to Canada, R. W. Dunning (1959) was probably the first to draw attention to the role of marginal man in ethnic relations. In this type of relation the ethnic minority is viewed in sharp contrast to a non-ethnic society, and the marginal man assuming the capacity of intermediary is without exception recruited from the non-ethnic majority. Dunning does not problematize the reason for this, but no doubt it has to do with actual power relations. An ethnic minority cannot form a basis for recruitment to middleman positions; that would be contradictory to the very nature of the minority situation. The holders must both possess 1) competence in the two cultures to a varying degree, and be able to obtain 2) the confidence of the two parties, which usually oppose one another because of conflicting interests. Presumably it is this need for mutual trust and firm recognition of competence appropriate to the middleman role that inhibits members of the minority, regardless of their capability, from assuming such positions. Moreover, the status is not particularly attractive; 1) the career tends to be rather shortlived, and

2) the dilemma of serving two masters at the same time will neutralize the range of activity for any marginal man emerging from a minority. The expectations and aspirations of the minority group cannot be fully satisfied, and if they were met, the trust and respect of the larger society would rapidly decline, leading to termination of the interethnic relation in this form. To avoid the predicament of leaving the niche open for individual exploitation, the minority can employ its own carefully selected incumbent, as the Sámi did in Sweden by establishing their own office of Sámi ombudsman (SO). In the long run, however, even such a strategy may cause unexpected problems for the minority, as will be shown later on.

At the initiating stage middlemen ordinarily play the role of broker, and this is most beneficial for both minority and majority. Once the position of broker is well established, the incumbents tend progressively to develop authority and power of control over those on whose behalf they act as mediators, thus transforming the relationship into dependency. The broker has then become a patron, steadily increasing his power and prestige vis-a-vis his clients (cf. Paine, 1971). People entering a patron-client relationship do not accept the expansion of the patron's influence beyond a certain point. In ethnic minority situations the pattern of patronage is especially sensitive and subject to revaluation, as patrons who usurp too much power will violate the idea of cultural autonomy. In the following I will expand on this last point illustrating with two different kinds of middlemen both ending up as influential patrons.

Traditionally, the most common roles that have led towards establishing real middleman status appear to be those of merchant or missionary. Persons with such status are often innovative, holding entrepreneurial skill that eventually will trigger social and economic change at the same time as individual career positions are built up (Barth, 1963).

Among the Naskapi in Labrador a missionary gradually developed an influential position in many important sections of daily life. All information flowing in and out of the community was controlled by him, and, because of his competence in the native language and in local culture generally, all contacts between the authorities and the local Naskapi were channelized through the missionary. In one sector of life, however, the missionary was unable to exercise control, and that was during the recurring winter hunting seasons, when the Naskapi migrated long distances entirely out of reach of the missionary and his supervision. By continuing their hunting way of life the Naskapi put an effective check on the patron role; thereby they also managed to maintain continuity in their traditional way of life and system of values (Henriksen, 1971).

In 1962 the National Union of Swedish Sámi (SSR) engaged a legally trained councilor as their ombudsman. Mainly he was to act on behalf of the Sámi in different legal contests, especially in the courts. In addition his duty was to advise the Sámi as to appropriate measures to be taken, style of articulation, etc., and to assist them in all kinds of ethnopolitical actions. For strategic reasons the office of SO was set up in Stockholm, offering easy access to all political and administrative institutions concerned with Sámi matters on the national level as well as to leading sections of the mass media. His expertise was eminent and most relevant for the role of partial broker. As he was deliberately selected by the Sámi he could act from a solid base of authority; this was paired by his special legal training and versatile experience which provided him with the recognition necessary to performance as intermediary. As long as SO was able to offer the Sámi coveted prizes he was assured of the complete reliance and appreciation as counter prestations. Thereby he could continue to develop his position, expanding his range of influence in all spheres of Sámi politics, and eventually his role performance became more patron-like. His career probably culminated in 1968 when the institutionalization of the office of SO was completed, the first Sámi Political Programme was adopted, for which SO bore the heaviest burden and, finally, the favourable verdict came in the Norwegian Supreme Court concerning the Altevatn Case. The latter case opened the way for launching the huge and very comprehensive trial of principles, the Taxed Mountains Case, which tested the landrights issue between the Sámi and the Swedish State, on a broad scale.

Over the years SO developed a network of important personnel, who could be used in various activities to promote Sámi political concerns. Some of these people were members of the Swedish Riksdag who frequently, on signals given by SO, were willing to introduce a debate in parliament in favour of Sámi interests. He also maintained contact with officials in relevant cabinets and other governmental institutions. His source of power, indispensable for minority political actions, expanded immensely. With the extension of his activity and his initiating power he became to a very large extent the brains behind Sámi politics; meanwhile ethnopolitical action got its present form. Exactly at this point a reaction among the Sámi was noticed. To the Sámi elite SO was no longer the partial broker they once employed. Sámi political activities were very much reflected by SO, and in a way he personified Sámi politics. This transformation of the SO status was entirely unacceptable to the Sámi.

Due to the Taxed Mountains Case, which was not completed until 1981, SO could very much have his way, although his position started to decline. When the case was concluded and the outcome turned out to be mainly negative and unfavourable to the Sámi, i.e. there were no more attractive prizes to be extended, they were immediately prepared for a redefinition of the entire institution of SO. In 1982 SO retired prematurely, i.e. five years early but with full economic compensation. He was then to devote most of his remaining time to legal historical research, especially adapted for a critical analysis of the verdict in the Taxed Mountains Case and the premises on which it was based. In this way it was believed the Sámi could obtain the greatest benefit from SO and his unique and highly valued expert knowledge. By this new and rather unconventional contract, the career of SO as patron came to an end.

In order to avoid the repetition of such role expansion, the Sámi have decided to employ a legal council, förbundsjurist (SSR-councilor), who is to act exclusively in the field of legal affairs. His office is relocated to Umeå, one of the towns for regional administration in the North. The SSR-councilor will assume the role of partial broker with no opportunity for Sámi politicizing on his own. The Sámi have learnt a lesson, and they are extremely cautious and fully aware of the danger with middlemen, consequently they do not wish to experience once again a concealed development recreating a patron-client relationship. Even at the price of being heard less intensively and expressing themselves politically somewhat less pronouncely, the Sámi prefer to guard and protect their own authority. The question of autonomy is crucial in this respect, for irrespective of the good intentions and proficiency in carrying out assignments, any middleman assuming a patron role will eventually meet negative reactions.

Ethnic minorities are reluctant to accept any form of tutelage, i.e. they do not want to be subjected to persons who always seem to know whatever is best for them. In consequence, the Sámi did not react against SO because he was doing the wrong thing, but because he was doing whatever was being done and because he was playing the role of protagonist in the continuous ethnopolitical game.

The problem of tutelage has been taken up by Robert Paine and others in the book White Arctic (1977). Many bureaucrats, especially those assigned to administer and assist ethnic minorities on the local and regional level, tend to adopt the role of guardian for the natives. These officials are always working with the best intentions, They believe their capability and appraisement are unequalled, and therefore they know what is of advantage to the Sámi/Inuit, etc. In the special Sámi administration that came about in the 1880's, an attitude of unquestioned superiority prevailed for a very long time. "The Sámi are like little children, they do not always understand what is good for them. We are here to serve the Sámi!" The officials also advocated an ideal of maintaining ethnically pure boundaries in absurdum (Svensson, 1976). When these bureaucrats take up patron-like features they play a new role, that of bureau-patron (Paine, 1977). In such instances, the Sámi/Inuit appear as clients or wards to the bureau-patron, depending on how the situation is defined. The possibility of carrying on ethnopolitical activities will necessarily be complicated by this relational framework.

Based on ethnicity the Sámi and many other ethnic minorities have recently reacted firmly against any form of tutelage. One of the main goals of the ethnopolitical strategy at present is to remedy this anomaly, undermining the effect of tutelage for the purpose of attaining cultural autonomy. This process is closely related to the realization of political autonomy. the ultimate aim of which is directed towards an ethnically plural situation. The attack on various middlemen, including SO, reflects penetratingly the form and objective of crucial ethnopolitical processes currently taking place. Taking up the lead from Paine (1977), therefore, I want to emphasize firmly the utility and expediency in focusing on middlemen in all studies of ethnopolitics.

In order to make its political action legitimate each ethnic group must be in possession of a set of consistent symbols effective in differentiating it from other groups. i.e. furnishing the group identity and exclusiveness (A. Cohen, 1974). Presently the Sámi and many other indigenous peoples return to old symbols more frequently than ever before. In the current situation, in which the Sámi are severely strained, such symbols are given a new, impressive content. The struggle for cultural survival, where the landrights issue appears as the Leitmotif, may be viewed as a process of symbolization as well as of politicization. A minority culture unable to refer to such symbols today would seem rather destitute; the use of symbols procures legitimacy and gives extra strength to ethnopolitical demands put forward by the minority.

The Taxed Mountains Case which refers to ownership rights to land and water, was primarily a legal struggle in formal terms; viewed from a Sámi perspective it was just as much a question of ethnopolitical action. The ultimate aim was not a court victory per se but to attain improved landrights legally codified, which would provide the Sámi with a minimum power base necessary to carry out political actions. The well-known Alta Case in Northern Norway which concerned a hydro-electric development project ended up in the Supreme Court, but it is similarly considered an ethnopolitical action. In both cases ethnic symbols were salient; the legal argumentation was intermingled with symbolic statements marking ethnic distinctiveness.

With reference to the Taxed Mountains Case, after close deliberation the Sámi decided to go to court with the predetermined goal of acquiring sufficient power to assure themselves culture viability. Viewed in Sámi historical perspective this event is quite unprecedented, and it lasted for 15 years, bringing about a total confrontation between the Sámi and the Swedish State. (For a detailed account including the Supreme Court Decision see Jahreskog ed., 1982)

Three key elements will explain this particular form of action; resources, power, and ethnicity (Despres, 1975). Any action leading to confrontation with the majority must be based on ethnic criteria, of which marking culture difference appears as the main objective. The Sámi could never have gone to court in the first place, if they did nor relate their action to ethnicity. In other words, as indigenous people the Sámi claim culturally defined rights to land, rights which are historically founded as well. Access to resource development is required to sustain a particular way of life, in this case to reindeer pasture suitable for the varying seasons, migrating routes, fishing waters, hunting grounds, campsites, etc. The ecological niche of the Sámi has been severely curtailed as a result of increasing encroachments in the Sámi Home Area by alternative resource developments from the industrial society; these consist of hydro-electric developments, industrial forestry, mining, and include certain side-effects of this form of exploitation. In certain areas the Sámi today are living under considerable strains. Their niche is especially vulnerable to extensive changes; only with great difficulty, therefore, can the Sámi pursue their special form of resource development. Control of the access to traditional resource development can never be secured unless the Sámi manage to obtain a certain power, which may be used as protection against continuous heavy exploitation. On the other hand, the Sámi will never acquire any real power if they do not relate their claims to ethnic uniqueness. And this is exactly what the Taxed Mountains Case was all about; a legal codification of fundamental rights should give the Sámi negotiating power so they could have a real say and the ability to check new instances of development whenever these violate the maintenance of the particular Sámi way of life.

In the Taxed Mountains Case and the Alta Case the Sámi went to court for the same reasons and with comparable strength; by claiming ethnic distinctiveness and aboriginal rights they tried to establish a satisfactory power base. That the Sámi failed in the two attempts does not make the events less ethnopolitical. The general process of Sámi political mobilization in modern times can be elucidated correspondingly by applying the three interdependent elements; resources, power and ethnicity (see e.g. Svensson, 1976).

For ethnic minorities the legal strategy of confronting the majority is hardly feasible. The courts are more reluctant to undertake drastic changes than are most other official institutions, and the judges consider themselves guardians of the existing system of laws. But the legal arena should not be ruled out entirely as an option for ethnopolitical tactics, as the James Bay Project revealed. In this case the Cree succeeded in obtaining significant gains in court, and these became paramount prerequisites for carrying out favourable negotiations with the authorities in the next phase. The Cree could not prevent this huge hydro-electric development, but as a result of the negotiations a protection regime regarding their landrights has been confirmed. By this procedure the Cree are guaranteed the authority and control of enough land to maintain their special hunting and gathering way of life and to transmit this land to future generations of Cree (La Russic, 1979, Feit, 1982). Such a protection regime would hardly have been authorized had not the issue been legally examined in advance.

As an aftermatch to the two cases concerning the Sámi the governments in both Norway and Sweden were forced to appoint special Sámi Rights Committees to investigate thoroughly the complex nature of Sámi rights. In 1984 the Norwegian Committee presented its first report, that on the SÁMI LEGAL STATUS (NOU 1984: 18). In response to Sámi pressure, and among many other matters, the Committee was to examine the question of ethnicity. The Committee complied with its mandate and presented a most constructive view on the Sámi as an ethnic group (see chapt. 4). Six basic factors were identified as necessary to the support of Sámi ethnicity, i.e. for maintaining Sámi comprehension of self and marking of identity. These factors are: kinship relations, native theory of territory, traditional means of sustenance, cultural values (language, costume, music, arts and crafts, etc.), and social organization (sii'da). In view of these criteria the Committee concludes that the Sámi people constitute a viable ethnic group. It is also pointed out that these factors not only exist internally but have a decisive impact on the continuous interaction between the Sámi and the larger society. So far as I know this is the first time a government committee has stated explicitly that the Sámi constitute an ethnic group. This argumentation is a breakthrough to political goals which the Sámi have aimed at for quite some time, and a formal recognition, if obtained through legislation, will have a real as well as a symbolic value to the Sámi.

Another point worth mentioning is that the Sámi Rights Committee turned to the Nordic Sámi Institute in Kautokeino for an opinion on which the Committee could then base its own statement. The final text is clearly influenced by this authorized Sámi participation, but it should not be regarded as a partial petition inasmuch as it is incorporated as part of the general report of the Committee. Many minorities in the North lack local government structures. Therefore, the forming of effective political bodies appears as a primary objective, in addition to the use of litigation. In Fennoscandia in the post World War II era there is a similar process going on among the Sámi, but until now no real ethnopolitical institutions have emerged in any of the three countries. Neither the nation wide Sámi organizations in Norway or in Sweden can act with political force against the majority society due to insufficient sources of power. Power relevant to the Sámi is closely related to codification of fundamental rights; the small advances the Sámi have experienced in the legal arena so far reflect the restricted power base of the Sámi organizations. The Sámi Parliament in Finland is no more political than the above mentioned organizations; similarly it lacks essential decisionmaking power and remains an advisory body, although its representation is strongly based on ethnicity (Müller-Wille, 1979). The proposed national Sámi Parliament, Sameting, in Noway will be ascribed only advisory powers as well (NOU 1984: 18). On the other hand, the second report of the Sámi Rights Committee, dealing with rights to land and water, may contemplate giving additional powers to the Sameting.

d) Ethnic Art

To ethnic minorities different forms of aesthetic manifestations tend to become more and more important. Ethnic art in a wide sense is closely related to communication. Ideas and knowledge about a specific culture can be transmitted through objects of art both internally and as external expressions. Within the group ethnic identity is reinforced and essential values that are shared by the members are strongly emphasized. The external function of art is to present an image which is ethnically adequate and telling; the art forms are some of the symbols defining ethnic boundaries (Graburn, 1976). In return for distinctive artistic expressions the ethnic minority receives respect and appreciation from the outside world, both for the arts themselves and for the culture from which they derive. In addition, there is a flow of inspiration and ideas to the minority about new aesthetic forms. As a result of culture contact ethnic art is constantly revalued and reshaped. Irrespective of change, however, everything created must represent something ethnically unique. This form of revitalization of aesthetics is connected to viability of the ethnic group.

Arts have a very special informative power which is used more frequently in present times. Genuine customs and traditions can be mirrored in arts peculiar to the group. This underscores the value of that which is "ours", an extremely important concept for people living under severe social pressure from the outside and struggling to preserve self esteem and respect for their own culture. The prerequisite for communications, however, is that both the producers and receivers of aesthetic messages view these arts similarly; they must agree on the meaning the various forms of art convey. In general terms ethnic art can be confined to two processes each having an impact on interethnic relations; 1) art is viewed as a means of expressing cultural community and shared value orientations; 2) art is regarded as a means of articulating to others ethnic distinctiveness, of communicating identity and insight into a particular culture.

Increasingly attention is paid to ethnic art by museums and official institutions as well as by many private collectors. At the same time members of native groups become more and more aware of the significance of their own specific arts, and for decorative purposes and out of genuine interest they acquire different art objects, such as books, records, handicraft and paintings, which are incorporated as natural items into their homes.

Ethnic art can be divided into four main parts: handicraft, music, literature, and fine arts. Both handicraft and music are original art expressions, which recently have been renewed and refined considerably. Fine arts, consisting of paintings and graphic together with sculptures, represent new kinds of art objects; notwithstanding this, they still have a close link with tradition, mainly in choice of theme, and partly in use of technique and material. The illustrative elements often derive from ornamentation of traditional artefacts made for use. The efficiency of the message contained in the art objects depends very much on the standard and quality of the products. Everything made by a Sámi, an Inuit or a Cree does not stir up an interest; the qualitative measures that prevail in the larger society must be met; similarly the objects must have a clear cultural identification. A positive consequence of meeting these criteria can be an urge of increased knowledge and understanding. Inuit prints and sculptures have developed into powerful instruments in interethnic relations; the demand for such arts is increasing all the time. The interethnic relation is, however, not only confined to art producer vs. customer; far more important is the explicit reference aboriginal peoples frequently make to their distinctive fine arts. In confrontations of various sorts, in political or administrative institutions as well as in the legal arena, articulation may be accentuated by referring to representative objects of art which are especially well known and highly valued among the natives themselves.

Pictures by the Sámi artist John Savio were brought up and related to many new contexts in the course of the Alta debate, the simplified and very stylized picture "Sámi" being the most expressive. In a few crude pen strokes this striking face summarizes a clear message. First, it gives an impression of anxiety about the uncertainty of the future; secondly it shows how the Sámi is securely anchored in the culture of his ancestors. This anonymous portrait also radiates full vigour and courage; it gives assurance that the Sámi will continue their struggle for improved rights and that they will remain as a special people, despite the obstacles created by increasing pressure from industrial development and extended control exerted by the larger society. More than any other single work of art, this picture succinctly epitomizes the Sámi culture and presents the Sámi as a viable aboriginal people in the Fourth World.

A fairly young Sámi artist, Hans Ragnar Mathiesen, has recently taken up Savio's lead, using similar graphic technique inspired by Japanese woodcuts. His motives are more explicitly political in the use of pointed contrasting effects. In many of his later pictures Sámi and reindeer are placed in the front with lines of factory chimneys symbolizing the industrial society penetrating into the Sámi land diffusely imagined in the background. In another sketch an eagle is grabbing a defenceless reindeer calf, a common occurrence in late spring; this is placed opposite an immense helicopter which seizes and carries off a Sámy baby lying in a qietka, the traditional portable Sámi cradle.

Literature, finally, is a novelty; the three forms novel, poetry and drama represent new means of artistic articulation. The acquisition of a written language, either the native tongue or the language of the larger society, enables members of an ethnic group to produce creative works of letters. The literary products add a dimension to the continuous flow of communication; they increase insight and acknowledgement of the dominant society vis-a-vis an ethnic minority; they also reinforce cultural self-esteem, vitalize and renew the native language and even enrich political argumentation. Regardless of language used, the style and theme of the literature must show unmistakable identity to have an impact on interethnic relations. All literary works having a definite function in polyethnic situations should be referred to as ethnoliterature (Svensson, 1984). This literature awakens an awareness

among its own people; thereby they can get an inside view of their own traditions and current problems. In various ethnopolitical confrontations the literature is referred to by native actors at opportune moments to emphasize and make their articulation more highly coloured.

Among the Sámi the poems by Paulus Utsi from Jokkmokk have become classical in this sense. In their laconic and concise form these poems remind one of the original song form, yoik. Utsi is preoccupied primarily with universal problems concerning aboriginal peoples everywhere; he offers a lyrical and refined, though unobtrusive, protest against the devastating encroachments in the Sámi land. In court cases, in negotiations with the government and other authorities and on many official occasions the poems by Utsi are common features. In particular, he has drawn attention to hydroelectric developments which over time cause severe and unmeasurable damage to the Sámi. His poems were never actualized with such force as during the Alta Case; traditional yoiks and Utsi's poems formed the basic artistic traits in the most dramatic confrontation with the larger society the Sámi have experienced in modern times (Charta 79, 1980: 4-5).

Novelists have taken up problems connected to the common dilemma most Sámi face at present in their everyday life. Usually these novels build on self-experience, and they are both epically telling and provocative. For this reason they are an important source of inspiration for the Sámi, who are helped both to contemplate more profoundly their own situation and to act in an articulate way. The conflict of interests in resource developments and the issue of tutelage have been highlighted in a dramatized but nearly documentary form. Other subjects treated are the latent conflict between reindeer Sámi and non-reindeer Sámi; and fair attention has also been given to the personality dilemma many Sámi encounter on trying to adjust to a life as Sámi in an urban milieu (Svensson, 1984).

To conclude this section with a word on drama, the very active Tukaq theatre from Greenland, founded in 1975, should be mentioned. The name Tukaq is symbolic and means harpoon point, implying strength and purpose, i.e. something which is aiming ahead, whereas the harpoon line represents continuity with ancient Inuit culture. In a very effective way the plays performed by the Tukaq theatre blend traditional Inuit mythology with contemporary minority political issues. Lately, even the Sámi have founded their own drama groups. By making use of an artistic medium, which derives from the larger society, and acting through their own idiom, the Inuit and the Sámi are able to mark the ethnic boundary in a new and hitherto untried fashion. Whenever the public consists mainly of native people, apart from being entertained they receive impulses which further an understanding of their own situation. Ethnic art in any form possesses this twofold communicative function; in different kinds of ethnopolitical actions creative and vivid art appears as a supportive asset for minority groups. In a non-controversial way the art demonstrates the inherent strength and value of cultural distinctiveness.

Concluding remarks

The purpose of the preceding discussion has been to give a comprehensive, although in no way complete, presentation of current trends in anthropological research concerning ethnicity. In exploring the field of ethnicity I have confined myself to elaborating a few basic concepts, which continually form an essential framework in advancing theory. The quality and usefulness of ethnic studies relate both to pragmatic and theoretical concerns. In elucidating ethnicity we are focusing on certain cultural processes - those of symbolization, communication and politicization, all of which influence the establishment and maintenance of an ethnic boundary as well as the forming and use of ethnic identity in interethnic relations. The emphasis laid on such fundamental processes, related to a dynamic and frequently changing setting, enables us to increase and broaden our knowledge of both culture and society. A culture theoretical approach ought to be given attention equivalent to that which is devoted to understanding and explaining interethnic relations per se. Moreovever, the context in which ethnicity appears as a variant form of social organization must be uncovered and properly defined. Ethnicity as an analytical construct is mainly situational; i.e. we have to look for specific situations in which ethnicity is a predominant feature. In the above exposition ample examples of this kind of situation have been presented. Ethnopolitics as a form of explicit goal oriented activity and ethnic arts, viewed as expressive, value oriented articulation, are especially feasible approaches in pursuing theoretical intentions outlined in this paper.

What possible directions can be discerned for ethnicity studies in the near future? One lead may be to try to generalize on the concept of competition, beyond that indicated by Leo Despres and others. In a heavy and very substantive volume Michael Banton has recently argued for generalized competition, by which ethnic relations should be explained in terms of rational choice theory. The attempt to fuse racial and ethnic relations in the same theoretical approach may be more convincing and commendable than the somewhat tiring discussion of competition (Banton, 1983). Competition certainly remains one of many elements influencing ethnic relations. I doubt, however, it can be accorded any superordinate place in building and refining ethnicity theory.

Following Clifford Geertz (1966) and his conception of religion as a cultural system, Lee Drummond has suggested that ethnicity should be considered a cultural system. The content and interrelated ideas contained in such a system emerge from a set of transformations rather than being formal elements in a fixed system. Ethnicity viewed as a cultural continuum may, according to Drummond, help merging idealist and materialist points of view. The transformations relate to questions such as how do people communicate distinctiveness, how do they assign ethnic identity and how do they act and feel once an interethnic relation is established? (Drummond, 1980) This challenge deserves serious consideration, and it is in line with the culture theoretical emphasis already pointed out.

Quite a different way of problematizing ethnicity is to return to the idea of plural society and look at cultural plurality and how it may be conceptualized. In urban settings, for instance in the Middle East, India and Africa, it is not sufficient to focus too narrowly on ethnic boundary maintenance, ethnic identity expression and ethnic group mobilization. In such milieus, as has been demonstrated by Fredrik Barth (1984), there are many kinds of boundaries which have to be spanned, and many identities, derived from diverse backgrounds and circumstances, which can be actualized in varying social contexts. Ethnicity, then, appears as only one of several social distinctions, and may not always be the most significant one. Here ethnicity is one aspect of plural society, which can in no way explain cultural plurality in its entirety. Simple polyethnic societies and ethnic minority situations are the empirical settings most appropriate for research concentrating on ethnicity; for comparative purposes and for theory development, however, one should be reminded of the connecting link to the question of cultural plurality.

References

Banton, M., 1983: Racial and Ethnic Competition. Cambridge University Press, Cambridge.

Barth, F. ed., 1963: The role of the entrepreneur in social change in Northern Norway. Årbok University of Bergen No. 3, Bergen, Oslo.

– ed. 1969: Ethnic Groups and Boundaries. The Social Organization of Culture Difference. George Allen & Unwin, London.

– 1984: Problems in Conceptualizing Cultural Pluralism, with Illustrations from Sohar, Oman in D. Maybury-Lewis ed. The Prospects for Plural Societies. Proceedings of the American Ethnological Society. Washington, D.C.

Berreman, G., 1983: Identity definition, assertion and politicization in the Central Himalaya, in Anita Jacobson-Widding ed. Identity: Personal and Socio-Cultural. Almquist & Wickseel International, Uppsala.

Cohen, A., 1969: Custom and Politics in Urban Africa. Routledge & Kegan Paul, London.

– 1974: The Lesson of Ethnicity in A. Cohen ed. Urban Ethnicity, ASA Monographs 12, Tavistock Publ., London.

– R., 1978: Ethnicity: Problem and Forms in Anthropology. Annual Review of Anthropology, Vol. 7.

CHARTA 79, 1980: Charta 79, No. 4-5.

Despres, L., 1975: Toward a Theory of Ethnic Phenomena in L. Despres ed. Ethnicity and Resource Competition in Plural Societies, Mouton, The Hague.

Drummond, L., 1980: The Cultural Continuum: A theory of intersystems, MAN No. 5 Vol. 15.

Dunning, R.W., 1959: Ethnic Relations and the Marginal Man in Canada, Human Organization Vol. 18: 1.

Eidheim, H., 1969: When Ethnic Identity is a Social Stigma in F. Barth ed. Ethnic Groups and Boundaries. George Allen & Unwin, London.

Epstein, A.L., 1958: Politics in an Urban African Community. Manchester University Press, Manchester.

– 1978: Ethos and Identity. Three Studies in Ethnicity, Tavistock Publ., London.

Evans-Pritchard, E.E., 1940: The Nuer, The Clarendon Press, Oxford.

Feit, H., 1982: Protecting Indigenous Hunters: The Social Environmental Protection Regime in the James Bay and Northern Quebec Land Claims Agreement. In G. Geisler et al. eds. The Social Impact Assessment of Regional Resource Development on Native Peoples. Indian SIA Monograph No. 3, University of Michigan.

Fortes, M., 1945: The Dynamics of Clanship among the Tallensi. Oxford University Press, London.

Geertz, C., 1966: Religion as a Cultural System in M. Banton ed. Anthropological Approaches to the Study of Religion. ASA Monographs 3, Tavistock Publ., London.

Goffman, E., 1963: Stigma. Notes on the management on spoiled identity. Prentice Hall Inc., Englewood Cliffs, N.Y.

Graburn, N., 1976: Arts of the Fourth World in N. Graburn ed. Ethnic and Tourist Arts - Cultural Expressions of the Fourth World. Univ. of California Press, Berkeley.

Gregory, J., 1976: The modification of an interethnic Boundary in BELIZE, American Ethnologist Vol. 3.

Henriksen, G., 1971: The Transactional Basis of Influence: White Men among Naskapi Indians in R. Paine ed. Patrons and Brokers in the East Arctic. ISER publ. No. 2, Memorial University, St. John's Newfoundland.

Jacobsen-Widding, A. ed., 1983: Identity: Personal and Socio-Cultural, Almquist & Wicksell International, Uppsala.

Jahreskog, B., ed., 1982: The Sami National Minority in Sweden, Almqvist & Wiksell International, Stockholm / Humanities Press, N.J. U.S.A.

Kennedy, J., 1982: Holding the Line - Ethnic boundaries in a Northern Labrador Community, ISER Publ. No. 27, Memorial University, St. John's, Newfoundland.

Kleivan, H., 1970: Culture and Ethnic Identity. On Modernization and Ethnicity in Greenland. Folk Vol. 11-12.

LaRussic, I. et al. eds., 1979: Negotiation a Way of Life. Initial Cree Experience with the Administrative Structure Arising from the James Bay Agreement, Montreal ssDcc.

Leach, E. R., 1954: Political Systems of Highland Burma. A Study of Kachin Social Structure G. Bell & Sons Ltd. London.

Mitchell, C., 1956: The Kalela Dance: Aspects of Social Relationships among Urban Africans in N. Rhodesia. The Rhodes-Livingstone Papers No. 27, Manchester.

Mitchell, C., 1974: Perceptions of Ethnicity and Ethnic Behaviour: An Empirical Exploration in A. Cohen ed. Urban Ethnicity, ASA 12, Tavistock Publ., London.

Moerman, M., 1965: Who are the Lue: Ethnic Identification in a Complex Civilization. Amer. Anthrop. Vol. 67.

Müller-Wille, L., 1979: The Sámi Parliament in Finland: A model for ethnic minority management? Etudes INUIT Studies Vol. 3: 2.

Nadel, J., 1984: Stigma and Separation: Pariah Status and Community Persistence in a Scottish Fishing Village, Ethnology 1984: 2.

Nagata, J., 1974: What is a Malay? Situational selection of ethnic identity in a plural society. American Ethnologist Vol. 1: 2.

Norges Offentlige Utredninger, 1984: Om Samenes Rettsstilling. Innstilling fra Samerettsutvalget NOU 1984: 18, Universitetsforlaget, Oslo Bergen Tromsø.

Okamura, J., 1981: Situational Ethnicity. Ethnic and Racial Studies. Vol. 4.

Paine, R., 1971: The Theory of Patronage and Brokerage in R. Paine ed. Patrons and Brokers in the East Arctic, ISER publ. No. 2, Memorial University, St. John's, Newfoundland.

– 1977: Tutelage and Ethnicity, a Variable Relationship in R. Paine ed. The White Arctic - Anthropological essays on tutelage and ethnicity. ISER publ. No. 7, Memorial Univ., St. John's, Newfoundland.

Pierson, J., 1981: Aboriginal migration, ethnicity and adaptations in Adelaide, Ethnic Groups Vol. 3: 2.

Svensson, T.G., 1976: Ethnicity and Mobilization in Sámi Politics. Stockholm Studies in Social Anthropology No. 4, University of Stockholm, Stockholm.

– 1979: Culture Communication and Sámi Ethnic Awareness. Ethnos Vol. 43 1978: 3-4.

– 1984: Sámi Literature and Handicraft as a Means of Communication. CULTURE Vol. 4: 2.

Tanner, A., 1983: Canadian Indians and the Politics of Dependency in A. Tanner ed. The Politics of Indianness, ISER publ. No. 12, Memorial Univ. St. John's, Newfoundland.

van der Berghe, P., 1975: Ethnicity and Class in Hihgland Peru in L. Despres ed. Ethnicity and Resource Competition in Plural Societies, Mouton, The Hague.

Vincent, J., 1974: The Structuring of Ethnicity, Human Organization Vol. 33.

Wallman, S., 1978: The Boundaries of 'Race': Processes of Ethnicity in England, MAN. No. 5 Vol. 13.

Address of the author:
Tom. G. Svensson
Ethnografisk Museum
Frederiks gate 2
Oslo 1
Norway

Native Ethnicity in the Canadian North
A Geographer's Perspective

William C. Wonders

Abstract: The Canadian North differs from the national ecumene in that native peoples still constitute a significant proportion of the local population, especially in the territories. In the N.W.T. they even make up a majority. Improved health and housing conditions in recent decades have reversed the decline in their numbers so that to-day they are increasing more rapidly than other ethnic groups. Inclusion of "aboriginal rights" in the new Canadian constitution and pressure for land claims settlements have strengthened the native role in the North. This is having significant repercussions on social, economic and political conditions in the North, with important implications for the future. The proposed division of the N.W.T. and creation of a new "Arctic" political unit (Nunavut) is an illustration of these developments. This paper examines some of the changes that have occured and their impact on the Canadian North.

Résumé: Le Nord du Canada diffère de l'écoumène national à cause d'une proportion importante des groupes indigènes parmi la population locale, surtout dans les territoires. Dans les territoires du Nord-Ouest ces groupes constituent même la majorité. L'amélioration des conditions de santé et d'hébergement dans les dernières décennies ont renversé la tendance au déclin et aujourd'hui ils s'accroissent plus rapidement que tout autre groupe ethnique. L'inclusion des droits aborigènes dans la nouvelle constitution Canadienne et les pressions pour les droits de colonisation des terres ont renforcé le rôle des populations indigènes du Nord. Ce développement a des repercussions importantes sur les conditions sociales, économiques et politiques et des implications pour le future. La division proposée des territoires du Nord West et la creation d'une unité politique nouvelle (nunavut) illustrent ces devéloppements. Cet article examine certains des changements qui ont survenu et leur impact sur le nord Canadien.

Zusammenfassung: Der kanadische Norden unterscheidet sich insofern von der Ökumene des Landes, als hier der Anteil der Urbevölkerung innerhalb der Gesamtbevölkerung nach wie vor bedeutend ist, besonders in den Territorien. In den N.W.T. ist sie sogar in der Überzahl. Verbesserte Gesundheits- und Wohnbedingungen haben in den letzten Jahrzehnten die Entwicklung in dem Sinne umgekehrt, daß ihre Zahl nicht mehr sinkt, sondern sogar zunimmt. Die Einbeziehung der "aboriginal rights" in die neue kanadische Verfassung und der Anspruch auf Land haben die Rolle der Eingeborenen im Norden gestärkt. Dies hat bedeutende Rückwirkungen auf soziale, wirtschaftliche und politische Strukturen im Norden mit wichtigen Auswirkungen für die Zukunft. Die vorgeschlagene Unterteilung der N.W.T., um eine neue "arktische" politische Einheit (Nunavut) zu bilden, ist ein Beleg für diese Entwicklungen. Einige dieser Veränderungen und ihrer Auswirkungen auf den kanadischen Norden werden in diesem Beitrag untersucht.

Ethnicity often means different things to different individuals and fields of studies. In Canada it displaced the earlier "racial origins" in federal government terminology as recently as the 1961 Census. Nevertheless the official Canada Year Book 1961 continued to use the previous phrasing, and while "ethnicity" now is firmly established some government officials and publications still persist in using "racial" in an ethnic sense.

Although anthropologists and sociologists may have their own definitions, cultural geographers generally would agree with Jordan and Rowntree: "Ethnicity - possessing ethnic quality or affiliation; the state of being ethnic. Ethnic group - a cultural group possessing a common (ancestry and) tradition and strong feeling of belonging, living as a minority in a larger host society of a different culture" (1982: 298).

Canada draws much of its cultural character from France and Britain, its historic parents. After two hundred years of sharing this northern expanse the offspring still largely co-exist in their "two solitudes", though there are encouraging signs of greater understanding in recent years. Meanwhile another distant relative joined the household with no direct ties to either France or Britain, coming from an increasingly varied background and usually identified collectively as "other" in official records. Such people have been present in Canada from its earliest years but they have increased dramatically over the past century, from 11 per cent of the national population in 1881 to 33 per cent in 1981 (Table 1). In most cases they have affiliated themselves with the English-speaking population rather than with the French, thereby contributing to the latter's fears for their cultural survival in an increasingly English-speaking continent. Yet the ethnic mix in Canada has reached such diversity that more and more even the British element is considered simply another ethnic group - especially if the Irish segment is treated separately! No other northern nation exhibits the ethnic diversity of Canada to-day. In this particular paper however "ethnic" will refer only to the native peoples, as opposed to the European or "white" populations (1).

Table 1: Major Ethnic Groups in Canada, 1871-1981 (%)

Ethnic Group	1871[+]	1881	1901	1911	1921	1931	1941	1951	1961	1971	1981
British	60.6	59.0	57.0	54.1	55.4	51.9	49.7	47.9	43.8	44.6	40.0
French	31.1	30.0	30.7	28.5	27.9	28.2	30.3	30.8	30.4	28.7	26.7
Other	8.3	11.0	12.3	17.4	16.7	19.9	20.0	21.3	25.8	26.7	33.3
(Native	0.7	2.5	2.4	1.5	1.3	1.2	1.1	1.2	1.2	1.5	1.7)

+) Four original provinces only

Date source: Census of Canada

"It has been estimated that before the Europeans came to Canada there were 200,000 Indians and 10,000 Inuit (Eskimo) belonging to many different and distinct cultures" (Statistics Canada, 1974: 237). War and disease subsequently reduced those numbers perhaps to half, though in the present century they again have increased to almost 500,000 (1981 Census of Canada), more than double their original numbers. Nevertheless the native peoples also have become one of the smallest minorities numerically in Canada, accounting for less than two per cent of the total population, very much an ethnic group separate from the mass of European decendents now occupying the country. In this respect Canada reflects much the same conditions as other northern nations with surviving indigenous peoples. Where it differs, except in the case of Greenland, is in the much larger native population compared with white population in its northern regions.

Problems of Definition

Difficulties are encountered in defining both "native" and the "Canadian North". In the latter case the geographic reality of the North does not conform with the artificial political boundaries which have been drawn over time (Wonders, 1984a). The results are frustrations for the researcher seeking a common statistical framework, for the officials seeking to implement policies in the North, and above all for the northerners living in the region and trying to cope with an often contradictory plethora of rules and procedures depending on which side of a political line they find themselves.

Hamelin's delineation of the Canadian North is widely used by Canadian geographers as one of the most satisfactory recent attempts to define the region (1979). On this basis well over two-thirds of Canada is "northern". All provinces except for the Maritime Provinces include significant amounts of "northern" lands (Figure 1), in total some 3.2 million square kilometers. A further 0.5 million square kilometers are included within the Yukon, and 3.4 million square kilometers within the Northwest Territories.

Figure 1:   The Canadian North

Source: After Hamelin (1979)

The sheer geographic enormity of the region and the many political authorities involved create significant local variations within the total geographic region. In my own case I shall focus primarily on the Northwest Territories (N.W.T.), which even within its own boundaries includes greater diversity than is often appreciated "outside", making up as it does one-third of the total area of Canada.

The aboriginal or native population of northern Canada includes three major groups: Indians, Métis (mixed bloods), and Inuit (Eskimos). Significant numbers of all three live in the Northwest Territories, though not in all parts of the Canadian North. The strong correlation between native ethnicity and the two major geographical regions of the North still persists, with the Inuit occupying the Arctic, and the Indians and Métis the Subarctic (Figure 2).

Figure 2: Native Peoples of Northern-Canada

Source: After Jenness (1977) and Helm (1981)

Native Numbers

Identification of native peoples in Canada is not quite as straight-forward as census data might suggest (Table 2). Government authorities distinguish between "status or registered Indians" and "non-status Indians". The former refers to those persons who are registered under the Indian Act of 1876 revised in 1951, as belonging to a registered Indian band and possessing a band number. Some but not all live on "reserve" land. (There are 561 separate Indian communities or "bands" in Canada, including 10 basic linguistic groups.) "Non-status Indians are persons of Indian ancestry who do not have the legal status of Indian ... either because they were never registered or are enfranchised, i.e. have voluntarily given up his or her rights under the Indian Act" (Lindsay, 1980: 175). One of the inequities to the present at least, is that white women marrying status Indians acquire Indian status for themselves and their children while status Indian women marrying white men become non-status Indians.

No such distinctions are made in the case of the Inuit, as Canadian Eskimos now prefer to be designated. In large measure this reflects their former geographic remoteness from other regions of Canada and the shorter period of permanent contact between them and the whites. The federal government has administered Inuit affairs, particularly since a Supreme Court of Canada decision in 1939 assigned to it exclusive legislative jurisdiction over Inuit. However, Ottawa has never passed a special act to appropriate provincial jurisdiction over the Inuit as it did for the Indians (Crowe, 1974: 161). Amongst the Inuit themselves scant attention is paid to an individual's ethnic background so long as he or she is accepted as an integral part of the Inuit community (Freeman, 1983).

Table 2: Native Peoples in Canada, 1981

	Inuit	Status or Registered Indian	Non-status Indian	Métis	Total Natives	Native Peoples & Other[+]	Total Population
Canada	23,200	266,420	47,235	76,520	413,380	78,085	24,083,495
Nfld.	1,365	715	930	215	3,230	1,205	563,750
P.E.I.	25	310	65	40	440	190	121,220
N.S.	50	5,270	530	460	6,305	1,485	839,800
N.B.	5	3,885	445	275	4,610	910	689,375
Que.	4,775	32,215	4,115	5,750	46,855	5,540	6,369,070
Ont.	565	60,635	14,130	8,530	83,860	26,200	8,534,260
Man.	140	38,055	4,695	17,025	59,920	6,355	1,013,705
Sask.	105	36,040	3,505	15,070	54,720	4,480	956,440
Alta.	315	32,645	5,420	21,625	60,005	12,040	2,213,655
B.C.	290	47,680	11,575	5,150	69,215	17,945	2,713,615
Yukon	70	2,450	740	150	3,430	630	23,070
N.W.T.	15,495	6,520	1,090	2,225	25,355	1,105	45,535

+) Includes 2,190 Inuit and other; 26,280 Status or Registered Indian and other; 49,610 Non-status Indian/Métis and other.

Source: 1981 Census of Canada

The idenfitication of "Métis" is the most complicated of all, as has been noted by numerous scholars, including historians (Foster, 1976) and anthropologists (Slobobodin, 1966; Asch, 1984). They are mainly people of mixed aboriginal and European ancestry. Slobodin states that "a working definition of the Mackenzie District Métis (in the western N.W.T.) is that they are persons of known Indian-European or Eskimo-European ancestry, for the most part occupying the legal status of Whites, who consider themselves and are considered to be Métis" (1966: 6). Almost all of the Eskimo-European ancestry people have considered themselves to be Inuit of the Western Arctic (the "Inuvialuit") in recent years however. Although the European ancestry is primarily French, it also includes British, and there are some Métis of non-European ancestry (Japanese, Polynesian, black). Furthermore, Asch notes that "Metis groups range widely in their cultural patterns and include, in some instances, groupings that are not readily separable from ways of life of certain 'Indian' nations, on the one hand, or patterns of European settlement, on the other" (1984: 5). There are well known cases where people who on the basis of their ancestry might be considered Métis but who are status Indians and others who might be considered status Indians who are Métis. "At the time of the northern treaty agreements some Métis people were given a choice of signing the treaty and thus becoming 'official Indians', or of taking a payment for their land rights, after which they would be treated as European Canadians" even though they continued to follow an Indian way of life (Crowe, 1974: 159). Others may even identify themselves as Métis or as white depending on the relative perceived advantages at a particular time.

The actual numbers of native peoples in Canada and in the Canadian North are not really known therefore. The 1981 Census data gives a total for Canada of 413,380 with a further 78,085 "native people and other", for an overall total of 491,466 persons of varying degrees of native ethnicity. Asch notes that estimates of total native population in Canada between 1971 and 1980 have ranged from 491,460 (census) to as much as 3,000,000, and suggests a total of roughly 840,000 based on statistics provided by the Secretary of State - almost double the 1981 Census figures (Asch, 1984: 3). Hamelin also agrees that there might be more than 800,000 native people in Canada (Hamelin, 1979: 213). However, for comparative purposes census data are used here.

Native peoples constitute an ethnic minority in the total Canadian population (Table 1). Contrary to popular opinion, the great majority of the indigenous peoples do not live in the North, but in the ecumene ("Base Canada") or settled part of Canada (Hamelin, 1979: 212). Although only one-fifth on them live in the North, their greater relative numbers in this region of small total population create a very different situation than in the southern parts of the country. While nationally they form less than two per cent of the population, in the North generally they make up about 10 per cent (Bone, 1972: 103). In the Yukon they make up 17.6 per cent of the total population, and in the Northwest Territories they make up 58.1 per cent of the total population. The majority situation of native people in the N.W.T. is unique in Canada and has major political and economic implications, especially since the devolution of government from Ottawa to the Territories. Of the 24 members elected to the N.W.T. Legislative Council in November 1983 for example, 13 are natives. In January 1984 that Council chose five native members and three non-natives to make up the eight-member Executive Council, with a native member serving as its head. Nowhere else in Canada do native people play such a leading political role. It means that increasingly matters of particular interest and concern to the native community will take priority over other considerations.

Demographic Considerations

Greatly improved health facilities in postwar years have been a major factor in the resurgence in the numbers of native peoples in the North. There now are nursing stations in every N.W.T. community of 200 or more people and hospitals in several large centres. In 1982 of the births in the N.W.T. 99.9% of Indians, 98.5% of Inuit and 99.6% of others were born either in hospital or nursing stations, with no recorded maternal deaths. Although the national average birthrate has fallen from 28.0 per thousand in 1951-56, to 15.4 per thousand in 1976-81, that of the N.W.T. has been slower to follow a similar trend. As recently as 1970 it was 40 per thousand, and in 1982 it was still 27 per thousand (Dept. of Information N.W.T., 1984: 60). Native women across Canada have larger numbers of children than non-native – in 1981 the averages were 3.8 and 2.5 respectively and as high as 4.6 amongst Inuit – but this is particularly significant in the N.W.T. where the native population forms the majority.

Canada's northern population is not only a rapidly growing one, but it is also a youthful one. The median age of the total Canadian population is 29.6 years, but in the N.W.T. it is only 22.0 years, and in the Yukon 26.6 years. Improved health conditions actually have lowered the death rate in the N.W.T. below the national average – 4.9 per thousand in 1982, compared with the 1976-81 national average of 7.2 per thousand (Dept. of Information N.W.T., 1984: 60; Statistics Canada, 1984: 43). Injury and poisoning still account for 31 per cent of deaths in the N.W.T. reflecting the hazards of traditional native life styles. Along with poorer earlier health facilities and out-migration of many older whites this helps explain the fewer old people in the N.W.T. The resultant population pyramid (Figure 3) reflects the typical broad-based model of third-world, underdeveloped areas.

Government has been obliged to provide expensive health services and a massive housing improvement programme primarily for the native population, in order to rectify past neglect and bring those facilities up to acceptable national levels. A similarly expensive and comprehensive education system has had to be implemented to meet the needs of this youthful population. Some 70 government-operated schools now exist, with over 700 teachers and over 12,000 students enrolled in the N.W.T. (double the student numbers two decades earlier). The predominance of native children and the increasing pride in traditional native culture have resulted in greater control by native communities, increased use of native languages, use of native classroom assistants, etc.

As the growing numbers of formally educated young natives leave school they expect employment opportunities to be available to them. More of them now are found in government offices and agencies, and they are particularly numerous in

Figure 3: Age/Sex Structure for Canada, Northwest Territories and the Yukon, 1981

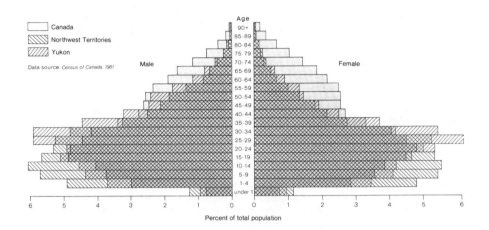

Source: 1981 Census of Canada statistics

local administration. In the long run however only increased private resource development probably offers employment prospects on the necessary scale. For some time past the companies involved in such development have been encouraged or obliged by government to employ natives among their work force. Half the workers at the Nanisivik lead-zinc mine opened in 1976 on Strathcona Sound on Baffin Island, for example, are Inuit. Half the work force currently involved in construction of the oil pipeline from Norman Wells in the Mackenzie Valley are northerners, the majority natives, and a native-owned and staffed drilling company is participating in the project.

Resource development projects usually involve environmental disruption. In their enthusiasm for development as a means of offsetting the high cost of social programs and of providing employment for the youthful northerners, authorities are faced with a basic problem. "Governments find themselves in the difficult if not impossible situation of trying to reconcile the need for northern resource development with their responsibility for protecting the environment" (Wonders, 1984b: 202).

Settlement Dwellers and Native Identity Problems

The original pattern of dispersed native population distribution has been abandoned since 1945 in favour of agglomerated settlement life. In part this reflected economic pressures with declining fur prices and rising costs of purchased goods. In part it reflected government encouragement (and at times pressure) in order to provide essential services. Considering the small total population involved and the formidable environmental conditions of the N.W.T. provision of those services is expensive.

"The small size and large number of the communities make for still more costly services. Sixty per cent of the 80 main settlements in the N.W.T., for example, have less than 300 inhabitants (Hamelin, 1979: 50). A similar situation in northern Scandinavia resulted in considerable rationalization of the settlement pattern in recent years, but this model has not been taken up in the Canadian North despite the potential advantages. (The one similar program involving Newfoundland outport relocations was discontinued.)" (Wonders, 1984a: 229). Aircraft are the only practical method of transportation to serve these communities in much of the N.W.T., particularly in the Arctic. In the late 1970s a joint Federal/Territorial program was completed to provide airport and aviation support services for all communities in the N.W.T. with populations over 100. There now are 184 airfields in the Territories!

It must be conceded that on purely economic grounds it is difficult to justify the continuance of the large numbers of small communities, mostly inherited from the fur trade era. On the other hand it may be argued that continuance is justified to demonstrate national territorial sovereignty based on occupance of this remote part of Canada. Only two Inuit communities exist in the Queen Elizabeth Islands, at Resolute and at Grise Fjord. Both of these were established in postwar years after weather stations were put in place on these northernmost islands. (The white personnel of the government scientific stations on these islands are not usually permanent residents.)

It also may be argued that continuance of these many small communities is justified in order to preserve at least something of the native culture. The rate and degree of cultural change experienced by many of the native people in the N.W.T. can not be overemphasized. "There are people today who have watched films of men walking on the moon, but who remember striking fire with stones" (Crowe, 1974: 152). Thanks to satellite technology no community of over 150 population in the N.W.T. is without radio and television to-day, even in the most remote northerly situations. After enjoying a traditional evening meal of caribou meat the family settles back to watch its favorite TV game programme and frequently succumbs to hucksters' inane commercial promotions. Currently no young native person in the North is well dressed without a "Walkman" plugged into his or her ear. Space shuttle flights are watched on television by northern natives as well as by other Canadians, yet their language has no words for many of the elements of technology involved, requiring ingenuity in translation. Thus in Inuktitut "space shuttle" becomes "aircraft like a star" and "astronaut" becomes "a person who flies where it is very still".

White cultural pressures on natives are most acute in the larger centres. It may be noted that the planned papal visit to the N.W.T. in the summer of 1984 to meet the native population resulted in a shift of locale from Yellowknife the capital, to Fort Simpson, despite the many practical problems involved with the latter's small size. Yellowknife was considered by the natives to be too much a white community.

"Town life" often results in great stress on native people whose ancestral values have been based on living off the land. Accustomed to an easy replacement of traditional dwellings, they may not be concerned with basic maintenance of their housing and certainly not with the whites' obsession with external neatness. An entire house was lost by fire in Ft. Chipewyan recently due to a spark while repairs being made by a native to a snowmobile. The fact that the snowmobile was in the living room may startle the non-native who would never consider such a work place, but be considered perfectly practical by the native. Many of the older natives find their traditional skills of no use in town and suffer a loss of pride and identity, while younger ones find it difficult to reconcile the lessons of school and the media with the views of their elders.

Such stressful situations have contributed to and been aggravated by alcohol and drug problems amongst natives in many northern communities. While social problems may not have reached the proportions experienced in some of the larger Greenlandic centres (Schuurman, 1976), they are serious. In 1983, 18 young males

15 to 24 years old were reported to have committed suicide in Inuvik (population 3,147); in Spence Bay (population 430) seven young men were reported to have attempted suicide within a two-month period in the fall of 1984 (Edmonton Journal, 19 October 1984). In an effort to reduce social problems many smaller northern native communities have imposed local prohibition of liquor sales, but such a course is much more difficult if not impossible in the ethnically-varied larger communities. It may be suggested therefore that government has a responsibility in the North to maintain on social and moral grounds, the smaller predominantly native communities despite the economic costs involved.

The popularity of the Territorial Government's "outpost camp programme" over the past ten years attests to the renewed importance of traditional native ways of life in the N.W.T. Such camps, providing up to a limited level of service, are staged out from the settlements. Most hunters continue to live in the settlements for varying periods of time but some now live in the outposts year-round. There presently are 109 such camps, involving a total population of 1300 people.

Aboriginal Rights and the Canadian Constitution

White settlement across Canada generally has been permitted only after native land rights were ceded by treaty in accordance with British and then Canadian government policy for over 200 years. In to-day's territorial North however, treaties came late and involved only part of the area. Treaty No. 8 in 1899 included that part of the Northwest Territories south of Great Slave Lake, and Treaty No. 11 in 1921 took in the N.W.T. Indians north of that Lake, to the Arctic coast. The Indians of the Yukon Territory and the Nishga Indians of northwestern British Columbia have never signed land treaties with the government. Neither have the Inuit.

"The native peoples of the Northwest Territories were influenced very deeply by two developments of the 1970s: the effective lobbying of Alaska's native peoples culminating in passage of the Alaska Native Claims Settlement Act in late 1971, and the extensive local hearings of the Mackenzie Valley Pipeline Enquiry ("The Berger Commission"). The latter recommended that no pipeline be constructed for ten years in order to permit settlement of native land claims and adjustment to new conditions (Berger, 1977)" (Wonders, 1984c). About the same time there was increasing general interest in the area by Canadians, concerned about environmental protection particularly in the North. For their part the Indians argue that the past treaties in the N.W.T. were "treaties of friendship" only, and that they did not give up their aboriginal rights in signing them.

Following a divided opinion by the Supreme Court of Canada in 1973 on whether the Nishgas' original title to their ancient tribal lands had ever been "lawfully extinguished" the federal government announced its willingness to deal with native claimants and with other levels of government to resolve all outstanding claims. In 1974 a special Office of Native Claims was established within the Department of Indian Affairs and Northern Development to deal with such matters. It should be noted that since 1970 the federal government has been funding native claimant groups and associations to enable them to research, develop and negotiate claims (Anon., 1982: 12). Native rights have been further recognized recently by government, through inclusion of "aboriginal rights" in the new Canadian Constitution of 1982, though the precise definition of these remains to be established. While the federal government is responsible for co-ordinating policies and programmes only for status Indians and Inuit as defined under The Indian Act, non-status Indians and Métis are recognized for their aboriginal descent. They therefore form part of certain claimant groups with whom the department negotiates for land claims settlements (Anon., 1982: 1).

"Claims for the Northwest Territories have been dealt with separately from adjacent political units despite native objections that political boundaries ignore their traditional and current areas of use and occupancy. Thus the westward extension of the native peoples into the political area of to-day's Yukon is not considered in N.W.T. negotiations, nor is the northward extension of present-day native residents of northern Saskatchewan and northern Manitoba into the N.W.T." (Wonders, 1984c)

Four associations represent the native people of the Northwest Territories. The Inuit Tapirisat of Canada (I.T.C.) originally represented all N.W.T. Inuit. Because of more immediate pressure of resource development in the Western Arctic, since 1976 the Inuit of that sector (the Inuvialuit) have been represented by the Committee for Original People's Entitlement (C.O.P.E.). In 1982 the I.T.C. established the Tungavik Federation of Nunavut (T.F.N.) to negotiate the Inuit Claims in the Central and Eastern Arctic. The Indian association is the Dene Nation, the various tribes of which are included within the Athapaskan linguistic family. The Métis are represented by the Métis Association of the N.W.T. For purpose of negotiation the Dene and Métis function as one group at government's insistance.

Practical Considerations

The native people of the Northwest Territories find themselves in a relatively strong position to influence if not control developments in that part of the Canadian North. Since 1966 there has been major political devolution of jurisdiction from Ottawa to Yellowknife (named Territorial capital in 1967), and native peoples form the majority of the population in the N.W.T. as has been noted. Their views on a variety of topics are increasingly important for the future of this area. Amongst these, four may be noted here: overlapping native land use and occupancy, protection vs. development, territorial division, and native/white relations.

Land Use Overlap

Although there is approximate conformity traditionally and currently between the geographic distribution of the majority of the native peoples of the Northwest Territories and its two major geographical regions as noted previously, it is not a perfect match. In defining their respective areas of claim, there have been areas of overlap where more than one native group have claimed the same land.

The position of the federal government has been that wherever such overlap exists, agreement has to be reached among the different users before claims could be settled. Although some bilateral meetings on the matter had occurred between the native organizations since 1980, no confirmed agreements had resulted by 1983. Until land claims are settled both government and private companies are uncertain about the ramifications for any possible large development project though it can be noted that the expansion of the Norman Wells oilfield (where no overlap was involved) has proceeded following mutual agreement between the company and the natives. The imminence of a federal election and the obvious political advantage of having achieved some concrete progress in settling land claims probably added to pressure on government.

In an effort to resolve the impasse in the overlap problem, the Minister of Indian Affairs and Northern Development with the approval of the native associations appointed an impartial fact-finder (the author) to inquire into, assess and report upon the extent (geographical and concentration) and nature of the traditional and current overlapping land concentration) and nature of the traditional and current overlapping land use and occupancy of the Dene, Métis, Inuvialuit and Inuit respectively of the Northwest Territories. The process was to rely on available documentary evidence, supplemented by oral or written evidence from the communities concerned where the fact-finder deemed it necessary. Despite the complexity and sensitivity of the task only five months time was allowed. The report was transmitted to the Minister in January 1984 (Wonders, 1984d). Figure 4 shows the generalized summary of the overlap areas - greater detail was provided in the report concerning specific sectors.

Figure 4: Areas of Overlapping Land Use by Native Peoples of the Northwest Territories.

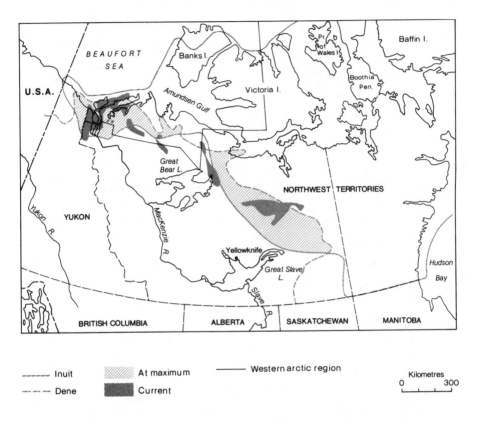

Source: Wonders (1984c)

The Dene and Métis were particularly concerned about overlap in the Western Arctic/Mackenzie Delta area where they saw a 1978 agreement-in-principle between C.O.P.E. and the federal government threatening their rights in the area. The fact-finding process served a useful purpose in that it did bring the contending native associations together to resolve their differences in that area. This made possible a satisfactory completion of the first comprehensive land claim settlement in the Northwest Territories. In March 1984 Cabinet approved "The Western Arctic Claim" agreement and it was ratified in Parliament in June 1984 (Anon. 1984). Under its terms the 2500 native peoples concerned will receive benefits similar to those in the Alaskan native lands settlement, including title to 91.000 km² of land, $ 45 million in 1977 dollars, $ 10 million economic enhancement fund, wildlife harvesting and management, etc.

Protection vs. Development

It must be conceded that most of the northern resource development which has occurred to date has been for the primary economic advantage of those outside the North. Even when there have been spin-off benefits for the North, until recently these have gone mainly to the white populations. Many of these in turn come to the North only as short-term "residents" in order to accumulate funds for ultimate use "outside", though there is an increasing number of whites who regard the North as their permanent home.

In recent years more native residents are finding employment in a widening range of economic opportunities, particularly as they have acquired more varied skills through formal education. This trend should increase with land claims agreements, establishment of native corporations to administer resources, etc. Indeed, one segment of the native population favours immediate active participation in development projects (such as the Norman Wells oilfield expansion) while another favours settlement of the claims before major economic development.

A more fundamental problem confronting the native population in the long run is the need to reconcile the potential conflict between those who seek to protect the natural environment even if it costs the loss of significant economic benefit, and those who would rate economic development as the higher priority. The first group sees the need to preserve traditional values and way of life against the increasing "alien" pressures as their primary concern. The second sees economic development as the only long range solution capable of providing employment for the increasing numbers of well educated native youth. To date native leaders have stated that it should be possible for them to provide a balanced future incorporating elements of both these viewpoints. It is to be hoped such can be the case but it remains to be seen.

Territorial Division

The sheer geographic enormity of the Northwest Territories complicates administration of it. In the 1960s bills were actually put before Parliament calling for division of the N.W.T., but these suggestions were ended in 1966 when an advisory commission into self-government in the N.W.T. came down in favour of the Territories remaining under one administration. In February 1976 the Inuit Tapirisat of Canada proposed that the area north and east of treeline be separated out as a new Territory (and future province) "Nunavut" ("Our Land"), to be governed by the Inuit. In October 1976 the Indian Brotherhood of the N.W.T. called for dismemberment of the N.W.T. and for establishment of a native province centred on the Mackenzie Valley, along with two other new provinces for Inuit and for whites respectively. In August 1977 the Prime Minister rejected the proposals in a policy statement, on the grounds that "Legislative authority and government jurisdiction are not allocated in Canada on grounds that differentiate between people on the basis of race ..." (Edmonton Journal, 4 August 1977).

The issue refused to die, at least so far as the Inuit were concerned. A territorial capital in Yellowknife has proved almost as unsatisfactory for them as when it was in Ottawa, removed both physically and culturally from the realities of the Arctic region. "The Inuit now realize that their culture and language cannot be protected by law books in Yellowknife or preserved in a museum. The Inuit realize that the protection, preservation and development of their culture is their responsibility and theirs alone ... (and that) they have a right to determine how things are done on their lands" (Amagoalik, 1978: 4). Under continuous pressure from the Inuit, the Legislative Assembly of the N.W.T. agreed in principle to the division in November 1980. In April 1982 a Territories-wide plebescite on the issue saw the Eastern Arctic support the proposal by 82 per cent though less endorsement in the western Subarctic pulled the pro-division territorial average down to 56 per cent. Ottawa approved the split in principle in November 1982 though it saw no provincial status "for the foreseeable future" because of the small populations and weak economies. Amongst conditions imposed was that all land claims in the N.W.T. must be settled, that the location of the boundary between the two territories (Nunavut and perhaps "Denendeh") had to be agreed upon, and territorial powers had to be suggested.

Figure 5: Boreal Forest and Arctic Tundra Regions of Canada

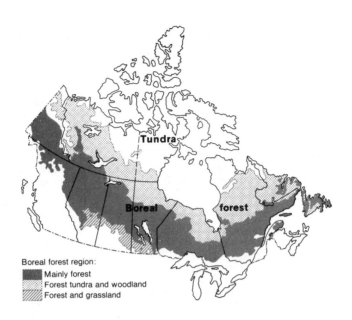

Source: After Hosie

Two regional organizations in the Northwest Territories are currently engaged in this process - the Nunavut Constitutional Forum in the Arctic, and the Western Constitutional Forum in the Subarctic. If treeline is accepted as the boundary there will be the problem of accurately delineating this feature which may appear obvious on a generalized map (Figure 5) but which is highly complex in reality. The Dene and Métis in the west so far have rejected this, preferring possibly a northward continuation of the Saskatchewan/Manitoba boundary line to the Arctic coast, in order to place under their jurisdiction the oil and gas resources of the Beaufort Sea area.

Native/White Relations

Finally it should be noted that native/white relations have been pointed up as well as those between the native peoples of the Northwest Territories by recent events. Some amongst the whites see the benefits to natives in land claims settlements as overly generous and potentially restrictive for further development. (Already some currents of dissatisfaction may be noted, though only amongst a minority of whites to date, for the favoured treatment perceived to native as opposed to non-native northerners in grants, employment, etc.).

The full implications of a territorial split are cause for concern amongst some whites. They are generally reassured about future prospects for the ethnically heterogeneous Mackenzie Valley, but much less so for the Arctic where the Inuit make up the overwhelming majority of population. The Inuit have frequently stressed that they do not seek to establish an ethnic government from which whites would be excluded and that Nunavut "would be wholly within the political norms of the

Canadian nation" (Nunavut Constitutional Forum, 1983: 55), though some proposals such as a minimum three-year residency qualification for voting, introduction of Inuktitut as an official language, have aroused criticism.

Clearly native/white relations have become of increasing importance in the Northwest Territories and will need to be handled carefully to ensure smooth relations between the various ethnic groups.

Conclusion

A large, and in places dominant native presence has always characterized the Canadian North and particularly the Northwest Territories. Historically, the influx of large numbers of whites led to the progressive carving off of new territories and provinces in Canadian political evolution. If present plans come to fruition it may well see the disappearance of the formal "Northwest Territories" after over a hundred years' existence and their replacement by two new political entities. It seems unlikely however that the native population will ever be reduced to the minority level characteristic of southern Canada because of the distinctive geographic nature of the North. In this situation it is to be expected that developments and policies will reflect native cultural values to an increasing degree. Hopefully mutual respect and consideration will result in a harmonious future for all parties concerned.

Footnote:

(1) "Whites" is commonly used throughout northern Canada to refer to the non-native population, with no discriminatory connotation between native and non-native. It is so used here. Unless otherwise indicated statistics are from the 1981 Census of Canada.

References

Amagoalik, J., 1978: Inuit Nunangat, The People's Land. Frobisher Bay: Inuit Land Claims Commission.

Anon. 1982: Native Peoples and the North, A Profile. Ottawa: Indian and Northern Affairs Canada.

— 1984: The Western Arctic Claim: The Inuvialuit Final Agreement. Ottawa: Indian and Northern Affairs Canada.

Asch, M., 1984: Home and Native Land. Toronto: Methuen.

Berger, T.R., 1977: Northern Frontier, Northern Homeland: The Report of the Mackenzie Valley Pipeline Inquiry, 2 vols. Ottawa: Minister of Supply and Services Canada.

Bone, R.M., 1972: "The Population of Northern Canada", in The North, ed. W.C. Wonders. Toronto: University of Toronto Press, 91-116.

Crowe, K.J., 1974: A history of the Original Peoples of Northern Canada. Montreal: Arctic Institute of North America/McGill-Queen's University Press.

Dept. of Information, 1984: Government of the Northwest Territories 1982 Annual Report. Yellowknife: Government of the Northwest Territories.

Foster, J.E., 1976: "The Origins of the Mixed Bloods in the Canadian West", in Essays on Western History, ed. L.H. Thomas. Edmonton: University of Alberta Press, 71-80.

Freeman, M.M.R. 1983: Personal communication, 2 September.

Hamelin, L.-E., 1979: Canadian Nordicity: It's Your North Too. Montreal: Harvest House.

Helm, J. (ed.), 1981: Handbook of North American Indians. Volume 6. Washington, D.C.: Smithsonian Institute.

Hosie, R.C., 1969: Native Trees of Canada (7th ed.). Ottawa: Canadian Forestry Service, Dept. of Fisheries and Forestry/Queen's Printer.

Jenness, D., 1977: The Indians of Canada (7th ed.). Ottawa and Toronto: University of Toronto Press.

Jordan, T.G., and Rowntree, L., 1982: The Human Mosaic (3rd ed.). New York: Harper and Row.

Lindsay, C., 1980: "The Indians and Métis of Canada", in Perspectives Canada III. Statistics Canada. Ottawa: Minister of Supply and Services Canada, 173-176.

Nunavut Constitutional Forum, 1983: Nunavut. Yellowknife: Northwest Territories Information.

Schuurman, H.J.C., 1976: Canada's Eastern Neighbour: a View on Change in Greenland. Ottawa: Minister of Supply and Services Canada.

Slobodin, R., 1966: Metis of the Mackenzie District. Ottawa: Canadian Research Centre for Anthropology, Saint-Paul University.

Statistics Canada, 1974: Perspective Canada. Ottawa: Information Canada.

— 1982-84: 1981 Census of Canada. Ottawa: Supply and Service Canada.

— 1984: Canada Handbook. Ottawa: Minister of Supply and Services Canada.

Wonders, W.C., 1984a: "The Canadian North: Its Nature and Prospects", Journal of Geography, Vol. 83 (5), Sept.-Oct., 226-233.

— 1984b: "Northern Canadian Resources Development" in China in Canada: A Dialogue on Resources and Development, ed. R.L. Gentilcore. Hamilton, Ont.: Dept. of Geography, McMaster University, 196-205.

— 1984c: "Our Land, Your Land - Overlapping Native Land Use and Occupancy in Canada's Northwest Territories", a paper presented at a Symposium of the International Geographical Union's Study Group on Development in Highlands and High-Latitude Zones, Innsbruck, 21-25 August.

— 1984d: Overlapping Land Use and Occupancy of Dene, Métis, Inuvialuit and Inuit in the Northwest Territories. Ottawa: Indian and Northern Affairs Canada.

Address of the author:
William C. Wonders
University of Alberta
Dept. of Geography
Edmonton
Canada T6G 2H4

Indian and Federal Government Relationship in Canada: The Constitution and the Mental Well-Being of Indian People in Northwestern Ontario

Edward M. Bennett

Abstract: Two major clusters of problems are identified in relationship to the mental well-being of native persons and communities: (i) community power-loss attributed to economic, social, religious, political and legal disenfranchisement, and (ii) the establishment of norms based on the myth of white superiority, which in relationship to the above diminish the identity and self-esteem of native persons and result in individual and collective power-loss. A review of recent events which have led to positive developments in Indian and Federal Government relations are discussed. While the author feels that the Indian Act and government structures continue to restrict Indian people in Canada the paper concludes that in the context of the 1982 Constitution Act of Canada the restoration of Indian power is more possible now than ever before in Canadian history.

Résumé: A propos du bien-être psychologique des autochtones et de leurs communautés, on a identifié deux ensembles de problèmes: 1) l'impuissance de la communauté attribuable à la perte des droits économiques, sociaux, religieux, politiques et légaux; 2) l'établissement de normes fondées sur le mythe de la supériorité des Blancs, ce qui diminue l'identité et l'estime de soi des autochtones et amène une perte de pouvoir individuelle et collective. On commente les récents événements qui ont conduit à des développements positifs dans les relations entre les Indiens et le gouvernement fédéral. En dépit du fait que la Charte des Indiens et les structures gouvernementales continuent d'imposer des restrictions aux populations autochtones, l'article conclut que, dans le contexte de la Charte canadienne de 1982, la restauration du pouvoir amérindien est maintenant davantage possible que jamais auparavant dans l'histoire canadienne.

Zusammenfassung: Bezüglich des psychologischen Zustandes der Urbevölkerung und ihrer Gemeinschaft kann man zwei Problembereiche erkennen: 1) der Machtverlust der Gemeinschaft aufgrund des Verlustes von wirtschaftlichen, sozialen, religiösen, politischen und legalen Rechten und 2) die Erstellung von Normen, die sich auf den Mythos von der Überlegenheit der Weißen stützt, was zur Einschränkung der Eigenidentität und der Selbsteinschätzung bei der Urbevölkerung führt und den Verlust an individueller und kollektiver Macht herbeiführt. Der Beitrag behandelt jüngere Entwicklungen, die das Verhältnis zwischen Indianern und Bundesregierung positiver gestaltet haben. Trotz der Tatsache, daß der Indian Act und die Regierungsstruktur nach wie vor Einschränkungen der autochthonen Bevölkerung bedeuten, schließt der Beitrag unter Bezug auf die kanadische Verfassung von 1982 mit der Feststellung, daß die Möglichkeit zur Erneuerung von Rechtspositionen der Urbevölkerung heute größer ist als je zuvor in der kanadischen Geschichte.

The theme of this paper is the identification and examination of some of the economic, political, religious and social structures created by the dominant white culture which effect the mental well-being of Indian persons living in Northwestern Ontario and the implications of the 1982 Canadian Constitution Act and the roles Indian people have played to restore their power loss. The Cree and Ojibwa peoples of Northwestern Ontario derive from a common Potro-Central-Algonkian stock. Furthermore, they share a common uniform sub-Arctic hunter/gatherer socio-economic cultural tradition and many fundamental features in their belief systems. The discussion which ensues describes how the psychological well-being of these people has been effected by the tensions resulting from the conflict between their common value systems and those of the white Euro-Canadian.

Author's Note:
The first section of this paper is a revised version of material previously published in the Canadian Journal of Community Mental Health, Vol. 1 (2), 1982.

Statement of Problem

Context

There is a tragic contradiction at the heart of much administrative behaviour in relation to the original inhabitants of Northwestern Ontario. There is on the one hand a belief that Indians have social, economic and educational needs which are best provided for by the white man. On the other hand, there is a belief that Indians are too dependent on the Canadian Government and that provision of material goods and services only furthers their continuing dependency.

It is indeed true that the majority of the Indians in Northwestern Ontario are materially dependent on the Canadian Government. On some Indian reserves the unemployment rate is over 90%. The hunting, fishing, and trapping which remain are usually limited to supplementing a form of survival which is dependent on government subsidies. Yet, the "fact of life" which embraces Indian persons living in Northwestern Ontario cannot be explained away by saying that they are lazy, ignorant, and indifferent - labels that are often applied to explain the situation. Nor is it correct to believe that the white civil service bureaucracy responsible for the administration of programs for native people, is composed of lazy, indifferent, or insensitive human service personnel. In my view the policies, programs and persons involved, for the most part, come by their problems honestly and are trying to alter the very evident dehumanizing conditions.

Unfortunately these programs and most of the Canadian tax dollars spent on Indian persons are directed at the consequences and not at the causes of their circumstances. The purpose here is to share with the reader a particular view of the problem, some of the underlying causes and to review some recent actions of positive change.

European Settlers

The Europeans who colonized what is now regarded as Canada regularly developed policies and treaties to meet the specific situation and political experience of their colonization. The issue of land and land use is at the heart of native identity. Moreover, the concept of land ownership is foreign to the Indian culture which viewed land as a part of nature to be shared by all people. A treaty system evolved as a primary means of land administration and a way to reconcile the conflict of the two cultures.

European economic and political value systems were vastly different than those of the Indian Nations. As a result, the Indians did not understand the economic and political implications inherent in the solicitation of their signatures. Generally, the Indians viewed the treaty primarily as a guarantee to continue their traditional life style and to maintain friendship and peace with the white man whose numbers were rapidly increasing. Consequently, many of them now find themselves living on land to which the Crown has exclusive rights (Cumming & Mickenberg, 1972).

Legislation

Smith, in his study of the preconfederation legislation on Indian matters in Canada, characterizes it as being based on the "moral premise ... (that) ... Indians who choose to live an Indian style of life are to be considered uncivilized". Witness the proscription of the use of alcohol, the potlatch, the Sun Dance and other traditional ceremonies, together with the determination that Indians be encouraged to develop "agriculture and other civilizing pursuits ..." (xvii)

Smith further points out that the 1857 standards set for native persons wishing to acquire full civil rights surpassed the requirements many other enfranchised Canadians were able to meet. To be eligible for full civil rights, one must be an ...

"Indian of the male sex and not under twenty-one years of age, is able to speak, read and write either the english or french language readily and well, and is sufficiently advanced in the elementary branches of education and is of good moral character and free from debt ..." (p. 51 citing 20 Victoria, 1857, CAP 26, Province of Canada).

The intention and inequality of the preconfederation law set the stage for the physical and psychological containment of native persons. As we shall see, this legislation is but one amongst a longer string of structural events which tell native persons they are different than, and inferior to, the white culture.

Economic Values

Like any group faced with the dynamics of acculturation, the original inhabitants lacked a conceptual perspective from which to understand how a capitalistic system would alter the social and moral foundation of their culture. Although the selling of furs and individual labor may have temporarily added to their economic base, it was also disruptive to the traditional basis of their community.

The acquisition of Euro-Canadian goods in particular tore at the roots of their culture as it contributed to the gradual modification of their concept of property. The trapping of fur bearing animals for example, was transformed from an activity shared with others in the community to a "competitive" enterprise and a potential means to increase individual wealth. At the same time, other traditional economic activities such as food gathering and manufacturing suffered from lack of manpower resources (Rogers, 1962). As the traditional resource exchange system diminished, the adoption of a more capitalistic system failed to maintain a satisfactory level of economy.

Religious Values

Native solidarity and their cultural, religious, and economic values were further weakened through the introduction of European Christianity. Missionaries did not encourage native persons to maintain their own culture. The Cree and Ojibwa believed that spirituality was inherent in the natural world. Man was but one component of that integral and dynamic system. The Christian belief system of the Euro-Canadian that man was dominant in a world which was created to serve him was radically opposed to the native belief system. The various church groups often badgered native persons to adopt European ethical and religious values. European work and property values were given as much emphasis as the gospel (McCullum, 1975).

Many of the reserves today are geographically sectioned and divided according to Christian church affiliation - one more institutional structure which divides native persons, their culture and communities.

Education and its Inherent Cultural Values

In school settings native people were constantly told their culture was inferior by: directives which discouraged or did not allow them to speak their native tongue; instructions and constant messages to adopt new values (different form of dress, work, concept of time, property, etc.); being taken away from their homes at an early age for ten months of the year to attend school; and directly or indirectly reminded that life with their family was dirty, uncivilized and pagan.

There are many Indian persons who have vivid recollections of literally being swept up in a plane and away from their homes at an early age, without any preparation as to why, where, or what for. Some of these people now living in Sioux Lookout described their first day at a residential school as involving a mass line up to a change room, undressing, being doused with a shower, having their hair shaved, and being given a foreign set of clothes to wear. One of the first school rules introduced was that talking in one's native tongue was a punishable offence. Although the administration of the school may have acted with the best of intentions, the experience described seems akin to many coercive institutional scenes designed to alter a person's identity. Current school policies, curricula, instruction, administration and financing for native children in the North are still white dominated. By definition, the predominant message communicated is that the white man still knows what is best for native persons.

Indirect Rule

The proliferation of white agencies appearing on Indian reserves, dispersing programs and money has amounted to a form of indirect rule by the white man. Indirect rule is administered by the orders and policies which emanate from Ottawa and Toronto, implemented through the local native chiefs at the reserve level. The white man who does not speak the native language, and who does not want to live in an isolated area, finds it convenient to have a local chief administer his policies. The Indians already uprooted from their historical ties and subdued economically, politically and socially, are vulnerable and dependent, making it easy for the white administrators to give the essential orders. The chiefs elected by their community, along with a council, fall somewhat short of fulfilling their traditional roles as leaders since they are always accountable to the white man and his policies. When there is a disagreement between the chief and the community the white program administrator is asked to adjudicate.

Rogers (1962), in his discussion of the Round lake Ojibwa, notes that under the influence of Euro-Canadian contact the older leader whose authority stemmed from the integration of political, religious, and economic roles was replaced by an elected "leader". The role of the chief was established by the Euro-Canadians as a purely political role. Rogers also notes that the political leader is not referred to as "Okima" meaning chief but as "Okimahka" meaning boss-like, a further achowledgement that the real authority resides outside of their control and community.

Summary of Ideological Structure

Starting with the introduction of a new economic system, traditional native religious beliefs, healing practices, kinship ties, and forms of social roles and organizations as interdependent systems were gradually eroded. The ideology which shaped the responses of native persons to the new values, beliefs and social organizations was the perceived inferiority of native belief systems to those of the Euro-Canadian. This ideology of native inferiority governed and continues to govern most of the relationships which the dominant white culture has with native persons and communities. As we shall see, this psychologically devastating ideological structure is further reinforced by the human service organizations in Northwestern Ontario.

Human Service Organizations and Native Persons

The mental health of native persons is inextricably tied to the physical, economic, social and cultural containment described in the previous section. The government organization of human services for native persons in Northwestern Ontario is a phenotype of the seemingly pervasive containment by the dominant culture.

The Federal and Provincial human service organizations appear to the people in the North (as they do in the South) as large, very specialized bureaucracies with characteristics somewhat akin to those outlined by Weber (1947). They differ from the Weberian monocratic bureaucracy because as government bodies they are sometimes responsive to various internal and external pressures and thus adapt and change (Gouldner, 1959; Etzioni, 1964). Nevertheless, policy and budget decisions established in Ottawa and Toronto are clearly separated from administrative practices in the field. The District Health Councils created by the Ontario Ministry of Health, are an excellent example. Defined as decentralized, local bodies to plan and co-ordinate health services for a district, the councils: (i) do not have any fiscal authority, and (ii) do not review and comment on the use of dollars for programs already in existence. With only limited funds allocated for new programs, one might ask what purpose the Councils were created to serve. The frustration of these limitations and the perceived futility of their efforts were apparent when the author participated in the planning meetings of the Kenora-Rainy River District Health Council Mental-Health Sub-Committee. As one member stated after the group had reviewed a proposal submitted by one native group, "Why did we allow these people to travel 150 miles, build up their hopes and expectations, when we know there is no new money to spend for at least two years?"

Although the above illustrates that native and non-native persons both experience the frustration of bureaucratic domination, the native persons received a double blow - being the victim of the white cultural domination as well.

Concurrently, Health and Welfare Canada isolates medical content (i.e., disease) from the Indian person's total life style, culture and environment. The highly specialized, legal-rational bureaucratic approach differs dramatically from the historical pattern of traditional relationships and authority systems of native persons and communities. Moreover, the treatment of health problems differs from the holistic perspective taken by native healers who view the problem as part of the patient's existential reality.

The dominant culture's attitudes toward the North and its people are perhaps the stumbling blocks. Medical personnel are seldom invited to view the North as a homeland or native culture as having something to teach or give them. Instead, policies are introduced which create a psychology about the North as an isolated, harsh, cold, foreign environment needing to be conquered. Special pay and living allowances are provided to physicians; other external incentives, such as priority in application to postgraduate training have been proposed by prominent and influential medical authorities (Bain, cited in McKinney, 1973).

The impact of the Medical Services in Northwestern Ontario on the health of native persons is distressingly inadequate (Concerned Citizens Committee, 1974; Goldthorpe 1975; Giesbrecht & Brown, 1977). This is consistent with other Canadian data on the health of Indian persons (Booz-Allen & Hamilton, 1969; Indian Self-Government, 1983; Conference of First Ministers, 1983). The incentives do not get at the heart of the problem, i.e., the lack of western trained native doctors, white professionals who speak the native language, and the limited acceptance and integration of native belief systems, life patterns and medicine men.

Overview of Problem

Two major clusters of problems have been identified in relationship to the mental well being of native persons and communities: (i) community power-loss attributed to economic, social, religious, political and legislative disenfranchisement and (ii) the establishment of norms based on the myth of white superiority, which in relationship to the above, diminish the identity and self-esteem of native persons and result in individual and collective power-loss.

Two types of changes are required: (i) Indian people must be given access to and control over their own resources and government to ensure their cultural survival. Control over such areas as finances, health, education and welfare, restoration of a land and resource base, and a meaningful form of self-government are essential elements of the proposed changes in the structural arrangements. (ii) A new set of norms must be established based on a view of Indian people and nations as productive, intelligent and spiritual civilizations at the time of first contact with the European settlers.

New Directions in Indian and Government of Canada Relations

Introduction - Key Events Influencing Change 1969-1984

While the Indian Act and complex government structures continue to restrict Indian people in Canada and the many examples of social deprivation and social disintegration noted earlier continue to prevail in Northwestern Ontario and elsewhere in Canada, some significant changes have occurred in the structural relations between Indians and the Federal Government during the period between 1969-1984. It may be some time before these changes percolate down to the reserve level in communities such as those of Northwestern Ontario. At this time, however, there is more hope for positive structural change and optimism for the restoration of self-direction, control and government at the community level, for Canadian Indians than ever before in Canadian history.

In the remaining pages of this paper I shall identify and briefly discuss the major events and developments in relations between Indian peoples and the Federal government, as follows: The White Paper, 1969; Property Rights and Native Land Settlement; The Organization of Indian Peoples in Canada; Indian Leaders, and Aboriginal Rights in the Canadian Constitution.

The White Paper

When Trudeau came to power in April, 1968, a new approach was applied to the "Indian Problem". The approach was closely aligned to Trudeau's views on the French situation, particularly his rejection of separate and special rights for both cultural groups. In regard to Indians, Trudeau's belief in political realities and power rather than historical rights prevailed. The political fact for Trudeau was that Quebec's secession would destroy confederation. Indians with one per cent of the population did not have such political power (Trudeau, 1968).

In 1969, shortly after Trudeau became Prime Minister, the Canadian Federal Government produced a White Paper on Indian policy which Indian people rejected and the Government eventually withdrew. The White Paper proposed the termination of the special treatment of Indian people, including the Indian Act. Although Indian people were also critical of the Act, they recognized it protected their Charter rights which had been granted or promised prior to Confederation in 1867.

The White Paper policy said "that the legislative and constitutional basis of discrimination should be removed", as the key ingredient in a solution to the problems of Indians. The Paper argued that the special rights of Indians had been the major cause of their problems (Diand, 1969).

It took a while for Indian organizations to evaluate the response of their memberships to the federal government's White Paper. When the response came it arrived with unprecedented unity among Provincial and National Indian Organizations. Cardinal's, The Unjust Society (1969) asserted the White Paper was an attempt to exterminate Indians through assimilation. Cardinal was especially troubled and angered by the proposal to transfer federal responsibility for Indian Affairs to the provincial governments.

The Indian Chiefs of Alberta presented a second document, "Citizens Plus" to Prime Minister Trudeau in June 1970. The first sentence of the Indian Chiefs of Alberta's response to the Federal Government's White Paper reaffirmed the importance of their treaties, their lands and the well-being of future generations. With the perception that the intention of the White Paper would extinguish all of the above, the Alberta Indian Chiefs concluded the contents offered despair instead of hope. As well, the Alberta Chiefs felt stung and hurt by the government's concept of "consultation". They challenged the government to identify the group of Indians who asked for the contents of the White Paper.

The preamble to their response comments on the government's consultation process and sets the stage for their counter policy as follows:

"... What Indians asked for ownership that would result in provincial taxation of our reserves? What Indians asked that the Canadian Constitution be changed to remove any reference to Indians or Indian lands? What Indians asked that Treaties be brought to an end? What Indians asked for a Commissioner whose purview would exclude half of the Indian population in Canada? The answer is not Treaty Indians asked for any of these things and yet through his concept of "consultation" the Minister said that his White Paper was in response to things said by Indians.

We felt that with this concept of consultation held by the Minister and his department, that if we met with them to discuss the contents of his White Paper without being fully prepared, that even if we just talked about the weather, he would turn around and tell Parliament and the Canadian public that we accepted his White Paper" (pp. 1-2).

'Citizen Plus' cited the report of the federally established Hawthorn Committee which proposed: "Indians should be regarded as Citizens Plus; in addition to the normal rights and duties of citizenship, Indians possess certain additional rights as charter members of the Canadian Community" (p. 20).

Showing great astuteness to the politics of language the Indians rejected the White Paper policy which said:

"that the legislative and constitutional basis of discrimination should be removed ... we say that the recognition of Indian Status is essential for justice. Retaining the legal status of Indians is necessary if Indians are to be treated justly. Justice requires that the special history, rights and circumstances of Indian people be recognized ... the Chretien (government) policy says, Canada cannot seek the just society and have key discriminatory legislation on its books ... this statement covers a faulty understanding of fairness ..."

The Indian Chiefs of Alberta cited author L. Green in arguing a counterpoint:

"Equality <u>in fact</u> may involve the necessity of different treatment ... to maintain that the rights of Indians result in discrimination against them or are evidence of a denial of their equality in the sense that their status is reduced is to indulge in an excessively narrowing meaning of the words, of the purpose of equality, and the nature of discrimination ... The legal definition of Indian must remain ... we believe that to be a good useful Canadian we must first be a good, happy and productive Indian" (pp. 4-5).

On March 17, 1971, in a speech given at Queen's University, Jean Chrétien, Minister of Indian Affairs, formally withdrew the White Paper.

Property Rights and Native Land Settlement

The native land rights issue involves the relationship between majorities and minorities and there are no quick or easy means of resolving the relationship. Although native people have always believed that they owned their land it was not until the 1970's that the notion of "aboriginal land rights" gained a measure of legal support, in part due to the judgements of those Supreme Court of Canada justices ruling in the Nishga case (Calder, et al., 1973).

Although the Nishga lost the case by a 4 to 3 decision, the case nonetheless became an important landmark because it determined: (1) the Nishga had aboriginal rights at the time of contact that were reconcilable with Canadian law, and (2) at least one of their rights - the usufruct title - had not been extinguished by colonial legislation. Other judges since the Nishga case have tended to support the aboriginal rights of other groups such as the James Bay Cree and the Baker Lake Inuit.

The importance of the Nishga decision is that it established a new frame of reference for Canadian legal practice, one which accepts the principle of cultural relativity in which one cultural group is not seen as inferior to another. Thus the Nishga were viewed as equal before the law with the right to property and title and protection thereof until extinguished by legislation (Asch, 1983).

In addition, the massive publicity associated with the James Bay Land Settlement and the Berger Inquiry on the proposed MacKenzie Valley pipeline brought the question of Native Land Rights and Property Claims into the consciousness of many Canadians. The James Bay Land Settlement of 1975 also served as a lesson for the aboriginal people of Canada. The settlement, which was the first in Canada, was subsequently perceived by many to be unfair to the aboriginal people affected by it. As such, it sensitized the nerve endings of other Indian nations and generated a great deal of public consciousness, concern and aid, including active assistance among the non-Indian people of Canada.

The aforementioned were important items in the string of events which contributed to the symbolic acknowledgement of aboriginal people and aboriginal rights in Section 35 of the Constitution Act - a complete reversal of the assimilationist-oriented "White Paper" published in 1969

Organization of Indian Peoples in Canada

A new chapter in the history of the Canadian Indian began to open in the 1960's and throughout the 1970's. Previously, various forces made the organization of Canadian Indians difficult if not impossible. These forces included: interference by the RCMP and Indian Agents, adult illiteracy, poverty, geographic differences and isolation, the lack of a common language, and a section of the Indian Act (1927) which prohibited political organizing.

Early efforts to organize Canadian Indians nationally had only moderate success. One of the most successful interprovincial settings was the annual conference for Indians and Metis. Initiated in 1954 by the Community Welfare Planning Council of Greater Winnipeg to focus attention one Native peoples' social and economic needs, the conference founded the National Indian Council (NIC) in 1961. The primary purposes of the NIC were: "... to promote unity among Indian people, the betterment of Indian ancestry in Canada, and to create a better understanding of Indian and non-Indian relationship" (Patterson, 1972: 177). The NIC tended to represent the interests of non-status Indians and middle class Indians residing in urban areas other than those of status Indians. Further, the non-status Indians came under provincial rather than federal jurisdiction and non-treaty Indians were concerned with aboriginal rather than treaty rights.

As a result of these differences, the NIC split into two separate organizations in 1968: The Canadian Métis Society and The National Indian Brotherhood (NIB).

In the next decade and a half the NIB was instrumental in broadening the base of contact and influence of Indians with the Federal Government of Canada. Most prominent among their efforts of influence were a parliamentary liaison group and a Joint NIB/Cabinet Committee (JNCC) which primarily served as a political lobbying group.

Activities of the liaison group included:
- monitoring the progress of legislative bills and budget estimates
- educating Indian Chiefs, and NIB leaders and staff about parliamentary

- procedures and expectations
- developing individual profiles of key MP's, cabinet ministers, senators, and others concerned with Indian matters
- involvement in selling agreements between NIB and the government to the broader parliament.

Paramount in their work were efforts to ensure that the language in government legislation did not undermine the protection of Indian rights defined under the BNA Act. The parliamentary interest group was instrumental in launching the NIB as a political interest group (Ponting and Gibbons, 1980).

The JNCC was an ad-hoc subcommittee of cabinet designed to deal exclusively with Indian matters. The committee was formed as a conflict-regulating mechanism in response to the 1974 violent confrontation on Parliament Hill between the RCMP and the Native Peoples' Caravan. As a subcommittee of cabinet it provided NIB with direct access to Cabinet not available to any other Canadian ethnic group.

Although the JNCC may not have made a single major decision, its establishment greatly increased NIB's penetration into the Federal Government bureaucracy. Regular liaison and involvement with the government bureaucracy enabled the NIB to consult with the government on a regular basis on important substantive issues such as land claims negotiations and revisions of the Indian Act. It also enhanced the respectability of Indian leaders of the NIB and the legitimacy of their concerns (Ponting and Gibbons, 1980).

Indian Leaders

The impetus for the development of Provincial and National Indian Organizations in the late sixties and throughout the 1970's came from talented Indian leaders. Although statistical probability would suggest that Indian people could possess their fair share of exceptionally talented leaders, the myth of the imcompetent, lazy Indian was so pervasive that the sudden presence of political, competent Indian leaders on the federal scene, came as a surprise to many government bureaucrats. The arrogance of the White Paper Policy provoked some Indians to assume leadership roles in order to organize a response to the government's policy of assimilation. Although crisis events such as the White Paper can influence the emergence of leaders, Manuel, a three term president of the NIB, cautions that it would be a mistake to assume that Indian leaders are a recent phenomena and that Indian resistance to the oppression of the European culture has just emerged. Manuel asserts that Indian leaders have been around since time memorial and telling their people for a very long time to resist the forces destructive to their lives and communities.

> "... The fact of the matter is that there was never a time since the beginning of colonial conquest when Indian people were not resisting the four destructive forces besetting us: the state through the Indian agent; the church through the priests; the church and the state through the schools, the state and industry through the traders. Today's renaissance can be seen in the resurgence of our languages, in the growth of political institutions both old and new, in the revival of Indian religion in urban Indian centres as well as on reserves, in the growing numbers of young people seeking out the wisdom of the grandfathers and finding ways to apply it in their own lives ... The renaissance of today is the fruit of the accumulated labour of our grandfathers. If it appears that we are only now awakening and discovering a new strength, it is because the current climate of political, social and economic forces is allowing what was always beneath the surface to emerge into the light of day" (Manuel and Poslums, 1974: 69-70).

Testimony of the enormous influence and effectiveness of Indian leadership and organizations in Canada is best observed in the following section on aboriginal rights in the Canadian Constitution.

Aboriginal Rights in the Canadian Constitution: Establishing Self-Government for Aboriginal Peoples.

In 1982, the Constitution Act of the Government of Canada acknowledged for the first time the aboriginal people and their aboriginal rights. Prior to this time all primary legislative powers "were deemed to be vested either in parliament or in provincial legislatures. The inclusion of existing aboriginal and treaty rights in the constitution may have altered this situation. If, as many assert, the right so self-government exists as an aboriginal right, there could be a substantial re-ordering of powers. Indian Governments may have implicit legislative powers that are now unrecognized" (Indian Self-Government in Canada, 1983: 43).

The inclusion of aboriginal rights in the Canadian Constitution represents an enormous reversal of government policy and is a major step forward towards achieving fundamental change in the relationship between Indian peoples and the Federal Government.

While the Constitution Act of 1982 recognized and affirmed existing aboriginal and treaty rights it did not define those rights.

The definition of these rights has already been the subject of two constitutional conferences (Ottawa, March 15-16, 1983 and March 8-9, 1984). In the 1983 Constitutional Accord on Aboriginal Rights, there was agreement to hold further conferences on aboriginal constitutional matters including self-government.

A key point of contention at this time concerns the question of legislative authority. Indian First Nations would like to be recognized as a sovereign government accountable to their peoples but the Federal Government has been reluctant to locate a third level of sovereign authority in Canada (First Ministers Conference, March, 1984).

An ideological explanation of the impasse has been presented by Weaver (1983). Weaver suggests aboriginal rights are problematic within the liberal-democratic ideology which assigns significance to freedom from discrimination and a universality form of equality regardless of race, religion and nationality.

A solution to the problem is suggested by the work of Lijphart (1969), McRae (1974) and Asch (1983) who note that there is more than one way for liberal-democratic communities to address differences or cleavages in their social structure and to incorporate their citizens. The most common method, which, founded on "universalism" is assimilative in orientation and assumes that sub-national entities will have no formal recognition by the state.

A second form of incorporation, defined by Lijphart (1969) as consociational democracy or consociationalism, provides mechanisms to guarantee the survival of cultural-linguistic traditions rather than assimilating them into a melting pot. As long as there is equality, separate but equal is not considered antithetical to liberal-democratic ideals. Areas of jurisdiction such as education and social services are identified and a universalistic theory of incorporation is applied only within segmental boundaries such as with the entrenched segmental rights of the Dutch and French populations in Belgium or on the basis of complete universalism with the provision of consociational institutions to accomodate segmental political rights of heterogeneous cultures as is the case of Switzerland (McRae, 1974; 1983).

Asch (1983) points out that Canada like Switzerland relies on an indirect form of consociation, which is compatable with universalism. Asch notes that Canada is structured to accomodate two primary segments, French (30% of the population), and non-French (70% of the population). Canada's ideology is universalistic but through its provinces is organized so that one of them, Quebec, contains a majority of the French speaking population. Under the British North America Act of 1867 and the Constitution Act of 1982 the provinces have legislative control over matters in their jurisdiction such as Health, Education, Taxation, and Justice with certain universal guarantees contained in the federal constitution. Because the French segment is a strong majority in the Province of Quebec they would therefore have legislative control over a large area of powers in their region.

The 1982 Constitution Act guarantees the French minority group their autonomy through provisions which protect ethnonational entities through an amending formula which allows each segment to block the effect of a constitutional change within the territory under its political jurisdiction. The formula also includes provision for compensation to be paid to those segments who decide to opt out in those instances where transfer of powers relate to education and other cultural matters.

In the above noted context of segmental accomodation found within the Canadian Constitution Act, some form of Aboriginal Self-Government is possible.

There is no unanimity among aboriginal nations regarding the adoption of some form of consociation with the Government of Canada. Nonetheless, the Indian's representatives at the 1983 and 1984 First Ministers Conference seem to agree that the protection of the segmental rights, including legislative authority and a land base, is possible within the Constitution Act of Canada.

Several proposals of self-government using a direct method of consociation have been put forward by the representatives of the aboriginal nations. The basic approach contained in The Report of the Special Committee of The House of Commons, Indian Self Government (1983) relevant for the Indians residing in Northwestern Ontario would build on the Indian Reserve land base as an important component of the desired land base over which the Indians residing south of 60° would like to have political and legislative authority. The system of government would be determined on an ethnonational basis and would not be open to Canadian citizens on the basis of universalistic criteria. Only persons residing on a reserve or reserve-like territory would be given power to influence the government directly.

Unlike an apartheid type of government (such as exists in South Africa) which provides differential access to power among the ethnonational units, the aboriginal units, the aboriginal proposal for the Canadian Indian groups south of 60° would incorporate citizens on a consociational basis. Power-sharing would exist on a segmental basis and provisions would therefore be available to block legislation in conflict with segmental autonomy.

The Canadian Government supports the values of cultural relativity and diversity and an indirect form of consociation exists within the Canadian political system. In the above-noted context the ideological shift required at this time to support a direct form of consociation to permit the independence and self-determination of Indian people within the Country of Canada seems well within the mandate and reach of subsequent meetings of the First Ministers Conference on aboriginal constitutional matters.

Summary

In conclusion, this paper has attempted to identify some of the damaging social and structural conditions which limit the abilities of Indian people, diminish their identity and self-esteem and result in individual and collective power-loss. While the Indian Act and complex government structures continue to restrict Indian people in Canada and the many examples of social deprivation and social disintegration noted earlier continue to prevail in Northwestern Ontario and elsewhere in Canada, some dramatic changes have occurred in Federal and Indian relations in the past decade.

One of the most powerful methods and strategies for deliberate change commences with the identification of a discernable and achievable future and then builds a part of the future in the present (Waskow, 1968). For a meaningful resolution of the problems identified, the Indian leaders envisaged a future in which Indian people will be able to participate in and influence the major decisions that affect their lives (political, social, economic, legislative, etc.) and in which the integrity of native culture is enhanced. The litigation of land claims, the creation of strong national organizations and the successful lobbying of public and private groups in Canada as well as the International Community dramatically altered the Federal Government's view of the aboriginal people's claim to aboriginal rights.

It was noted that the constitutional recognition sought by aboriginal groups is consistent with the liberal-democratic Government of Canada. The direct form of consociation proposed by Indians south of 60°, of which the Indians who reside in Northwestern Ontario are a part, could be accomodated within the Canadian Constitution Act, 1982. The acceptance of this position is not without risk, but the costs and risks of further delay or possible rejection seem to be greater.

The entrenchment of political rights of Indian people in the Constitution Act is a necessary step towards accepting the value of cultural relativity in Canadian culture and establishing norms that Indian people and nations are productive, intelligent and spiritual people. Without the entrenchment of their political rights the power-loss of Indian people is bound to continue and the patriation of the Canadian Constitution would remain incomplete.

Reference Notes

(1) Jean Chrétien. The Unfinished Tapestry - Indian Policy in Canada. Speech given at Queen's University, Kingston, Ontario, March 17, 1971 (Ottawa: Diand Press Release).

References

Bain, H., 1973: In McKinney, W., The Sioux Lookout medical program. The Beaver, 303, p. 57.

Booz, Allen & Hamilton, 1969: Summary Report. Study of Health Services for Canadian Indians. Ottawa: Department of National Health and Welfare.

Calder et al, v. Attorney General of British Columbia, 1973: SCR 313 (1973), 4 WWRI, 34 DLR (3 d) 145.

Cardinal, Harold, 1969: The Unjust Society. Edmonton: M. G. Hurtig.

Concerned Citizen's Committee, 1974: While people sleep: Sudden deaths in the Kenora area: A study of sudden deaths amongst the Indian people of the Kenora area with primary emphasis on apparent alcohol involvement. Grand Council Treaty # 3.

Cumming, P. A. & Mickenberg, N. H. (Eds.), 1972: Native rights in Canada (2nd Edition). Toronto: The Indian-Eskimo Association of Canada in association with The General Publishing Co. Ltd.

DIAND (Department of Indian Affairs and Northern Development), 1969: "The White Paper". Statement of the Government of Canada on Indian Policy 1969. Ottawa: Queen's Printer.

— (Department of Indian Affairs and Northern Development), 1973: Statement of Claims of Indian and Inuit People. Press Release, August, 1973.

Etzioni, A., 1964: Modern Organizations. Englewood Cliffs, N.J.: Prentice-Hall, Inc.

Federal Provincial Conference of First Ministers on Aboriginal Constitutional Matters. Verbatim Transcript, 1983: Ottawa: Canadian Intergovernmental Conference Secretariat.

— 1984: Ottawa: Canadian Intergovernmental Conference Secretariat.

Giesbrecht, N. & Brown, J., 1977: Alcohol problems in Northwestern Ontario: Preliminary report: Consumption patterns and public order and public health problems. Toronto: Addiction Research Foundation.

Goldthorpe, W. G., 1975: The Sioux Lookout Project - culture and geography. Address to Community Health Division, University of Toronto, October, 1975.

Gouldner, A. W., 1959: Organizational analysis. In R. K. Merton, L. Broom, L. S. Cottrell, Jr. (Eds.). Sociology today: Problems and prospects. New York: Basic Books, Inc.

Green, L. C., 1969: Canada's Indians: Federal Policy. Government of Alberta.

Indian Chiefs of Alberta, 1970: Citizens Plus. A Presentation to The Right Honorable P. E. Trudeau, Prime Minister and The Government of Canada.

Lijphart, A., 1969: "Consociational Democracy". World Politics, 21 (2): 207-225.

Lysyk, Kenneth, 1973: The Indian Title Question in Canada: An Appraisal in the Light of Calder. Canadian Bar Review, 51: 450-480.

Manuel, S. and Poslums, M., 1974: The Fourth World: An Indian Reality. Don Mills: Collier-MacMillan Canada Ltd.

McCullum, H. & K., 1975: This land is not for sale. Toronto: Anglican Book Centre.

McRae, Kenneth D., 1974: Consociational democracy. Toronto: McClelland and Steward Ltd.

— 1983: Conflict and compromise in multilingual societies: Switzerland. Waterloo, Ontario: Wilfrid Laurier University Press.

Patterson, E. and Palmer, I., 1972: The Canadian Indian: A History since 1500. Don Mills: Collier-MacMillan Canada Ltd.

Ponting, J. R. and Gibbons, R., 1980: Out of Irrelevance: A socio-political introduction to Indian Affairs in Canada. Toronto: Butterworths.

Rogers, E. S., 1962: The Round Lake Ojibwa. Toronto: Published by the Ontario Department of Lands and Forests for the Royal Ontario Museum.

Smith, D. G. (Ed.), 1975: Canadian Indians and the law: Selected documents 1963-1972. Toronto: McLelland and Stewart Ltd.

Special Committee on Indian Self-Government, 1983: Indian Self Government. OHAWA: Department of Supply and Services.

Trudeau, Pierre Elliot, 1968: Pierre Elliot Trudeau: Federalism and the French Canadians. Toronto: MacMillan.

Waskow, A., 1968: Looking forward: 1999. New University Thought, 6, 3.

Weaver, S. M., 1981: Making Canadian Indian Policy: The Hidden Agenda 1968-70. Toronto: University of Toronto Press.

Weaver, S. M., 1983: "Difficulties with Aboriginal Rights Demands". In J. Anthony Long, M. Boldt and L. Little Bear (Eds.), Aboriginal Rights: Towards an Understanding. Lethbridge: University of Lethbridge, pp. 87-98.

Weber, M., 1947: The theory of social and economic organizations. Translated by K. Morris. New York: Harper and Row.

Address of the author:
Edward M. Bennett
Dept. of Psychology
Wilfrid Laurier University
Waterloo Ont.
Canada N 2 L 3 C 5

Canada's Indians:
from "bands" to "First Nations"

Peter R. Gerber

Abstract: In October 1983 the "Report of the Special Committee on Indian Self-Government in Canada" has been submitted to the House of Commons. In its report, the Committee recommends the granting of a wide autonomy to the Indian First Nations within the Canadian Confederacy. There is some food for controversy in the recommendation; this is shown among other things in the fact that the majority of the provincial governments rejected the recommendation of an Indian Self-Government for economic reasons in March 1984. The article contents comments and reflections on the legal substantiation of the demands for an Indian Self-Government. Recommending the introduction and constitutional incorporation of an Indian Self-Government means as much as challenging power structures on an ethical level not only within Canada. Therefore, the author tries to represent the position of the Indian First Nations, and deliberately looks at the rather political and legislative theme from an anthropological perspective.

Résumé: En Octobre 1983, le "Report of the Special Committee on Indian Self-Government in Canada" fût soumis au House of Commons. Dans ce rapport, le comitée propose d'accorder une large autonomie aux "Indian First Nations" dans l'ensemble de la confédération canadienne. Cette proposition a nourri des conflits, ce qui se prouve, entre autres, dans le fait de la rejection des recommendations concernant l'autonomie des Indiens par la plupart des gouvernements pour des raisons economiques. L'article contient quelques commentaires et considérations concernant la révendication légal d'une autonomie indienne. Cependent, cette révendication représente un défi éthique, qui ne concerne pas seulement le Canada. L'auteur essaye, en tant d'anthropologue, de défendre la position des "Indian First Nations" en considérant particulièrement les aspects politiques et legislatifs.

Zusammenfassung: Im Oktober 1983 wurde dem House of Commons der "Report of the Special Committee on Indian Self-Government in Canada" vorgelegt. In diesem Bericht empfiehlt das Komitee, den Indian First Nations eine weitgehende Autonomie innerhalb der kanadischen Konföderation zuzugestehen. Der Bericht lieferte mit dieser Empfehlung Nahrung für Kontroversen, was sich u.a. darin zeigt, daß die Mehrzahl der Provinzregierungen die Empfehlungen für eine indianische Selbst-Regierung aus wirtschaftlichen Gründen ablehnte. Der Beitrag umfaßt einige Stellungnahmen und Überlegungen über den legalen Anspruch der Forderungen nach indianischer Selbst-Regierung. Die Empfehlung zur Einführung und konstitutionellen Verankerung einer indianischen Selbst-Regierung bedeutet allerdings eine ethische Herausforderung, die nicht nur Canada betrifft. Daher bemüht sich der Autor, den Standpunkt der "Indian First Nations" zu vertreten und betrachtet dabei insbesondere die politischen und legislativen Aspekte aus einer anthropologischen Perspektive.

❋❋❋❋❋❋❋❋❋❋❋❋❋❋

Introduction

As it is known, in the summer of 1969 the Federal Government of Canada heralded in its "White Paper" a "new Indian Policy" with the ultimate aim of completely assimilating the aboriginal population into white culture and society.(1) The Indian reaction to this was exactly voiced with the words of Harold Cardinal, a Cree Indian, who maintained that this new policy followed a new version of the old maxim of the soldiers on the frontier: "The only good Indian is a non-Indian" (1969: 1). At that time, prime minister Pierre E. Trudeau could hardly have imagined that 15 years later just the opposite of a total disruption of aboriginal identity was to emerge: Even as to political matters, native peoples started to increasingly mark themselves out from the rest of Canada. Instead of further allowing white control of native affairs, today's catchword is "Indian Control of ..." and goes so far as to include controlling their own religions, or educating and training their children, or having control of economic issues like their own land and its resources, as well as of their political self-determination. (2)

Therefore, the last 15 years were marked by a growing confrontation between representatives of the aboriginal population on the one hand and the federal government in Ottawa on the other. In all these years, the government's way of acting has left much to be desired and has been characterised by treating the native peoples with an attitude of degrading condescension; and generally speaking, they were only granted the right to be consulted. Open negotiations on equal level were rather exceptional and took often only place if nothing interfered with "national interests", such as the exploitation of resources and energy production. (3)

Nevertheless, the native peoples' determined political struggle was crowned with a far-reaching success. Contrary to the intention of the federal government and the provincial governments the aboriginal population managed to be mentioned in the new Canadian Constitution of 1982. Admittedly, not everybody concerned was happy with it; yet, in my opinion, the rather vague formulation of the text, as for example in article 35(1) on "existing aboriginal and treaty rights", gives a certain leeway for further legislative work. (4)

In the meantime, considerable progress has been made with working out the report of the "Special Committee on Indian Self-Government in Canada". This Special Committee was set up by the House of Commons on December 22, 1982, and for the first time in the history of the Canadian Parliament, three representatives of the aboriginal peoples were called in. (5) The Special Committee was appointed "to act as a Parliamentary Task Force on Indian Self-Government to review all legal and related institutional factors affecting the status, development and responsibilities of Band Governments on Indian reserves" (Penner-Report 1983: V).

For 9 months, the Special Committee carried out extensive consultations and hearings, the results of which were compounded in a 200-page report, which had a rather sensational effect. The press mainly stressed the report's suggestion of closing and dissolving the Department of Indian Affairs within five years once the report's recommendations were passed. However, the press only summarised all radical political and legal recommendations for the benefit of the aboriginal peoples; possibly because there is some food for controversy. These recommendations were about nothing less than granting a wide autonomy to the Indian First Nations.(6) This right of self-determination includes a total control of land and resources; thus, no wonder that above all it was the resourceful provinces to object to the Penner-Report.(7)

In the following, I am going to make a few comments and reflections on the legal foundation of the demands for Indian Self-Government, from the point of view of an advocate anthropology.

The Royal Proclamation as a source of aboriginal rights?

It is striking to see the Penner-Report stating that the Indian policy of the last 110 years has been a mere failure; this is also shown in the socio-economic facts and figures.(8) Furthermore, the report stated that, pursuant to the Indian Act, federal authorities had patronized indigenous peoples as to result in total dependence and great apathy.(9) Therefore "the Committee recommends that the federal government establish a new relationship with Indian First Nations and that an essential element of this relationship be recognition of Indian self-government" (Penner-Report 1983: 41). This "new relationship" meant as much as a return to colonial policy of over 200 years ago. The Special Committee reasons that at that time the Royal Proclamation of 1763 was a means for the English Crown to legalize a relationship which took into consideration that "for thousands of years prior to European immigration, North America was inhabited by many different self-governing aboriginal peoples" (Penner-Report 1983: 39).

In legal literature, one can often read that "the Indians possess occupancy rights to all land which they have not formally surrendered", as Harper (1947: 134) wrote almost 40 years ago; and the Penner-Report (1983: 43) writes "(the Royal Proclamation) recognized aboriginal titel and rights to the land".(10)

To me, it is rather unique that the Royal Proclamation of 1763 should serve as a source of international law for the current discussion on "existing aboriginal rights". Yet, the Proclamation does not explicitly state any rights of the indigenous peoples; i.e. rights, assuming that indigenous peoples were organized in sovereign states. On the contrary: The English Crown used the Proclamation only to establish an exclusive control on all land of indigenous peoples living within the frontiers of the three colonies Quebec, East Florida and West Florida. The Proclamation says that the Crown only be empowered to annex Indian land by means of treaties; and the Crown only be entitled to have the same privilege concerning Indian land beyond colonial frontiers.(11)

When reading the Royal Proclamation and taking into consideration the historical context of the time it was made public, I start doubting whether it is the international law instrument suitable to put through the justified cause of the Indian First Nations, namely to be granted greatest possible independence within the Canadian Confederacy. One has to bear in mind that the Proclamation was not enacted to acknowledge the rights of aboriginal people, but to protect imperial claims of the English Crown, both within its own colonies and facing other European colonial powers. It was a deed of pure power politics.

Let me show why I see the Royal Proclamation in this way! Until this "Royal Will and Pleasure" was made public, it had been more or less up to the colonies how to deal with indigenous peoples. Frideres (1983: 16-18) described how the English Crown had conferred settlers land titles without even mentioning the indigenous peoples, or at best, mentioning them from an extremely racial point of view. Colonial politics at that time was strictly speaking nothing else but European countries having conflicts with one another and competing for oversea's resources in land, raw material and human labour; thus, European conflicts were shifted to the colonies.

The extended war between France and England about the North American colonies ended with the Treaty of Paris on February 10, 1763. Lasting more than 60 years, this conflict made it very clear to the English Crown that the colonies needed to be disciplined with a rigid control of the mother country. When, in May 1763, the Ottawa Chief Pontiac organized a remarkably strong alliance of several Indian peoples against England, another reason was given to tie the colonies closer to the mother country. The English-French war and Pontiac's resistance against the settlers' pressure to go west forced the English Crown to realize that the Indian peoples actually had certain military powers. Thus, enough reasons were given for a proclamation on October 7, 1763 (see, e.g., Zlotkin & Colborne 1977).

Yet, the mere fact that the English Crown selfishly proclaimed how land inhabited by indigenous peoples was to be used, clearly proves the Crown's arrogation of being the one and only owner of the North American continent. To my mind, the Proclamation is plain enough when stating that for the Indians within the colonies "Parts of our Dominion and Territories ... are reserved ... as their Hunting Grounds". The land beyond the colonies was also to be "(reserved) for the use of the said Indians". Such words can only be used in an ethnocentric paper which could by no means stand for a document of two equal partners mutually recognizing their existence as sovereign states. The Proclamation's only purpose was to establish the colonial frontiers and to settle immigration. To this end, it was necessary to unify the policy towards indigenous peoples. As troubles were not desired in the colonies, Indians were simply reserved hunting grounds, even those indigenous peoples who had never heard of the fortune which was given to them "by the grace of God".

For me, being an anthropologist and not a lawyer, it is most difficult to duplicate why the Royal Proclamation should represent an international recognition of the true rights of indigenous peoples. Its colonial and imperial intention became more evident in the constitution of the new British Dominion of Canada, in the British North America Acts of 1867. There, article 91(24) says that "the exclusive Legislative Authority ... (over) Indians, and Lands reserved for Indians" is assigned to the Parliament in Ottawa. Hence, the white Canadians' claim of being the predominant people was clearly defined and the indigenous peoples were degraded to mere wards of the state which started to be controlled with the Indian Act of 1876.

Going back to the Royal Proclamation to prove aboriginal people's rights, seems to me to be choosing the wrong way. At most, it could tactically be used in the discussion of the new Canadian Constitution, pointing out the fact that in 1763 the English Crown tried to acquire Indian land through treaty negotiations. Still, there is room for different interpretations in this context, too: England did not want to fight wars at its colonial frontiers, therefore the cheaper method of transfering land rights through treaties was chosen. To maintain that the indigenous peoples were recognized as such can only be said by a cynic.

Indian Self-Government and the Constitution Act

In my opinion, Indian Self-Government cannot be based upon the Royal Proclamation of 1763. Hence the question follows, on what the self-determination of Indian First Nations in modern time could be based upon. It is obvious to try the new Canadian Constitution. After years of confrontation and conflicts among themselves and especially with the federal government and the provinces, the indigenous peoples succeeded in explicitly incorporating their existence into the new constitution. However, nothing is mentioned about Indian Self-Government. Indian representatives, like for example the National Chief of the Assembly of First Nations (AFN), David Ahenakew, keep emphasizing that "Indian Governments already exist in this country and we are now merely changing our constitution to reflect this reality" (1983b: 10).

And on behalf of the Brotherhood of Indian Nations in Manitoba, Chief Louis J. Stevenson had similar things to say in a speech to the Minister of Indian Affairs, Mister John C. Munro, in March 1984. Chief Stevenson said how disappointed he was as the Second First Ministers Conference had not been successful, with the majority of the provinces turning down the recommendations of the Penner-Report. Stevenson himself is not fully convinced of the Penner-Report and sarcastically says (1984: 2):

"How can Federal Government grant self government authority to the Indian Nations when we never gave up that right in the first place? The Penner-Report and the Federal Government merely has to recognize our right. To do otherwise, would be hypocritical to its United Nations membership and a violation of principles of their own Canadian Constitution."

As anthropologist I have to bring up one of these "principles" of the Canadian Constitution which was explicitly mentioned in article 27 of the new constitution. The article says:

"This Charter (of Rights and Freedoms) shall be interpreted in a manner consistent with the preservation and enhancement of the multicultural heritage of Canadians".(12)

In fact, the principle of multiculturalism is a tradition of Canadian history and politics. Yet, it is doubtful whether this principle will ever be applied to all cultures existing in Canada, if the views of some white decision makers are going to prevail. These people think that the American principle of a cultural melting pot is more attractive. How else is it possible to explain Trudeau's "White Paper" of 1969, referring to article 7 of the Universal Declaration of Human Rights? To abolish the cultural existence of indigenous peoples by means of this article about equal rights is such a horrible thought that the Liberal Trudeau must only have realized its real meaning short before he resigned this spring, when he was highly in favour of adopting the recommendations of the Penner-Report. Well, Trudeau and his Liberal Party are probably not the only white Canadians to apply the principle of a cultural mosaic only to a few cultural varieties within occidental culture.

The concept "cultural mosaic" has a totally different meaning to the genuinely liberal standpoint of Indian peoples. In an answer to the "White Paper", the Indian Chiefs of Alberta wrote in their paper "Citizens Plus: The Red Paper" (1974: 10):

> "There is room in Canada for diversity. Our leaders say that Canada should preserve her 'pluralism', and encourage the culture of all her peoples. The culture of the Indian peoples are old and colourful strands in that Canadian fabric of diversity. We want our children to learn our ways, our history, our customs, and our traditions."

It cannot be denied that ethnographically speaking there is a multicultural population in Canada. Indian Affairs enumerates no less than "six major culture areas" and "ten linguistic groups" in its publication "Linguistic and Cultural Affiliations of Canadian Indian Bands" 1980. In said paper, only the 577 bands of the Status Indians are listed. Not merely an anthropologist may wonder why it had been possible to wipe out this ethnographic reality with a stroke of the pen only three years ago, when the notorious "Kitchen Accord" stroke it off the constitutional draft on November 5, 1981.

The only plausible explanation to this can be seen in Canda's growing economic dependence on Big Brother to the South of its border. After the first oil crisis in 1973, the presumed and later discovered vast resources, especially in the North of the continent, have constantly gained in economic significance. Granted through the Indian Act, the special rights of indigenous peoples, like the relatively unlimited hunting rights and the reserves, have been annoying obstacles to the undisturbed exploitation of these resources. "Termination policy", formulated in 1947, has been pursued more or less openly for almost 40 years and should have facilitated access to the resources. 1947 Parliament was tabled "a Plan to Liquidate the Indian Problem in 25 Years"; 1969 this policy was concealed with a human rights article, and 1981 the indigenous peoples were simply wiped out of the constitutional draft. Yet, it was too late to "liquidate the Indian Problem" - this language is rather perfidious - and resistance of the Indian First Nations had grown to be too massive. As it is known, Parliament made a positive turn on November 25, 1981 for which it has to be honoured.

In their speeches, Indian representatives keep saying that their demands for autonomy are nothing else than applying the principle of multiculturalism also on aboriginal peoples. AFN-National Chief David Ahenakew comments (1983a: 6):

> "Such concepts are not unfamiliar to more recent Canadians, who claim varying degrees of sovereignty and jurisdiction for themselves at the same time as they deny our position (...) For example, the province of Prince Edward Island, with far less land area, with 1/3 the population that Indians have, has sovereignty and jurisdiction over certain agreed upon matters affecting their citizens. They are empowered to legislate, to make original law, to exercise sovereignty, within an agreed upon constitutional framework, on matters affecting education, municipal institutions, health, social services, economic development and many other areas (...) And yet, with three times the population and a much larger land base, we have been called unrealistic when we assert that we seek recognition and entrenchment of Indian government control over our own lives, our own economies, and our own resources."

To this, I only add that globally there are many peoples being numerically smaller and having less land area than the aboriginal population of Canada that are independent nations and duly represented in the UN. And it is not even such an independence the aboriginal peoples are seeking. David Ahenakew (1983a: 6):

> "When we say 'sovereignty', we are not talking about extremes. We
> are talking about recognition and entrenchment of Indian sovereignty
> and jurisdiction within Confederation (...) We are not seeking to
> establish our own armies and our own foreign relations."

To accuse them of "separatism" is considered absurd and ridiculous by the indigenous people. In this connection, Chief Stevenson, who has been mentioned earlier, says (1984: 4):

> "Indian people have a stake in this country, this is our homeland,
> our country. Everyone else, whether they like to admit it or not,
> whether they immigrated here or were born here, everyone else
> is just a permanent guest or visitor to our land. We are the original people."

It is a long and strenuous way along the legislative process of incorporating precisely formulated aboriginal rights, including that of Indian Self-Government. The Canadian government seems not to be willing to accept Indian Self-Government, despite their lip services of late. This became for example truly evident in the "Statement by the Canadian Observer Delegation to the Third Session" of the UN-Working Group on Indigenous Populations in Geneva this summer. The Statement only grants the aboriginal peoples "greater control over" and "greater responsibility for matters which directly affect them", but no "full control over" or "full responsibility", as had earlier been recommended by the Penner-Report and what is persistently demanded by the indigenous peoples. The same Statement mentions the proposed bill to introduce Indian Self-Government and stresses:

> "(The proposed Bill C-52) respects the existing division of powers
> between the federal and provincial governments within Canadian
> federation".(13)

It is exactly this federalism, as much as it could be welcomed by a Swiss anthropologist, that is one of the biggest obstacles on the way to fulfill the Indians' demand for autonomy within the Canadian borders. The reason behind is mainly to be found in the economic sovereignty of the provinces.(14)

It might be possible to push ahead the constitutional incorporation of Indian sovereignty, if international pressure could be exercised on the Canadian Confederation. Here, I think of the efforts of various indigenous peoples and their organizations to strive for a solution under international law for their threatened existence. In this connection, the World Council of Indigenous Peoples tabled a new "International Covenant on the Rights of Indigenous Peoples" on the occasion of its conference in Canberra, Australia, in April 1981. In article 1 of this convenant it simply says:

> "All peoples have the right to self-determination. By virtue of that
> right Indigenous Peoples may freely determine their political status
> and freely pursue their economic, social and cultural development".(15)

Still, it will be a hard job to push such a covenant through every UN-body right up to the General Assembly. It is only for 2 1/2 years that the above mentioned Working Group on Indigenous Populations exists on the lowest level of the UN-hierarchy. The main job of this Working Group consists in finding out possible violations of indigenous peoples' human rights. It seems that this Working Group does not enjoy great popularity among UN-member states. This is easily revealed by choosing the concept of "Indigenous Populations" instead of the concept of "Indigenous Peoples", the latter being preferred by the aboriginal peoples but also being more controversial from the point of view of international law. There already is an international legal basis broad enough for the right of self-determination of "Peoples", however, not for the peoples in the so-called Fourth World, that is for aboriginal peoples living in nation states. And indeed, the last session of the Working Group this summer was not successful in trying to define the concept of "Indigenous Peoples". Yet, there are no definition problems for the Canadian aboriginal population. In their "Declaration of the First Nations" of November 18, 1981 it unequivocally says (1982: 62):

> "'Aboriginal people' means the First Nations or Tribes of Indians in Canada and each Nation having the right to define its own Citizenship."

Indian First Nations' policy over the last years impressively demonstrates that they meet the four basic conditions of a "Nationhood" according to international law: 1) they have a permanent population, 2) they live in defined territories, 3) they have their own governments and 4) they are able to establish contacts with other states.(16) The National Indian Brotherhood and the Assembly of First Nations have proved the latter with their lobbying in Europe between 1979 and 1982, when they struggled for constitutional recognition. This does not change afore-mentioned statement that the First Nations do not strive for complete sovereignty.(17)

The Canadian Confederacy has given itself time until April 17, 1987 to find a just solution to its "Indian Problem".(18) Hopefully, the good spirit of the Penner-Report is going to win. Indian Government has been existing since "(the) Creator has given us the right to govern ourselves and the right to self-determination", as it is said in above Declaration of the First Nations. To sum it all up, not only from an anthropological point of view does Indian Government fully deserve to be incorporated in the Canadian Constitution.

Acknowledgements

I would like to express my gratitude to John F. Leslie and Alma Lo, Indian and Northern Affairs Canada, Ottawa, for their help, when I visited Indian Affairs in 1981 and 1983 in order to collect information. I wish to extend my thanks to Brenda McGregor, Assembly of First Nations, Ottawa, who hounored my interest for more information by the AFN. Elisabeth Biasio, Zurich, read an earlier draft of the manuscript and offered constructive criticism, for which I express my appreciation. Helena Nyberg, Zurich, did a careful and committed translation of the manuscript from German into English. Last but not least, I thank Ludger Müller-Wille for the invitation to participate in the Symposium on "Ethnicity in Canada", held in Marburg in December 1984.

Footnotes

1. See the "Statement of the Government of Canada on Indian Policy, 1969", presented to the First Session of the Twentyeighth Parliament by the Hounorable Jean Chrétien, Minister of Indian Affairs and Northern Development, Ottawa.
2. See, e.g.: Gerber 1979, 1980 and 1984, NIB 1972 and 1979.
3. See especially Weaver's study on "Indian Policy" 1981.
4. Constitution Act 1982, Article 35. (1) "The existing aboriginal and treaty rights of the aboriginal peoples of Canada are hereby recognized and affirmed." (2) "In this Act, 'aboriginal peoples of Canada' includes the Indian, Inuit and Métis peoples of Canada."
5. "Indian Self-Government in Canada", Report of the Special Committee, House of Commons (Queen's Printer for Canada), Ottawa 1983 (Penner-Report). On page 4: "The Assembly of First Nations was asked to designate a representative to participate fully in the Committee's work as an ex officio member with all rights except that of voting" (nominated was Ms. Roberta Jamieson). "In addition, the Native Council of Canada" (representing the non-Status Indians; nominated was Mr. Bill Wilson) "and the Native Women's Association of Canada" (nominated was Ms. Sandra Isaac) "were invited to designate liaison members".
6. It is a remarkable change of terms describing the aboriginal social units

in Canada: The Indian Act of 1876 used the term "Indian bands", a term used for no other minority group in Canada. The majority of aboriginal representatives preferes today the term "First Nations". The Penner-Report writes (1983: 141): "In order to familiarize the general public with the term, the Committee decided to use Indian First Nations in this report."

7. The Canadian Government's response was astonishingly quite positive; see the "Response of the Government to the Report of the Special Committee on Indian Self-Government", Ottawa, March 5, 1984. - The Saskatchewan Indian (April/May 1984, Special Edition) commented in its Editorial "We Didn't Fail": "Prime Minister Trudeau made an impassioned plea to the Premieres to make some moves but he was met with no concessions. For Trudeau it was too little too late and for the Premieres it was too much too soon. The Premieres are obviously waiting for a Mulroney Conservative Government and are not willing to make any deals during the last few months of Liberal rule."

8. Some facts from the Penner-Report (1983:15):
   - Child Welfare: The proportion of Indian children in care has risen steadily to more than five times the national rate.
   - Education: Only 20 per cent of Indian children stay in school to the end of the secondary level; the comparable national rate is 75 per cent.
   - Facilities: In 1977, fewer than 40 per cent of Indian houses had running water, sewage disposal or indoor plumbing facilities; the national level of properly serviced houses is over 90 per cent.
   - Unemployment: The unemployment rate among the Indian people is about 35 per cent of the working age population; in some areas it is as high as 90 per cent.
   - Suicide: Indian deaths due to suicide are almost three times the national rate; suicide is especially prevalent among Indians aged 15 to 24.
   - Infant Mortality: The infant mortality rate (up to the age of four weeks) among Indian children is 60 per cent higher than the national rate.

9. The Penner-Report writes (1983: 17): "The Indian Act is a comprehensive piece of legislation that circumscribes activities in all sectors of Indian communities. It places constraints on the rights of Indian people and bands and limits their ability to govern themselves effectively (...) The first consolidated Indian Act was passed in 1876; the Act was last amended over thirty years ago (1951)."

10. Quite a different point of view is expressed by Douglas Sanders in his unpublished article; he writes (1983: 6): "The Proclamation did not grant rights to Indians. It confirmed the pattern of recognition of Indian territorial rights which had become established, and set out formal procedures for treaty making (...) In other words colonial sovereignty had been established." - However, this seems not to be the last word and the summary by Mickenberg seems to be valid (1971: 142): "(The) precise meaning of the Royal Proclamation has generated so much controversy as to further obfuscate an already inordinately complex subject."

11. I take more or less the same position as Douglas Sanders' in his article. - Parts of the text of the Royal Proclamation is published in Mickenberg 1971: 155-156: "Excerpts from the Royal Proclamation of 1763".

12. In this article of the Constitution Act 1982 the term "multicultural heritage of Canadians" is used, but not the term "multicultural heritage of Canadian peoples"!

13. See the "Statement by the Canadian Observer Delegation to the Third Session of the U.N. Working Group on Indigenous Populations", Geneva, July 30 - August 3, 1984: 4.

14. See Constitution Act 1982, Article 92A: "(1) In each province, the legislature may exclusively make laws in relation to (a) exploration for non-renewable natural resources in the province; ..." etc.

15. The Covenant is published in Opekokew 1982: Appendix A, I-VIII. - See for a broader discussion of aboriginal rights in international law, especially the historic development, Sanders 1983.

16. These "fundamental requirements of nationhood" have been declared in

the "Declaration of Principles for the Defense of the Indigenous Nations and Peoples of the Western Hemisphere", Geneva 1977, by 100 Native Nations, published, e.g., in Opekokew 1982: Appendix A, VIII-X.
17. See about the history of the Constitution lobby; Saskatchewan Indian, Constitution Special Edition, April 1982: 4-12. - In order to face the problem of a model of Indian Self-Government at a national level, the AFN agreed to work out a solution region by region (1984: 5).
18. The Assembly of First Nations is pleased of the nomination of David Crombie, the new Conservative Minister of Indian Affairs. He is "rated by Indian leaders as accessible, innovative and willing to get his 'hands dirty' to get a job done", and the AFN means that "Crombie may have a difficult time should he attempt to promote aboriginal rights" (1984: 4 and 10).

References

AFN-Declaration, 1982: Declaration of the First Nations of November 18, 1981, in: Saskatchewan Indian, Constitution Special Edition, April 1982, Saskatoon.

AFN-Anonymous, 1984: Assembly of First Nations BULLETIN, November 1984, Vol. 3, No. 1, Ottawa.

Ahenakew, David, 1983a: From the National Chief. Excerpts from his Statement to the First Ministers' Conference on aboriginal rights - 15 March 1983, Ottawa, in: Assembly of First Nations BULLETIN, April 1983, Vol. 2, No. 1, Ottawa.

– 1983b: From the National Chief. Excerpts from his Speech to the Public Service Administration of Canada - June 9, 1983, in: Assembly of First Nations BULLETIN, June 1983, Vol. 2, No. 3, Ottawa.

Cardinal, Harold, 1969: The Unjust Society. The Tragedy of Canada's Indians (Hurtig), Edmonton.

Frideres, James S., 1983: Native People in Canada. Contemporary Conflicts (Prentice Hall), Scarborough.

Gerber, Peter, 1979: Indian Control of Indian Education. Ein Bericht über die Erziehungspolitik kanadischer Indianer, in: Indianer Heute, Ethnologica Helvetica I, ed. by the Schweizerische Ethnologische Gesellschaft, Bern.

– 1980: Die Bedeutung der 'Religion' im Überlebenskampf der Indianer, in: Bulletin No. 44, ed. by the Société suisse des Américanistes, Geneva.

– 1984: Das Recht, Indianer zu sein. Die kanadische Regierung versus die Ureinwohner, in: Bulletin No. 48, ed. by the Société suisse des Américanistes, Geneva.

Harper, Allen G., 1947: Canada's Indian Administration. The Treaty System, in: America Indigena, Vol. 7, No. 2.

Indian Chiefs of Alberta, 1974: Citizens Plus. The Red Paper, June 1970, in: The Only Good Indian, ed. by Waubageshig (new press), Don Mills.

Mickenberg, Neil H., 1971: Aboriginal Rights in Canada and the United States, in: Osgoode Hall Law Journal, Vol. 9, No. 1.

NIB, 1972: Indian Control of Indian Education. Policy Paper presented to the Minister of Indian Affairs and Northern Development by the National Indian Brotherhood, Ottawa.

— 1979: To have what is one's own. Report from the President of the National Indian Socio-Economic Development Committee, October 16, 1979, Ottawa.

Opekokew, Deliah, 1982: The First Nations: Indian Government in the Community of Man (Midwest Litho), Saskatoon.

Sanders, Douglas, 1983: The Re-Emergence of Indigenous Questions in International Law, Manuscript, January 14, 1983.

Stevenson, Louis J., 1984: Presentation to John C. Munro, Minister of Indian Affairs, On Indian Self-Government Legislation, by Chief Louis J. Stevenson, Peguis Indian Band on Behalf of the Brotherhood of Indian Nations, Manuscript, March 20, 1984, Winnipeg.

Weaver, Sally M., 1981: Making Canadian Indian Policy. The Hidden Agenda 1968-70 (University of Toronto Press), Toronto.

Zlotkin, Norman and Donald R. Colborne, 1977: Internal Canadian Imperialism and the Native People, in: Imperialism, Nationalism, and Canada, ed. by Craig Heron (New Hogtown Press), Toronto.

Address of the author:
Dr. Peter R. Gerber
Völkerkundemuseum
Universität Zürich
Pelikanstr. 40
CH-8001 Zürich

Development Problems of Southern Albertan Indian Reserves

Claudia Notzke

Abstract: The two reserves under observation, the Stoney and Peigan Reserves, are located in southern Alberta, in an area encompassing the largest Indian reserves in Canada. Like other Indian reserves they constitute patches of a "third world environment" within the framework of a western industrialized nation. Historically the Stoney and Peigan Reserves are Treaty Seven Reserves. While sharing a common origin these reserves have been subject to quite different courses of development, due to differences in their culture, endowment with natural resources, in their leadership and local politics, and their dealings with provincial and federal government. Due to the discovery of natural gas on their land the Stoneys may be considered a relatively wealthy tribe, whereas the Peigan depend on a very narrow resource base, namely land and water. This basic difference is modified by a variety of other physical and human factors.

Résumé: Les deux réserves en question, celles des Stoney et des Peigan, se trouvent dans une région du Canada qui est fortement caractèrisée par l'existence de réserves indiennes. Elles représentent, dans l'ensemble d'une nation industrialisée, des tâches d'un "Environnement du Tiers-Monde". L'origin des deux réserves remonte au Traité No. 7. Ayant ainsi un point en commun, les deux réserves se sont développées de façon très différente par la suite. Les raisons en sont, entre autres, les différences de leurs civilisations, la disposition de ressources naturelles, la politique locale et les negotiations avec les gouvernements provincial et fédéral. En raison de la découverte du gas naturel, les Stoney peuvent être considérés comme tribu relativement à l'aise, tandis que la base de l'existence des Piegan est assez restreinte, étant surtout la terre et l'eau. Ces différences fondamentales sont encore influencées par de nombreuses facteurs de l'environnement physique et humain, aspects qui sont discutés dans cet article.

Zusammenfassung: Die hier betrachteten Stoney und Peigan Reservate liegen im südlichen Alberta und damit in dem Gebiet, das die größten Indianerreservate des Landes beherbergt. Wie andere Indianerreservate bilden sie geradezu Inseln eines "third world environment" im Rahmen einer modernen Nation westlich-industrieller Prägung. Historisch gesehen sind die Stoney und Peigan Reservate "Treaty Seven"-Reservate. Trotz dieses gemeinsamen Ursprungs waren sie sehr unterschiedlichen Entwicklungen unterworfen aufgrund von Unterschieden in ihrer Kultur, ihrer Ausstattung mit natürlichen Hilfsquellen, ihrer politischen Führung und ihren Beziehungen zu Provinz- und Bundesregierung. Aufgrund der Entdeckung und Förderung von Erdgas auf ihrem Land können die Stoney Indianer als relativ wohlhabender Stamm angesehen werden, wohingegen sich die Existenz der Peigan auf sehr begrenzten Rohstoffquellen begründet, nämlich Land und Wasser. Dieser grundlegende Unterschied wird noch durch eine Reihe anderer physischer und menschlicher Faktoren modifiziert.

1. Introduction

The two reserves under observation, the Stoney and the Peigan Reserves, are located in southern Alberta, in an area encompassing the largest Indian reserves in Canada. Like other Indian reserves which - to a varying degree - generally do not have the resources and/or the infrastructure to economically sustain their ever increasing population, they constitute patches of a "third world environment" within the framework of a western industrialized nation.

The Stoney Indians have a landbase of approximately 500 km² at their disposal. The Morley Reserve which is the main reserve and includes the uninhabited Rabbit Lake Reserve comprises 460 km² and centres around the township of Morley, roughly 56 km west of Calgary. The Morley Reserve as well as the small reserves Bighorn and Eden Valley to the north and south are all located in the foothills of the Rocky Mountains. The Stoney population totals 2.296. The 1.812 Peigan Indians inhabit approximately 450 km² in the southwestern corner of the province. The main reserve is centred around their administrative centre Brocket which is 80 km southwest of Lethbridge (see figure 1).

Historically the reserves in southern Alberta are Treaty Seven Reserves. This treaty, the so-called Blackfoot Treaty, was the seventh in a series of eleven post-confederation treaties, and was signed at Blackfoot Crossing on the Bow River in 1877 between the Crown and the native tribes occupying the area that today is southern Alberta. While sharing a common origin, the resultant reserves have been subject to quite different courses of development, due to differences in their culture, endowment with natural resources, in their leadership and local politics, and their dealings with provincial and federal government. Due to the discovery of natural gas on their land the Stoneys may be considered a relatively wealthy tribe, whereas the Peigan depend on a very narrow resource base, namely land and water. This basic difference is modified by a variety of other physical and human factors.

2. Aspirations for the Future

For almost a century after the signing of Treaty Seven in 1877 by the southern Albertan tribes and their subsequent settlement on reserves the federal Department of Indian Affairs was in absolute control of virtually every aspect of reserve life. It was only in the 1960s that reserves throughout Canada started pressing for more control of their own affairs. Band councils wanted to develop their own programs and administer their own funds. In 1966 the federal government finally yielded to the pressure and announced its program of local reserve self-government. The Peigan and the Stoneys were among the first in Alberta to accept the challenge of assuming administration of their own reserves.

The reserves functioning under the system of local self-government are by no means autonomous. They are still subject to the Indian Act; they are still under the final control of the Indian Affairs department, and they are subject to certain federal and provincial laws and regulations. But within these boundaries the band chiefs and councils now have a certain degree of freedom to identify and pursue the directions and goals of reserve development.

When we look at the aspirations and goals of the Stoneys, Peigan and other treaty Indians, we will find that the development of their reserves as ethnic homelands is a prominent theme. The concept of ethnic homelands is closely linked to the Indian people's desire to survive not only as individuals, but as a people. What the retention of group identity really means to them, is nowhere better expressed than by George Manuel: "Remaining Indian means that Indian people gain control of the economic and social development of our communities, within a framework of legal and constitutional guarantees for our land and our institutions" (G. MANUEL & M. POSLUNS 1974: 221 f). The evolution of Canadian Indian policy shows quite clearly that Indians as a collectivity as well as their reserves were (and are) regarded as a transitory feature of Canadian society. Reserves were not considered lands reserved for Indian people for their homelands but as lands granted by the government to be used as schools for civilization and to be done away with once this purpose had been fulfilled. On the other hand there can be no doubt that Indians still promote the idea of the reserve as an ethnic homeland. This is shown by the continued residence of the majority of western Indians on their reserves - with the Stoneys and Peigan the percentage living off-reserve is in fact negligible - and the retention of close ties to their home community by most of the urban migrants; it is also evident from the endeavour of Indian politicians on all levels. At the same time the retention of Indian homelands does neither imply the conservation of a museum culture nor the clinging to economically bankrupt refuges. Indian

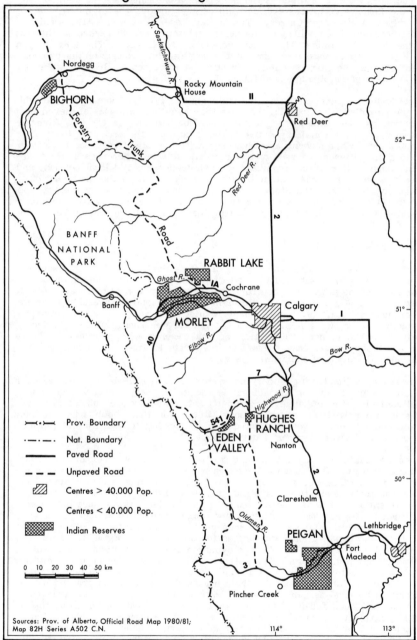

Fig.1

people want economic viability, but they want it on their own terms and in their own style:

> "Economic well-being does not necessarily mean a high standard of living or great wealth, but rather freedom from want achieved through meaningful activity. It means having available and being able to choose from the widest possible range of options respecting lifestyle" (NATIONAL INDIAN BROTHERHOOD 1977: 83).

Socio-economic development of their own making is seen as a means to satisfy new consumer tastes and to retain of their culture what seems desirable to them. Socio-economic development is broadly defined by Alberta Indian leaders as "people development in conjunction with economic development" (Eugene Steinhauer and Joe Dion cited by R. PRICE 1979: 7); this is different from mere natural resource development under profit-maximizing principles, as it went on under Department of Indian Affairs management before the onset of self-government.

3. The Factors of Production: Land, Labour and Capital

In their emphasis on human development and humane economic development which takes into account pre-existing socio-cultural features, the Stoneys and the Peigan are faced by a host of problems not all of which have been resolved yet. In order to clarify the conditions under which potential development is to take place, it is useful to consider the "factors of production" (as employed by W. B. MORGAN & R. J. C. MUNTON 1971: 46 ff) land, labour and capital one at a time.

3.1 The Land

The Indian land situation differs from the remainder of the province in several aspects: the existance of outstanding land claims, land shortage and the tenure system. Indian land claims have been a feature of almost all periods of Canada's history, but due to legal and political factors it has only been in the 1970s and 1980s that Indian people were really able to bring claims forward. There are various types of claims. In Alberta we are dealing with specific claims based on lawful obligations. These may be claims for land due to native people as part of a treaty agreement with the Crown, such as the Wesley Stoneys' claim of land in the Bighorn-Kootenay Plains area. Other claims involve lost land, surrendered under often dubious circumstances since the creation of the reserves, such as the forced sale of the northwest corner of the Peigan Reserve in the early 1900s. The question of water rights on the Peigan Reserve and the problem of mineral rights on land received by the Stoneys in exchange for the Transcanada Highway right-of-way are further contentious issues. Many of these cases involving millions of dollars have been before the courts for years without any solutions in sight.

All this "unfinished business" has far-reaching consequences for the development of the reserves. Not only does it directly affect the resource base and financial situation of the bands, but it also has an impact on their general relationship to government departments and thereby may influence decisions concerning not only the reserve communities but also the larger society. Examples would be the controversy over the eventual construction of a natural gas processing plant on the Morley Reserve and the question of where to locate an on-stream storage facility on the Oldman River on or near the Peigan Reserve.

There is an old African proverb: "Men and beasts beget, but land does not beget". In all its simplicity it very well characterizes the land situation on the reserves. Since the inception of the reserves the Stoney landbase increased by roughly 100 per cent. At the same time, according to available statistics, the Stoney population increased by 244 per cent. Due to the possibly illegal surrender the Peigan even experienced a reduction of their reserve lands, while their population grew by 113 per cent. A likely explanation for the striking difference between the Peigan and Stoney population is an inadequate enumeration of the latter due to their continued nomadic lifestyle in the early reserve days. In both cases there now is an obvious discrepancy between a stationary landbase and a rapidly growing population. It is not surprising, therefore, that the population density of both reserves is somewhat higher than that of the provincial census divisions the reserves are part of.

As to land tenure, Indians are opposed to any system of allotment that would give individuals ownership with rights to sell, but rather want the Indian Act changed to give Indians control of lands without changing the fact that the title is now held in trust of the Crown, because "The true owners of the land are not yet born" (INDIAN CHIEFS OF ALBERTA 1970: 10). With regard to individual tenure, many bands, particularly on the prairies and including the Peigan and Stoneys, choose not to use Certificates of Possession or any of the Indian Act provisions for internal Indian land holding on reserves. They adhere to what may be called "customary" or "traditional" land allotment patterns. These bands allot land to individual band members, but do so at the discretion of the band council. They avoid any Ministerial validation of the allotment. The allottee, on the other hand, has no more legal security of tenure than the band council is prepared to permit. The practice of this land policy and the problems encountered slightly vary from reserve to reserve.

On the Peigan Reserve 57 per cent of the reserve's landbase have been individually allotted. There are about 200 "landowners" (this somewhat incorrect term is chosen for convenience). Among these 160 have rights to arable land, 78 to grazing land, arount 60 per cent "own" both categories. The average size of a large holding is 390 ha, while small holdings average 65 ha. Small plots account for 75 per cent of all individual land holdings. A result of the uneconomically small size of even the large units with regard to both farming and ranching is the exorbitant leasing out of valuable land to non-band members with two-thirds of the revenue leaving the reserve and only one-third being paid to the owner. Sixty per cent of the individually allocated grazing land is being leased out, and 90 per cent of the arable land.

On the Stoney Reserve the division between landowners and landless band members is less pronounced than on the Peigan Reserve, as every family by custom has the right to fence off or use a parcel of land to graze some livestock. There are "acceptable" limits as to the size of holdings an individual may fence off for himself, the majority measuring under 65 ha. About 60 per cent of the main Morley Reserve have been taken up individually. Although there is a pronounced land shortage and the individual holdings are uneconomically small, all the individually used land is nevertheless used for grazing livestock, and none is leased to non-band members. Although leasing was practised before self-government, it was discontinued about a decade ago as a matter of policy, and thanks to their gas royalties band members do not depend on this source of income.

3.2 The People

The manpower characteristics of the Stoneys and Peigan are typical for so-called underdeveloped countries or groups who were subject to a colonial experience. The tribes are characterized by a young population and burdened with a high dependency ratio. However, whereas the dependent population 15 years and younger has declined since the 1960s, the young adult group 15-29 has grown considerably in proportion: The Indian labour force now experiences the full brunt of the Indian baby boom (which lagged behind the non-Indian one by several years and peaked in the mid-sixties).

Further features are low educational achievement (although there is an upward trend) caused by the social incoherence of the educational system throughout the decades - church control for most of a century and more recently the federal government's school integration policy -, its lack of quality and its imposition by one culture on another, and an occupational structure which is characterized by an overrepresentation in the so-called "unskilled" and "semi-skilled" area (e.g. service occupations, construction, forestry and logging, a variety of labour jobs) and underrepresentation in the managerial, professional, clerical and sales areas. The Peigan unemployment rate is 70 per cent; on the Stoney Reserve it is subject to seasonal fluctuations and varies between 50 and 60 per cent.

In fact the skill development and employment situation with the Peigan and Stoneys is characterized by a vicious circle. On the one hand the scarcity of employment opportunities, especially for more highly skilled individuals, does little to boost people's motivation to improve their skills. On the other hand, a reservoir of skilled manpower is one of the vital factors needed to establish the groundwork for a viable economy.

There are other less tangible factors involved. The Stoneys and the Peigan are poorly equipped by their culture to copy western industrial development. Life in white society is highly compartmentalized. The economy is disassociated from all other activities and in itself corporatized, bureaucratized, professionalized and governed by its own laws which are in some cases diametrically opposed to norms and behaviour patterns a native person is accustomed to.

A final factor which must be mentioned is the impact of the historical interactions and relationships of the Stoneys and Peigan with whites. Over more than a century the contact situation has been characterized by weakness in the bargaining power of the Indian, and growing dependence on whites. To a degree this dependency pattern established itself during the fur trade era, but it was virtually perpetuated after the treaties with the onset of the reserve period. A pervading paternalistic orientation and preemption of decision-making has characterized government policy towards Indian people. The continuing effect of such policy has not only been economic deprivation but also in many cases psychological crippling, evidenced in attitudes of dependency, apathy and irresponsibility. This phenomenon is one of the major roadblocks for those native individuals who work for the advancement of their people, and can only be understood in the light of history.

3.3 The Capital

The economic situation of Stoney and Peigan households is partly reflected by their occupational and employment situation. With an overrepresentation in unskilled and semi-skilled job categories and an unemployment rate between 60 and 70 per cent it is fairly evident that the average Stoney and Peigan income is considerably lower than the average Canadian income. The major portion of the Indian labour force on both reserves is without gainful employment and at the same time unable to sustain itself by ranching or farming. Consequently a large proportion of the Peigan population depends on the Department of Indian Affairs Social Assistance Program and receives an annual income considerably below the Statistics Canada Poverty Line.

The Stoneys are in a different position. Their natural gas royalties provide them with a substantial tribal income which is shared among the community by means of bi-weekly per capita payments, the investment in economic projects, and works of a capital nature. When the Stoneys started their full-time interest payments three years ago, thus enabling each single member of the tribe to benefit from the communally owned resource, they became independent from social assistance payments, and for the first time even unemployed reserve residents came to receive an annual income substantially above the poverty line.

As for all of Canada's Treaty Indians, the Stoneys' and the Peigan's band funds are held in Ottawa. Under federal direction their accumulated finance goes into what is commonly called the "trust fund". Governmental control over the bands' financial management is not confined to grants and appropriations out of the Indian Affairs budget - which often take the form of separate agreements with rigid guidelines and strict accountability -, but it includes the money accrued from Indian assets. Yet the extent of restraint exercised by the department varies according to the degree of financial independence achieved by the reserve.

Thanks to their gasroyalties the Stoneys are in the fortunate position of being virtually independent from Indian Affairs appropriations. The tribe controls its own revenue account, whereas the capital account is still adminstered by the Department of Indian Affairs. Although the Stoneys enjoy comparative freedom in deciding how their own money is invested, their situation is still characterized by strict accountability to Ottawa.

The Peigan are representative for those reserves - who are in the majority - that lack high revenue producing natural resources. They are dependent on the federal government; consequently most of their funds are non-discretionary, their allocation being determined by statute. Vital budgetary decisions are made thousands of miles away and have to be filtered through the district, regional and head offices of the Department of Indian Affairs. Even more disconcerting is the availability of funds for social assistance rather than for economic development. It must suffice here to say that for the fiscal year 1982/83 the respective ratio for the Peigan equalled 16:1, the money available for economic development being a mere token sum.

4. Economic Activities

With land being valued as such a vital asset among Indian people, it is not surprising that the land-based economy features prominently in the economic make-up of the reserves.

4.1 Livestock Production

The Peigan and Stoney Reserves are situated in one of Alberta's main rangeland areas, and the grazing of livestock may be considered as the main landuse for reasons of physical geography as well as for cultural preference. On both reserves there are band ranches as well as individual enterprises, almost exclusively cow-calf operations. While a small percentage of Stoneys can be classed as full-time ranchers, many other individuals with different sources of income also keep cattle in smaller numbers, this applies even more to the ownership of horses. An important characteristic of the Stoney ranching economy is the fact that half of the overheads of the individual operations are carried by the band; this way the Stoney cattle owners do not have to account for the normal operational costs of ranching enterprises. Ranches which would not be economical to manage off the reserve due to the small size of herds and the resultant high overheads and low margins of profit, may still pay their way for the Stoney ranchers one half of their overheads is carried for them. But there is more involved than just economics. It is necessary to consider here what role the Indian community plays for the individual. Communal ownership of resources is integral part of the maxim of the community's protection of the individual. With regard to land, its realization under modern circumstances is not without problems. But due to their wealth in natural gas the Stoneys are financially better off than the Peigan. Thus in a way the income accruing from a communally owned and quite substantial non-renewable resource is used to somehow offset resource shortages in other areas (such as land). There is no chance that the reserve could accommodate all those who want to engange in livestock raising on an economic unit basis. But in the protective environment of the reserve Euro-Canadian economic laws somehow cease to apply, and the individual - benefitting from a tribally owned resource - still has the freedom of engaging in an activity that would prove uneconomic under off-reserve competitive conditions.

On the Peigan Reserve, overheads are not carried by the band, but by the individual operator. Mutual integration of crop production and livestock economy restricts itself to the grazing of stubble. Because of the presence of so many non-Indian, owned cattle on the reserve and the practice of leasing out individual plots, livestock ownership by non-ranchers is less widespread among the Peigan than among the Stoneys. While there are some larger owners with about 200 animals, the average herd size is small. Unlike the Stoneys the Peigan do not have a source of continuous income which they could use to offset their shortage of land

and capital. Even if they had one, they might not use the same strategy. But when they received a $ 4 million settlement after a water rights dispute in 1981, part of the money was used to initiate a program to boost their ranching economy.

4.2 Farming

Limitations imposed by the natural environment all but preclude the cultivation of crops on the Stoney Reserves and create severe restrictions for the Peigan Reserve. Roughly one-third of the latter can be classified as arable land, three-quarters of which have been broken. Over 90 per cent of the tribe's arable land is being leased to white farmers, there being only one Peigan farmer on the reserve. As a result approximately $ 300.000 of rent money is distributed to land occupants with 20 per cent retained by the band for administration costs. Non-Indian farmers take as profits 600.000 - 800.000 $ from the reserve without any employment or other benefits for band members being generated. Consequently the Peigan landbase - their largest single non-human resource - is badly underutilized and does not even come close to producing an income for the tribe comparable to its productive capacity.

4.3 Forestry

Forest land occupies 52 per cent of the Morley Reserves (main reserve plus Rabbit Lake). The lumbering business being one of the oldest economic activities on the reserves, the Stoneys in 1977 established a new automated mill with a planer unit south of Morley beside the CPR mainline. At present the sawmill only turns out 0,5 million bf per year, and the main problem behind this low production is surprisingly enough a shortage of log cutters. Nevertheless the sawmill fulfills many purposes for the reserve community. Fifty to seventy-five per cent of its produce is used on the reserve for housing programs, public buildings and on ranches. Moreover, the Stoneys provide a variety of off-reserve customers with high quality dressed and graded lumber.

On the Peigan Timber Limit, northwest of the main reserve, a pilot project has been in operation since 1981 utilizing a portable sawmill, but logging has never furnished a sizeable contribution to Peigan economy.

4.4 Outdoor Recreation

Outdoor recreation is the most recent development of all the activities involving the renewable resource sector on the reserves. It goes without saying that the location of the Morley Reserve midway between Banff National Park and the City of Calgary has a most significant bearing on the potential for outdoor recreation activities. The recent development of Kananaskis Country as a recreational region bordering on both the Morley Reserve and Eden Valley attested to the need of alleviating congestion in the existing national parks and of providing greater recreational opportunities in the Eastern Slopes. The Stoneys are aware of this need and also of the great scenic beauty of many parts of their reserve. On the other hand, with a limited landbase at their disposal as it is, and valuing their privacy, they are understandably ambivalent about a large scale influx of foreigners in their midst. Chiniki Lake with its picturesque setting and view of the Rocky Mountains and Kananaskis Valley is regarded by many (potential developers) as the beauty spot of the reserve. On the other hand a large segment of the Stoney population is strongly opposed to any development at that place, as the lake has great cultural significance to the Stoney People themselves (f.i. as site for their annual sundance). At present, the only outdoor recreational enterprise in operation is the Stoney Indian Park, which was conceived and developed in 1970 as a campground and recreational area overlooking the Bow River Valley and providing camping facilities and rental teepees. Despite its obvious potential it seems to suffer from lack of promotion. The Peigan Reserve's potential for recreational and tourism development is more limited, and presently the Peigan are not deriving any income from this source.

4.5 Non-Renewable Resources

The Stoney Reserves are underlain by substantial natural gas reserves distributed in several fields. During the last decade royalties from this resource have contributed to a considerable rise in the Stoneys' standard of living. The gas fields are operated by Shell and PanCanadian Petrolum Limited, who acquire a working interest and send royalty and lease payments to the Department of Indian Affairs, which then deposits the money into the Trust Fund. Apart from occasional exploration leases the Peigan are not deriving any income from fossil fuels.

4.6 Secondary Industries

Activities evolving from the land-based economy - be it agriculture, forestry, outdoor recreation or mineral extraction - can still be interpreted as having some degree of continuity from the Indians' traditional mode of economy. The land as provider is a familiar concept to the Indian of old and new times alike. In contrast, the idea of manufacturing goods for a market rather than just satisfying personal subsistence needs was an alien one. Taking this factor into account plus the problems connected with labour and capital, it is hardly surprising that secondary industries established themselves among the Peigan and Stoneys only recently and on a small scale. On the Peigan Reserve there are two manufacturing enterprises, both located in Brocket: a garment factory employing 50 people and a smaller moccasin factory. On the Stoney Reserve handicraft production is the only secondary industry in operation; the number of Stoneys involved in this commercial activity though, has sharply declined in recent years after the per capita royalty payments set in.

4.7 Service Industries

Morley and Brocket constitute focal points of the reserves and provide certain goods and services for their hinterland. But upon closer investigation it becomes evident that they fulfill this function only to a rather limited degree.

In Brocket there are two service industries - both privately owned -: a grocery store and a service station. Besides, there are a few institutions catering to the band's recreational needs: an indoor hockey rink, a new community centre with gymnasium, poolroom and drop-in centre, and the Oldman River Cultural Centre. There is no doctor or nurse on the reserve. The health centre merely proves instruction in hygiene and related matters by community health and childcare workers. A daycare centre is located in the administration complex. Thus it is obvious that the Peigan have to satisfy many of their needs off-reserve. Recreational facilities - a decade ago virtually non-existant - have been considerably improved. But the Peigan still leave their reserve to do literally all their shopping, travelling to Pincher Creek and less frequently to Lethbridge.

The situation among the Stoneys is not too different. There is a small grocery store on the reserve, the so-called Stoney Trading Post, which is owned and operated by non-Indians. The Stoneys do most of their shopping at the Calgary Co-op. There are two band-owned service stations on the reserve. In 1981 the Chief Chiniki Restaurant was opened, scenically situated on the Transcanada Highway and specializing in native dishes. The Morley townsite contains a band hall, a multi-purpose recreation complex with a gymnasium, a swimming pool, a hockey arena and a drop-in centre, a daycare centre and a health centre. The latter is administered from the Foothills Hospital in Calgary and offers somewhat more comprehensive services than the one in Brocket. In addition the Stoneys own two facilities which they themselves use for a variety of purposes, but which also bring in revenue from outside the reserve when rented out: the Nakoda Institute, an educational-spiritual centre opened in 1981, and the Chief Goodstoney Rodeo Centre, a two million dollar facility just opened in summer 1983.

5. Conclusion and Outlook

The previous chapters have introduced two reserves which illustrate the development problems of a section of Canada's native population. These reserves differ culturally, economically and physically. As members of the Sioux and Blackfoot Nations respectively, the Stoneys and the Peigan are culturally distinct. Even today the Stoneys remain more secluded and self-contained than the Blackfoot tribes in comparison, while at the same time assuming an important role in Indian cultural revival as annual hosts of the Indian Ecumenical Conference.

In terms of natural resources the Peigan Reserve's main assets are its good agricultural and grazing land and its location on the Oldman River, a water body of vital importance for irrigation purposes. For this reason the Peigan have recently put up a strong stand in negotiations concerning land and particularly water, because these are the only potential sources for a much needed economic boost. The Stoney Reserve has a distinct potential for livestock economy, forestry and recreation, but its mainstay is a non-renewable resource, natural gas, which has a major impact on all other sectors of the reserve's economy.

Like the buffalo of old (an analogy the Stoneys like to draw on) gas has helped the Stoneys in a variety of ways, but unlike its predecessor it has not been able to provide its beneficiaries with that wholesome way of life which satisfies not only a people's economic needs but also its social and spiritual needs. The Stoneys are plagued with the same social problems as all the other tribes. Another difference is equally important: As a non-renewable resource gas is finite, and one has to ask what is going to replace it a few decades from now. But the Stoneys share this wealth among the community in a variety of ways, and a sizeable portion is invested for the future in terms of revenue and employment creating projects. Another portion is regularly being distributed among the population on a per capita basis and has served to make the Stoneys independent from the government's social assistance programs. Some might argue that these payments create the same syndrome as the welfare system - payment without gainful employment -, but for the people there is a crucial difference between the traditional sharing of a communally owned natural resource and the perpetuation of dependence on a paternalistic government. On the other hand it cannot be denied that these payments have served to curb economic activities, be it handicraft production (for the market) or realization of available employment opportunities at band enterprises like the band ranch, the sawmill or the restaurant. This may simply be "human nature", but it must not be forgotten that like other tribes, the Stoneys look back at a long "welfare tradition" which is not easily overcome.

The Peigan are engaged in a desparate struggle to break away from their almost total dependence on the federal government, but they are caught in a vicious circle. Without the creation of more and/or larger economic enterprises they cannot raise more investment capital, but for the establishment of economic projects they depend on a government that is prepared to pool millions of dollars into social assistance but only a token sum into economic development. Therefore, so much depends for the Peigan on the settlement of land claims and water-related agreements. This situation puts this tribe under much more pressure than the Stoneys are exposed to, and makes it even more difficult to realize any degree of true "self-government". It also limits the scope for experimentation with alternative ways of socio-economic development.

The question of exactly how certain cultural traits and economic development accomodate each other, still lacks a conclusive answer. It is impossible to arrive at any generalizations. In both tribes there is the effort to channel incoming capital to the wider community in various ways, be it per capita distribution or investment in economic development projects such as the cow-calf program of the Peigan or the sawmill of the Stoneys. They also try to alleviate social problems by creating outlets for recreational and cultural needs such as the community complex in Brocket or the rodeo centre on the Stoney Reserve. While the accumulation of capital is not a value in itself, nowadays money is needed and desired for the necessities of life and for other things native people have come to appreciate.

Whether a tribal enterprise is competitive in the outside world or not, in the long run (though not at the experimental stage) it will have to be able to sustain itself, unless the tribe is in a position to subsidize it permanently. Thanks to their income in royalties the Stoneys have experienced more freedom than the Peigan to experiment and to do things in their own way. By means of traditional sharing mechanisms they have offset resource shortages in some areas such as land and embarked upon a variety of economic projects while trying to accommodate their people's cultural traits and needs. Many developments here are too recent to offer any conclusions.

Nevertheless, after looking at these two reserves, it appears that the idea of tribal homelands is a feasible one, even in terms of economic viability. The Stoneys have reached this goal for the time being thanks to the riches beneath their land, and the Peigan could achieve it too, if they were given a fair chance at economic development and if their substantial land claims were settled in a just manner.

References

Cardinal, H., 1977: The Rebirth of Canada's Indian, Edmonton: M. G. Hurtig.

Carstens, W., 1971: Coercion and Change, pp. 120-132 in Ossenburg, R. J., ed. 1971: Canadian Society: Pluralism, Change and Conflict, Scarborough: Prentice-Hall of Canada Ltd.

Cumming, P. A., and Mickenberg, N. H., eds., 1972: Native Rights in Canada. The Indian-Eskimo Association of Canada in association with General Publishing Company Limited, Toronto.

Daniel, R. C., 1980: A History of Native Claims Processes in Canada, 1867-1979, prepared by R. C. Daniel, Tyler, Wright & Daniel Limited, Research Consultants for Research Branch, Department of Indian and Northern Affairs, February 1980.

Dempsey, H. A., 1978: Indian Tribes of Alberta, Calgary: Glenbow-Alberta Institute.

Frideres, J. S., ed., 1974: Canada's Indians. Contemporary Conflicts, Scarborough: Prentice-Hall of Canada Ltd.

Getty, I. A. L., and Larner, J. W., 1972: The Kootenay Plains and the Big Horn Wesley Stoney Band - An Oral and Documentary Historical Study, 1800-1970. Unpublished Research Report, Morley: Stoney Tribal Council.

Getty, I. A. L., and Smith, D. B., eds., 1978: One Century Later. Western Canadian Reserve Indians since Treaty 7, Vancouver: University of British Columbia Press.

Government of Canada, 1969: Statement of the Government of Canada on Indian Policy 1969 ("White Paper"), presented to the First Session of the 28th Parliament by the Honourable Jean Chretien, Minister of Indian Affairs and Northern Development.

Indian Association of Alberta, 1977: Joint NIB/DIAND Socio-Economic Study for Alberta Region, submitted by the Indian Association of Alberta, March 31, 1977.

Indian Chiefs of Alberta, 1970: Citizen Plus ("Red Paper"), a Presentation by the Indian Chiefs of Alberta to Right Honourable P. E. Trudeau, Prime Minister and the Government of Canada, June 1970.

Jenness, D., 1932: Indians of Canada, Ottawa: National Museum of Canada, Anthropological Series No. 15.

Manuel, G., and Posluns, M., 1974: The Fourth World, Donn Mills, Ont.: Collier - Macmillan Canada.

Morgan, W. B., and Munton, R. J. C., 1971: Agricultural Geography, London: Methuen and Co. Limited.

Morris, A., 1880, 1971: The Treaties of Canada with the Indians of Manitoba and the Northwest Territories, including the Negotiations on which they were based, and other Information relating thereto, Toronto: Willing & Williamson.

Nagler, M., ed., 1972: Perspectives on the Northamerican Indians, Toronto, McClelland and Stewart.

National Indian Brotherhood (NIB), 1977: A Strategy for the Socio-Economic Development of Indian People, Background Report No. 1, Ottawa, Sept. 1977.

Ossenberg, R. J., ed., 1971: Canadian Society: Pluralism, Change and Conflict, Scarborough: Prentice Hall of Canada Ltd.

Palmer Patterson, E., 1972: The Canadian Indian: A History Since 1500, Don Mills, Ont.: Collier-Macmillan Canada.

Ponting, J. R., and Gibbins, R., 1980: Out of Irrelevance. A socio-political introduction to Indian affairs in Canada. Toronto: Butterworth and Company (Canada) Limited.

Price, R., ed., 1979: The Spirit of the Alberta Indian Treaties, Toronto: Butterworth and Company (Canada) Limited.

Snow, J., 1977: These Mountains are our Sacred Places, Toronto: Samuel-Stevens, Publishers.

Tobias, J. L., 1976: Protection, Civilization, Assimilation: An Outline History of Canada's Indian Policy, The Western Canadian Journal of Anthropology 6,2, pp. 13-30.

Address of the author:
Dr. Claudia Notzke
Am Schnepfenhof 4
4000 Düsseldorf 1

Changing Inuit Ethnicity in Canada

Ludger Müller-Wille

Abstract: In nothern Canada, recent political and socio-economic developments have exerted a strong influence on the cultural identity of the Inuit. These noticeable changes in the expression of ethnicity are discussed in relation to the maintenance of cultural boundaries and of contemporary ethnic attributes and, finally, in relation to the political and organizational management of modern Inuit ethnicity. As a case study, the evolution of Inuit institutions and organizations in Canada is presented. In conclusion, the repercussions of these developments on ethnic survival are summarized.

Résumé: Au Canada septentrional, les développements politiques et socio-économiques récents ont exercé une influence profonde sur l'identité culturelle des Inuit. Ces changements perceptibles dans l'expression d'ethnicité sont discutés à l'égard du maintien des frontières culturelles et des attributs ethniques contemporains et, finalement, à l'égard de la gestion politique et organisationelle de l'ethnicité inuit moderne. L'evolution des institutions et organisations inuit au Canada forme la base de cette recherche. Finalement, les répercussions de ces développements sur la survie ethnique sont résumées sommairement.

Zusammenfassung: Die politischen und sozio-ökonomischen Entwicklungen der letzten Jahre haben einen starken Einfluß auf die kulturelle Identität der Inuit im nördlichen Kanada ausgeübt. Diese bemerkbaren Veränderungen im Ausdruck ethnischer Identität werden hier im Zusammenhang mit der Erhaltung kultureller Abgrenzungen und gegenwärtiger ethnischer Merkmale und schließlich mit der politischen und organisatorischen Handhabung moderner Ethnizität bei den Inuit diskutiert. Die kürzliche Entstehung verschiedener Organisationsformen bei den Inuit in ihren Beziehungen zur Regierung dient als Fallstudie. Die feststellbaren Rückwirkungen dieser Entwicklungen auf das Weiterbestehen ethnischer Gruppen werden am Schluß zusammengefaßt.

Changing Ethnicity and Maintenance of Cultural Boundaries

Ethnicity or ethnic identity according to Barth (1969: 10-11) is a concept to describe and define attributes shaping separate but related human populations in respect to biological descent, the sharing of fundamental social values (cultural forms), the interaction and communication within a territory, and, finally, the identification by the members themselves or by others as being a distinct cultural group. There cannot exist any fixed or stagnant ethnicity within a group or in the group's interaction with other neighboring groups. Therefore ethnicity undergoes constant changes in its definition and application in intra-ethnic and inter-ethnic relations. However, ethnicity as an important cultural form serves and reiterates the cohesiveness of a group and the continuation of ethnic groups and boundaries even within encompassing political structures which tend to equalize cultural differences. Over time, the identity of cultural groups has shown considerable survival skills in respect to losses and mobility in its clientele resulting in assimilation and integration into other groups. In fact, the continuing socio-political relations between groups of different stature across ethnic boundaries contribute to the maintenance of cultural dichotomies. These relations are a necessary element in the changes and redefinition of ethnicity internally and externally (Barth 1969: 9-10).

The understanding and acceptance of the dynamic nature of ethnicity is of particular importance to the discussion of ethnicity in the Fourth World, i.e. indigenous peoples living in their homelands which are today encapsulated by modern (nation) states in which they lack the political and economic base to control or even influence power relations and decisions. Despite this pessimistic or fatalistic statement (cf. Brody 1981) these indigenous peoples, who are by now usually ethnic minorities, are trying to maintain cultural integrity and distinctiveness and to redefine their ethnicity in order to preserve their perceived rights to land and cultural self-determination as a people or nation.

These premises based on Barth's concepts (1969) and reassessed so carefully by R. König and T.G. Svensson in this volume serve very well the discussion of changes which have occurred in the ethnicity of Inuit society in arctic Canada during the last quarter century. These relate to the important socio-political and cultural developments among the Inuit in particular, but even more, to the changing views on the rights and position of indigenous peoples within Canadian society in general. As a reference point I take the year of 1969 when the Canadian federal government issued its 'Statement on Indian Policy' on the termination of special status for indigenous peoples in Canada (Chrétien 1969). This document happened to be the beginning of a long thorny path to come to grips with the issue of indigenous affairs in Canada. For the Inuit of Canada as for the other indigenous peoples this policy was the turning point in the perception of their identity and how it could be projected in a broader context to achieve the secure continuation of their shared, but changing value systems, i.e. their own cultural forms. On the other hand, it is obvious that earlier contact with Europeans and later with Euro-Canadians had repercussions. But particularly the more recent political developments towards self-affirmation have caused a surge to reiterate and stress distinctiveness, i.e. ethnicity, pratically in all areas of concern to indigenous peoples versus the state.

Historic Inuit Ethnicity: Shaping an Image

Until more extensive contact with European explorers, American whalers, fur traders, missionaries and later Canadian administrators, particularly since the middle 19th century, Inuit identity was based on local family bands and groups that developed strong internal ties. Still, relations existed with neighboring groups in more distant areas; also, as Knud Rasmussen could establish in the 1920s, local Inuit had knowledge, if still vague, of other Inuit they never met. In the southern fringes of their culture area the Inuit also had experience with Athapascan and Algonkin Indians with whom relations were not usually easy or even peaceful. Therefore the perception of a unified Inuit culture or identity was very much localized and, in cases, even isolated. However, the increasing contacts with people of European origin gradually created cultural and ethnic dichotomies on which the future orientation of Inuit culture and society hinged (i.e. 'Inuit = The People' on the one side and the 'Qallunaat = The Big Eyebrows (Whites)' on the other side).

As of that time of increased contact, Inuit ethnicity and the evolving cultural image of the Inuit was influenced and shaped by external peoples, the Europeans, who took, e.g., the derogatory ethnic label 'Eskimo' = 'Raw Meat Eaters' from their southern neighbors, the Algonkin. The Inuit were seen as a peaceful people, content with the sparse, but intriguing environment of the arctic. For the Europeans they had become the epitomy of heroes of endurance and patience taxing the limits of humankind's capabilities to survive under extreme circumstance. In a sense, an image was created which would influence Inuit-Canadian relations until today.

Although Inuit moved large distances through arctic Canada meeting other Inuit, only since the time of exploration, whaling and, finally, the fur trade did Inuit obtain, through these external establishments, more knowledge about other Inuit groups. But it was left to the various religious missions and to the Canadian government to provide the base for an increased ethnic and cultural awareness among all Inuit of Canada. With the advent of government services and programs in welfare, housing, economic development and particularly schooling since the 1950s, a pan-Inuit image did gradually emerge for all Inuit throughout Canada. This projected image reiterated local identity of family groups and strengthened the Inuit cultural base, in spite of the rapid changes in their culture related to external factors. It is ironical to state that this process of evolving pan-ethnicity was supported in part by the very teaching of an externally perceived Inuit cultural image in the newly introduced schools. This image was based on the Qallunaat (White) perception of the Inuit way of life.

By the 1960s, the Inuit had realized that their lives were bound to the encompassing political system of Canada which had incorporated their homeland without their consent. The Inuit learned now, as well, that their survival as an ethnic group in their land (Nunavut = 'Our land') would depend very much on the relations that were to develop between them and the various governmental levels. The projection of ethnicity could no longer only surge from internal factors and strength, but rather would now also be shaped by external relations, which could not be assessed unless knowledge was obtained on the workings of the encompassing political and cultural Canadian system. It is also important to state that Inuit almost solely experienced the 'wider Canadian society' in a segmented way through a small number of representatives who came for special reasons and tasks. Thus inter-ethnic contact locally did not provide the opportunity for easy insight into the other culture(s). These relations were usually carried out in a formal way via institutions, such as the Department of Indian and Northern Affairs (DINA), which, in turn, created more and more dependency. It was arduous for the Inuit to appreciate and assess this intercultural situation. In order to prevail and manage, some Inuit engaged in 'cultural commuting' (Williamson 1981) to be able to mediate and possibly negotiate between the two cultures.

Attributes of Modern Inuit Ethnicity

It is not possible to describe the attributes of contemporary Inuit ethnicity in detail but major aspects come to mind which are important to the cultural survival and the development and expansion of a stronger ethnic base for the Inuit. These attributes are as follows:

(1) The land and the use of its resources as originated in the Inuit way of dealing with the environment;
(2) The Inuit language and its development through schooling and other means;
(3) The knowledge and acceptance of cultural distinctiveness versus other indigenous and immigrant cultures within the Canadian context;
(4) The urge to preserve and develop cultural heritage in combination with new influences;
(5) The expression of symbols of Inuit ethnicity in the arts and handicrafts (soapstone carvings, stone cut prints, literature, etc.);
(6) Political awareness and astuteness in dealing with internal and external factors and developments mainly in relation with government authorities.

These areas of a higher political ethnicity, as I would like to call it, draw their support from within and without contemporary Inuit society. Inuit ethnicity has thus become part of the multicultural setting and political structure of the state of Canada, which is based legally on the assumption of two founding nations - English-Canadian and French-Canadian, but obviously also faces the perceived rights and demands by a large number of indigenous peoples and other immigrant populations. For both the founding nations and the new immigrant Canadians the purpose for being in Canada has quite different dimensions than for the 'first' Canadians. By the 1980s, the Inuit have learned to understand that their cultural aspirations have to be adapted to and accommodated by the encompassing political framework of Canada. Thus, recently, ethnicity has become more of a political issue in inter-ethnic relations. It is this aspect of ethnicity that I want to discuss here in light of contemporary political processes among the Inuit and their impact on the survival of Inuit culture.

Political Organization and Management of Inuit Ethnicity

The last 15 years of indigenous affairs and politics in Canada - that is since 1969 - have altered the political context within which indigenous peoples can manoeuver in respect to their cultural self-determination versus Canadian society and the federal, provincial, and territorial governments presumably representing all societal sectors. With its 'Statement on Indian Policy' in 1969 the Canadian government sought the termination of special status for the indigenous sector of Canadian society. By the early 1970s the government, in turn, had to realize that the claims for aboriginal title to land and right to self-determination by indigenous people had legal merits. Therefore the government reversed its position and instead offered to negotiate with indigenous peoples and their respective organizations which in most cases did not yet exist (cf. Asch 1984).

In 1971, the Inuit founded 'Inuit Tapirisat of Canada' (ITC) to serve as a pan-Inuit voice in the emerging process of aboriginal land claims and cultural rights. But very soon it was realized that the already existing political institutions and territories did not allow for a consolidation of a large pan-Inuit organization with roots in all Inuit communities in Canada. Rather, up to 1984, the Inuit population has been politically gradually split by external factors and events:

(1) in the Northwest Territories: Inuit Tapirisat of Canada (ITC) and the Committee on Original Peoples' Entitlement (COPE or Inuvialuit);
(2) in Newfoundland-Labrador: Labrador Inuit Association (LIA) including white settlers who trace their local origins to the 18th century;
(3) in Québec: Northern Quebec Inuit Association (NQIA) which became Makivik Corporation under the James Bay and Northern Quebec Agreement in 1978.

These individual organizations have been funded by the Canadian federal government, being under legal constitutional obligations to provide for the well-being of Canada's indigenous peoples. The organizations represent an ethnic constituency within fixed political territories which does not necessarily reflect the existing cultural bonds. To be or remain a member of the constituency ethnic criteria are used; in some cases, like in northern Québec, membership in an ethnic group has been legalized under the land surrender agreements (e.g. so-called 'beneficiary').

Although pan-Inuit ethnicity has become accepted by the Inuit in all of arctic Canada and has been supported by increased dissemination of information (radio, television, telephone, etc.) and numerous ethno-political meetings, the Inuit organizations have negotiated separately with government authorities over land, benefits, compensation and socio-political rights. Thus the Inuit have become effectively divided despite the realization that a distinct cultural affinity exists among them. Negotiated agreements, e.g. in northern Québec and in the western Arctic, have even deepened the separation of the Inuit residing in different political entities.

The issues of aboriginal rights during the recent constutional debate leading to the Canada Act of 1982 provided a new impetus for joint representation for all Inuit in Canada through the 'Inuit Committee on National Issues' (ICNI). This ethnic lobby group is to look after all Inuit interests under the constitutional guarantee of 'existing aboriginal and treaty rights' (Section 35 in the Canada Act of 1982). The First Ministers Conference, representing the provinces and the federal government, has still to define these legally by 1987.

Additionally, Inuit organizations and politicians have developed other fora where ethnicity and the quest for cultural as well as political survival have become important and pressing issues. By founding the 'Inuit Circumpolar Conference' (ICC) with representatives from Alaska, Canada and Greenland in 1977, the Inuit of the Circumpolar North have pursued policies to be implemented on the international level. These recently formulated 'Inuit Arctic Policies' (Inuit Circumpolar Conference 1982-) draw from contacts and support from other northern indigenous peoples and from the 'World Council of Indigenous Peoples' (WCIP), founded in 1975. The ICC is a member of the UN Non-Governmental Agencies Organization through the WCIP. All these bodies act on the assumption of a perceived ethnicity that is the basis for their functioning and for the drive behind their actions, i.e. to maintain a breathing space for the preservation of what indigenous peoples consider their cultural attributes and distinctiveness.

These political endeavors on the national and international level have a solid purpose, which, however, cannot be furthered if the general ethnic population does not back the efforts. For that reason, Inuit ethnicity has to derive its strength from the Inuit individuals in the communities across the Circumpolar North. As has often occurred in ethnic politics of minorities versus central states, the instigators have become dangerously distant from the grass-root level of the general ethnic populace. In the case of the Inuit, certain measures have been taken to overcome this discernible internal dichotomy in the projection of continually changing Inuit ethnicity. For example, the 'Inuit Cultural Institute' (ICI) in the Northwest Territories and 'Avataq Cultural Institute' (ACI) in northern Québec are two institutions which have tried to close this gap on the cultural and scientific front by stressing both the preservation and the development of Inuit cultural heritage.

The mandate for these tasks, for which funds are often obtained from the governments, has been given to these institutes by the 'Inuit Elders Conferences' established in the two political entities, the Northwest Territories and Québec. These conferences draw from the resources of older women and men representing each Inuit community to enlighten the younger generation on the origin of their common cultural identity. Other organizations such as the newly founded 'Inuit Women's Association' (IWA) pursue similar cultural and ethnic issues along with more general concerns, such as equal opportunity. The 'Inuit Elders Conferences' originated in Inuit culture in which the elders always have been the carriers of knowledge and wisdom whose transmission was vital to cultural survival. Today, the deliberations and resolutions of these annual conferences are felt throughout the communities, and thus reinforce ethnic identity in the broadest sense.

The mandate for cultural development was clearly spelled out in the first resolution, passed unanimously by all Elders present at the first 'Northern Quebec Inuit Elders Conference' held in 1981 (Avataq 1983: 81):

'to discuss ways and means of revitalizing and preserving traditional Inuit culture';
'to retain tangible aspects of Inuit culture';
'to define how Inuit culture should be respected by Inuit and non-Inuit alike'.

Thus the Inuit are now directly involved in designing policies which shape the consolidation of Inuit ethnic identity on all levels.

Repercussions on Ethnic Survival

Although the developments mentioned above are very recent some repercussions can already be detected for the Inuit in the areas of cultural and socio-economic change:

(1) Despite changes in the northern economy and land use patterns, caused by modernization and mechanization, the relationship with the land has been maintained and preserved very strongly.
(2) The foundations of the Inuit language have been strengthened considerably by its introduction into the schools and by the development of Inuit oriented curricula; its future status as an official language is under discussion.
(3) Organizational planning and activities as well as almost constant mobility of Inuit politicians and the possibilities of instant communication have reinforced cultural distinctiveness in the Canadian context.
(4) The preservation of cultural heritage, i.e. the transfer of oral tradition to written tradition, has resulted in renewed esteem for one's culture, e.g. environmental knowledge through systematic mapping and place names.

These developments and processes have forced the Inuit to reexamine their cultural position within the ever present framework of inter-ethnic relations under the political umbrella of the Canadian state. For the Inuit, the political and organizational development based on ethnic identity is another step in their adaptation to a changing environment - be it physical or human - which is now also strongly influenced by external forces. One could bemoan the fact that the 'original Inuit ways' are vanishing. But does this not reveal a static image of culture, one which would not allow for a redefinition of one's identity - a task and challenge crucial to indigenous peoples in states they do not politically control. As for the Inuit, this is the dilemma and challenge all peoples of the Fourth World are confronted with.

Acknowledgements

My discussion of Inuit changing ethnicity has been shaped and influenced by my field work with the Inuit of Repulse Bay, N.W.T., August to December, 1973 and, more recently, by the cooperation with Inuit and their institutions during large scale Inuit place names surveys in northern Québec (Inukjuak, Kuujjuaq, Kangiqsualuujjuaq) and in the N.W.T. (Pangnirtung) between 1982 and 1984. For the latter work, financial support by the Volkswagenwerk Foundation and the Faculty of Graduate Studies and Research (McGill University), is gratefully acknowledged.

References

Asch, Michael, 1984: Home and Native Land, Aboriginal Rights and the Canadian Constitution. Toronto: Methuen.

Avataq, 1983: Northern Quebec Inuit Elders Conference, Kangirsuk (Payne Bay). Quebec. April 21-25, 1981. Inukjuak: Avataq Cultural Institute.

Barth, Fredrik (ed.), 1969: Ethnic Groups and Boundaries. Oslo: Universitetsforlaget.

Brody, Hugh, 1981: Maps and Dreams. Vancouver: Douglas and McIntyre.

Inuit Circumpolar Conference, 1982: Inuit Arctic Policy Review. Nuuk, Greenland.

Williamson, Robert R., 1981: The Notion of Cultural Commuting: Evaluation of Short-term Feasibility. Proceedings: Conference on Commuting and Northern Development. Feb. 15-16, 1979. Saskatoon: Institute for Northern Studies, University of Saskatchewan, pp. 220-263.

Address of the author:
Prof. Dr. Ludger Müller-Wille
Department of Geography
McGill University
805 Sherbrooke St. West
Montréal. Québec, Canada
H3A 2K6

Das Problem
der archäologischen und historischen Kontinuität
im Gebiet der Kupfer-Inuit

Hansjürgen Müller-Beck

Abstract: Experience from archaeology and history shows that even in cases where excellent sources are available, cultural, and from this ethnical, continuity can only be partially proved due to the complex dynamics of the processes involved. Long term continuity is apparently rare and correlated with special conditions. Reconstructions of this sort are more difficult where sufficient sources are still lacking. In the Copper Inuit area, the oldest traces of human activities come from the Arctic Small Tool tradition. This tradition is known from large areas of the North American Arctic and Subarctic. Regional adaption to the environment of the High Arctic is already clearly visible in this area at this time. The following Dorset is a technically defined archaeological complex which evolved in the Canadian Arctic. Developments in this complex can be clearly separated from those in Alaska beginning around the time of Christ's birth. During the Dorset Culture, technical skills which are characteristic of later Inuit cultures are invented. The area of the later Copper Inuit forms the most western wing of this Central and Eastern Arctic complex. New aspects are introduced by the Thule who apparently expanded from Alaska rapidly under improving climatic conditions during the eleventh century. The Thule complex is based mainly on the exploitation of larger whales. The relation between the Thule and the Dorset in our area is not clear. It seems rather unlikely that the Dorset people completely disappear. It is more likely that an acculturation of technological aspects takes place. If this is correct, the point at which the Dorset and Thule components begin to mix can be seen as an ethnogenetic threshold marking the begin of new units which are later called the Copper Inuit. The first archaeological traces of the Copper Inuit are known from the contact period of the 19th century. They document the passing of a second ethnogenetic threshold, somewhere between 1600 and 1800, which marks the ending of the previously mentioned development. These thresholds do not have clear cut boundaries, but exist within the flow of cultural continuity.

Résumé: L'expérience des archéologues et des historiens démontre que, même dans les cas où les meilleures sources sont disponibles, la preuve d'une continuité culturelle, et par là ethnique, ne peut réussir que partiellement à cause du dynamisme complexe du développement. Des continuités prolongées sont apparemment rares et se lient à des conditions particulières. La tâche devient encore plus difficile là où les sources sont encore mal explorées. Dans l'aire des Inuit de cuivre les premières traces d'une activité humaine se lient à la tradition des "Arctic Small Tool", couvrant en grande partie les régions arctiques et subarctiques centrales du Canada. Une adaptation à l'environnement des régions arctiques est déjà clairement observable à cette époque. Dans le sens archéologique, le complex technico-culturel des "Dorset" a commencé par se développen au centre de la haute région arctique du Canada. Cette unité culturelle s'éloigne vers l'an zéro des Inuit de l'Alaska. Dans la culture "Dorset" se sont developpées de nombreuses techniques de ce qui est devenu plus tard la culture Inuit. La région des Inuit de cuivre couvre la partie Ouest de cette culture nouvelle de l'arctique central. Au cours du onzième siècle se manifestent des influences de la culture "Thule" se répendant à partir de l'Alaska en profitant des conditions climatiques favorables à cette époque et en se basant sur l'utilisation de la baleine. Les interéchanges entre les "Dorset" et les "Thule" sont encore mal connus pour les époques postérieures, mais il semble invraisemblable que les fragments des "Dorset" auraient disparu totalement. On pourrait plutôt supposer qu'une acculturation se soit effectuée sur le plan technologique. Si ceci était vrai on pourrait parler du début de la culture des Inuit de cuivre, dans le sens d'un seuil ethno-génétique, au moment où les éléments des "Dorset" et des "Thule" se sont amalgamés. Malheureusement les premières traces archéologiques des Inuit de cuivre ne remontent qu'à la période de contact du 19e siècle. Elles démontrent l'existence d'un deuxième seuil ethno-génétique qui aurait terminé ce processus d'amalgamation quelquepart entre 1600 et 1800. En tout cas, ces seuils culturaux ne se caractérisent pas, au cours de l'histoire, pan des limitations strictes mais font plutôt partie d'une continuité culturelle.

Zusammenfassung: Die Erfahrungen der Archäologie und Geschichtswissenschaften zeigen, daß der Nachweis kultureller und damit auch ethnischer Kontinuitäten auch bei bester Quellenlage wegen ihrer komplexen Dynamik nur partiell erfolgreich sein kann. Langfristige Kontinuitäten sind offenbar selten und zudem an besondere Bedingungen geknüpft. Noch schwieriger werden derartige Nachweise bei noch unzureichend erschlossenen Quellen. Im Gebiet der Kupfer-Inuit gehören die ältesten Spuren menschlicher Tätigkeit in den Zusammenhang mit der Arctic-Small-Tool-Tradition, die weiträumig das arktische und auch erhebliche Teile des subarktischen Kanadas umfaßt. Eine regionale Anpassung an hocharktische Verhältnisse im hier behandelten Raum ist bereits klar erkennbar. Das anschließende "Dorset" ist ein technisch geprägter kultureller Komplex im archäologischen Definitionssinne, dessen Entwicklungszentrum in der kanadischen Arktis liegt. Diese Einheit trennt sich etwa seit der Zeit um Christi Geburt von den Erscheinungen in Alaska deutlich ab. Im "Dorset" werden weitere Nutzungstechniken der späteren Inuit-Kultur entwickelt. Das spätere Kupfer-Inuitgebiet bildet den westlichen Flügel dieses zentral- bis ostarktischen Komplexes. Neue Einflüsse bringt das offenbar rasch von Alaska aus im klimagünstigen 11. Jahrhundert ostwärts vorstoßende "Thule", das auf Nutzung größerer Wale basiert. Das anschließende Verhältnis zwischen "Dorset" und "Thule" im hier behandelten Raum ist noch ungeklärt. Es erscheint eher unwahrscheinlich, daß die Träger des "Dorset" vollständig verschwinden. Eher ist wohl eine technologisch begründete Akkulturation anzunehmen. Wäre dies richtig, würde als Beginn derjenigen Gruppen, die später als Kupfer-Inuit zusammengefaßt werden, im Sinne einer ethnogenetischen Schwelle, der Beginn des Zusammenwachsens der "Dorset"- und "Thule"-Komponenten zu bezeichnen sein. Manifest sind archäologisch bestimmbare Kupfer-Inuit-Spuren bisher erst aus der Kontaktzeit im 19. Jahrhundert, die damit das Überschreiten einer weiteren ethnogenetischen Schwelle dokumentieren, welche irgendwann zwischen 1600 und 1800 den vorgenannten Vorgang des Zusammenwachsens beendet hätte. Schwellen also, die im Ablauf des historischen Geschehens, das damit andeutbar wird, auf keinen Fall kategorische Grenzen darstellen.

<><><><><><><><><><><><>

Es ist ein immer wieder reizvolles Unterfangen, mit historischen und archäologischen Mitteln Siedlungskontinuitäten nachzugehen. Das bleibt solange relativ unproblematisch, als man einfach nur die in einer Landschaft aufeinander folgenden Zustände beschreibt und auf genetische Verknüpfungen verzichtet. Vor allem verbieten meist die allzu fragmentarischen archäologischen Quellen und ihre zudem oft nur unvollständige kulturhistorische Auswertung den Anschluß an durch Schriftquellen belegte Zustände. Und auch diese sind oft zur Definition sprachlicher, ethnischer oder gar politischer Regionen wegen ihrer Lückenhaftigkeit meist unzureichend. Wie schwierig derartige Definitionen selbst heute noch für interessierte zeitgenössische Beobachter sind, hat das hier publizierte Symposium sehr deutlich werden lassen. Das gilt keineswegs nur für die komplexen Zustände moderner Groß-Städte in Kanada, sondern auch für überlagerte Randgruppen, wie etwa die Samen im Norden des heutigen Finnlands.

Man sollte sich auch bewußt sein, daß wir an unsere begrenzten Quellen zur Rekonstruktion früherer Siedlungszustände mit Fragestellungen herangehen, die auf heute gänzlich anders begründeten Denkstrukturen fußen. Auch dies hat unser Symposium sehr deutlich unterstrichen. Gerade im gegenwärtigen Europa muß unbedingt darauf verwiesen werden, wie hier auf der Basis der Nationalvorstellungen der Romantik (die immer noch sehr stark die deutschsprachige archäologische und ethnohistorische Forschung beeinflußt) vor rund 100 Jahren gearbeitet worden ist. Nationen und Völker wurden nicht nur trotz unzureichender Quellenlagen in ihrer Genese über Jahrtausende hinwegverfolgt, sondern aus diesen Rekonstruktionsversuchen wurden konkrete politische Gebietsansprüche abgeleitet. Die Folgen für die europäische Geschichte sind ausreichend bekannt (J. R. v. SALIS 1980, Bd. I/1: 96). Es gibt nur sehr wenige Arbeiten, in denen es bisher überzeugend gelungen ist, mit archäologischen Mitteln Kontinuitäten zu rekonstruieren, die einmal an historisch bekannte ethnische Einheiten anschließen und sich andererseits bis an ihre Anfänge zurückverfolgen lassen. Dabei geht es vor allem um die ausreichende Dokumentation einer weitgehend gleichbleibenden materiellen Ausstattung als Gegenstand der Archäologie. Bei genügendem Umfang der zuordenbaren Funde dokumentieren sie nicht nur unveränderte technisch-konstruktive Traditionen, sondern auch die damit verbundenen Lebensstrategien und endlich auch die sie tragende geistige Weltsicht. Das mögen zum Teil mit zunehmender Zeittiefe nur noch Andeutungen sein, die aber ausreichen müssen, um den postulierten kulturhistorischen Anschluß zu sichern. Überzeugend ist das etwa D. W. CLARK (1974) in einer gerade in dieser Hinsicht noch unausgeschöpften Arbeit über die Koniag-Prähistorie auf Kodiak Island gelungen. Hier findet sich der Anschluß der historischen Gegebenheiten an die vorhergehende prähistorische Entwicklung bis hinunter zu deren Beginn. Grundlage dafür ist eine Synthese aller Funde von den Faunenresten über die materielle Ausstattung für die Nahrungsbeschaffung, die Haushaltsführung und rituelle Manifestationen bis hin zu Bestattungspraktiken. Sie sind durchgehend in allen Grundzügen identisch mit jenen bei den seit dem 18. Jahrhundert von Europäern kontaktierten Koniag. Eine offene Frage bleibt freilich dennoch die tatsächliche Ethnogenese dieser Population. Dazu fehlen die notwendigen regional und zeitlich angrenzenden archäologisch umfassenden Aufarbeitungen der Quellen.

Betrachten wir nach diesen Vorbemerkungen das hier interessierende Gebiet der historischen Kupfer-Inuit: dort lassen sich Spuren einiger weiträumig definierter technohistorischer Stufen archäologisch nachweisen. Wir werden sehen, daß sogar auch der Anschluß der jüngsten prähistorischen Phase an die tatsächliche Frühgeschichte der Kupfer-Inuit möglich ist. Unsicher bleibt aber selbst deskriptiv der Beginn dieser kulturellen Einheit, und dies vor allem deshalb, weil die Wertigkeit des von außen geprägten Begriffes "Kupfer-Inuit" undeutlich bleibt. Hier wäre vor allem zu klären, ob sich tatsächlich regional faßbare Verbände zu einer entsprechend funktionalen übergeordneten Einheit autochthon zusammengefunden hatten. Doch dieses Problem soll besser zurückgestellt werden. Wir folgen der geographischen Definition, wie sie D. JENNESS (1922 und 1946) gegeben hat und wie sie von M. FREEMAN (1976) übernommen wurde. Die Gesamtfläche umfaßt etwa 250.000 Quadratkilometer und entspricht damit ziemlich gut der Fläche der Bundesrepublik Deutschland. Hauptachse ist der meist eher schmale Kanal, der von Union Strait, Dolphin Strait, Coronation Gulf and Queen Maud Gulf südlich von Victoria Island gebildet wird. Die historisch überlieferte Landnutzung reichte vom nordöstlichen Banks Island über den größten Teil von Victoria Island bis hinüber zur Baumgrenze auf dem Festland. Zu Beginn des 20. Jahrhunderts bestand die Bevölkerung aus wenig mehr als 700 Personen. Die jeweils aktuelle Nutzung verschob sich innerhalb des Gesamtareals jeweils nach den periodisch verfügbaren Nahrungsquellen.

Das gilt sicher auch für das früheste archäologisch faßbare kulturelle Niveau dieses Raumes, welches einen Teil des Pre-Dorset beinhaltet, das seinerseits zum länger andauernden Abschnitt der Arctic-Small-Tool (AST)-Komplexe gestellt wird (R. McGHEE 1978). Die relativ umfangreich ergrabene Station von Umingmak im zentralen Banks Island (H. MÜLLER-BECK 1977a, S. MÜNZEL 1983) zeigt, daß vor rund 3.200 Jahren auch im größeren Umfang während der wärmeren Jahreszeiten die Inlandsresourcen genutzt werden konnten. Dabei standen das Sammeln von Eiern, die Jagd auf Vögel und vor allem auf Moschusochsen im Vordergrund. Die genaue Analyse eines Ausschnittes der geborgenen Faunenreste (S. MÜNZEL 1983) beweist, daß zumindest partiell die Reproduktionsverhältnisse dieser an arktischen Bedingungen extrem angepaßten großen Säuger noch günstiger waren als in rezent beobachteten optimalen Perioden. Das potentielle Nahrungsangebot war also auch im Inland so groß, daß ein derart weites Hinausgreifen der menschlichen Nutzung offensichtlich riskiert werden konnte. Das war auch deswegen möglich, weil das Flucht- und Verteidigungsverhalten der Moschusochsen die Jagd über nur kurze Distanzen erleichterte. Das Risiko einer Versorgung auf Basis der sehr flüchtigen und zudem stark zersplitterten hocharktischen Karibu-Bestände wäre im Sommer sicher zu groß gewesen. Auch das oft schwankende Angebot an Vögeln und Fischen allein hätte wohl kaum ausgereicht. Schon der Gerätebestand in Umingmak bezeugt durch die Anwesenheit von Knebelharpunen (H. MÜLLER-BECK 1977b), daß eine gewisse Nutzung der Seesäugerresourcen erfolgte. Wahrscheinlich nahm diese im Winter zu. Allerdings läßt sich dies im Gegensatz zu den saisonal tatsächlich bestimmten Moschusochsenresten von Umingmak (S. MÜNZEL 1983) vorerst noch nicht durch konkrete Faunenanalysen nachweisen. Immerhin bestätigen die Sondagen von W. E. TAYLOR (1967) im südlichen Victoria Island für das Pre-Dorset generell die Seesäugernut-

zung durch Faunenreste.
Wir können also sicher sagen, daß das spätere Kupfer-Inuit-Gebiet in der Zeit des Pre-Dorset vor rund 3.500 bis 3.200 Jahren bis weit hinauf in den Norden genutzt worden ist. Wann diese Nutzung begann, ist noch unklar. Entsprechende frühere Funde fehlen bisher. Aber man muß im Auge behalten, daß nur dort Spuren von oft nur kurzfristigen Lagerplätzen bewahrt werden, wo deckende Sedimentbildungen sie ausreichend schützen. Das ist vor allem dann der Fall, wenn beginnende Klimaverschlechterungen zur Verstärkung der Massenbewegungen führen, wie das am Ende des vierten Jahrtausends vor heute weltweit der Fall war (Y. VASARI, H. HYVÄRINEN and S. HICKS 1972). Außerdem ist dort die Wahrscheinlichkeit größer, entsprechende Spuren zu entdecken, wo sich Lagerplätze durch günstige Bedingungen für die Nahrungsbeschaffung verdichten. Das ist in Umingmak auf einer Gesamtfläche von rund 10 Hektar gegeben (H. MÜLLER-BECK 1979). Andere Fundstellen aus der gleichen Zeit, wie etwa jene aus dem südlichen Victoria-Island, sichern die Ausdehnung dieser Nutzung ab. Sie stellt damit einen Ausschnitt aus der von R. McGHEE (1978) rekonstruierten Zone der Arctic-Small-Tool-Komplexe dar (Abb. 1).

Abbildung 1: Die erschlossene Verbreitung der "Arctic Small Tool Tradition" nach R. McGHEE 1978 mit Einzeichnung des historischen Kupfer-Inuit-Gebietes

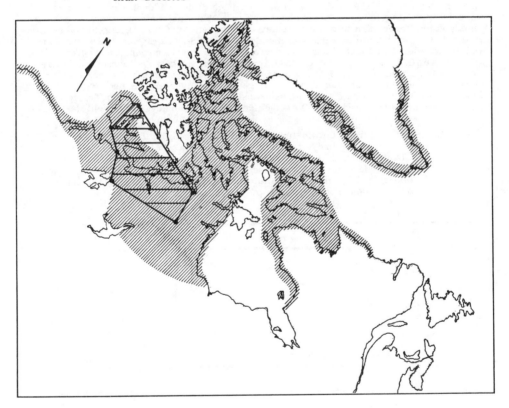

Wie groß in unserem Gebiet die damalige Population war, läßt sich nur schwer abschätzen. Sie hat kaum diejenige der dort historisch beobachteten Bevölkerung erreicht und war zugleich sicher Schwankungen unterworfen. Beachtlich ist die eindeutige Tatsache, daß zumindest in den letzten Jahrhunderten des vierten Jahrtausends vor heute eine Bejagung der nördlichsten Huftierfaunen noch jenseits der klassischen Lebensräume der Inuit mit ihren Karibu-Großherden möglich war. Welchen Umfang die Nutzung von Seesäugern schon besaß, bleibt vorerst unklar. Es wäre denkbar, daß im Sommer und bis zum Frühwinter ausreichende Vorräte angelegt werden konnten, um den Winter auch bei nur geringer ergänzender Jagd auf Robben im Eis zu überstehen. Es ist also nicht auszuschließen, daß gelegentlich die Inlandlager auch über den ganzen Winter beibehalten werden konnten. Daher sollten sich eigentlich Spuren festerer Behausungen finden, die bisher aus Umingmak noch nicht bekannt sind, wo allerdings auch noch kein ganzer Ar ausgegraben wurde. Derartige Fragen können durch Verdichtung der archäologischen Daten entschieden werden, die nur durch weitere Plangrabungen zu gewinnen sind. Das gilt etwa auch für das Problem der damaligen regionalen Untergliederung oder die Umreißung größerer übergeordneter Einheiten. Bei zu erwartender dünnerer Bevölkerung ist dabei keineswegs auszuschließen, daß derartige Großeinheiten zwei- bis dreimal so umfangreich waren wie das der historisch definierten Kupfer-Inuit. Es könnte aber auch sein, daß schon die Grundeinheiten selbst noch größere Flächen nutzten und zugleich autarker waren als später. Darüber hinausgreifende Einheiten mögen zwar vorhanden gewesen sein, aber daneben kaum besonderes funktionales Gewicht besessen haben.

Was nach 3200 zunächst in unserem Raum geschah, ist bisher wegen des Fehlens eindeutig hierher zu verweisender Funde unklar. Wahrscheinlich ist bei zunehmender Ungunst des Klimas ein Zurückweichen nach Süden anzunehmen, das bis zur vollständigen Aufgabe eines Abschnittes des schmalen Küstenstreifens auf dem Festland geführt haben könnte sowie zu einer erheblichen Ausdünnung der Bevölkerung in der Tundra nördlich des zurückweichenden Borealwaldes. Erst vor 2.300 ^{14}C-Jahren ist im südlichen Banks Island wieder eine Station nachweisbar, die Lagoon Site (CH. D. ARNOLD 1981). Sie hat gewisse Ähnlichkeiten mit dem Pre-Dorset auf Banks und dem Dorset der Ekalluk-River-Zone auf Victoria sowie auch mit dem dortigen Pre-Dorset. Es gibt aber auch sehr deutliche Züge im Fundinventar, die nach Westen und über die Mackenziemündung nach Alaska weisen und als Choris-Norton-Tradition definiert werden, welche sich vom Dorset eindeutig unterscheidet (Übersicht 1).

Übersicht 1: Die kulturelle Entwicklung von der "Arctic Small Tool Tradition" über die Trennung in "Norton" und "Dorset" bis zum Ausgreifen des "Thule" nach Osten und der ersten ethnogenetischen Schwelle im 11. Jahrhundert sowie der wahrscheinlichen Kombination von "Thule" und "Dorset" über die zweite ethnogenetische Schwelle im 17./18. Jahrhundert zu den historischen Kupfer-Inuit.

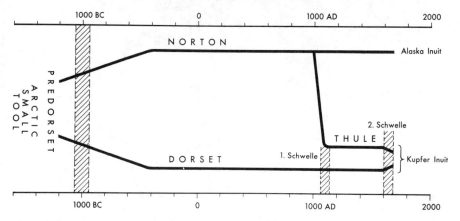

Besonders interessant ist die Zusammensetzung der Jagdfauna der an der Küste liegenden Lagoon Site. Im Vordergrund stehen hier mit insgesamt 55% der bestimmten Fragmente Schneegans und Schneehuhn, 21% Ringelrobbe, nur 0,1% Bartrobbe und noch immer mehr Moschusochsen (9%) als Karibus (0,5%). Wahrscheinlich wurden die Robben eher am Eisrand im Spätwinter und Frühjahr gejagt als mittels hochwinterlicher Atemlochtechnik. Das könnte einerseits bedeuten, daß auch hier schon ausreichende Wintervorräte anzulegen waren, andererseits daß die See-Eisjagd an Atemlöchern im Winter an einem anderen Ort, etwa weiter südwestlich, stattfand, wo dafür im ruhigen Flacheis günstigere Bedingungen herrschten als im sich am Eingang des Amundsen Gulf sich leichter aufstauenden Packeis. Der relativ hohe Anteil von Moschusochsen spricht wieder dafür, daß wir uns eher in der Nähe der damaligen Nordgrenze der menschlichen Ökumene befinden und daß die Großherden bildenden Karibus auch damals Banks nicht erreicht haben. Nach den bisher ausgewerteten bekannten Daten ist es wahrscheinlicher, daß für den heute ergrabenen Teil der Station die Schneegansjagd und Ringelrobben-Küstenjagd bzw. See-Eisrandjagd eher für eine Frühjahrs- bis Sommerjagd sprechen. Die genauere Bestimmung des Individualalters der Beutetiere steht noch aus, so daß keine definitive Aussage dazu gemacht werden kann, wie das in Umingmak möglich war.

Die Inventare im südlichen Victoria Island, die in der Ballentine Site auf 2450 + 220 und 2200 + 140 und in der Joss Site auf 1860 + 100 ^{14}C-Jahre vor heute datiert werden, gehören alle einem deutlich ausgeprägten frühen Dorset-Komplex an, der keine ausgeprägteren Stilzüge des Norton aus dem Westen besitzt (CH. D. ARNOLD 1981, W. E. TAYLOR 1967). Diese Inventare ähneln vielmehr stark jenen im Foxe Basin, einem der Kerngebiete der anschließenden Dorset-Entfaltung. Es sieht am ehesten so aus, als ob wir jetzt einer Trennung der Entwicklung in eine westliche Komponente, die aber doch über die Mackenziemündung nach Osten greift, und einer östlichen, dem klassischen Dorset der kanadischen Arktis, gegenüberstehen. Die Stilareale im Westen werden zum Teil sehr kleinräumig, offensichtlich in Abhängigkeit von der durch die Gunst der Resourcen möglichen Verdichtung (H.-G. BANDI 1965). Im Osten sieht es dagegen so aus, als ob der ganze kontinentale Küstenstreifen eine große Einheit bildet, die auch die gegenüberliegenden Inseln mit einbezieht, während einerseits nur Neufundland und seine Nachbarschaft, das damals auch Teil der Dorset-Entwicklung ist, und andererseits das südliche Grönland eine gewisse Eigenständigkeit besitzen.

Wir können daraus schließen, daß in der zweiten Hälfte des dritten Jahrtausends vor heute und auch noch zu Beginn des vorletzten im Gebiet der späteren Kupfer-Inuit die technische, stilistische und damit nach archäologischen Maßstäben auch kulturelle Tradition des Dorset vorherrscht. Nur im äußersten Westen mögen auch Elemente aufgetreten sein, die eher zu Traditionen gehören, die ihre Hauptentwicklung in Alaska besitzen. Auch dieser Befund entspricht noch immer den Rekonstruktionsvorschlägen von R. McGHEE (1978) in ihren Hauptzügen. Allenfalls könnte das westliche Norton im Winter es bis hinüber zu den ruhigen See-Eisflächen des Minto Inlet oder des Prince Albert Sound im westlichen Victoria Island ausgegriffen haben (Abb. 2).

Danach scheint die Funddichte in unserem Raum nachzulassen. Jedenfalls fehlt nach rund 100 n.Chr. oder etwa 1850 ^{14}C-Jahre vor heute das Mittlere Dorset. Ob es sich ganz nach Osten zurückgezogen hat oder ob seine Spuren bei insgesamt schlechteren Klimabedingungen zu dünn wurden, daß sie nicht wieder aufgenommen haben, ist noch unklar. Auch das spätere Norton fehlt. Es hat sich mit seinem Schwergewicht jetzt in Alaska und den dort günstigeren Jagdgründen etabliert. Die Eigenständigkeit des Dorset ist jedenfalls unübersehbar. Auch die Endphasen des Dorset sind in den Randzonen nicht allzu gut belegt, tauchen aber wieder auf dem südlichen Victoria Island auf (W. E. TAYLOR 1967) und lassen sich etwa auch auf Ellesmere (R. McGHEE 1978) oder neuerdings sogar kurz vor Beginn des 12. Jahrhunderts (etwa vor 850 ^{14}C-Jahren) auf Bathurst Island, nördlich von Victoria, das allerdings am einfachsten auch von Südosten her erreichbar ist, erkennen. Ob sich darin eine Ausdehnung der eingeengten Siedlungszone des Mitteldorset, verursacht durch verbesserte klimatische Bedingungen, andeutet, ist noch ungewiß. Es könnte auch aus den gleichen Gründen eine Verdichtung der Siedlungspunkte bei zunehmender Bevölkerung erfolgt sein, die dann eher aufzufinden wären. Ebensowenig ist auszuschließen, daß wieder spezielle Sedimentationsbedingungen zum Auffinden führen. So sind die genannten Spätdorset-Spuren von Bathurst als Spolien und sekundäre Einbettungen im Zusammenhang mit einer frühen Thule-Siedlung beobachtet worden (R. McGHEE 1984 b).

Immer deutlicher wird jedenfalls, daß das späte Dorset wieder weit verbreitet war und auch im späteren Kupfer-Inuit-Gebiet nicht fehlt. Das anschließende frühe

Abbildung 2: Die erschlossene Verbreitung des "Dorset" nach R. McGHEE 1978 als eigenständige zentral- und ostarktische Erscheinung mit Einzeichnung des historischen Kupfer-Inuit-Gebietes

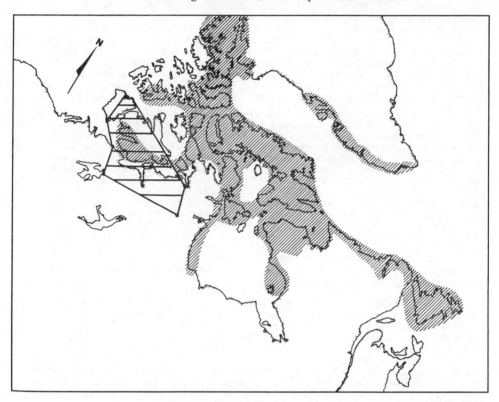

Thule überlagert offensichtlich mit kurzer zeitlicher Distanz zumindest in Teilregionen das spätere Dorset, wie etwa gerade die eben erwähnten Funde dieses auf Entwicklungen in Kanada fußenden Kulturkomplexes in Brooman Point auf Bathurst Island bei etwas mehr als 75° Nord dokumentieren. Von dort liegen zwei ^{14}C-Datierungen vor für eine gut gegrabene frühe Thule-Siedlung mit 870 ± 30 BP (BM-1803) und 800 ± BP (BM-1804), also 1080/1150 im Mittelwert n.Chr.Geb. (R. McGHEE 1984b). Es spricht einiges dafür, daß die Expansion dieses Komplexes, der offensichtlich mit auf der Jagd auf größere Wale von Hautbooten aus fußt, recht plötzlich erfolgt ist. R. McGHEE (1985) nimmt sogar an, daß es sich um regelrechte Explorationsvorstöße handelt, die sich in die Bereiche lockeren Eises eben gerade nördlich von Banks und Victoria auf Melville und Lancaster Sound bis zur Baffinbay bewegten. Hauptgrund für diese Vorstöße sieht er in der Suche nach Metall, das tatsächlich in Nordwest-Grönland bei Cape York in Form von Meteor-Eisen vorkommt. Dies steht damit in Übereinstimmung, daß bereits das frühe Thule in ganz erheblichem Umfang - vor allem für feinere Schnitzarbeiten - tatsächlich eiserne Klingen einsetzte und zugleich das Steingerätinventar gegenüber demjenigen des Dorset sehr rasch vor allem in den kleineren Einsatzformen verarmte. Es spricht sehr viel dafür, daß schon um 1150 Elemente der Thule-Kultur auch auf Grönland anzutreffen waren, wie etwa gerade die Walnutzung und der Bau von Walhäusern (unter Verwendung von Rippen und Kiefern), von denen al-Idrisi auf Sizilien für die "innersten Inseln des Nordatlantiks" bereits weiß (R. McGHEE 1984a). Der erste Direktkontakt zwischen den nach Nordwesten vorstoßenden Wikingern und den Thule-Inuit (Abb. 3) ist erst auf 1266 an der Westküste Grönlands anzusetzen (R. McGHEE 1984a). Daß die Beeinflussung Grönlands von Europa aus ebenfalls in erster Linie durch wirtschaftli-

Abbildung 3: Die erschlossene Verbreitung von Merkmalen des "Thule-Komplexes" nach R. McGHEE 1978 mit Einzeichnung des historischen Kupfer-Inuit-Gebietes

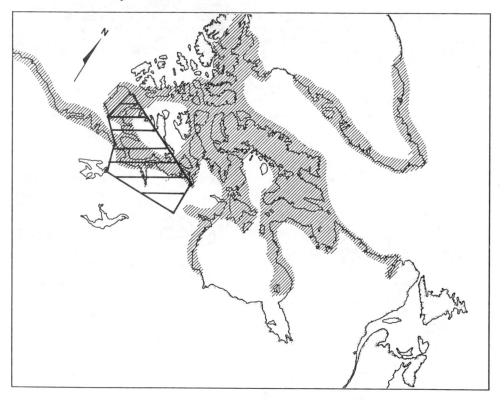

liche Interessen ausgelöst wurde, ist gut belegt (H. STEINERT 1982). Im Vordergrund stand dabei das wertvolle Walroß-Elfenbein. Aber selbst Grönlandfalken spielten als Exportgut für die Beizjagd im Orient eine Rolle.

Unklar ist vorerst das Verhältnis zwischen diesen neu nach Osten sich ausbreitenden Thule-Komponenten. In der Regel wird aber angenommen, daß diese neue Welle die alten Populationen völlig ersetzte (R. McGHEE 1978). Archäologisch läßt sich das aber keineswegs bestätigen. Vor allem geht es dabei um das Problem des Verbleibs der autochthonen Dorset-Gruppen. Eine ganze Anzahl von Befunden gerade im Kupfer-Inuit-Gebiet könnte auch für eine reine technische Beeinflussung und damit partielle Akkulturation der bisherigen Dorset-Jäger sprechen. So zeigt etwa die Bloody Falls Site am Westufer des Coppermine Rivers, etwa 10 Meilen landeinwärts, nicht nur eine intensive Fisch-, sondern zugleich auch eine starke Karibu-Nutzung. Neben zwei relativ leichten Häusern im Stil der Thule-Konstruktionen wurden zwei Zeltringe untersucht. Die Datierung in den Zeitraum des Thule zwischen 1200 und 1600 ist ausreichend gesichert. Natürlich wäre hier einfach auch eine Landaktivitätszone der Thule-Leute anzunehmen. Aber derartige Befunde häufen sich auch an anderen Stellen unseres Raumes. So fanden sich in der Memorana Site am Ende des Prince Albert Sounds unweit von Holman nur wenig Walknochen, aber 72% Ringelrobbe und 26% Karibu neben wenig Resten von Bartrobbe, Schneehase, Eisfuchs, Vögeln und Fischen (R. McGHEE 1971), also ein Inventar, das auch der Dorset-Tradition entsprechen könnte. Andererseits gibt es Walknochen-Depots der Kupfer-Inuit noch etwas weiter nördlicher am Minto-Inlet (R. McGHEE 1971). Weiter südlich auf Victoria hat die Clare Site vor allem Karibu erbracht (W. TAYLOR 1972), ebenso die Pembroke Site (W. TAYLOR 1972), während die Bell Site dazu noch Seesäuger, Füchse, Moschusochsen, Vögel und Fisch enthielt (W. TAYLOR 1972). Das gilt auch für die Station am Lady Franklin Point, wo bei guter Knochenerhaltung zeitlich aus dem Frühen Thule 82% der Reste dem Karibu und 17% den Robben zuzuordnen waren. Das ist besonders bemerkenswert, da diese Station am Meer liegt, aber in einem Gebiet, in dem später die Kupfer-Inuit vor allem ebenfalls Karibu gejagt haben (W. TAYLOR 1972, D. R. FARQUHARSON 1976). Dagegen liegt 15 Meilen WNW von Bernard Harbour eine Thule-Station, die Wale erbracht hat (W. TAYLOR 1972) (Abb. 4).

Abbildung 4: Die Hauptnutzungsareale der Kupfer-Inuit am Minto-Inlet und am Prince-Albert-Sound um die Jahrhundertwende

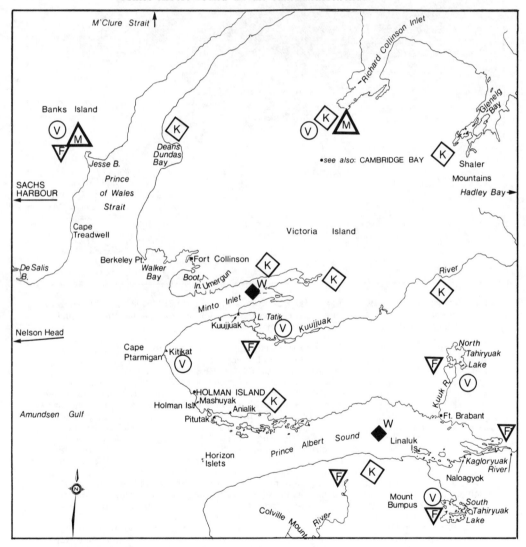

W=Winterlager auf dem See-Eis (Robbenjagd), K=Karibujagd, M=Moschusochsenjagd, V=Vogeljagd, F=Fischfang in Seen und Flüssen. Kartenunterlage aus D. F. FARQUHARSON 1976, Eintragungen des Autors nach FARQUHARSON 1976 mit Ergänzungen.

Es würde an dieser Stelle zu weit führen, auf diese Problematik näher einzugehen. Zudem sind die meisten hier genannten Stationen bisher nur in sehr kleinen Ausschnitten ergraben. Dabei geht es um eine der archäologischen Grundfragen. Aber erwähnt sei doch wenigstens ein Beispiel, wo eine ähnliche Frage als gelöst angesehen werden kann. Im Neolithikum der Schweiz war es über Jahrzehnte eine klare archäologische Vorstellung, daß das durch einen Keramikstil definierte jungsteinzeitliche Cortaillod der Westschweiz durch das aus Nordwesten einwandernde - ebenfalls durch seine Keramik definierte - Horgen abgelöst wurde, also eine Mechanik, die ganz derjenigen der Dorset-Thule-Folge entspricht. Neuere Grabungen mit einer über 800jährigen Stratigraphie haben nun in Twann am Bielersee gezeigt, daß die Horgener Keramik allmählich die Cortaillod-Gefäße ersetzt haben (H. MÜLLER-BECK 1984). Dahinter steht ein technischer funktioneller Wandel, dessen Zentrum tatsächlich weiter nördlich liegen dürfte. Und genau dies ist auch für die Thule-Beeinflussung denkbar, die zwar auch echte Einwanderungskomponenten außerhalb des ständig festen Eises aufweist, wie R. McGHEE (1984b) recht überzeugend nachweist, aber eben auch eine Übertragungskomponente auf die autochthone Dorset-Grundbevölkerung sehr wohl enthalten kann.

Interessant ist in diesem Zusammenhang, daß sich die historischen Kupfer-Inuit, deren Lebensweisen erst zu Beginn dieses Jahrhunderts näher erforscht wurden (D. JENNESS 1922, D. R. FARQUHARSON 1976, H. MÜLLER-BECK 1982), bewußt betont hart geben. Tatsächlich ähnelte ihre Lebensweise nach 1600 - also mit der einsetzenden und dann anhaltenden Klimaverschlechterung - eher wieder der der Dorset-Leute (R. McGHEE 1978). Die großen Seesäuger, die für das klassische Thule so kennzeichnend sind, fehlen nahezu vollständig zwischen Union Strait und Queen Maud Gulf. Erste Kontakte mit Europäern erfolgten hier erst zu Beginn des 19. Jahrhunderts. Diese brachen noch einmal zwischen 1850 und 1900 im Zuge der starken Klimaverschlechterungen ab, um dann seit der von d. JENNESS (1922) geleiteten Expedition um 1916 nicht mehr aufzuhören. Zu den Mackenzie-Inuit im Westen, die durch Krankheiten nach dem Kontakt mit amerikanischen Walfängern praktisch nahezu erloschen, bestand keine Beziehung mehr. Wahrscheinlich war sie auch vor 1800 nur noch gering. Weniger klar ist die Abgrenzung nach Osten, die aber auf keinen Fall so deutlich war wie die nach dem Westen. Stärker war sicher auch die Abgrenzung gegen die Indianer der Taiga im Süden, die sich noch durch den Eingriff europäischer Wirtschaftsinteressen verschärft haben dürfte. Insgesamt lassen sich die Kupfer-Inuit in der Definition von D. JENNESS (1922) auf vier bis sechs Lokalgruppen verteilen (D. R. FARQUHARSON 1976, H. MÜLLER-BECK 1982), die zwischen gut 200 und 50 Individuen umfaßten oder grob zwischen etwas über 40 und 10 Familien. Die größte Gruppe lebte am Minto Inlet und am Prince Albert Sound, wo im Winter auf dem Eis die Atemlochjagd auf Robben, im Frühjahr und Sommer die Vogeljagd und der Fischfang in aufgelockerten Gruppen im Inland wie ebenso die Jagd auf Moschusochsen auch auf Banks und, eher im Herbst, auf Karibus betrieben wurden (Abb. 4). Dazu kamen noch einmal herbstlicher Fischfang und herbstliche Vogeljagd, bevor jede der beiden Gruppen wieder enger auf dem Eis von Minto Inlet und Prince Albert Sound mit je 20 Familien zusammenkam, um, gut bevorratet, die großen Feste des Winters zu feiern.

Die bisherigen archäologischen Daten nach 1600, die den Kupfer-Inuit zuzuordnen sind (R. McGHEE 1978, P. SCHLEDERMANN 1975, J. HAHN 1976, I. CAMPEN 1977, C. G. HICKEY & D. G. STEELE 1978), stehen mit diesen Beobachtungen im Einklang. Allerdings sind sie vorläufig noch sehr sporadisch und gehören offensichtlich meist in das 19. Jahrhundert. Ganz eindeutig wurde die Nutzung auf Banks stark ausgedehnt, was zugleich mit der Verwendung des in der Mercy Bay aufgegebenen Schiffes "Investigator" als Rohmaterialquelle zusammenhängen dürfte (C. G. HICKEY 1984). Zu Beginn des 20. Jahrhunderts wurde die Nutzung von Banks fast ganz aufgegeben. Im Zuge der Schul- und der damit zusammenhängenden Siedlungspolitik der kanadischen Regierung seit Mitte des Jahrhunderts kam es zu den Konzentrationen in Holman Island, Coppermine, Bathurst Inlet und Cambridge Bay, die tatsächlich alle historisch als Kupfer-Inuit-Orte anzusehen sind. Dies gilt nicht für Sachs Harbour auf Banks Island, das vor allem von Neusiedlern aus Alaska und aus noch größeren Distanzen besiedelt wurde, und genausowenig für Tuktuyaktuk, das ebenfalls vor allem eine Siedlung von Neueinwanderern darstellt und auch nie im Bereich der Kupfer-Inuit, sondern im Siedlungsraum der Mackenzie-Inuit lag. Welche politischen Komponenten hier heute eine Rolle spielen, schildert ausführlich der Beitrag von W. C. WONDERS in diesem Band.

Wir aber haben unser Thema damit erschöpft, soweit dies in einem kurzen Aufsatz möglich ist. Der gesamte Ablauf besitzt also eine über drei Jahrtausende hinweg erkennbare Dynamik. Sie ist naturgemäß anders mit archäologischen Mitteln zu beschreiben als in den späteren frühgeschichtlichen Phasen, die freilich noch kein Jahrhundert umfassen. Nach der weiträumigen Phase der Arctic Small Tools, zu denen die Inlandmoschusochsenjäger von Banks und zeitgleiche Stationen weiter östlich gehören, folgt das auf die Ostarktis beschränkte Dorset. Dieses trennt sich offenbar an der späteren Grenzlinie von Mackenzie- und Kupfer-Inuit vom Westen um Christi Geburt ab. Möglicherweise verdünnt sich in der Folge bei schlechteren Klimabedingungen die autochthone Bevölkerung, die jetzt die typische See-Eis-Jagd schon in größerem Umfang betreibt. Um 1000 ist sie aber mit Verbesserung der Umweltbedingungen und damit der Säugerproduktivität in der Lage, sich wiederum weiter auszudehnen und zuvor aufgegebene Streifgebiete bis hinauf nach Bathurst wieder zu nutzen. Erst im 11. Jahrhundert wird durch den Vorstoß der Walfänger aus Alaska eine neue Entwicklung ausgelöst, die aber alte Traditionen eher ergänzt und gerade im Kupfer-Inuit-Gebiet kaum zu einem vollen Populationsaustausch geführt hat. Es werden aber derart viele technische Komponenten, bis hin vor allem zur Metallnutzung, übernommen, daß jetzt das Thule als technische Komponente vorherrscht und als Zeitstil das bisherige Dorset vor allem in der Werkzeugausstattung ersetzt oder ergänzt. Gerade hierzu wären größere Grabungen und genauere Objektanalysen notwendig. Mit dem Ausklang des Thule bilden sich dann endlich erst jene Komponenten, die als typisch für die historischen Kupfer-Inuit gelten können, deren Lebensstrategien sich von denjenigen der Thule-Leute schon wegen der Änderungen im Ökosystem der Meersäuger vor allem deutlich unterscheiden.

Irgendwo zwischen 1600 und 1800 würde man also die "endgültige" Ethnogenese der Kupfer-Inuit ansetzen müssen, wenn man einen solchen Schwellenwert sucht. Im wirklichen Fluß des Lebens scheint das dem Autor aber wenig sinnvoll. Denn diese Marke wird von einem Kontinuum der Raumnutzung und damit auch der lokalen Kulturentwicklung zugleich überbrückt. Dabei ist auch unwichtig, wie stark die Dorset-Komponente nach dem Jahre 1000 in unserem Raum noch weiterlebte und sich gegen Thule-Aspekte behaupten konnte. Zugleich müssen wir uns daran erinnern, daß auch der Begriff Kupfer-Inuit regional gefaßt ist und nach Osten hin eher verschwommen wirkt. Historisch und damit auch politisch konkreter wird die Diskussion, wenn man sich auf die kleineren Nutzungszonen konzentriert. Hier ist etwa der Zusammenhang zwischen den Gruppen vom Minto Inlet und Prince Albert Sound mit der modernen Kommune auf Holman Island über mindestens zwei Jahrhunderte gesichert. Es mögen auch vier oder gar ein ganzes Jahrtausend sein - eingerechnet die Wiederausbreitung des späten Dorset und die anschließende kontinuierliche Akkulturation in das Thule. Größenordnungen also, die auch europäische Gemeinden selten nachweisen können.

Anders verhält es sich in Sachs Harbour und Tuytuyaktuk. Hier haben wir mit Orten zu tun, die erst in den letzten 50 bis 60 Jahren neu entstanden sind und in denen allfällige lokalhistorische Traditionen nur geringes Gewicht besitzen. Insgesamt sind sie auf andere Art historisch-politisch und damit auch durchaus faktisch begründet. Das spricht sicher nicht dagegen, daß etwa Tuk, Sachs und Holman, wie man heute dort oben sagt, miteinander eine übergeordnete politische Einheit bilden. Es wären auch andere Kombinationen denkbar, in denen etwa Holman stärker mit Coppermine, Bathurst oder sogar Cambridge Bay verbunden wäre. Das aber sind Entscheidungen, die nur unter Mitwirkung der ansässigen Bevölkerungen gefällt werden können. Wie sich danach das kommunale Recht an den jeweils zugehörigen Landnutzflächen und angrenzenden Küstengewässern entwickelt, wird die Zukunft zeigen. Eine sachgerechte Berücksichtigung historischer Gegebenheiten wird dabei auch für diese politisch wichtigen Entscheidungen nur förderlich sein.

Literatur

Arnold, Charles D., 1981: The Lagoon Site (OjRl-3): Implications for Paleoeskimo Interactions. Mercury Series No. 107. Nat. Mus. of Man, Ottawa.

Bandi, Hans-Georg, 1965: Urgeschichte der Eskimos. Gustav Fischer, Stuttgart.

Campen, Ingo, 1977: Head Hill Flat Site, ein Herbstlagerplatz der Kupfer-Eskimos auf Banks Island, N.W.T. Polarforschungen 47, 38-46.

Clark, Donald Woodford, 1974: Koniag Prehistory: Archaeological Investigation at Late Prehistoric Sites on Kodiak Island, Alaska. Tübinger Mon. Urgeschichte 1. Kohlhammer. Stuttgart.

Farquharson, Don F., 1976: Inuit Land Use in the West-Central Canadian Arctic. In: Milton M. R. Freeman, 33-61.

Freeman, Milton M. R., 1976: Report: Inuit Land Use and Occupancy Project. Department of Indian and Northern Affairs, Gov. of Canada, Ottawa.

Hahn, Joachim, 1976: Ein Eskimo-Werkzeug-Cache von Banks Island, N.W.T., Kanada. Polarforschungen 36, 95-105.

Hickey, Clifford G., 1984: Ethnohistoric Research among the Copper Inuit: Combining Archaeology, History and Ethnography to Understand Cultural Change. Report Conference on Regional Studies in the Archaeology and History of the Canadian Arctic. Bamberg/Tübingen.

— & Steele, Gentry D., 1978: Of Man and Muskox: New light on a very old relationship. Paper Annual Meeting Can. Archaeol. Ass. Quebec City.

Jenness, Diamond, 1922: The Life of the Copper Eskimos. Canadian Arctic Expedition 1913-1918, Volume XII, Ottawa.

— 1946: Material Culture of the Eskimos. Canadian Arctic Expedition 1913-1918, Volume XVI, Ottawa.

McGhee, Robert, 1971: An Archaeological Survey on Western Victoria Island, N.W.T. Canada. Nat. Mus. Canada Bull. 232, 158-191.

— 1972: Copper Eskimo Prehistory. Publications in Archaeology, No. 2. Nat. Mus. of Man, Ottawa.

— 1978: Canadian Arctic Prehistory. Nat.Mus. of Man, Ottawa.

— 1984: Contact between Native North Americans and the Mediaeval Norse. Amer. Antiquity, 49, 4-26 (1984 a).

— 1984: The Thule Village at Brooman Point, High Arctic Canada. Mercury Series No. 125, Ottawa (1984 b).

— 1984: The Timing of the Thule Migration. Polarforschung 55 (in press).

Müller-Beck, Hansjürgen, 1977: Excavations at Umingmak on Banks Island, N.W.T., 1970 and 1973. Preliminary Report. Archaeol. Venatoria Urgeschichtliche Materialhefte 1, Tübingen (1977 a).

— 1977: Bone Tools from Umingmak I A and I D. In: H. Müller-Beck, 58-71 (1977 b).

Müller-Beck, Hansjürgen, 1979: Das Ökosystem der Moschusochsenjägerstation Umingmak. In: A. Pletsch und C. Schott (Hrsg.): Kanada: Naturraum und Entwicklungspotential. Marburger Geogr. Schriften 79, 97-112.

— 1982: Naturräumliche Nutzung als Basis kultureller Gliederung im arktischen und subarktischen Kanada. Zeitschr. Ges. Kanada Studien 2, 45-62.

— 1984: Besprechung von Prähistorischer Zeitschrift 55, 1980. Tribus 33, 214-216.

Münzel, Susanne, 1983: Seasonal Activities at Umingmak, a Muskox-Hunting Site on Banks Island, N.W.T., Canada. With Special Reference to the Bird Remains. In: J. Clutton-Brock & C. Grigson (Eds.): Animals and Archaeology: 1. Hunters and their Prey. British Archaeol. Reports, Intern. Series 163, Oxford, 249-257.

Salis, Jean R. v., 1980: Weltgeschichte der Neuesten Zeit, Bd. I. 1: Die deutsche Vormachtstellung in Europa. Orell Füssli, Zürich.

Schledermann Peter, 1975: Muskox Hunters on Banks Island and other Considerations. Paper Conference on Archaeology of Western Canada, Calgary.

Steinert, Harald, 1982: Tausend Jahre Neue Welt. Auf den Spuren der Wikinger in Grönland und Amerika. Deutsche Verlags-Anstalt, Stuttgart.

Taylor, William E. Jr., 1972: An Archaeological Survey between Cape Perry and Cambridge Bay, N.W.T. Canada. Mercury Series No. 1, Nat. Mus. of Man, Ottawa.

Vasari, Yrjöi, Hyväkinen, Hannu & Hicks, Sheila, 1972: Climatic Changes in Arctic Areas during the Last Ten-Thousand Years. Univers. Oulu. Oulu.

Address of the author:
Prof. Dr. Hansjürgen Müller-Beck
Institut für Urgeschichte
(Jägerische Archäologie)
Schloß
7400 Tübingen 1

Sami and Ethnicity Problems in Finland

Marjut and Pekka Aikio

Abstract: The authors discuss the importance of language maintenance and reindeer herding as elements of the ethnicity of the Sami people as indigenous people and ethnic minority in northern Fenno-Scandia (Finland, Norway and Sweden). Sami language and Sami reindeer herding have long been considered the cultural hallmark of Sami identity internally and externally in relation with neighboring cultures. Based on the examination of historical records and recent surveys conducted in Vuotso, a Reindeer Sami village in the Sami Home Region of northern Finland, the authors argue that Sami ethnicity does not solely rely on language and reindeer herding but that ancestry and other characteristics play an important role in the maintenance of ethnicity.

Résumé: Les auteurs de cet article discutent l'importance et de la maintenance de la langue "Sami" et de l'économie nomade pour l'ethnicité des "Sami" comme population autochthone en même temps que minorité ethnique dans la partie septentrionale de la Fennoskandinavie (Finlande, Norvège et Suède). La langue ainsi que le nomadisme pastoral de rennes ont été depuis longtemps, considérés comme élements de base les plus importants, internément et externément, de l'identité "Sami". Utilisant des documents historiques et se basant sur une enquête effectuée auprès de la population "Sami" à Vuotso, village dans la Laponie finlandaise centrale, les auteurs élaborent l'hypothèse que "langue" et "nomadisme pastoral" ne suffisent pas comme critères d'ethnicité "Sami", mais que la descendence et d'autres critères jouent également un rôle important.

Zusammenfassung: Die Autoren dieses Beitrages erörtern die Bedeutung der Erhaltung der samischen Sprache und Rentierwirtschaft für die Ethnizität der Sami als Urbevölkerung und ethnische Minderheit im nördlichen Fennoskandien (Finnland, Norwegen und Schweden). Sprache und Rentierwirtschaft sind seit langem als die wichtigsten kulturellen Kernelemente der samischen Identität angesehen worden, die nach innen und außen gleichermaßen wirken. Anhand der Überprüfung historischer Unterlagen und einer Untersuchung der heutigen Ethnizität der samischen Bevölkerung in Vuotso, einem Dorf im mittleren Finnisch-Lappland, kommen die Autoren zu der Auffassung, daß Sprache und Rentierwirtschaft nicht allein als Kernelemente samischer Identität anzusehen sind, da Abstammung und andere Kriterien eine Rolle spielen.

Ethnicity and Language

The questions focussing on Sami ethnicity have been touched upon in several works (e.g. Asp 1965, 1966; Eidheim 1969; Svensson 1976). Especially during the last few years new results have been published that diverge from the traditional trends in research on the Sami (Müller-Wille 1974; Bjørklund 1983).

According to Allardt and Starck (1981), an ethnic group consists of a number of people having certain cultural, linguistic or other characteristics, e.g. 'racial', having also - at least partly - a common genesis and sharing a feeling of togetherness. That definition gives us several indicators of ethnicity, such as cultural characteristics, origin, ancestry and identity. The same authors, with reference to Frederik Barth (1969), stress it is not their cultural content but the boundaries between them that make groups ethnicly distinct. Since the boundaries are not permanent, the mechanisms creating and maintaining them are important in the study of ethnic groups. These mechanisms operate with classifications made by others and by the groups themselves. People use their ethnic identification to classify themselves and others, in order to regulate personal interactions. That is where, Barth suggests, ethnic groups come into existence.

Ethnic groups are not everlasting. Because of the nature of ethnic groups, both ethnic feelings and the social meaning of ethnic groupings can change quite quickly and fundamentally. According to sociolinguist Joshua Fishman (1965, 1972, 1977), we should not forget the dynamics of ethnicity and the perpetual differences in degrees of belonging to an ethnic group, neither should we make rash resolutions about inaccuracy of boundaries. Boundaries between groups may be unclear and difficult to study, but the cores of groups may, nevertheless, be clear. Belonging to an ethnic group is characterized by Allardt and Starck (1981) as follows: There can be different reasons for belonging to the same ethnic group. Further, grounds relevant to every member for belonging to an ethnic group do not exist. However, some portion, usually the majority, of the members of a minority must fulfill certain conditions in order for us to be able to speak of an ethnic group. For example, Allardt and Starck say, it is peculiar to speak about a linguistic group or a linguistic minority unless at least some members of the group do not master that language. It is language that is a necessary condition for the existence of linguistic minorities. However, every member of the minority need not command it. Some people are considered to belong to a group because of their ancestry or because they are regarded by themselves or others as members of the group. According to the same authors, we can identify four such necessary conditions - and at least some members of the minority must fulfill them - before we can speak about an ethnic group. Further, everybody considered to belong to the group must fulfill at least one of these four conditions.

1. Self-identification based on one's classification:
2. Ancestry;
3. Special cultural characteristics, e.g., command of a language;
4. Existing social organization for interaction among members.

Sociolinguists are usually satisfied with the first three conditions; social anthropologists emphasize the fourth condition as well, that is the meaning of the social organization regulating interaction between ethnic groups. The viewpoints of both sociolinguists and social anthropologists are worthy of consideration. The conditions are differentiated by their nature, because, among other things, the first three requirements pertain to individual characteristics, the fourth to properties of groups. The central question about which is a person's language, his or her mother tongue or first learned language, best spoken or mostly used, is not so easy to answer.

The Sami People and Ethnic Criteria in Northern Fenno-Scandia

In the Fenno-Scandian context, the language of the Sami is divided into several major dialects - some linguists speak of independent languages. Traditionally, nine dialects were distinguished starting in the southern Sami areas with Southern Sami and ending in the northeastern parts with Russian Sami on the Kola Peninsula. In respect to ethnicity, there always has been a strong connection between belonging to the Sami people and having Sami as the first learned language. This connection, e.g., has entered the official definition of a Sami in Finland; in Norway and Sweden this ethnic definition is under discussion.

There are no reliable population figures for the Sami in Fenno-Scandia. The confusion is probably the result of the terms referring to a Sami: in Norway the terms has been 'finn', in Sweden 'lapp' and in Finland 'lappalainen'. The designation 'Sami' is the genetive plural form and comes from the word 'sabmi'. 'Sami' means the Sami people and the land of the Sami; it is this term the Sami themselves prefer as the officially accepted name for themselves as the indigenous people of northern Fenno-Scandia. In Norwegian and in Finnish 'saamelainen'.

Recent historical research in Finland has suggested that the term 'lappalainen' (Swedish 'lapp') was a legal term at least until the end of the 18th century (Hyvärinen 1982). It referred to a person who had the legal right to engage in the so-called 'Lapp livelihood' based on reindeer herding, hunting and fishing. One vestige of this is that, to this day, in Sweden (as well as Norway) only Sami engaged in reindeer herding are considered ethnic Sami (Wikman 1960). Obviously, a large number of other ethnic Sami are not included in this definition.

Varying figures on the number of Sami have been presented based on different criteria: language, ethnic origin and Sami livelihood, particularly reindeer herding (Table 1). The traditionally accepted figures are disregarded today because official census figures were provided on the Sami population in both Finland and Sweden during the 1960s and 1970s.

Table 1: The Sami Population in Northern Fenno-Scandia and USSR

	Traditionally Accepted Figures	Minimum Figures in the 1970s	Actual Figures in the 1980s	Estimates by Sami
Finland	3,000	4,500 (1)	5,000	
Norway	20,000	27,500 (2)	40,000	
Sweden	10,000	17,000 (3)	20,000	
USSR	1,500	2,000	2,000	
Total	34,500	51,000	67,000	100,000

(1) Komitea 1973: 46; Asp 1965; Nickul, E. 1968
(2) Aubert 1978
(3) Samerna ... 1975

The largest Sami population lives in Norway, where the data on the number of the Sami people perhaps contains the most deficiencies. The study by Aubert (1978) covers the central area inhabited by Sami, that is, almost the entire province of Finnmark (88.7% of the total area), and part of the provinces of Troms (22.9%) and Nordland (6.1%).

While the Swedish Sami population numbers between 17,000 to 20,000 individuals, only 10 to 20% of them are reindeer herders. Norway was found to have approximately 2 500 Sami reindeer herders, i.e. 5 to 10%. It is apparent that the number of reindeer herders is only a fraction of the Sami population, although reindeer herding is seen as an important element in Sami ethnicity.

The Swedish Sami Delegation to the Nordic Sami Conference has traditionally been nominated by the National Association of Swedish Sami which mainly represents reindeer herders. Previous to the conference held in Ohcejohka (Utsjoki), Finland in August 1983, the discussion of the nomination of the Swedish Sami Delegation was rather heated. At debate was what portion of the representation should belong to the traditionally powerful reindeer herders' organization and what portion to the other Sami institutions, above all to Sami Ätnam, a cultural organization. At the Ohcejohka Conference the representation of these two main Swedish Sami organizations was equally shared, but for the future the problem has still remained unsolved.

The Norwegian Sami Delegation to the conference has been nominated by both the National Association of the Norwegian (Reindeer) Sami and the Central Union of the Norwegian Sami. In Finland, the Sami Parliament, elected by the Finnish Sami, since its establishment under law in 1973, has formed the conference delegation with its 20 members. Since the Ohcejohka Conference all Nordic Sami delegations are equal in size, all having 20 delegates.

Finland is the only Nordic country whose official legal definition of a Sami is on a linguistic basis. A person is a Sami if she/he speaks or has spoken Sami as the first language or if at least one of her/his parents or grandparents has spoken it (cf. Finnish statute for the establishment of the Sami Parliament - Asetus ... 1973). This legal situation in Finland influences Sami cooperation across Nordic national boundaries because the Finnish Sami are the only ones who base their representation in the Sami Parliament on elections. In Norway and Sweden, national organizations look after Sami matters. Still the interest in electing Sami representatives is strong in Norway and Sweden. At this time, various committees are working towards a definition of the legal status of the Sami population in the Nordic countries including Sami self-government in Norway and Sweden. In Norway the Committee on Sami Rights just submitted its report in June 1984 (Om Samenes ... 1984).

In Finland, according to the Sami Parliament, there might be at present about 5,000 Sami based on the linguistic criterion. Usually it has been assumed that two thirds of the Finnish Sami speak Sami, but this figure seems to be too optimistic. The figure of 5,000 Sami consists of the various categories of Sami from those who master the language completely, speaking, reading, and writing, to those with only one grandparent who speaks or spoke Sami. The more reliable population figures for the Finnish Sami go back to 1962 when the census area - the so-called Sami Home Region - was restricted to the northernmost Finnish counties - Enontekiö, Inari, and Utsjoki - and the northern parts of Kittilä and Sodankylä (Nickul, E. 1968). Since 1973 the Kittilä portion of the region has been excluded. All of the Sami Home Region lies in the reindeer herding areas of Finland. It comprises approximately one third of the total Finnish reindeer herding districts. Outside the Sami Home Region, however, there live people who do not belong to the officially defined Sami population but could belong according to the linguistic definition or, perhaps even more, according to the definition based on the right to the so-called 'Lapp livelihood' as mentioned above. If these people were included in the census the Sami population in Finland would certainly number more than 5,000 individuals.

Linguistic acculturation and the decrease in reindeer herding pastures because of spatial conflicts have weakened the basis of Sami ethnicity. Nevertheless the Sami are the same people as before. When considering the inadequate censuses of Sami, especially in Norway and Sweden, the existence of the coastal Sami, and the broad concept of 'Lapp and Lapp livelihood', it is quite obvious that the real number of Sami in northern Fenno-Scandia in fact comes closer to 100,000 than to the lower estimate of 51,000 (Table 1).

The best or most natural starting point for defining Sami ethnicity is offered by the fact that the Sami do exist as a cohesive population with their own idea or consciousness of a Sami nation and a distinct Sami identity. The most recent discussion on problems of defining Sami ethnicity is offered in the report by the Norwegian Committee on Sami Rights which states that the concept of Saminess must contain both measurable and immeasurable characterics (Om samenes ... 1984: 18). Such measurable properties are language competence, family bonds and cultural ancestry. The core of Sami ethnicity also contains such items as territorial and occupational engagements, group consciousness, kinship relations, special cultural characteristics, and expressing one's own personality through one's own language, music or other kind of creative expression. In practice it is difficult to take these factors into consideration. In addition the definition ought to describe what it is like for a person to be Sami or how the individual experiences it.

The Nordic Sami Conference held in Tromsø, Norway in 1980 adopted by resolution the Sami Political Program which included a definition of a Sami with 'certain social rights' as follows (Samiraddi 1980).

As Sami, with such social rights, we regard a person, who

(1) learned Sami as his/her first language or whose mother, father, grandmother or grandfather learned Sami as their first language; or

(2) considers himself/herself to be Sami and has totally adapted himself/herself to the Sami society after having been accepted as Sami by a representative Sami organization; or

(3) has either mother or father as a Sami according to the above conditions.

In the case of Finland, the use of Finnish as the administrative language in reindeer herding has accelerated the linguistic acculturation of the Reindeer Sami. It is ascertained that some reindeer herding families who generally are considered Finnish both inside and outside the Sami Home Region, are in fact of Sami origin. The same phenomenon often appears when considering the official statistics and censuses of the Sami population. It is therefore difficult to define exactly where the line should be drawn for establishing Sami ethnicity.

Sami Ethnicity in Central Finnish Lapland

At the end of the 1970s the Academy of Finland (Suomen akatemia) started a comprehensive research project called 'Cultural Adaptation to Northern Environments' under the directorship of Pekka Sammallahti (Department of Finnish and Sami Languages, Oulu University). The aim of the project was to study the adaptation of Sami culture to changing conditions in the northern areas of Finland (Aikio and Aikio 1983). The authors have studied the change in Sami culture within a specific part of the Sami cultural area, the reindeer herding district called 'Lapin paliskunta' with its center, the village of Vuotso (Fig. 1). This region is the southernmost area

Figure 1: Reindeer Herding District 'Lapin paliskunta', Central Finnish Lapland

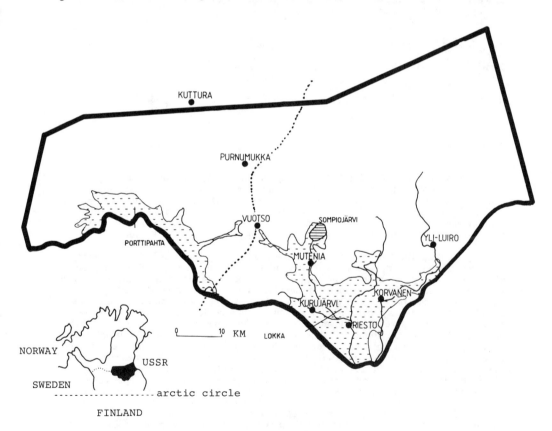

of the Sami Home Region in Finland. The major emphasis of the study was put on Sami language, reindeer herding practices and the ecological conditions of the reindeer and their pastures.

Traditionally the Sami language has been considered the most obvious criterion for identifying Sami; in addition, reindeer herding has been seen to maintain Sami language use and support its development. Alf-Isak Keskitalo (1981: 153), following K. Nickul (1970), believes the definition used in Finland for Sami based on first language serves as a more or less perfect indicator of ethnicity. We disagree on the basis of our research which is presented in more detail below (cf. Aikio, M. 1984).

The case study dealt with the concepts of mother tongue, first language learned, and language best spoken. These are the terms employed when censuses of the Sami population are taken in Finland. In the 1950 census, people were requested to indicate the language they felt they spoke best. In 1962, when a special study of the Sami population in Finland was conducted upon the recommendation of the Nordic Sami Council, the language learned first was used as an indicator (Nickul, E. 1968). The 1977 survey asked for mother tongue. When comparing the figures of 1962 and 1977 for the village of Vuotso the conflict and discrepancies between first language and mother tongue become apparent for the 51 informants in both years (Aikio, M. 1984).

Table 2: Discrepancies Between First Learned Language and Mother Tongue in Vuotso in 1962 and 1977

First Learned Language		Mother Tongue		People
Sami	Finnish	Sami	Finnish	n
x		x		10
x			x	36
	x		x	4
	x	x		1
Total				51

In a survey in 1982 of 199 Sami living in Vuotso only 15 informants reported Sami as their mother tongue. So in reality, these criteria and the figures connected with them are unreliable and inconsistent. Although officially Sami ethnicity is still defined by linguistic criteria in Finland, this situation means that the present definition does not represent the cultural reality (Aikio, M. 1984). The fact is that the Sami people of Vuotso have changed their language from Sami to Finnish.

By plotting the Sami population of the study area - here defined by ancestry - on concentric circles by the year of their birth, it is possible to follow the process of language change as seen in language use as well as other ethnic indicators, such as ancestry and dispersal of reindeer herding. Here we can give the example of one large Vuotso Sami family. The circle (Fig. 2) illustrates Matti Ponku's family, his grandparents, parents, three wives, and all his descendants including the spouses. Ponku was a famous reindeer herder, who owned several thousand reindeer. There are more than 400 individuals on this circle, of which almost 60 are spouses of Finnish origin. When the assumed or verified knowledge of the language of every single person on the time circle is plotted, a comprehensive picture of the process of language shift is shown. The circles of increasing size indicate the time from the 1800's to the 1970's. A small rounded area, either alone or in a 'sausage', represents one individual. The dotted figures indicate those persons, 60 in all, who use or have used Sami as their home language. The vertically hatched figures indicate those persons, 59 in all, who have used or use both languages - Finnish and Sami - in their personal contacts. The cross hatched figures indicate the unilingual Finnish-speaking persons, who form the majority, namely 310 persons.

Figure 2: Language Shift in the Ponku Family of Vuotso Between 1800 and 1982 (see text for explanation)

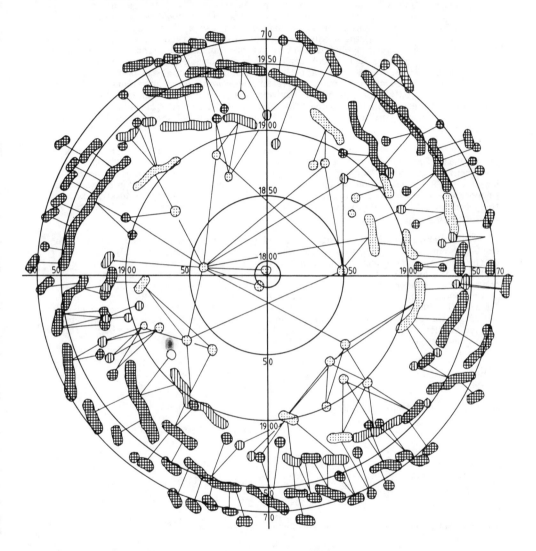

What is remarkable is that the great majority of all adults, at least those born before the 1940's, still command the Sami language but do not use it. Of all those Ponku family members drawn on the circle, about 140 are ethnically mixed and more than 200 are Sami by origin. The Sami people traditionally are connected with reindeer herding. This might support the earlier argument that reindeer herding helps to maintain the use of the Sami language. Let us reexamine these two statements.

The Ponku family is a real reindeer Sami family. More than 200 adults among the 429 persons included in the circle (Fig. 2) are alive at present; but only 60 persons work with reindeer herding to any extent. The majority of the 60 reindeer herders uses only the Finnish language even in reindeer herding. This is undoubtedly due to the fact that Finnish is the official language and must be used even in the administration of reindeer herding - it is not possible to use Sami to file reports, but perhaps only herding activities in the forest and in the mountains. In other words, the majority of all descendants of the richest Sami reindeer herding family in Vuotso are no longer reindeer herders nor users of the Sami language. Still all of them including their children (in all 370 persons) are nevertheless Sami. Their ethnic origin has not changed. Ethnicity and culture maintenance, as Fishman (1972: 58) says, appear to be much more stable phenomena than language maintenance. Linguistic competence, although it too may undergo changes in both directions, persists longer than language use. Native language and bilingualism must be looked upon a process; only ethnic origin is a circumstance that cannot change. By contrast linguistic competence, language use and identification may always change as stressed by various authors (Fishman 1972; see also Skutnabb-Kangas 1981; Aikio, M. 1984).

Reindeer herding has been generally accepted as being the cultural hallmark of the Sami. Originally reindeer herding was, of course, part of Sami life and environment. A special terminology has evolved around reindeer herding in the Sami language. The same can be said of vocabulary related to weather and other natural phenomena. The reindeer herding Sami people of Vuotso have almost totally lost their command of this linguistic repertoire now that the language used in reindeer herding has changed from Sami to Finnish.

In Finland, reindeer herding conducted by Finns has a particularly long tradition, although the origins of reindeer herding were Sami. This probably depended on the 'old Lappish' concept that Finnish reindeer herding rights and traditions originated in the legal rights and status of the former 'Lapp villages'. Therefore the recent past of reindeer herding shows some complicated features. It is not quite easy to understand why there are at present more Finnish than Sami reindeer herders in Finland. Reindeer herding is considered as one most important criterion of Sami ethnicity; in the other hand, reindeer herders of Sami as well as non-Sami origin form also an acknowledged separate professional group in Finland. This shows that reindeer herding has been fennicized to a large extent.

Table 3: Ethnic Background of Reindeer Herders in Vuotso

A. 1911-14 (Poronlaidunkommissioo 1911-14)

	Families		Family Members		Reindeer Owned	
Settler	8	21.6	70	39.5	1313	16.7
Other Occupation	3	8.1	3	1.7	13	0.2
Reindeer Sami	26	70.3	104	58.8	6514	83.1
Total	37	100.0%	177	100.0%	7840	100.0%

B. Reinvestigation Based on Same Sample (Aikio and Aikio 1983)

	Families		Family Members		Reindeer Owned	
Settler	-		-		-	
Other Occupation	1	2.7	1	0.6	10	0.1
Reindeer Sami	28	75.7	122	68.9	7711	98.4
Forest Sami	7	18.9	53	29.9	118	1.5
Fisher Sami	1	2.7	1	0.6	1	
Total	37	100.0%	177	100.0%	7840	100.0%

Table 4:   Spatial Distribution of Descendants of Vuotso Reindeer Sami in 1982
           (cf. Fig. 3)

Region/County	Individuals	Total (%)
Sami Home Region	252	252 (54.3)
Northern Finland (excl. Sami Home Region)	112	112 (24.1)
Province of Lappi		
Kemi	10	
Pelkosenniemi	1	
Ranua	3	
Rovaniemi	19	
Salla	3	
Savukoski	4	
Sodankylä	47	
Tervola	4	
Tornio	2	
Province of Oulu		
Kalajoki	1	
Kempele	3	
Oulu	15	
Southern Finland		37 (8.0)
Kokkola	3	
Toholampi	3	
Vaasa	1	
Iisalmi	3	
Siilinjärvi	4	
Jyväskylä	3	
Mikkeli	3	
Pieksämäki	2	
Nokia	4	
Ylöjärvi	3	
Ranua	3	
Turku	3	
Kouvola	2	
Helsinki and Gulf of Finland Coast Region		36 (7.8)
Espoo	2	
Hanko	13	
Helsinki	17	
Kirkkonummi	2	
Tammisaari	1	
Vantaa	1	
Foreign Countries		27 (5.8)
Norway	2	
Sweden	24	
Turkey	1	
Total:		464 (100)

The report of the first Finnish state commission to look into the conditions of reindeer pasture in Lapland (1911-1914) shows how the Vuotso Reindeer Sami were divided into groups (Table 3, A). According to that report, there were, at the beginning of this century, 37 families in Vuotso, of which 70.3% were Sami who owned 83.1% of the reindeer herded in the district.

The authors have reinvestigated the material in the state archives in Helsinki (Table 3,B) and could notice that fewer than 3% of the reindeer herding families fell outside the Sami definition and there were no Finnish settlers at all. All 8 families reported to be settlers by the Commission, in fact were reinder Sami (2 families) or forest Sami (6 families). This may reflect the competence of the authorities to judge Sami ethnicity at that time.

In 1982 there were 464 descendants of the Vuotso Sami which the authors surveyed in respect to ethnicity. Of those 45.7% (N = 212) lived outside of the designated Sami Home Region in Finland (Fig. 3 and Table 4). Most of them resided in a Finnish speaking environment and their language contacts were entirely in Finnish. In the census a large number of theem indicate their mother tongue as Finnish. Although based on the language criterion of first learned language they should be identified as Sami. Also they no longer recognize their family members as Sami. It seems that, on occasion, it might be advantageous for a Sami to report Finnish as his/her native or first language, for example, to avoid stigmatization and social pressure, although such information might not always reflect the facts.

Conclusion

Research on ethnicity has so far not been successful from the Sami's viewpoint, because it generally has not produced enough analytical data on ethnicity and secondly has not benefitted the Sami. In a number of studies on Sami, the size of the Sami population was usually the main topic which was never solved satisfactorily either in Finland nor other countries. In Finland, a special Sami registry was established for the election of the Sami Parliament. However, not all Sami living in Finland are included in the registry. Also the ethnicity of some persons included in the registry is still unclear.

During the last century Sami reindeer herding and other Sami occupations were strongly protected within the boundaries of Lapland. Today reindeer herding no longer has the protection afforded by property rights, but only by land use rights. As a result, herding and pasture areas have diminished. Since Sami ethnicity was strongly defined by reindeer herding Sami identity partly changed and weakened versus other cultures.

In Sweden and especially in Norway, in the Sami core areas, the use of the Sami language is still strong, but even there the process of language shift is noticeable. These changes and transitions make it very difficult to get a reliable picture of Sami ethnicity by examining language and reindeer herding, based on official statistics. Language and reindeer herding as criteria for ethnicity do not, in fact, reflect the various characteristics of modern Sami culture and identity.

Acknowledgements

The authors acknowledge gratefully the editorial efforts by Linna Müller-Wille and Ludger Müller-Wille, Montreal (Quebec, Canada).

Figure 3: Distribution of 464 Descendants of Vuotso Sami in Finland in 1982 (cf. Table 4; mm² = one person)

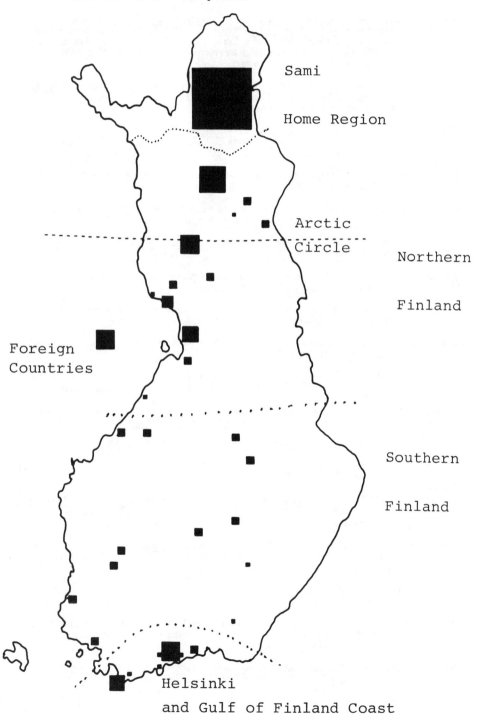

References

Aikio, Marjut, 1984: The position and use of the same language: historical, contemporary and future perspectives. Second international conference on minority languages. June 1983, Turku/Åbo, Finland. Journal of multilingual and multicultural development. Volume 5, Nos 3&4. Ed. by B. Molde and D. Sharp.

— and Pekka Aikio, 1983: Kulttuurin sopeutuminen arktiseen ekologiaan (Cultural Adaptation to Arctic Ecology). Academy of Finland. Unpublished Project Report.

Allardt, Erik and Christian Starck, 1981: Vähemmistö, kieli ja yhteiskunta. Suomenruotsalaiset vertailevasta näkökulmasta (Minority, Language and Society. Finland Swedes in Comparative Perspective). Juva.

Asetus Saamelaisvaltuuskunnasta, 1973 (Statute to establish the Sami Delegation): Asetus (Statute) No. 824/73. Helsinki.

Asp, Erkki, 1965: Lappalaiset ja lappalaisuus (The Lapps and Lappishness). Turun yliopiston julkaisuja C, 2. Turku.

— 1966: The Finnicization of the Lapps. Turun yliopiston julkaisuja B, 100. Turku.

Aubert, Vilhelm, 1978: Den samiske befolkning i Nord-Norge. Artikler fra statistisk sentralbyra No. 107. Oslo.

Barth, Fredrik, 1969: Introduction, in: Ethnic Groups and Boundaries. Ed. by Fredrik Barth. Oslo: Universitetsforlaget.

Bjørklund, Ivar, 1983: Etnisk identitet som økonomisk tilpassning blant kvaener paa 1700-tallet. Fra 'Bøgdelap' til 'gvaen'. Heimen.

Eidheim, Harald, 1969: When Ethnic Identity is a Social Stigma, in: Ethnic Groups and Boundaries. Ed. by Fredrik Barth. Oslo. Oslo: Universitetsforlaget.

Fishman, Joshua, 1965: Varieties of Ethnicity and Varities of Language Consciousness, in: Monograph Series of Language and Linguistics 18: 69-79.

— 1972: Language in Sociocultural Change. Stanford.

— 1977: Language and Ethnicity, in: Language, Ethnicity and Intergroup Relations. Ed. by M. Giles. London.

Hyvärinen, Heikki J., 1982: The legal status of the reindeer-keepers in Finland. Third International Reindeer/Caribou Symposium 1982. Saariselkä. Manuscript.

Keskitalo, Alf Isak, 1981: The Status of the Sami Language, in: Minority Languages Today. Ed. by E. Haugen, J. D. McClure and D. S. Thomson. Edinburgh: Edinburgh University Press.

Komitea, 1973: Saamelaiskomitean mietintö (Report of the Sami State Committee). Helsinki.

Müller-Wille, Ludger, 1974: Lappen und Finnen in Utsjoki (Ohcijohka) Finnland. Eine Studie zur Identität ethnischer Gruppen im Kulturkontakt. Westfälische Geographische Studien 30. Münster.

Nickul, Erkki, 1968: Suomen saamelaiset vuonna 1962 (Finland's Sami 1962). Pro-gradu thesis, Department of Statistics, Helsinki University.

Nickul, Karl, 1970: Saamelaiset kansana ja kansalaisina (The Sami as People and Citizens). Helsinki: Finnish Literature Society.

Om Samenes Rettstilling, 1984 (Report by the State Committee on Sami Rights). Norske Offentlige Utredningsserie (NOU) 1984: 18. Bergen.

Poronlaidunkommissioo 1911-14: Porolaidunkomissioonin asiakirjat 1911-1914 (Reindeer Pasture Commission. Minutes 1911-14). Virallinen Arkisto (Official Archives). Helsinki.

Samerna I Sverige, 1975: Stöd at sprak och kultur. Statens Offentliga Utredningar (SOU) 99-100. Stockholm.

Skutnabb-Kangas, Tove, 1981: Tvasprakighet. Lund.

Samiraddi 1980 (Sami Council): Sami Political Program of the Nordic Sami Council. Manuscript.

Svensson, Tom G., 1976: Ethnicity and Mobilization in Sami Politics. Stockholm: Department of Social Anthropology, Stockholm University.

Wikman, Ake, 1960: Natural Resources, in: Lapps To-day in Finland, Norway and Sweden, Vol. I. Paris: Mouton.

Address of the authors:
Marjut Aikio
Finnmarks distrikshögskole
(Finnmark's Regional College)
N-9500 Alta
Norway

Pekka Aikio
Suomen Akatemia
(Academy of Finland)
Project 'Cultural Adaptation
to Northern Environments'
Valtakatu 2 C 4
SF-96010 Rovaniemi 10
Finland

L'Ethnie Bretonne en France et ses problèmes d'aujourd'hui

Robert Omnès

Abstract: Brittany has a surface area of just over 35.000 sq. kilometers and a population of 3.800.000. In the 4th to 7th centuries A.D. this land was invaded by the Britons. They managed in 845 to create a unified state (first a Kingdom, then a Duchy), independent until the end of the 15th century. Finally, Brittany was annexed after bloody defeats, but kept its status of autonomy until the revolution in 1789. The reforms in administration carried out during the French Revolution met with strong opposition in Brittany. In the 19th century, objecting people were mainly regionalists. Since 1911, nationalist and even separatist movements have come into being. Now, the great majority of Bretons feel that a more positive form of regionalisation would be a means of solving its economic and its cultural problems. The Third Republic (1871-1940) openly opposed "regional" languages. The number of Breton speakers has, in 60 years, declined from 1.300.000 to 600.000. Now, the government allows only a few hours teaching of the Breton language on a voluntary basis and very little place is devoted to Breton on radio or television. Fortunately, Breton public opinion is, to some extent, waking up to these anomalies.

Résumé: La Bretagne a une surface un peu supérieure à 35.000 km2 et une population d'environ 3.800.000 habitants. Elle fut peuplée par les Bretons (venus de Grande Bretagne) entre le 4e et le 7e s. après J. C. Ceux-ci parvinrent à créer en 845 un Etat unifié (royaume, puis duché), qui réussit à garder son indépendance jusqu'à la fin du XVe s. Finalement, la Bretagne fut annexée par la France après de sanglantes défaites, mais conserva un statut d'autonomie jusqu'à la Révolution de 1789. Les réformes administratives de la Révolution Française rencontrèrent de vives résistances en Bretagne. Au XIXe s., les protestataires furent surtout des régionalistes. Depuis 1911, se manifestèrent des tendances nationalistes et même séparatistes. Actuellement, la grande majorité des Bretons voit, dans une régionalisation hardie, un moyen d'apporter de meilleures réponses aux problèmes culturels et économiques. La 3e République (1871-1940) combattit ouvertement les langues "régionales". Le nombre des bretonnants est passé en 60 ans d 1.300.000 à 600.000 environ. Actuellement, le gouvernement autorise seulement quelques heures facultatives d'enseignement du breton et une très petite place est réservée à cette langue à la radio et à la télévision. Une partie de l'opinion bretonne, heureusement, se mobilise pour mettre fin à ces abus.

Zusammenfassung: Die Bretagne hat eine Größe von mehr als 35.000 km² und eine Bevölkerung von 3,8 Mio. Einwohnern. Vom 4. bis 7. Jahrhundert n.Chr. wurde dieses Land von Bretonen überflutet. Ihnen gelang im Jahre 845 sogar die Errichtung eines eigenen Staates (zunächst Königreich, später Herzogtum), das bis Ende des 15. Jahrhunderts unabhängig blieb. Nach blutigen Auseinandersetzungen wurde die Bretagne annektiert, behielt aber ihren Autonomiestatus bis zur Revolution von 1789. Die Verwaltungsreformen im Zuge der Französischen Revolution stießen in der Bretagne auf heftigen Widerstand. Während des 19. Jahrhunderts wurde dieser Widerstand vorwiegend von "Regionalisten" weitergeführt. Seit 1911 kam es dann zunehmend zu nationalistischen und separatistischen Bestrebungen. Heute besteht verbreitet die Auffassung, daß sinnvollere Regionalisierungsansätze die wirtschaftlichen und kulturellen Probleme der Region lösen könnten. Die "Dritte Republik" (1871-1940) widersetzte sich heftig dem Gebrauch "regionaler" Sprachen. Die Zahl derer, die bretonisch sprechen, ist innerhalb von 60 Jahren von 1,3 Mio. auf 600.000 gefallen. Heute werden offiziell nur wenige Unterrichtsstunden in "bretonisch" auf freiwilliger Basis zugestanden, und nur wenig Möglichkeit ist der bretonischen Sprache in Radio oder Fernsehen eingeräumt. Ein Teil der bretonischen Öffentlichkeit ist heute glücklicherweise entschlossen, diese Verhältnisse zu ändern.

I. Le cadre géographique

Située à l'extrémité occidentale du territoire français, la Bretagne a une surface un peu supérieure à 35.000 km2 et environ 3.800.000 habitants. Sous la Révolution Française, elle a été divisée en 5 départements, dont les limites, très arbitraires, ne correspondent à aucune réalité historique, ethnique ou économique. En 1941, le gouvernement du Maréchal Pétain, au moment de la création des régions administratives, a séparé du reste de la Bretagne Nantes, sa capitale historique, et le département de la Loire Atlantique (le plus riche et le plus peuplé). Depuis, cette mesure n'a jamais été rapportée, malgré les innombrables protestations des élus, les manifestations unitaires et la volonté de la population du Pays Nantais, qui a souvent été qualifié d'"Ulster Breton". Cette division de la Bretagne n'empêche pas les représentants du Pays Nantais de participer à la vie de certains organismes économiques, comme le CELIB (Comité d'Entente et de Liaison des Intérêts Bretons) ou culturels, comme l'Institut Culturel de Bretagne, mais elle constitue une gêne sur le plan administratif et compromet gravement le développement de la Région.

II. Les origines des Bretons; leur personnalité ethnique

Personne n'oserait affirmer aujourd'hui sérieusement que les Bretons constituent une race bien définie, même si certains caractères physiques se rencontrent avec une remarquable fréquence dans telle ou telle région de Bretagne (la "race" de Téviec, très brachycéphale, dans le sud du Morbihan) et si le groupe sanguin O est fortement représenté dans les 5 départements.

L'ethnie bretonne est définie par un certain nombre de facteurs:

- Le sentiment d'appartenir à une même communauté historique et géographique.

- Une certaine vision du monde, dont la langue bretonne reste la plus pure expression (même si, aujourd'hui, moins de 20% des Bretons ont une connaissance courante du celtique, il ne faut pas oublier que le breton fut parlé du IXe au XI s. dans presque toute la Bretagne et a laissé des traces importantes dans les dialectes romans de l'est du pays et dans le "français de Bretagne").

- Des traditions populaires communes et toujours vivaces (jeux et sports, musique, danses, fêtes, contes et légendes ...), tout ce que l'on entend par "folklore" au sens propre du terme.

- enfin le désir de continuer de vivre ensemble et la volonté de défendre des intérêts communs sur tous les plans (économique et culturel, en particulier).

Il nous semble que l'appartenance d'un individu à l'ethnie bretonne dépend beaucoup plus de son adhésion à un certain "milieu culturel", de son immersion dans une certaine "société", que de ses origines raciales. A la limite, si l'on n'est pas né Breton, on peut le devenir. Il y a en Bretagne des personnes tout-à-fait étrangères à la région par leurs origines, qui se sont si bien intégrées, qui ont si bien adopté les "façons" de la société bretonne, qui manifestent un tel intérêt pour la langue et la culture du pays, qu'elles peuvent revendiquer l'appartenance à notre ethnie; par contre un Breton émigré à Paris ou à New-York, qui a perdu tout lien avec sa patrie d'origine et est bien intégré dans son nouveau milieu, nous est devenu complétement étranger (1).

Nous pourrions citer le cas d'un écrivain japonais, dont le breton est la langue littéraire (et l'une des langues journalières). Comment ne pas le considérer comme un "Breton à part entière"?

Ces remarques ne nous dispensent pas de nous pencher sur le problème des origines historiques de la Communauté Bretonne.

Notre presqu'île forme, à l'une des extrémités de l'Europe, une sorte de "cul-de-sac", qui a servi de refuge à de nombreux peuples chassés d'autres régions par des invasions; mais, en même temps, grâce à ses estuaires et à ses innombrables ports naturels, elle a toujours été largement accessibles aux influences venues d'Outremer, et, en particulier de Grande-Bretagne, d'Irlande et d'Espagne.

Les Bretons d'aujourd'hui sont, tout à la fois, les descendants des peuples de la Préhistoire (en particulier, des constructeurs de dolmens et de menhirs, qui vivaient en Bretagne entre le quatrième et le deuxième millénaire avant J.C.), des envahisseurs Celtes (VIIe - IIe s. avant J.C.) qui donnèrent aux rivages occidentaux de la Gaule le nom de "Paremorica" ("pays situé devant la mer", devenu "Aremorica") et des "Bretons" qui débarquèrent sur nos côtes (surtout de IVe au VIe s.) et donnèrent à l'extrémité occidentale de l'"Aremorica" le nom de Bretagne.

Les recherches du Professeur F. Falc'hun (Universités de Rennes, puis de Brest) l'ont conduit à la conclusion que l'Armorique, conquise par César en 58 av. J.C. et occupée pendant plus de 4 siècles par les légions, n'avait jamais été entièrement romanisée. La langue celtique s'y est maintenue pendant la période romaine et le latin n'a guère été en usage que dans quelques centres urbains, comme Rennes, Nantes, Vannes, Aleth (Près de St Malo) ...

Ce maintien du celtique a pu favoriser l'établissement des Bretons en Armorique et, par la suite, la fusion des différents éléments de la population.

De son côté, le Professeur Fleuriot (Univ. de Rennes) a démontré que l'on avait étudié jusqu'ici les migrations bretonnes dans un cadre historique et géographique beaucoup trop étroit. Ces migrations ont commencé au cours des derniers siècles de l'Empire Romain. D'ailleurs, elles ont été favorisées par les Romains, qui considéraient à juste titre les Bretons comme d'excellents soldats et les utilisèrent pour combattre les invasions "barbares". C'est pourquoi l'on retrouve les traces de contingents bretons à l'embouchure de la Seine, sur les bords de la Loire, en Espagne et dans les "Champs Décumates", région particulièrement menacée. Notons que ces migrations n'ont jamais eu l'ampleur ni la durée de celles qui ont concerné l'Armorique (surtout à partir du IVe s.). Aucune d'entre elles n'a abouti à une colonisation durable et à la fondation d'un Etat.

L'émigration des Bretons en Armorique s'est intensifiée au Ve s., lorsque les Angles et les Saxons se sont établis dans l'île de Bretagne, repoussant les Bretons vers les terres pauvres et montagneuses de l'Ouest et du Nord-Ouest. Beaucoup d'entre eux ont alors décidé de prendre la mer pour rechercher des terres plus accueillantes. Ajoutons que les échanges entre les deux rives de la Manche sont restés intenses jusqu'au XIIe s. et que ce n'est guère que vers cette époque que les divers parlers brittoniques (Gallois, cornique, breton) se sont différenciés (2).

Au moment des invasions anglo-saxonnes, les Bretons se trouvèrent géographiquement divisés en 5 groupes:

- Ceux du Nord-Ouest de l'actuelle Angleterre et du Sud de l'Ecosse (royaume de Strathclyde).

- Ceux du Pays de Galles (dont la vallée de la Severn constitua pendant un certain temps la frontière orientale).

- Ceux de Devon et de Cornwall (ces deux régions doivent leurs noms, respectivement, aux Dumnonii et aux Cornovii, deux tribus bretonnes) (3).

- Ceux qui s'étaient établis en Armorique.

- Enfin, ceux qui, volontairement ou non, avaient débarqué sur les côtes septentrionales de la Galice et des Asturies et y avaient fondé l'évêché de Bretoña, qui exista de 560 à 840 environ.

Ainsi, au sens large, le nom de "Breton" peur être appliqué à plusieurs communautés ethniques actuelles. Si ceux de Galice, du Devon et du Cumberland semblent avoir perdu leur identité culturelle et ont été assimilés par les peuples

Les Migrations des Bretons
(V^e - VIIe s.)

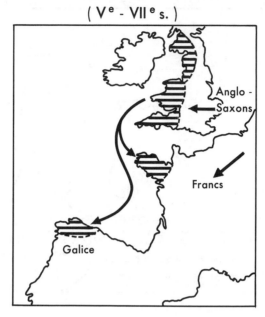

voisins, les habitants du Pays de Galles, du Cornwall et de l'Armorique peuvent être considérés comme des représentants de l'ethnie bretonne (4).

Dans le cadre de cet exposé, nous nous limiterons à l'étude de l'histoire politique et culturelle des Bretons d'Armorique et de leur situation actuelle.

III. Les Bretons d'Armorique: bref rappel historique

Les Francs, à la suite des Romains, favorisèrent dans un premier temps l'établissement en Armorique des Bretons, dont ils s'etaient fait des alliés contre les Wisigoths et les pirates nordiques et irlandais.

Cependant, des conflits éclatèrent entre Francs et Bretons lorsque ces derniers dépassèrent les limites orientales du territoire sur lequel les Francs désiraient les confiner et notamment après la prise de Vannes (577) par le chef Waroc'h.

Diverses tentatives franques contre le territoire breton échouèrent. En 845, après l'effondrement de l'Empire carolingien, les Bretons parvinrent à constituer un Etat unifié (5), qui, à la fin du IXe s. annexa le Cotentin, l'Avranchin, et une partie de l'Anjou et du Maine. Divers souverains bretons portèrent à cette époque le titre royal. Après les invasions normandes et la perte des territoires annexés, leurs successeurs durent se contenter du titre de Duc. Jusqu'à la fin du XVe s., la Bretagne parvint à garder son indépendance et connut à la fin du Moyen-Age, grâce au developpement de l'industrie des toiles et au commerce maritime, une remarquable prospérité.

De sanglantes défaites, les deux mariages de la Duchesse Anne avec le roi de France Charles VIII, puis avec le roi Louis XII et surtout l'union de sa fille Claude, héritière du Duché, et de François Ier, entraînèrent l'annexion de la Bretagne (6).

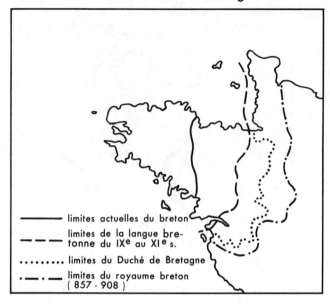

Les Frontières de la Bretagne

—— limites actuelles du breton
– – – limites de la langue bretonne du IXe au XIe s.
········ limites du Duché de Bretagne
·—·—· limites du royaume breton (857 - 908)

En 1532, un traité d'Union fut signé par le roi de France François Ier et les députés bretons (7). "Province réputée étrangère", la Bretagne, malgré les tentatives centralisatrices du pouvoir royal - surtout sous Louis XIV - conserva un statut d'autonomie jusqu'à la Révolution de 1789 (8). Celle-ci supprima les anciennes provinces et les divisa en départements, à la tête desquels Napoléon Ier plaça plus tard des "préfets", représentants du pouvoir central. Quand la Monarchie fut restaurée en France, le nouveau système fut maintenu et survécut à tous les changements de régimes du XIXe s.

De récentes réformes ont apporté quelques correctifs à ce système de gouvernement:

1) La Région est redevenue une unité administrative (mais, dans le cas de la Bretagne, il y a eu un démembrement du pays).

2) Depuis 1981 (victoire de François Mittérand aux élections présidentielles) les pouvoirs des élus communaux, départementaux et régionaux ont été théoriquement renforcés. Malheureusement, ils disposent de moyens financiers dérisoires, par rapport au budget de l'Etat. La décentralisation reste surtout un thème favori de discours officiels.

3) Aujourd'hui existent des Assemblées Régionales. Mais elles sont composées de personnalités élues au second degré (par les villes ou les Conseils Généraux des Départements), de parlementaires nationaux (députés, sénateurs ...) ... Le président Mittérand a promis lors de son élection qu'un vote aurait lieu pour désigner de nouveaux élus régionaux au suffrage universel direct, mais ce vote a été constamment différé (il a été question de l'organiser en 1984, puis 85, puis 86 ...). En attendant, les administrations centrales gardent l'essentiel du pouvoir et opposent à toute tentative de changement leur puissante force d'inertie.

IV. Deux siècles de combats pour la reconnaissance de l'identité bretonne

Les réformes administratives de la Révolution Française ont immédiatement rencontré de vives résistances en Bretagne, tant de la part des "Chouans" (partisans de l'ancien régime) que des "Girondins" (ou fédéralistes, qui revendiquaient pour les Assemblées Départementales une large autonomie et s'opposaient au centralisme parisien). De véritables guerres civiles éclatèrent en Bretagne et dans tout l'Ouest de la France. Girondins et Chouans furent victimes d'une sanglante répression.

Au milieu du XIXe s. nacquit le régionalisme politique, qui accompagna le renouveau littéraire et lingüistique (9). C'est en 1911 qu'apparurent les premières manifestations séparatistes (Création du Parti Nationaliste Breton). Le mouvement s'amplifia jusqu'à la guerre de 1914-1918. La mobilisation, puis la disparition d'un certain nombre de militants (parmi lesquels le poète Jean-Pierre Calloc'h) pendant la Iere guerre mondiale brisa cet élan.

Le mouvement nationaliste reprit quelques années plus tard. Tout en gardant des proportions encore modestes, il inquiéta vivement les gouvernements français de l'époque par ses publications (parmi lesquelles la revue "Breiz Atao" est restée célèbre) et par les attentats de sa branche clandestine "Gwenn ha Du" (Blanc et Noir, couleurs du drapeau breton). En 1932, le Monument de l'Union de la France et de la Bretagne, érigé devant l'Hotel de Ville des Rennes, fut détruit par une explosion; il ne fut jamais reconstruit.

En 1940, lors de l'invasion de la France par les troupes allemandes, le bruit courut que les occupants étaient favorables à la restauration de l'Etat Breton. C'est à cette époque que certains fonctionnaires, soucieux de préserver ou d'améliorer leur situation, firent des avances au mouvement politique breton. En fait, le gouvernement allemand hésitait entre deux politiques: démembrer la France en s'appuyant sur les mouvements séparatistes de diverses régions ou jouer la carte de la collaboration avec le gouvernement du Maréchal Pétain et les représentants ultra-nationalistes de l'extrême droite française. C'est cette deuxième stratégie qui fut retenue. Bien entendu, lorsque Pétain rencontra à Montoire le chancelier Hitler, il exigea le respect de l'intégrité du territoire français.

La célèbre poignée de main de Montoire eut de nombreuses conséquences pour le mouvement nationaliste breton:

1 - Il cessa d'être encouragé par les occupants et resta seulement toléré.

2 - Les éléments les plus extrémistes et les plus favorables aux forces d'occupation furent éliminés de la direction du P.N.B. (parti national breton) et remplacés par des dirigeants modérés, qui entendaient tenir le mouvement à l'écart de toute compromission, afin de préserver les chances de celui-ci, quelle que soit l'issue du conflit international.

3 - On assista, parallelement, à une renaissance du régionalisme, dont les objectifs apparaissaient comme plus réalistes, au moment même où Pétain créait les Régions et dotait la Bretagne d'un "Comité Consultatif".

Tous ces faits échappèrent à l'ensemble de l'opinion publique bretonne, mal informée. Le climat général ne se prêtait guère aux jugements nuancés. Dans leur immense majorité, les Bretons étaient hostiles au Nazisme et aux troupes d'occupation. Cette hostilité s'accrut lors des represailles dont furent victimes les résistants en 1943 et 1944 (prises d'otages, exécutions, déportations ...). Après l'occupation, le souvenir des tentatives avortées de 1940 fut systématiquement exploité par ceux qui voulaient porter un coup fatal au mouvement breton et même à ses expressions les plus modérées. Sous prétexte que quelques nationalistes avaient collaboré avec les occupants, de nombreux militants bretons furent emprisonnés. Il y eut même une vingtaine d'éxécutions et des condamnations aux travaux forcés. Il suffisait d'avoir été abonné à un journal breton pour être arrêté, de jouer du biniou pour être suspect (10).

Malgré les conseils de modération donnés par le général De Gaulle, une véritable "chasse aux sorcières" fut organisée: elle a laissé des traces chez les plus de 60 ans. Les générations qui ont connu la guerre ont été soigneusement "conditionnées". Par contre, les jeunes générations abordent aujourd'hui le problème politique breton sans complexe et avec une information plus objective et une grande liberté de jugement.

Les événements de 1944-1945 expliquent la prudence qui marqua la renaissance vers 1950 du mouvement politique breton.

C'est à cette époque que les parlementaires, les élus communaux et départementaux et les cadres économiques de Bretagne, généralement favorables à un regionalisme modéré, créèrent, sous l'égide de René Pléven, ancien résistant qui participa à plusieurs gouvernements, le "Comité d'Entente et de Liaison des Intérêts Bretons". Quelques années plus tard fut fondé le "Mouvement pour l'Organisation de la Bretagne" (M.O.B.), d'inspiration fédéraliste. Puis apparurent, à la suite d'une scission du MOB, qui provoqua plus tard sa disparition, des partis plus ouvertement autonomistes, comme l'Union Démocratique Bretonne (U.D.B.) et "Strollad ar Vro" (S.A.V.). Le premier de ces partis se proclame de gauche et aujourd'hui ses élus (quelques maires et maires-adjoints et un nombre non négligeable de conseillers municipaux) participent à la direction des certaines communes aux côtés des socialistes et des communistes (11). Quand au second, qui connait actuellement une éclipse, il se veut à la fois "nationaliste breton et fédéraliste européen".

L'audience des partis spécifiquement bretons aux élections (législatives ou autres) reste assez limitée. Mais un examen plus approfondi montre que les idées exprimées avec force, jadis ou naguère, par les principaux théoriciens du nationalisme et du régionalisme bretons, ont pénétré dans des milieux qui votent, par tradition ou par souci d'éfficacité, pour des partis politiques "français". En fait, presque personne en Bretagne ne souhaite le maintien du système centralisateur issu de la période napoléonienne. Beaucoup de Bretons voient, dans une régionalisation plus hardie, un moyen d'apporter de meilleures réponses aux problèmes économiques actuels (industrialisation insuffisante, crise de l'agriculture, chomage, émigration des jeunes ...).

Ajoutons qu'il y a des jeunes Bretons qui ne font pas confiance à l'action légale et ont formé un mouvement clandestin, le "Front de Libération de la Bretagne", qui s'est manifesté, depuis 1970 surtout, en faisant sauter des monuments ou des établissements symbolisant à ses yeux "l'occupation française": perceptions, palais de justice, casernes ...

Ces manifestations semblent excessives à la majorité de l'opinion bretonne. Elles n'en traduisent pas moins un malaise ...

V. Le problème culturel et lingüistique

Le recul de la langue bretonne (qui fut parlée dans la presque totalité de la Bretagne du IXe au XIe s.) commença dès le XIIe s. Jusqu'à cette époque, le breton était la langue de la cour ducale et de toutes les classes sociales. Cette langue possédait un riche vocabulaire dans tous les domaines, même savants. Des changements dynastiques (avènement de Ducs de la Maison Plantagenet, puis de Ducs Capétiens) entraînèrent la francisation de la cour, puis celle de la noblesse et de la bourgeoisie. Le breton devint de plus en plus la langue des classes populaires; son vocabulaire courant s'apauvrit; en l'absence d'enseignement, il se dialectalisa de plus en plus. Cette dialectalisation gêne l'intercompréhension, sans toutefois la rendre impossible. Le recul "social" du breton fut accompagné d'un recul géographique (dans tout l'Est de la Bretagne). Sauf dans les classes dirigeantes, de plus en plus francisées, ce recul se fit au profit des parlers romans de Rennes et de Nantes, dont les spécialistes ont souligné recemment l'originalité (et les rapports avec le breton). Le "britto-roman" est lui même en recul rapide dans les campagnes de l'Est, malgré les efforts d'un nombre croissant de militants.

Les gouvernements de la 3e république (1871-1940) combattirent ouvertement toutes les langues régionales (breton, basque, corse, occitan ... etc. ...), considérées comme des idiomes barbares, des véhicules de l'"obscurantisme et du cléricalisme", et surtout des obstacles à l'Unité Nationale, au moment même où l'on célébrait le culte de la "France Une et Indivisible". "Pour l'Unité de la France, déclara le ministre de l'Instruction Publique de Monzie, la langue bretonne doit disparaître:". L'école primaire obligatoire reçut la mission d'accomplir ce que l'on a appelé à juste titre le "génocide culturel".

La méthode était simple: les enfants étaient invités à se surveiller les uns les autres et à dénoncer ceux qui faisaient usage de la langue régionale dans la cour de récréation. Les contrevenants étaient sévèrement punis. Cette méthode (aussi anti-éducative sur le plan moral que sur le plan culturel) porte en elle-même sa propre condamnation, mais elle fut couronnée par la réussite. Elle suscita les réactions indignées d'un petit nombre d'écoliers, qui devinrent souvent plus tard d'ardents défenseurs de la langue bretonne, mais il faut avouer que, dans l'ensemble, les masses se résignèrent, voyant dans le français un moyen de promotion sociale. La plupart de ceux qui avaient été punis parce qu'ils faisaient usage du breton décidèrent de ne parler qu'en français à leurs propres enfants, "pour leur éviter les mêmes ennuis". Le nombre des bretonnants est passé la une soixantaine d'années de 1.300.000 à 650.000 environ. On cite le cas de familles (de moins en moins nombreuses, à mesure que les anciens bretonnants disparaissent) où la vieille grand-mère, qui ne connaît pratiquement pas le français, est obligée de faire traduire ses paroles par ses enfants (parfaitement bilingues) pour communiquer avec ses petits-enfants, auxquels on s'est abstenu d'enseigner "la langue des ancêtres".

Depuis 1950 environ, les gouvernements français ont adopté une attitude plus libérale envers les langues régionales. Mais le mal est fait et il est bien difficile de "remonter la pente".

La volonté des gouvernements français de la 3e République de détruire les langues minoritaires et d'en effacer les traces se manifesta de multiples façons dans d'autres domaines que celui de l'école:

- Tous les actes administratifs étaient, bien entendu, rédigés en français. L'Etat central ne recourut aux "idiomes barbares" qu'en deux circonstances: pour inciter les Bas-Bretons (et d'autres minorités de l'hexagone) à lui prêter de l'argent et à aller coloniser l'Afrique!

- Les noms de lieux furent souvent francisés, soit en fonction d'une volonté délibérée, soit, plus souvent, par simple ignorance (les fonctionnaires chargés d'établir les cartes et la signalisation n'avaient la plupart du temps aucune notion de breton). C'est ainsi que les "carrefours" ("Kroaz-Hent" en breton) devinrent des "Croissants", que le lieu dit "Ar Zalver" (Le Sauveur) devint "La Salle Verte", que "An Tri Person" ("Les 3 Personnes" ... de la Sainte Trinité) devint "Les Trois Curés" ("Person" signifie également "curé" en breton).

- Les noms de famille furent généralement respectés (12). Il y eut tout de même des noms qui furent francisés. Un cas curieux de double francisation fut celui d'une famille "Gwern", dont le nom fut traduit par "Le Mât" (le mât de navire). Or "Mat" signifie "Bon" en breton. Une génération plus tard, les "Le Mat" étaient devenus des "Le Bon!"

- Pour les prénoms, l'administration tomba dans d'autres aberrations. Pendant longtemps, la coutume en Basse-Bretagne fut d'inscrire à l'état-civil la forme française du prénom (quand elle existait); mais, dans la vie courante, la plupart des Jean étaient appelés "Yann", les Alain étaient "Alan" ou "Lanig" (diminutif), les Vincent étaient "Visant" ... etc. ... Le prénom officiel (celui de l'état-civil) était souvent inconnu des plus proches voisins de l'intéressé eux-mêmes.

Des conflits éclatèrent avec l'administration, surtout entre 1950 et 1965, lorsque des parents bretons, de plus en plus nombreux, voulurent inscrire à l'état-civil les prénoms qu'ils avaient choisis pour leurs enfants sous leur forme bretonne.

Certains procureurs de la République donnèrent des consignes sévères aux employés de l'état-civil, qui refusèrent des prénoms rares, ou dont seule la forme bretonne était connue; lorsque les prénoms avaient une forme française, on voulut l'imposer aux parents. Mais les temps avaient changé et bien des parents refusèrent de s'incliner. Certains cas furent réglés à l'amiable, grâce à l'intervention des élus locaux. Parfois, des procès eurent lieu. On peut citer le cas d'une famille, dont plusieurs enfants restèrent pendant quelques années sans état-civil (et sans aucun droit aux prestations sociales, puisqu'ils n'avaient pas d'existence légale). Il fallut l'intervention de la Cour Internationale de La Haye pour mettre fin au conflit (13).

Depuis une dizaine d'années, de nouvelles consignes ont été données aux administrations et les Bretons, grâce à leur ténacité, se sont vus reconnaître le droit de choisir librement les prénoms de leurs enfants.

VI. Le combat culturel

Le combat pour la reconnaissance de la langue et de la culture bretonne a commencé au XIXe s. Des grammaires furent publiées, ainsi que des dictionnaires et des ouvrages littéraires. Parmi ces derniers, le plus célèbre fut un recueil de chants populaires, le "Barzaz Breiz" de La Villemarqué, qui fit naître de nombreuses vocations d'écrivains. A partir de 1870, se multiplièrent les pétitions en faveur de l'enseignement des langues régionales.

Le XXe s. a été marqué par le développement des associations favorables à l'enseignement du breton. Le "Bleun Brug" (catholique) et "Ar Falz" (laïque) organisèrent des concours de chant, de poésie, de rédaction etc. ... en breton, malgré l'hostilité du ministère de l'Instruction Publique jusqu'à la fin de la 3e République. Le mouvement "Ar Brezoneg er Skol" (Le breton à l'école) recueillit entre les deux guerres de très nombreuses signatures d'élus locaux. Parallèlement, les éditions "Gwalarn" publièrent des ouvrages littéraires et scientifiques, démontrant ainsi que le breton pouvait être utilisé dans tous les domaines.

Ces actions furent poursuivies après la seconde guerre mondiale. L'une des réalisations les plus spectaculaires a été la création des écoles "Diwan", où tout l'enseignement est donné en breton. Ces écoles, qui connaissent un succès croissant, sont tolérées, mais très peu aidées par le ministère de l'Education Nationale. Elles vivent grâce à la générosité des parents et des militant bretons (14).

Dans l'enseignement public et privé, la place du breton reste très réduite, malgré les innombrables projets de lois déposés par les parlementaires bretons de toutes les tendances. Il n'existe guère que quelques cours facultatifs, donnés par des professeurs à-demi bénévoles. Au baccalauréat, les langues régionales ne peuvent être choisies que comme langues complémentaires.

A l'Université, une licence de celtique a été créée, mais il n'est pas question de former des professeurs spécialisés pour les lycées et les demandes de création d'une agrégation et d'un CAPES (concours du pressorat) de breton sont restées sans réponse.

La place du breton à la radio (malgré les efforts de certains studios privés) et à la télévision (en moyenne 2h par semaine) reste très réduite. Les Bretons ne peuvent s'empêcher de comparer leur situation et celle des Gallois, qui disposent d'une chaîne de télévision utilisant uniquement leur langue.

Le combat pour la reconnaissance de l'identité culturelle bretonne continue, malgré des conditions bien difficiles. Deux fédérations, "Kuzul ar Brezhoneg" et "Emgleo Breiz" diffusent des livres en breton. Des ouvrages en breton ou sur la Bretagne sont également édités par la Coopérative "Breizh", créée par la puissante fédération folklorique et culturelle "Kendalc'h". Enfin, l'"Institut Culturel de Bretagne" assure le préfinancement d'ouvrages scientifiques ou de vulgarisation concernant la matière bretonne. "Skol an Emzao" ("l'école du Mouvement") fait porter ses efforts sur l'enseignement de la langue et de l'histoire.

Récemment s'est créée une association des élus bretonnants de toutes tendances, à laquelle ont adhéré des maires et des conseillers municipaux de diverses régions de Bretagne. Cette association se propose de donner au breton une place dans la vie publique, dans les actes administratifs, dans la signalisation routière, de faire rectifier tous les noms de lieux déformés ou francisés, d'encourager l'enseignement du breton ... etc...

VII. Bilan et perspectives - l'avenir de l'ethnie Bretonne

La pénétration dès le XIIe s. de la langue et de la culture française en Bretagne, loin d'être une sorte de "malédiction historique", aurait pu constituer une chance, si les deux cultures s'étaient contamment enrichies par des contacts mutuels. Que des échanges fructueux aient eu lieu à certaines époques, c'est incontestable: songeons à l'importance prise par la "matière de Bretagne" dans la littérature française médiévale ou encore à la contribution des Bretons aux lettres françaises pendant tout le XIXe s. La sensibilité d'un Chateaubriand, d'un Renan, d'un Lamennais, pour ne citer que ces exemples, porte la marque des origines celtiques de ces trois écrivains.

La volonté des gouvernements de la 3e République de faire disparaître les langues minoritaires et d'uniformiser la culture sur toute l'étendue du territoire français n'a pas seulement abouti à un véritable "génocide culturel"; elle a nui à la culture française elle-même. D'autre part, le breton étant, selon les spécialistes, la langue vivante la plus proche du gaulois (qui fut parlé en France avant la romanisation et a eu sur le français une influence considérable), la préservation du seul parler celtique subsistant dans l'héxagone devrait être l'un des soucis majeurs de tout français cultivé. Aujourd'hui, certains responsables politiques le comprennent et le gouvernement a adopté une position plus libérale; mais un peu tard, au moment où la langue "dominante" est devenue le parler maternel de l'immense majorité des jeunes Bretons.

Certains faits sont, tout de même, de nature à tempérer notre pessimisme:

1) Si le breton est de moins en moins parlé, il est de plus en plus étudié: chaque année, environ 1.000 candidats choisissent le breton comme 2e ou 3e langue au baccalauréat (il n'est toujours pas possible de la prendre comme 1ere langue) (15). Des milliers de personnes ont appris le breton en classe, par correspondance ou grâce à des cours du soir.

2) Le breton populaire s'était "dialectalisé" et souvent abatardi (invasion de mots français techniques ou savants). Celui des néo-bretonnants est unifié, ce qui facilite beaucoup sa diffusion (16), et comporte un vocabulaire adapté à la vie moderne.

3) Les techniques actuelles (magnétophone, méthodes audio-visuelles ...) sont mises de plus en plus au service de l'enseignement du breton.

4) Les néo-bretonnants sont nombreux, non seulement en Basse-Bretagne, mais également dans l'Est du pays (dans des régions où l'usage du breton s'était perdu depuis plusieurs siècles). La fameuse opposition Bretagne romane / Bretagne bretonnante est en train de s'estomper.

Si cette évolution se confirme, le danger pour le breton n'est pas de disparaître, mais de devenir une langue de culture (comme le gaelique d'Irlande, dont un million environ de personnes ont une connaissance "scolaire"), et de cesser d'être le véhicule de la vie courante. Le breton parlé a constamment "nourri" le breton littéraire. Il serait grave que celui-ci perdît ses racines populaires.

C'est pour celà qu'il convient d'attacher la plus grande importance au développement des écoles "Diwan" et à toutes les tentatives visant à refaire du breton la langue de la vie quotidienne. Cet objectif peut paraître démesuré, voire utopique, mais il donne tout son sens au combat pour la langue bretonne.

Bien entendu, tout dépend de la volonté des Bretons eux-mêmes. Tout dépend aussi de l'évolution économique de la région (si les jeunes sont condamnés pour la plupart à émigrer vers des pays de langue française ou de langue anglaise, ils oublieront vite le breton et ne transmettront pas à leurs enfants une langue dépourvue de toute utilité dans le domaine des communications internationales). Tout dépend enfin de certaines réformes institutionnelles. Les élus locaux se sont constamment montrés favorables à l'enseignement du breton; mais ils se sont heurtés au mauvais vouloir ou à la force d'inertie des administrations centrales. Ainsi, l'avenir de la culture bretonne dépend en grande partie du degré d'autonomie auquel parviendront les futures Assemblées Régionales.

L'Allemagne fédérale a ses "Länder"; l'Espagne post-franquiste a ses "Communautés Autonomes". La construction de l'Europe ne se conçoit pas sans une harmonisation des institutions de ses différents Etats.

L'espoir des militants bretons est de voir la France, qui a accepté une timide régionalisation, tourner résolument le dos au "modèle napoléonien" et procéder aux réformes profondes qui permettront l'épanouissement de ses régions et, en particulier, de celles qui ont gardé, comme la Bretagne, malgré toutes les tentatives d'assimilation, une forte personnalité.

Annotations

(1) Signalons, toutefois, que les Bretons (comme les Basques et les Galiciens) ont tendance à se regrouper en associations, que ce soit à Paris, à New-York ou à Dakar, et gardent en général des liens étroits avec leur pays d'origine.
(2) Le vocabulaire de base et la numération sont restés à peu près identiques dans les trois langues brittoniques. Le cornique, dont l'usage avait disparu au XVIIIe s., connait aujourd'hui, une véritable renaissance, en tant que langue littéraire et langue parlée.
(3) Au moment des émigrations bretonnes, le nord de notre presqu'ile forma une principauté, la Domnonée, qui devait son nom aux "Dumnonii"; quant aux "Cornovii" établis en Armorique, ils fondèrent autour de Quimper, le royaume de Cornouaille ("Kerne" en breton).
(4) Les Gallois se désignent eux-mêmes, dans leur langue, par une terme qui signifie "les compatriotes"; ceci explique l'étymologie du nom gallois du Pays de Galles (Cymru).
(5) Entre le Ve et le IXe s. (et selon les époques), il y eut en Armorique 3, 4 ou 5 petit "royaumes" bretons; par ailleurs, chaque paroisse (Plou, Lan, ...) semble avoir joui d'une certaine autonomie, sous la direction d'u chef civil ou religieux.
(6) Par son contrat de mariage avec Louis XII, la Duchesse Anne avait exigé le retour du Duché à l'indépendance après la mort des deux époux. Ce calcul fut déjoué lorsque Claude épousa François Ier et renonça à ses droits sur la Bretagne.
(7) La Bretagne ducale étant une monarchie constitutionelle, l'annexion ne pouvait se faire sans l'accord des députés des "Etats"; ceux-ci négocièrent les conditions de l'annexion.
(8) Le traité de 1532 ne pouvait pas être abrogé sans l'accord des "Etats" (or ceux-ci ne furent jamais consultés, et unilatéralement dissous). Dès 1789, des voix s'élevèrent en Bretagne pour protester contre cette décision illégale. Aujourd'hui encore, il y a des Bretons qui refusent d'être jugés par un tribunal "français" (La Bretagne avait sa propre cour de justice en vertu du traité de 1532).
(9) Le mouvement romantique fut accompagné d'une renaissance des cultures et des langues régionales. Des phénomènes assez semblables ont pu être observés à peu près à la même époque en Ecosse, en Irlande, en Galice, en Bretagne et dans d'autres pays.
(10) On peut citer le cas d'un responsable départemental du P.N.B., membre d'un réseau de Résistance, qui fut condamné à mort à la fois par les occupants allemands et par un groupe de résistants hostiles aux autonomistes; bien entendu, il ne pu être tué qu'une fois. Autre cas, parmi tant d'autres:

celui de Yann Le Mitour, de Quimper, qui, bien qu'évadé d'un stalag allemend, fut condamné pour son action bretonne et passa trois ans et demi en prison.
(11) Alors que le mouvement politique breton passait, en général, jusqu'en 1950, pour conservateur, une évolution vers la gauche de la plupart de ses jeunes militants se dessina ensuite. En 1981, le Président Mittérand, qui semblait d'ailleurs disposé à prendre des mesures favorables à la décentralisation et à l'enseignement des langues régionales, bénéficia du soutien de nombreux militants bretons; ces derniers se déclarent souvent déçus aujourd'hui par la gauche française.
(12) Il n'en fut pas de même au Pays de Galles. Les anglais obligèrent les Gallois à renoncer à leurs noms de famille celtiques, qui presque tous disparurent (d'où les patronymes "John's", "Davie's", "William's" ... etc...).
(13) Un jour, un certain M. Moulin se présenta à l'état-civil pour déclarer la naissance d'un fils, auquel il voulait donner le prénom de Yann. L'employé n'accepta qu'à la condition que ce prénom fût suivi d'un second prénom "bien français". " - L'Algérie est bien française?", demanda alors M. Moulin. " - Mais, certainement"!, repondit l'employé. " - Dans ce cas, 'reprit le déclarant', je l'appelerai Yann Mohamed!"
(14) L'expérience "Diwan" s'est inspirée des réalisations semblables menées à bien au Pays de Galles et au Pays Basque (les "ikastolak").
(15) Il y a quelques années, un candidat a refusé de passer son baccalauréat dans une autre langue que le breton. Après hésitation, les autorités académiques ont désigné des examinateurs bretonnants dans toutes les matières et ont déclaré le candidat reçu.
(16) Trois des quatre dialectes bretons restent assez proches de la langue littéraire; le quatrième, celui du pays de Vannes, a sa propre littérature.

Bibliographie

Bernier, G., 1982: Les Chrétientés celtiques continentales. Rennes.

Borderie (A. de la) et B. Pocquet, 1896-1914: Histoire de Bretagne. 6 volumes.

Chadwick, N. K., 1969: Early Brittany (University of Wales Press - Cardiff 376 p.)

— The colonization of Brittany from Celtic Britain. Proceedings of the British Academy. LI PP. 235-289.

Delumenau et collaborateurs, 1969: Histoire de Bretagne. Privat-Toulouse, 542 p.

— 1971: Documents de l'Histoire de Bretagne. Privat, 402 p.

Duchatellier, A., 1836: Histoire de la Révolution dans les départements de l'ancienne Bretagne. Nantes. 6 volumes.

Durtelle de Saint-Sauveur, 1935: Histoire de Bretagne des origines à nos jours. Plihon-Rennes. 2 volumes, 435 et 508 p.

Falc'hun, F., 1963: L'histoire de la langue bretonne d'après la géographie linguistique. Presses Universitaires de France. Paris. 2 volumes, 437 p.

Fleuriot, L., 1980: Les Origines de la Bretagne. Payot, 353 p.

— 1964: Le vieux breton, éléments d'une grammaire. Paris-Klincksieck.

Fouéré, Y., 1977: Histoire résumée du Mouvement Breton. Les Cahiers de l'Avenir de la Bretagne, no 4, 155 p.

Galliou, P., 1983: L'Armorique Romaine". Les Bibliophiles de Bretagne-Braspars, 310 p.

Giot, P. R., Fleuriot et Bernier, 1982: <u>Les Premiers Bretons - La Bretagne du Ve s. à l'an 1.000.</u> Editions JOS-Chateaulin, 36 p.

Giot, L.: <u>La Bretagne avant l'Histoire.</u> Ed. Kendalc'h-La Baule-Collection "Breiz hor Bro, 110 p.

Giot, L'Helgouarc'h et Briard, 1962: <u>La Bretagne préhistorique et protohistorique.</u> Paris Arthaud.

Grenier, A., 1970: <u>Les Gaulois.</u> Paris.

Hubert, H., 1932: <u>Les Celtes.</u> 2 volumes (403 et 368 p). Paris, collection: L'Evolution de l'Humanité.

Kervella, F., 1974: <u>Anviou-lec'h ar vro vrezhoneg.</u> Hor Yez-Tome 96, p. 5-30.

Le Lannou, M., 1950-52: <u>Géographie de la Bretagne.</u> 2 volumes. Rennes-ed. Plihon.

— 1978: <u>La Bretagne et les Bretons.</u> P.U.F. collection "Que sais-je?" 126 p.

Le Roux, F., 1972: <u>Keltische Religion</u> in "Handbuch der Religion Geschichte". Göttingen, Vandenhoek und Ruprecht, pp. 245-276.

Lloyd, J. E., 1939: <u>History of Wales.</u> 3e édition-Londres. Tomes I et II.

Lot, J., 1883: <u>L'émigration bretonne du Ve au VIIe s. de notre ère.</u> Rennes-Imprimerie de Baraise.

Phlipponneau, M., 1970: <u>Debout, Bretagne!</u> St Brieuc-Presses Universitaires de Bretagne.

Planiol, M., 1953-55: <u>Histoire des Institutions de la Bretagne.</u> Rennes. 3 volumes.

Poupinot, Y.: <u>Les Bretons à l'heure de l'Europe.</u>

Sanquer, R. (depuis 1972): <u>Chroniques d'archéologie antique et médiévale</u> in Bulletin de la <u>Société d'Archéologie du Finistère.</u>

"Skol Vreiz", 1974-84: <u>Histoire de la Bretagne et des Pays Celtiques.</u> 5 volumes. Plourin-Morlaix.

Tanguy, B.: <u>La limite linguistique de la péninsule armoricaine à l'époque de l'émigration bretonne</u> (Annales de Bretagne. 87.3. p 426-462).

Touchard, J., 1967: <u>Le Commerce maritime breton au Moyen-Age.</u> Paris. Belles Lettres.

Waquet, H., 1948: <u>Histoire de Bretagne</u> (PUF "Que sais-je?" 127 p.).

Adresse de l'auteur:
Robert Omnès
Ti Lanig Kergoff.
29000 - Plomelin - Breiz -
(France)

Recent Trends in Immigration Policy in Canada: Some Remarks on the 1981 Census

Jean-Michel Lacroix

Abstract: It is generally believed that Canadian society is, in many respects, ideal. We willingly continue to use the embellished metaphor of the ethnic mosaic. But this idealism should be somewhat adjusted. Based on the recent statistics provided by the 1981 Census, this article takes a close look at non-white immigrants who are tremendously increasing in number. This might seriously alter the nation's perspectives and this article tries to observe the impact of the changes recently incorporated in Canadian legislation relating to immigration. The difficulties created by certain recent waves of immigration have raised the issue of a multicultural society which is becoming multiracial as well.

Résumé: La métaphore valorisante de la mosaïque ethnique caractérise assez bien la société canadienne mais il convient toutefois de nuancer. Les toutes dernières données statistiques du recensement de 1981 marquent clairement le poids accru des minorités visibles au Canada. Cet article analyse plus particulièrement l'augmentation sensible des "non-blancs" qui risque de modifier sérieusement les perspectives, puis essaye d'évaluer l'impact des changements introduits récemment dans la législation canadienne en matière d'immigration. La problématique est désormais celle d'une société multiculturelle qui devient une société multiraciale.

Zusammenfassung: Allgemein wird angenommen, daß die kanadische Gesellschaft in vielerlei Hinsicht ideal ist. Wir benutzen bereitwillig die beschönigende Metapher des "ethnischen Mosaiks". Diese Idealvorstellung sollte jedoch teilweise korrigiert werden. Auf der Grundlage der Statistiken, die durch die Volkszählung 1981 geliefert wurden, werden in diesem Beitrag die "nicht-weißen" Immigranten betrachtet, deren Zahl in den letzten Jahren enorm anstieg. Dies könnte die Zukunftsentwicklung der Nation tiefgreifend verändern, daher werden in diesem Beitrag besonders die jüngeren Veränderungen behandelt, die in der kanadischen Gesetzgebung bezüglich der Immigration erfolgten. Die Schwierigkeiten, die durch die letzten Einwanderungswellen entstanden sind, bestehen überwiegend darin, daß aus einer "multikulturellen" eine "multirassische" Gesellschaft zu werden scheint.

I would like to start off with the 1981 Census — the results having just been published (1) — in order to make the most of recent data on the subject of immigration and to put forward some critical remarks from a foreign observer's point of view.

My goal will be to attempt to interpret the meaning of the evolution of the ethnic composition of Canadian society, and to evaluate the problems that have arisen, or that may arise in the very near future.

It would seem unnecessary to remind you of the importance of the demographic realities of a country which would have a radically different character if it were more densely populated. As far as the evolution of the population is concerned, there are two areas which merit our close attention: on one hand, the rate of natural growth, and on the other hand, the actual contribution of immigration, that is to say net migration. I have already had the occasion to write (2) that natural growth has played a more important role than immigration in Canada's demographic expansion, and that the rate of this growth has just experienced a new and perturbing decline during the decade from 1971 to 1981. Given this fact, there is a general tendency to continue believing that Canadian society is, in many respects, ideal. Besides retaining an image of a pluralistic democracy safe from terrorist attacks, we willingly continue to use the embellished metaphor of the ethnic mosaic. Admittedly, despite the extreme variety and extreme heterogeneousness of this ethno-cultural pluralism, Canadian society has never experienced the problems that have plagued Great Britain or the United States concerning race relations or ethnicity. But this idealism should be somewhat adjusted as it has little to do with reality.

Outline of the subject

An examination of the 1981 Census can give way to all sorts of analyses and I will exclude right away a study of the comparative situations of the two founding peoples, or of their linguistic evolution. I would prefer to centre my attention on the "third force", or more precisely on the "visible minorities" whose numbers are rising significantly.

The accrued weight of this third force is what, initially, surprised the observers of social change over the past few decades. Let us briefly recall that in 1867, English Canadians represented more that 61% of the total population, French Canadians 31% and "others" 8%. In 1971, the English made up only 44.62%, the French 28.65% and the others represented 26.73%. In 1981, this evolution was even more pronounced: the percentage of English had fallen to 40.17%, the French 26.74% and the others had increased to 33.09%.

It has often been stated that one of the essential differences between the United States and Canada is precisely the colour element. To prolong the metaphor, we might say that, as opposed to the mosaics of Antiquity, the Canadian mosaic is to the naked eye very pale or even colourless.

But the growing importance of visible minorities within the third force, relegating the French to third place, might even seriously alter the nation's perspectives and it will be interesting, in this respect, to observe the impact of the changes recently incorporated in Canadian legislation relating to immigration. Just over twenty years after the passage of racist laws in 1962, a bit more than ten years after the introduction of an official Multiculturalism Programme, and with the hindsight that we are beginning to acquire, we can ask ourselves if Canada's multicultural society is the product of an ideal model or if it is embodied in an ordinary reality. The concrete difficulties encountered and created by certain recent waves of immigration have raised the issue of a multicultural society which is becoming multiracial as well.

I. The Evolution of Canada's ethnic composition and particularly of the percentage of visible minorities within the third force.

During the past twenty years radical changes have been noted as to the geographic and ethnic origin of immigrants to Canada. Until 1961, the colour element was negligible when we analyse the composition of the Canadian population. The proportion of visible minorities is infinitesimal. The 1961 Census mentions 121,753 Asians (0.66% of the total population) and 32,127 Negroes (sic!) (or 0.17%). In all, non-whites represented less than 1% of the total. We will not dwell on the history of these groups or on the official policies of the Canadian government concerning immigration before the beginning of the 1960's, due to the existence of numerous studies which have already been published on the subject.

The first signs of change appeared with new legislation introduced in 1962, which no longer perpetuated the racially discriminatory practices of the past, for the Immigration Act of 1962 lay stress exclusively upon criteria such as education and skill. However, the effects of the political will on reality are rarely immediate, and until about 1965 or 1966, a more or less preferential treatment was still given to those immigrants arriving from Europe and particularly Great Britain. Even the location of immigration offices reveals the favourable consideration enjoyed by Caucasian nations: of the 32 offices situated in 21 countries, only 4 were in non-white countries.

The White Paper released by the government in October 1966 reformulated the proposals which were to lead to the adoption of the Immigration Act of 1967 which provided for a unique "points system" which would, from then on, take into consideration factors such as age, skill, education and employment possibilities. The law vigorously reaffirmed the government's desire not to fall back on discriminatory practices and, beginning in 1967, non-white immigrants began their massive entry into Canada. Since then, the percentage of Europeans versus non-whites has evolved in a significant fashion. Despite the fact that in 1966, Canada's newly-admitted immigrants were 76% European, and only 15% Black and Asian, the percentages were almost equal in 1973/74: 39% and 36.6% respectively (3). Even though the placement of recruiting offices was still quite selective, we can nonetheless conclude that by 1967 onward the Canadian government had abolished all racist restrictions.

It is quite difficult to obtain precise and, above all, comparable statistics, given the variations introduced during successive censuses (notably regarding the formulation of questions, the chosen criteria, the processing of information, and the names used to designate the various ethnic groups), but we can, however, estimate that between 1966 and 1974, 408,000 Blacks and Asians entered Canada. We can fully grasp the impact of the 1967 legislation when we consider that just for the decade spanning from 1967-77, non-white newcomers numbered 556,000.

At this stage in our chronological presentation, we should remind ourselves of the importance of the world economic crisis, which began in 1974 and was not without effect upon Canada's own particular economic situation. Indeed, certain socio-economic criteria will be forced to play an increasingly fundamental role with regard to federal immigration policy; legislation passed in 1976 confirmed this erosion of the job market. Due to Bill C-24, proposed in November 1976 (and proclaimed in April 1978), the borders began to close on foreigners. It is unquestionable that Canada now selects candidates based purely on socio-economic criteria, but we must also note that these criteria do not favour non-whites.

We should emphasize that a gap always exists between official government policies and the practices of an entire society, and we may underline that the check placed on the entry of large numbers of non-whites has not yet made its impact fully felt; Canadian society is presently experiencing more and more acutely the effects of the accrued presence of visible minorities which is established by the statistics of the 1981 Census. Indeed, with the increase in numbers of Blacks and Asians in Canada we have seen reappear, starting in 1976/77, the first signs of discrimination which had been somewhat forgotten, true enough, since the nativism of the 1920's and 30's. The euphoria created by the Multicultural Programme launched in 1971 did not hide the core of the problem, but it is helpful to qualify and distinguish carefully the components of a group which is too often over-simplified to "non-whites". Let us consider the evolution of the statistics of the last three censuses (table 1):

Table 1: Blacks and Asians in Canada's population

	Blacks		Asians		Total	
1961	32,127	(0.17%)	121,753	(0.66%)	153,880	(0.83%)
1971	34,445	(0.16%)	285,540	(1.32%)	319,985	(1.48%)
1981	45,215	(0.19%)[+]	785,715	(3,26%)	830,930[++]	(3.45%)

+) This figure only includes Africans.
++) This figure includes West Asians and North Africans, Indo-Pakistanis, Far East Asians, Africans, and people from the Pacific Islands.

Source: Statistics Canada

In reality, if we define visible minorities as non-whites we cannot limit ourselves to just Blacks and Asians, and we can therefore reasonably estimate the non-white population of Canada to be 1,864,000, or close to 7% of the total population (4). This figure includes the members of the first nations and the Métis as well as those Canadians originating from African and Asian countries, and from China, India, Pakistan, Japan, Korea, Southeast Asia, Latin America, the Pacific Islands, the West Indies and the Philippines. We can see that during each of the decades noted above the total amount more than doubles and reaches, in 1981, a percentage that ranks visible minorities at a level much higher than that of the larger communities of the third force.

The first remark that should be made is to emphasize the relative stability of the African group versus the spectacular rise of the Asian group. The difficulty involved in a rigorous evaluation of the data depends essentially upon the evolution of the terms employed by the Census to designate the various ethnic or racial communities. This lexical evolution is, moreover, quite revealing of the mentality of the times. In 1961, the concepts "Asians" and "Negroes" were used. These schematized and oversimplified categories can be found again in 1971, whereas by 1981 they have been refined and diversified, not without, however, some surprising regroupings; the Asian and African category is separated into five sub-groups: the Western Asian and North African group, which includes Armenians, Lebanese, Palestinians, Syrians, Egyptians, Iranians, Turks and Israelis; the Indo-Pakistani group; the East-Asian group, including among others the Chinese, Indochinese and Japanese; the Pacific Islands group including Fijians, Indonesians, Filipinos and Polynesians and, finally, the African group.

Immigrants from the Caribbean (81,605) are rather curiously placed in the Latin American category. Their remarkable influx has constituted one of the major events in immigration of the two decades spanning from 1961 to 1981 (5). Until 1960, less than 1% of all immigrants came from the West Indies. From then on the percentage continued to increase: 1.6% in 1961, 2% in 1962, 2.4% in 1963, 3.8% in 1967, 8.8% in 1969, 9.2% in 1970, 9.9% in 1971. After this peak, the numbers began to drop in 1972 (7.5%) and, despite the figures in 1973 (11.8%) and 1974 (10.3%), the economic crisis had a spectacular effect upon entries from the Caribbean: 7.4% in 1975, 4.3% in 1979 (6).

The largest recent influx of immigrants is therefore that of the Asian group, and it is ironic to note that the country that battled the "yellow peril" at the turn of the century has more recently witnessed a constant expansion of its Chinese and Indochinese population. Indeed, within the East Asian group, it is the Japanese group which has remained the most stable: +27.78% from 1961 to 1971 but only +10.02% from 1971 to 1981.

Table 2: East-Asians in Canada's population

	Japanese	Chinese	Indochinese and other Far East Asians	Total
1961	29,157	58,197	34,399	121,753
1971	37,260	118,815	129,460	285,540
1981	40,995	289,245	455,475	785,715

Source: Statistics Canada

On the other hand, Canada's humanitarian policies toward refugees were to reach their height during the decade of 1971-1981. South Vietnamese and Cambodians have entered the country at a rate of 10,000 per year since 1975, and the percentage increased beginning in 1979. Canada was to welcome more than 60,000 boat people in the space of 18 months between mid-1979 and the close of 1980. The effect was immediately reflected by the 1981 Census statistics which showed an increase in Chinese population of 104.16% between 1961 and 1971 and of 143.44% from 1971 to 1981, and an increase of Indochinese and other East Asians of 276.35% between 1961 and 1971, and of 251.83% from 1971 to 1981.

The latest figures from the 1980's reinforce this trend: in 1981 Canada welcomed 48,483 Asians out of 128,421 entries (37.75%); in 1982, 41,686 Asians out of 121,147 entries (34.41%) and, in 1983, 36,734 Asians out of 88,846 entries (41,35%). We should note in this regard that even if we fear an increase of racial discrimination in Canada due to the accrued presence of visible minorities, we might still think that Asians would integrate themselves relatively easily if we simply consider the example of the U.S. where they benefit fully from the effects of a mobile society. This is not yet entirely true in Canada even though those Japanese who have had more time to establish themselves than other Asian groups have already benefitted from this mobility (7).

II. Some Remarks about racism and racial discrimination derived from an analysis of official government statements since 1971

Canada's "humanitarian" policies have led her to welcome within her borders thousands of refugees and foreigners of other races. The re-distribution of the two hemispheres does indeed have an effect upon the philosophy of political decisions and the attitudes of their citizens. In the mid-1960's, the percentage of European immigrants was double that of Asians; in the mid-1970's the two figures were equal, and at the beginning of the 1980's we find 27% of Europeans versus more than 40% of Asians. The reversal of this trend is quite significant. In fact, the percentages do not drastically change the overall figures because they are actually higher percentages that are based on decreasing numerical quantities. Thus, in 1983, 41.35% of Asians represented only 36,734 people, whereas in 1982 34.40% of Asians represented 41,686 people.

It is nonetheless difficult to tell whether it is sociological realities and attitudes which condition official government policies, or whether it is the latter that shape concrete individual practices. Be that as it may, it is interesting to review the official line of reasoning in order to grasp the evolution of federal policy since 1971.

It is surely unnecessary to remind ourselves that it was, ironically enough, the province of Quebec that originally inspired the soul-searching which was to lead to the launching of a programme which was not necessarily in her best interest. The strained relations between the English and the French, the vigorous if not violent affirmation of Québécois nationalism initially gave rise to the creation of a Royal Commission on Bilingualism and Biculturalism. The Commission began its work in 1963, at the height of the Quiet Revolution, and the first volumes of its Report were published in 1969. Another irony of this sort was the fear experienced by Canadians of neither French nor British origin, of being relegated to the status of second-class citizens; this anxiety led to the publication of volume IV, dealing with the cultural contribution of the other ethnic groups. It was therefore the B and B Commission which suggested initially that a multiculturalism policy be adopted, responsive enough to facilitate the harmonious integration of the various ethnic groups into Canadian society. Thus Prime Minister P. E. Trudeau unveiled on October 8, 1971 the official programme of the federal government adopting a policy of multiculturalism within the framework of a reaffirmation of bilingualism (8). The goal of this initiative was to aid the members of various ethnic communities to "overcome cultural barriers" and to resolve those difficulties encountered while learning at least one of the two official languages; all this in hope of facilitating a "total participation". The political initiatives on the institutional level provided for, among other projects, the creation in 1972 of a Multiculturalism Directorate as a Department of the Secretary of State and the establishment in 1973 of the Canadian Consultative Council on Multiculturalism (CCCM). Biennial conferences held on a national level as well as regional meetings would aid the formulation of specific recommendations.

In reality, starting in November 1973, the Canadian government initiated a series of restrictive measures in the face of a decline in economic growth. Each application for entry had, from then on, to be sent from the country of origin, and it was no longer possible to enter Canada as a visitor in order to later obtain residency status. The Green Paper of 1974 and the preparation of Bill C-24 would endow the government with a very effective means of control because the number of immigrants to be admitted was fixed annually and each admission category was subjected to rigorous planning.

Legislation passed in 1976 clearly established three admission categories: independent immigrants chosen on the basis of their professional qualifications and a variety of factors aimed at determining their capacity for assimilation, such as age and education; sponsored immigrants whose entry application is handed in by an immigrant having already settled in Canada, and designated immigrants, selected on the basis of their ability to enter the job market. Until about 1974 visible minorities entered Canada mainly as independents; after this date the entries were mainly sponsored. We must not, of course, forget all those who, having entered illegally, benefitted from amnesty, or those who, having entered as visitors or students, were granted admission while already in Canada.

Despite the introduction of these restrictions which are more of a socio-economic nature, we must recognize that the 1976 lawmaker was, for the first time, concerned about the plight of refugees. The United Nations Convention of 1951 and the 1967 Protocol expressed the international community's desire to officially recognize these refugees. Despite having helped to draft the 1951 document, Canada did not sign the Convention until 1969, and the initial effects were only felt in 1973, and made into law in 1976. The objectives of Bill C-24, concerning immigration, are characterized by a generous idealism: to facilitate the recruiting of families and to maintain a humanitarian attitude toward refugees and displaced persons (sections 45 to 47). In a more general manner, section 3 (f) reminds us that those who seek admittance to Canada on a permanent or temporary basis are chosen based on non-discriminatory standards, regardless of race, ethnic or national origin, colour, religion or sex.

The entry of over 100,000 people, notably Indochinese, under refugee status has given rise to an awareness campaign led by citizens and non-governmental organizations who have been encouraging the government to adopt even more lenient admittance regulations. The declaration of intent contained in the 1976 law already mentioned, was reiterated in 1982 in the Charter of Rights and Freedoms:

> "15.(1) Every individual is equal before and under the law and has the right to the equal protection and equal benefit of the law without discrimination based on race, national or ethnic origin, colour, religion, sex, age..."

> "27. This Charter shall be interpreted in a manner consistent with the preservation and enhancement of the multicultural heritage of Canadians".

Because of structural changes in the area of immigration, and due to the present economic problems, the Multiculturalism Directorate has, since the start of the 1980's, sought to stimulate actions and initiatives taken to reduce tensions and cultural barriers and promote the principles of integration and equality. Rather than contenting itself with merely favouring cultural preservation by addressing itself solely to ethno-cultural minorities, it seems that the government has chosen as its aim to sensitize the Canadian population to its multiculturalism policies and particularly to the various economic and social factors. Collective thought seems to orient itself toward the problems of interracial relations. The fight against racism and discrimination has become, ever since a national symposium on race relations and the law was held in Vancouver in April 1982, one of the priority objectives of the Multiculturalism Minister.

In the same vein, Jim Fleming, who was then in charge, created in May 1983 an all-party Special Parliamentary Committee to study the participation of visible minorities in Canadian society, and assigned this Commission of inquiry the task of recommending positive programmes which would "promote understanding, tolerance, and harmony among races". Chaired by MP Bob Daudlin, this committee just released its report in March 1984, entitled <u>Equality, Now</u>!

This study reflects a new-found awareness of the challenge that faces a society which is becoming more and more multicultural but above all more and more multiracial. The report reminds us of the federal efforts in 1981 to create a Unit for interracial relations within the Multiculturalism Directorate, due to the appearance of overtly as well as latently racist attitudes. It is clear that the 1980s opened new perspectives, and it is not just by chance that the analyses of racism have multiplied in the past several years (9). Our theory of a possible Asian integration would be confirmed if we considered the committee's interpretation which explains the growing racism as a reaction to Canadian immigration policy, notably concerning the arrival of immigrants from the Caribbean and India (10).

The latest development in the subject area is without a doubt the proposed Bill C-48, an Act respecting multiculturalism presented for first reading to the House of Commons on June 21, 1984. We should pay keen attention to the justification of this law which clearly introduces the concept of race (without actually defining it). It is still a matter of the preservation and development of the cultural patrimony but opinions on the question have evolved to the point of insisting upon the necessity of giving members of all the visible minorities of Canada an equal chance:

> "national unity is founded on the will of all cultural and racial groups in Canada to coexist and on their need for full confidence in their own identity ... it is in the public interest to promote a cultural policy for Canada encompassing equitable treatment of all such cultural and racial groups" (11).

The law has as its objective to "assist in the removal of barriers that inhibit the full and equal participation of cultural and racial groups in the social, cultural, political and economic life of Canada" (section 3 b) and to "encourage, in Canadian society and its institutions, awareness of and appreciation for Canada's cultural and racial diversity" (section 3 d).

As we have seen, Canada has, in the space of 20 years, seen fit to abolish all racist legislation and invite a much more diversified flow of immigrants than just Europeans. This ideological opening-up of the floodgates, which has given Canada her unique character, was unfortunately interrupted by socio-economic factors which have begun to close the gates. The generosity of Canada's humanitarian policies was ambiguously thwarted by the realities of the job market. We have known for quite a while that the ethnic mosaic is a vertical mosaic, but the real significance of the evolution of the last few years was the emerging importance of interracial relations. The era of the <u>multicultural</u> society which P. E. Trudeau's liberal government held so dear seems to be giving way to the era of the <u>multiracial society</u>, and it is still difficult at this point to predict how B. Mulroney's conservative government will choose to handle it.

Even though the decennial Census of 1981 did not give visible minorities the recognition they deserve, we can only hope that the next Census will include supplementary questions which will provide us with more precise data on visible minorities.

Let me conclude with a quote from Ramcharan:

> "Finally, one can note that the type of intergroup relations that develop in Canada in the eighties will depend on the way the majority society reacts to the solution of the legitimate grievances of people who perceive themselves at present as second-class citizens ... The difficulties involved in eradicating discriminatory

practices that have developed over centuries are immense but not insolvable ... We have the opportunity at the present time to avoid the cataclysmic confrontations and conflict that have marked interracial relationships in the United States and Great Britain ... A truly multiracial state can emerge, but only if institutional and attitudinal changes are introduced, and if the majority of citizens mobilize their efforts to fight injustice and discrimination in the society" (12).

If Canada succeeds in so doing, then it will be really different from other countries.

Footnotes

1. Population: 1981 Census of Canada (Ottawa: Ministry of Supply and Services, Statistics Canada, 1984). Catalogue 92-910 (Mother tongue, official language and home language); Catalogue 92-911 (Ethnic origin); 92-913 (Place of birth, citizenship, period of immigration).
2. J. M. LACROIX, "Diversité ethnique et unité nationale au Canada" in: P. GUILLAUME, J. M. LACROIX, P. SPRIET, eds., Canada et Canadiens, Presses Universitaires de Bordeaux, 1984, p. 197.
3. A. RICHMOND, "Recent Developments in Immigration to Canada and Australia: A Comparative Analysis", International Journal of Comparative Sociology, 17, n°s 3-4 (1976), p. 188.
4. Cf. Equality Now!, Report of the Special Committee on the Participation of Visible Minorities in Canadian Society, Supply and Services Canada, Hull, Quebec, March 8, 1984, p. 2.
5. 1951:   3,888 Caribbeans
   1961: 12,363 Caribbeans
   1971: 68,090 Caribbeans
   1981: 81,605 Caribbeans.
6. For full details, see Micheline LABELLE, Serge LAROSE, and Victor PICHE, "Politique d'immigration et immigration en provenance de la Caraïbe anglophone au Canada et au Québec, 1900-1979", Canadian Ethnic Studies, vol. XV, n°2, 1983, pp. 1-24.
7. Subhas RAMCHARAN, Racism: Nonwhites in Canada, Toronto, Butterworth, 1982, pp. 67-72.
8. For an assessment of this policy, see J. M. LACROIX, "A propos des Hispaniques: Bilinguisme et multiculturalisme au Canada", in: J. CAZEMAJOU, ed., Les Minorités hispaniques en Amérique du Nord (1960-1980), Presses Universitaires de Bordeaux, 1984, pp. 71-82.
9. V. DOYLEY, ed., Black Presence in Multi-Ethnic Canada, Vancouver, 1978. K. V. UJIMOTO and G. HIBAYASHI, eds., Visible Minorities and Multiculturalism; Asians in Canada, Toronto, 1980. S. RAMCHARAN, op.cit. Anthony B. CHAN, Gold Mountain: The Chinese in the New World, Vancouver, New Star Books, 1983. Peter S. LI and B. Singh BOLARIA, eds., Racial Minorities in Multicultural Canada, Toronto, Garamond Press, 1983.
10. In 1982, Indians were the fourth largest group of immigrants to Canada.
11. Bill C-48, an Act respecting multiculturalism, 32-33 Elizabeth II, 1983-1984, first reading, June 21, 1984, p. 1.
12. S. RAMCHARAN, op.cit., pp. 112-113.

Address of the author:
Jean-Michel Lacroix
professeur à l'Université de Bordeaux III
6, rue Jean Racine
33170 Gradignan (France)

Les Québécois et le continent, ou la transformation progressive d'une identité construite en identité réelle

Eric Waddell

Abstract: The novel Maria Chapdelaine serves as the point of departure in a review of the debate over québécois identity. The national elite has historically emphasized its Frenchness and hence transplanted nature as well as an attachment to the St. Lawrence lowlands, thereby ignoring the long tradition of continental mobility and of a sentiment of being American that is expressed by the population at large. The reasons for this dichotomy are considered, and the 1980 Referendum is seen as a turning point in its confrontation of contrived and real identities, the latter prevailing. Subsequent attempts, by geographers and others, to circumscribe the essential Americanness of québécois identity are considered, the concept of a dual attachment, to both Québec and the continent, being advanced.

Résumé: Le roman Maria Chapdelaine sert de prétexte pour aborder la question de l'identité québécoise. L'élite nationale a traditionnellement insisté sur les origines françaises, donc outre-Atlantique, aussi bien que sur un attachement à la vallée du Saint-Laurent, faisant donc fi d'une longue tradition de mobilité continentale et d'un sentiment d'américanité chez les gens du peuple. Une explication de cette dichotomie est proposée, et le Référendum de 1980 est présenté comme point de non-retour dans cette confrontation entre identité construite et identité réelle, ce dernier ayant gain de cause. Pour terminer, les tentatives de la part de certains géographes et autres intellectuels en vue de circonscrire l'essentielle américanité québécoise sont passées en revue, une attention toute particulière étant apportée à la notion de double appartenance, au Québec et au continent, chez ce peuple.

Zusammenfassung: Der Roman Maria Chapdelaine dient als Ausgangsbasis für die Frage nach der Identität Quebecs. Die nationale Elite hat in der Vergangenheit immer die französische Herkunft, und damit eine vom europäischen Kontinent übertragene kulturelle Identität hervorgehoben, ebenso wie deren enge räumliche Bindung an das Sankt-Lorenz-Tal. Sie hat dabei übersehen, daß eine lange Tradition innerkontinentaler Mobilität besteht, verbunden mit einem Gefühl der breiten Bevölkerung, Amerikaner zu sein. Der Beitrag untersucht die Gründe für diese Dichotomie. Das Referendum von 1980 wird als das Schlüsselereignis in dem Widerstreit zwischen "künstlicher" und "wirklicher" Identität verstanden, seit dem die "wirkliche Identität" das Übergewicht erlangt hat. Die Versuche von Geographen und anderen Wissenschaftlern, die "Amerikanität" der Quebecer zu analysieren, werden abschließend betrachtet, wobei dem Aspekt der Doppelzugehörigkeit der Bevölkerung zu Québec als Provinz und zum Kontinent als ganzem besondere Aufmerksamkeit geschenkt wird.

✧✧✧✧✧✧✧✧✧✧✧✧✧

"Je crois qu'ils cherchent, sans trop s'en rendre compte, quelle est la place que la conscience française occupe en Amérique, ou peut-être, quelle est la part de l'âme québécoise qui est américaine."
- Jacques Poulin à propos des deux personnages principaux de son roman Volkswagen Blues, cité dans Nicole Beaulieu "L'écrivain dans l'ombre", L'Actualité, 10 (4): 73-78, 1985

Illustrations hors texte. Bois originaux de Jean Lébédeff, tirés de: Maria Chapdelaine, Ed. Le Livre de demain, Librairie Arthème Fayard, Paris 1947, p. 7 et 83

Un récit canadien-français

Classique de la littérature du 20e siècle, Maria Chapdelaine est peut-être le premier grand roman canadien, un roman du terroir centré sur la soi-disante paysannerie canadienne-française, mais surtout une oeuvre dont on s'est servie abondamment pour évoquer 'le destin d'une race':

> Nous sommes venus ici il y a trois cents ans, et nous sommes restés ...
> Nous avions apporté d'outre-mer nos prières et nos chansons: elles sont toujours les mêmes ...
> Nous avions apporté dans nos poitrines le coeur des hommes de notre pays ...
> Nous avons marqué un pan du continent nouveau ...
>
> Autour de nous des étrangers sont venus, qu'il nous plait d'appeler des barbares; ils ont pris presque tout le pouvoir; ils ont acquis presque tout l'argent; mais au pays de Québec rien n'a changé. Rien ne changera, parce que nous sommes un témoignage. De nous-mêmes et de nos destinées, nous n'avons compris clairement que ce devoir-là: persister ... nous maintenir.
>
> C'est pourquoi il faut rester dans la province où nos pères sont restés, et vivre comme ils ont vécu ...
> - Hémon, réedit. 1967: 250-51.

Maria Chapdelaine était fille de défricheur, d'assoiffé de terres neuves, enfant d'un homme soumis à l'appel du bois et du Nord, en fuite perpétuelle des vieilles paroisses ... donc femme appelée à poursuivre la même vocation.

Toutefois, à la lecture du roman, on constate qu'il y avait trois hommes dans la vie de Maria, trois prétendants ... et trois destins possibles. Eutrope Gagnon, le colon, lui proposait de l'amitié et, en plus, la possibilité de "... continuer la vie d'à présent, dans une autre maison de bois, sur une autre terre mi-défrichée" (op. cit.: 190), soit une vie encerclée de la forêt:

> Le bois ... toujours le bois, impénétrable, hostile, plein de secrets sinistres, fermé autour d'eux comme une poigne cruelle qu'il faudrait desserrer peu à peu, année par année, gagnant quelques arpents au printemps et à l'automne, année par année, à travers toute une longue vie terne et dure ...
> - op. cit.: 190-91.

Mais il y avait, également, deux hommes qui lui proposaient, chacun à sa façon, de défoncer les murs du Royaume et de partir à l'aventure continentale. D'une part, François Paradis, garçon témeraire et pur, coureur de bois et des régions lointaines, ami des Indiens et homme "... en qui le vaste pays sauvage avait réveillé un atavisme lointain de vagabondage et d'aventure" (op. cit.: 50). D'autre part, Lorenzo Surprenant, celui qui avait pris 'le chemin des Zétats' et du travail dans les manufactures de la Nouvelle-Angleterre et qui, à titre de citadin, fut porteur 'd'un autre mirage', de "... la magie mystérieuse des cités, l'attirance d'une vie différente, inconnue, au centre même du monde humain et non plus sur son extrême lisière" (op. cit.: 183-84).

Le destin a fait que François Paradis lui soit enlevé, arraché 'par le norouâ impitoyable', laissant ainsi à Maria deux futurs possibles, celui du sédentaire ou celui du pionnier, d'ouvreur de pays ou de coureur de 'facteries'. L'un représentait la voie de la souffrance, mais aussi des valeurs sûres et la continuité parmi les siens, et l'autre le bonheur matériel - une sorte de délivrance étatsunienne. Mais:

> Là-bas c'était l'étranger: des gens d'une autre race parlant d'autre chose, dans une autre langue, chantant d'autres chansons ...
> - op cit.: 247.

Voilà pourquoi, en dernier lieu, cette fille de colon n'avait pas la liberté de choisir. Son devoir de canadienne française lui imposait une seule voie vers l'avenir, celui de:

> ... rester dans la province où nos pères sont restés, et vivre comme ils ont vécu, pour obéir au commandement inexprimé qui s'est formé dans leurs coeurs, qui a passé dans les nôtres et que nous devrons transmettre à notre tour à de nombreux enfants: Au pays de Québec rien ne doit mourir et rien ne doit changer ...
> - op. cit.: 251-52.

Et ce roman de début de siècle, avec son mélange doux-amer de ténacité et de tragédie, est passé à l'histoire pour devenir 'un chef d'oeuvre catholique' de lecture obligatoire pour des générations d'écoliers québécois.

Le discours de clercs ... et la volonté du peuple

Dès la fin du 19e siècle la voie est clairement tracée pour le peuple québécois, et ce, à quelques nuances près, jusqu'à tout dernièrement. Les bornes ont été mises en place par ses clercs - prêtres, intellectuels et membres de la classe politique - dont le discours se résume ainsi. Les Canadiens français, devenus des Québécois, sont issus de la Nouvelle-France. Accrochés aux rives du Saint-Laurent, ils sont profondement imprégnés par leurs origines et également par leur terre d'adoption et marqués non seulement par une langue et une histoire propres mais également par des valeurs différentes. Ce sont des Français d'Amérique placés par le destin outre-Atlantique et restés fidèles à une terre devenue simple espace d'appartenance, dont les limites se rétrécissent inéluctablement pour se cantonner au seul Québec. Autrement dit, ce discours prône un nécessaire enracinement dicté par les lois irréfutables de la géopolitique.

Et pourtant le peuple qui est issu de cet espace a toujours été tenté par l'aventure continentale. Welland et Moonbeam, Ontario, Saint-Boniface, Manitoba, Gravelbourg et Falher, Saskatchewan, Gentilly, Minnesota, Bourbonnais, Illinois, Saint-Joseph, Kansas, Maillardville, Colombie-britannique, Lowell, Massachusetts, Woonsocket, Rhode Island, Lewiston, Maine ... et Fort Lauderdale, Floride; la diaspora québécoise est le témoin vivant de cette tradition de partance. De cette dichotomie est née la constatation récente de Morissonneau d'un "peuple en mouvance et une élite qui la nie" (Morissonneau, 1983: 16).

Toutefois, pendant la plus grande partie du 19e siècle ces départs furent admis, voire même encouragés, par une partie importante de l'élite qui rêvait encore de bâtir une Amérique française à même les décombres de la Nouvelle-France. Il s'agissait d'une époque où le peuple participait volontiers au développement du continent, jouant souvent des rôles-clef dans des secteurs aussi diversifiés que le commerce dans le Midwest et jusqu'au Sud-ouest américain, l'exploration de l'Ouest, les négociations avec les Indiens, le transport le long de la frontière, l'industrie du textile en Nouvelle-Angleterre, la forêt, les mines, la colonisation agricole ...

Mais les voix qui exprimaient cette dimension de la vie d'un peuple se sont tues progressivement à partir de la deuxième moitié du 19e siècle. Pourquoi? D'abord il y a eu le retour en force de l'Eglise catholique en Amérique francophone à partir des années 1840, une Eglise marquée par des influences ultramontaines qui faisait des Canadiens français un rameau de la civilisation française et un peuple d'élus avec une mission providentielle en Amérique. Ensuite il y a eu la création d'un cadre institutionnel distinct pour la formation de plusieurs générations de clercs, laïques et religieux, le collège classique veillant à la création d'une élite qui s'est démarquée clairement de ses semblables d'expression anglaise en Amérique. Finalement, pour la classe politique il y a eu l'échec de la Confédération canadienne, évoqué notamment par la pendaison à Régina en 1885 de Louis Riel, chef spirituel et politique de la nation métisse, suivie par toute une série de législation répressive dans les provinces canadiennes-anglaises à l'égard des francophones.

Le rétrécissement idéologique

Donc, c'est surtout à partir de 1885 que l'univers institutionnel et idéologique canadien-français commence à se rétrécir, d'abord vers l'intérieur des quelque 2000 paroisses nationales saupoudrées sur l'espace immense qui est l'Amérique, pour ensuite se coaguler en deux grands versants élaborés autour de la frontière canado-américaine; le Québec d'en Haut (la vallée du Saint-Laurent) et le Québec d'en Bas (la Nouvelle-Angleterre). Finalement, à partir des années 30 (et suite à la Crise ... et la crise Sentinelliste) cet espace se résume au seul Québec. De ce retranchement progressif, allié à une formation intellectuelle spécifique, est né la mentalité d'assiégés propre à une grande partie de l'élite et de l'intelligentsia québécoises. Or, il s'agissait non seulement de lancer l'affirmation 'Hors du Québec point de salut' mais également de manifester un profond mépris à l'égard des partants, évoqué notamment par le jugement retentissant de Georges-Etienne Cartier à l'égard de ceux qui quittaient la province en fin de 19e siècle pour s'installer en Nouvelle-Angleterre: "Laissez les partir, c'est la canaille qui s'en va." Plus tard c'est le quolibet 'vendus' qu'on lançait à ceux qui ont osé quitter le Québec pendant la Révolution tranquille pour travailler à Ottawa ou au Canada anglais.

En ce qui concerne l'enseignement et la recherche en sciences humaines un intérêt prédominant s'est vite manifesté pour la Nouvelle-France ainsi que pour tout l'héritage de cette époque, en termes de langue, de folklore, d'institutions et, par conséquent, de la dimension rurale de la société québecoise dans son ensemble. Ainsi, pendant des décennies, les historiens ont largement ignoré le 19e siècle, les géographes la Nouvelle-Angleterre, et les sociologues l'univers des Petits Canadas, à un tel point qu'un historien renommé s'affirmait être 'homme de l'Ancien Régime' tandis qu'un porte-parole d'une discipline voisine parlait de 'nous les géographes de la vallée du Saint-Laurent', et d'autres encore défendaient 'une intellectualité farouchement européenne'. De telles préoccupations intellectuelles servaient à nourrir le discours des élites religieuse et politique, et donc à renforcer la stratégie de retranchement aussi bien que la mentalité d'assiégés.

Le Québec a également connu, à travers cette démarche, une certaine convergence entre l'identité proposée par une grande partie de l'élite canadienne-française et celle imposée par la majorité anglo-américaine. Si, d'une part, on insistait sur le nécessaire attachement aux terres d'origine, à la langue, aux institutions et aux aspirations collectives, d'autre part on parlait, dans les récits de voyageurs et des guides touristiques, des expériences 'in old Québec' et on dressait le portrait des 'proud, loyal peasants, descendants of the pioneers of New France'. Mission providentielle pour les uns et survivants d'une autre époque pour les autres, on a réussi, par cette conjoncture de discours et de préoccupations, à effacer pendant les premiers deux-tiers du 20e siècle la partie urbaine et moderne de la civilisation canadienne-française des livres d'histoire et de géographie. En se limitant au versant rural de cette civilisation et à l'espace politique québécois, la partie urbaine et moderne, soit le Québec d'en Bas, a été condamnée à l'oubli. Et quand il s'agit, plus tard, de circonscrire 'la spécificité québécoise' il est peu surprenant de constater que les chercheurs trouvent les racines de cette identité exclusivement en milieu rural, en Nouvelle-France ... et dans la vieille France également.

L'essor nationaliste et l'ouverture sur le monde ... outre-Atlantique

Qu'il porte l'épithète 'moderne' ou non, force est de constater que le mouvement nationaliste des années 60 et 70 a été profondément marqué par cette démarche intellectuelle avec ses préoccupations vis-à-vis l'histoire lointaine et l'environnement immédiat, et avec son ambivalence manifeste à l'égard du continent nord-américain. Ce

poids du passé s'exprime de diverses façons dont la rupture des relations avec la
francophonie hors Québec et la politique 'd'ouverture du Québec sur le monde'.
Scellée en 1967 à l'occasion d'un débat sur le droit du Québec à l'autodétermination
aux Etats généraux du Canada français, cette rupture n'était qu'une manifestation
de plus du mépris et de l'ignorance réciproques qui se sont imposés au niveau des
relations entre Québécois et francophones de la diaspora. A partir des années 60
les Québécois ont sombré dans une telle amnésie collective à leur égard qu'il n'était
même plus question pendant un certain temps d'admettre et d'assumer les liens de
filiation qui enjambaient les frontières politiques. Ayant des destins différents il
fallait nécessairement faire abstraction des origines communes.

Valable en soi, la politique québécoise d'ouverture sur le monde péchait par sa
préoccupation outrancière du monde outre-Atlantique au dépens du continent nord-
américain. Il s'agissait non seulement de former des fonctionnaires (en termes de
mentalité et de connaissances) pour travailler essentiellement en Europe ou en Amérique latine plutôt qu'en Amérique du Nord, mais surtout de miser sur les Délégations situées en Europe. Or, même en 1984 la seule Délégation du Québec à Paris
coûte plus cher à l'Etat que l'ensemble des délégations aux Etats-Unis ... et pourtant les deux-tiers des échanges économiques extérieures (en termes de valeur)
se font avec le voisin du sud, les émigrants québécois se dirigent surtout vers les
Etats-Unis (actuellement entre 250.000 et 500.000 sont installés en permanence en
Floride contre quelques centaines à Paris), et les Québécois préfèrent largement les
mass-média américains à leur contre-partie française.

                                Et vint le Référendum

L'an 1980 assumera avec le temps les dimensions d'une date-charnière dans
l'histoire du Québec, le référendum sur son avenir politique ayant servi à amorcer
une réflexion en profondeur sur l'identité réelle d'un peuple. Rejeté par 60% de la
population, dont 50% des francophones, le projet de souveraineté-association semble
avoir échoué moins à cause d'une formulation boiteuse de la question et beaucoup
plus à la suite d'une configuration erronée de l'identité québécoise. Car, le Parti
Québécois avait fait fausse route en proposant un modèle à la fois trop axé sur la
France métropolitaine et incertain dans ses relations avec le reste du continent, donc
un modèle qui laissait entrevoir la notion d'un certain échec américain. Léandre Ber-
geron, originaire de Saint-Boniface, Manitoba, tenant d'un diplôme de troisième
cycle en études françaises, et Don Quichotte des intellectuels québécois a bien dé-
crit cette impasse:

> Les grands défenseurs du Québec français poussent donc les Québé-
> cois à l'assimilation. Car ils n'ont pas compris, ces grands pourfen-
> deurs de dragons, que le Québécois veut un Québec québécois et
> non pas français. Plus on tirera le Québécois vers le mandarinat
> français, plus il s'enracinera dans sa conviction qu'il est améri-
> cain. Si la québécitude est interdite, si le seul choix c'est
> d'être Français d'Amérique ou Américain, le Québécois va choisir
> l'Américain.
> - Bergeron, 1982: 15.

Autrement dit, ce moment de décision a suscité chez les gens du peuple le sentiment d'être en train de se faire couper du reste du continent. La coupure se faisait sentir beaucoup plus en termes de sentiments d'appartenance qu'en choix politiques. Il s'agissait là d'un drame réel, le continent nord-américain constituant pour
l'ensemble du peuple québécois un espace référentiel fondamental, partie intégrante
de leur histoire et leur vécu. Champ des possibles depuis toujours, le nouveau
pouvoir politique, à travers un discours mélancolique, était en voie de transformer
cet univers d'espérance en territoire d'échec cuisant. Un tel projet ne pouvait pas
concorder avec les aspirations profondes de la population.

L'identité repensée

Avec l'échec du Référendum le débat s'amorce en milieu académique et dans la presse écrite sur l'identité réelle québécoise, et les géographes y figurent largement. Déjà, vers la fin des années 70, Christian Morissonneau avait commencé à élaborer une thèse sur 'la mobilité québécoise'. Réagissant aux thèses classiques et s'inspirant de plusieurs séjours dans des régions de colonisation agricole, Morissonneau (1979/1983) avance la proposition que les Québécois sont surtout 'peuple de passage et non d'enracinement', en mouvance perpétuelle et donc coureurs de 'facteries' aussi bien que de bois. Et pour cet auteur, leur spécificité réside justement dans cette mouvance, et dans le fait qu'on se trouve devant 'un peuple sans frontières' qui a toujours refusé la mobilisation imposée.

La journaliste Lise Bissonnette a poussé cette réflexion plus loin, tout en y apportant une nouvelle dimension, en constatant que les Québécois constituent:

... un groupe distinct par sa langue et par ses origines plus lointaines sur ce continent, qui a participé à tous les courants du siècle passé et présent, qui contenait en ses rangs toute la diversité des peuples qu'il côtoyait.
- Bissonnette, 1983.

Autrement dit, plutôt que de s'attarder aux différences, elle commence à faire ressortir les ressemblances entre Québécois et autres nord-américains.

Une communication sur la langue et culture françaises de Fernand Dumont, une des têtes de file de l'élite intellectuelle québécoise, reprise en partie dans Le Devoir, fournit l'occasion à Bissonnette d'approfondir sa pensée. Outrée de l'incapacité chronique de voir 'la réalité en face', Bissonnette accuse Dumont d'être obsédé par 'le péril américain', de maintenir la tradition de vouloir chercher 'l'être véritable québécois' à travers le refus de l'Amérique, et donc de proposer 'la vocation du martyre comme destin et spécificité' (avec, comme modèles, l'Irlande et la Pologne!). Pour elle, cette réalité flagrante, tant niée par des générations d'intellectuels québécois, est:

... celle d'une américanité que nous partageons, sans nous porter plus mal que d'autres, avec une vaste partie de la planète. Nous le faisons simplement en français ...
- Bissonnette, 1982.

Cet échange sur 'l'éternelle question existentielle' entre journaliste et universitaire a suscité un débat passionné dans les pages du Devoir. C'était comme si d'autres attendaient dans les coulisses cette occasion de crever une abcès collectif.

Parmi les chercheurs c'est Pierre Anctil qui a le plus fait pour approfondir les idées lancées par Morissonneau et Bissonnette, dans sa volonté de cerner l'essentielle américanité québécoise. Il trace une première esquisse de cette américanité à l'occasion d'une conférence aux Etats-Unis en 1983 (Anctil, 1983). Il note que la culture québécoise est avant tout une 'culture de convergence' ayant 'assimilé les influences externes pour les faire siennes', qu'elle est une culture marquée par 'la migration et le recommencement à chaque génération', et également par 'l'absence totale de barrières sociales. C'est aussi une culture marquée par l'oralité et par l'importance qu'on y accorde à l'innovation technologique. Enfin, pour Anctil la liste est très longue, mais:

Il en découle que nous partageons avec la culture american un certain nombre de traits et de sensibilités qui nous la rendent familière (là où la culture française est étrangère), du moins au niveau de l'ensemble des couches populaires ... En choisissant l'influence américaine les Québécois se rapprochent du centre de leur expérience historique.
- Anctil, 1983: 3.

Et voilà que l'engouement pour les produits culturels américains (télévision, musique, cinéma, périodiques) devient compréhensible:

> Ce que les intellectuels perçoivent être un impérialisme odieux apparaît par ailleurs à la masse québécoise comme un message singulièrement près de leur vécu.
> - Anctil, op. cit.: 3.

En guise de conclusion

Pour la génération montante d'intellectuels, formée dans la foulée de la Révolution tranquille, Eutrope Gagnon n'est plus le portrait-témoin d'un peuple, sa place ayant été prise par un être qui affiche sans complexes son américanité, une sorte d'heureux mélange de François Paradis et de Louis Surprenant peut-être. Mais les générations précédentes ne peuvent pas avoir entièrement tort, une élite québécoise plutôt européanisée ayant toujours existé, tout comme une longue tradition indépendantiste. L'occasion est donc propice à un début de lecture critique du nouveau discours.

Lise Bissonnette ouvre timidement la voie en commentant la réaction négative des chercheurs américains devant une conférence d'Yvan Lamonde sur l'influence culturelle étatsunienne au Québec:

> Il aurait fallu, selon eux, définir le concept de culture, montrer comment les "valeurs" d'un peuple diffèrent de celles d'un autre et absorbent dès lors autrement "La petite maison dans la prairie" ou le dernier "Rocky".
> - Bissonnette, 1982.

Or, Anctil, tout comme Lamonde, a peut-être fait fausse route en confondant Amérique et Etats-Unis, américanité et culture étatsunienne. Le Québec exprime sa différence "... toujours sur un arrière-plan ou un substrat d'américanité" (Spriet, 1984: 41) (1). Il est donc normal que les gens apprécient le cinéma et les émissions télévisées américains. Ils sont attirés, toutefois, plus par la signification derrière les symboles, ces derniers restant étrangers et aliénants puisque de facture étatsunienne. Victime de sa faiblesse démographique et économique, et donc de sa marginalité, le Québec doit nécessairement se tourner vers les Etats-Unis faute d'une production culturelle locale adéquate. Le problème est double. Les Québécois ont-ils les moyens de fabriquer leurs propres symboles? Existe-t-il chez l'élite québécoise une volonté réelle de concevoir des symboles décrivant adéquatement le vécu américain du peuple? Jacques Poulin fait figure de pionnier ici avec son dernier roman Volkswagen Blues dans lequel Jack Waterman et son amie, la Grande Sauterelle, traversent le continent de Gaspé à San Francisco à la recherche d'un frère perdu, tout en empruntant "... les principales voies de pénétration des découvreurs de jadis et ... (retrouvant) les traces de l'ancienne présence française en Amérique" (Poulin, cité dans Beaulieu, op. cit.). Et chose certaine, la démarche des générations de migrants québécois, leur discours, leurs préoccupations et leurs choix seront une source d'information importante dans cette nouvelle recherche d'une identité québécoise située à l'intérieur de l'américanité retrouvée.

Dorenavant il sera possible d'admettre ce que Louis Dupont appelle 'la double appartenance' des Québécois (Dupont, 1984) et Paul Painchaud le 'système allégeances multiples' (Painchaud, Le Devoir, 12 novembre 1984) qui les relient à la fois au Québec et au continent. Dans sa thèse, récemment déposée à l'université Laval, Dupont dresse le portrait de cette double appartenance: un peuple qui, d'une part, partage la même culture économique que les autres habitants du con-

---

1) Ce texte fort révélateur de Pierre Spriet s'intitule "Les Etats-Unis et les origines de la culture canadienne". Même si l'auteur s'intéresse surtout à la culture anglophone sa pertinence pour le Québec ne fait aucun doute.

tinent et qui, d'autre part, possède un foyer culturel - une mère-patrie - dans la vallée du Saint-Laurent où ils sont linguistiquement majoritaires. Donc, d'une part, un espace économique fait d'aspirations individuelles et, d'autre part, un espace politique, expression d'aspirations collectives, où il y a recherche du pouvoir. Donc, également, le nécessaire survie et développement du foyer collectif et la nécessaire mobilité autour du même foyer.

Plus que tout autre, Dupont touche à l'identité réelle d'un peuple, identité qui a été marquée depuis 25 ans par la transformation d'une identité ethnique (plus ou moins fictive mais sans doute nécessaire à la survie de la collectivité) en identité d'état. Autrement dit, avec la Révolution tranquille et le mouvement nationaliste des dernières décennies ethnie canadienne-française est devenue peuple québécois. Devenus 'définisseurs' de l'identité officielle et norme pour l'ensemble de la population de l'espace politique qui est le Québec, les Canadiens français ont cessé, politiquement, de se comporter en ethnie. Par le fait même ils arrivent, idéologiquement, à s'insérer d'une façon non-équivoque dans la trame continentale. Et en ce faisant, les départs ne font plus peur, la collectivité québécoise devient plus visible et 'réelle', et elle risque de devenir avec les années un bercail pour les 13,000,000 d'Américains de souche française.

Sources

Anctil, Pierre, 1983: "Today's Québec - True to its origins?" Texte d'une communication présentée à l'occasion du Congrès de la Western Social Science Association, Albuquerque (Nouveau-Mexique). 27 avril. Manuscrit. 10 p.

Beaulieu, Nicole, 1985: "L'écrivain dans l'ombre", L'Actualité, 10(4): 73-78.

Bergéron, Léandre, 1982: "Peuple québécois, langue québécoise", p. 5-15 dans Imposer la batârdise francophone, numéro spécial de Anthropologie et Sociétés, 6(2).

Bissonnette, Lise, 1983: "Préface", p. ix-xi dans Du continent perdu à l'archipel retrouvé: Le Québec et l'Amérique française publié sous la direction de Dean R. Louder et Eric Waddell. Québec: Presses de l'Université Laval.

— 1982: "De notre agonie", Le Devoir, 11 septembre.

Dupont, Louis, 1984: Le fait social de partir, ou la migration québécoise vers la Floride. Thèse de maîtrise, Département de géographie, Université Laval.

Hémon, Louis, 1967 réedit. (Edition originale, 1914) Marie Chapdelaine: Récit du Canada français.

Morissonneau, Christian 1983: "Le peuple dit ingouvernable du pays sans bornes; mobilité et identité québécoise", p. 11-24 dans Du continent perdu à l'archipel retrouvé: Le Québec et l'Amérique française publié sous la direction de Dean R. Louder et Eric Waddell. Québec: Presses de l'Université Laval.
(Première version publiée dans les Cahiers de Géographie du Québec, 23(58), 1979).

Spriet, Pierre, 1984: "Les Etats-Unis et les origines de la culture canadienne", Annales du Centre de Recherches sur l'Amérique anglophone, Nouvelle série No. 9, Séminaires 1983: 19-41. Bordeaux: Maison des Sciences de l'Homme d'Aquitaine.

Adresse de l'auteur:
Eric Waddell, professeur
Dépt. de Géographie
Université Laval
Cité Universitaire
Québec, P.Q.
Canada G1K 7P4

French and English Settlement in the Eastern Townships (Québec) – Conflict or Coexistence

Alfred Pletsch

Abstract: This article discusses two key-questions of the historical development of a conflict which characterizes the neighbourhood of French Canadians and Anglo Canadians in the province of Quebec. In a first part the question is asked whether this conflict has influenced the cultural landscape of Central Canada. Based on documents from the Canadian Archives it is shown, that the maintenance of French jurisdiction after the Treaty of Paris (1763) has had, in this respect, a decisive influence, especially regarding the layout of the Townships in the later province of Ontario and even more within the Eastern Townships of Quebec. The second part discusses the demographic changes within the Eastern Townships and especially within three townships, a process through which the anglocanadian population became systematically replaced by French Canadians. This process is still going on as can be seen from the analysis of real estate transfers.

Résumé: L'article concerne deux questions fondamentales du développement historique du conflit qui caractérise le voisinage des Canadiens-Français et des Canadiens-Anglais dans la province du Québec jusqu'à l'heure actuelle. Dans une première partie, la question est abordé, dans quelle mesure ce conflit a-t-il marqué la physiognomie du paysage dans la région du Canada central. Basé sur les documents des Archives du Canada, l'auteur essaye de prouver une telle influence, devenue possible par le maintenance du Droit Français après le Traité de Paris (1763), et étant particulièrement visible dans l'arpentage des Cantons dans la région devenant plus tard l'Ontario, mais encore plus dans la région des Cantons de l'Est du Québec. La deuxième partie de l'article concerne le processus de substitution démographique d'une population anglophone par les Franco-Canadiens à l'exemple de trois Cantons, processus qui est toujours en cours et qui peut être observé par l'analyse des transfers immobiliers.

Zusammenfassung: Dieser Beitrag behandelt zwei Grundfragen der historischen Entwicklung des Konfliktes, der das Nebeneinander der Frankokanadier und der Anglokanadier in der Provinz Quebec bis heute prägt. In einem ersten Teil wird der Frage nachgegangen, inwieweit dieser Konflikt in der Kulturlandschaft Zentralkanadas seinen Niederschlag findet. Auf der Grundlage historischer Dokumente des Canada-Archivs kann belegt werden, daß die Beibehaltung französischen Rechts nach dem Frieden von Paris (1763) diesbezüglich einen entscheidenden Einfluß gehabt hat, insbesondere bei der Township-Vermessung sowohl im Gebiet des späteren Ontario als in noch stärkerem Maße in den Eastern Townships von Quebec. Der zweite Teil behandelt den demographischen Verdrängungsprozeß im Gebiet der Eastern Townships an drei konkreten Beispielen, ein Prozeß, durch den die anglokanadische Bevölkerung systematisch durch die frankokanadische substituiert worden ist. Der Vorgang ist bis heute anhand der Grundstückstransaktionen nachvollziehbar.

Studies on ethnicity seem to be primarily the field of sociologists, anthropologists or historians, and less the interest of geographers. However, the traditional understanding of geographical research, strongly influenced by German geographers of the late 19th and the early 20th century has always emphasized the argument, that any human influence on the physical or cultural landscape provokes and has to provoke the geographers' interest. Nobody would deny, that ethnic structures in a country like Canada, or in other countries having a similar cultural mosaic, do have a very distinct impact on the shaping of a cultural landscape pattern, being the result of the most divergent influences exercised by the different ethnic groups. To describe as well as to explain these influences is still a very important realm of geographers' work. During the past, there has been some research in this field, although in general the

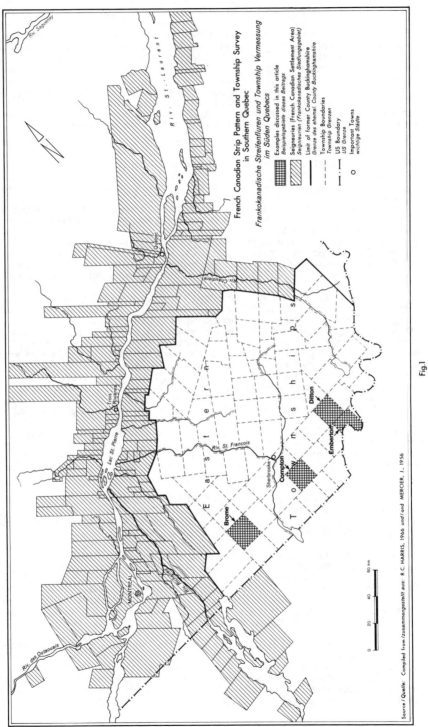

Fig.1

aspect of ethnic influences on the cultural landscape has been neglected.

The reason for this might be that in many cases the question could be considered trivial. Chinatowns, to give an example, are easily detectable even for people without any geographical or other scientific knowledge. But there are many more aspects to be considered than the purely physiognomical features, indeed these features are not always that evident. A very exiting area for examining ethnic influences on the cultural landscape lies in Southern Québec between the St. Lawrence River, the Chaudiere River and the US Boundary. This region covers part of the early settlement areas of the French Canadians in the St. Lawrence Lowlands and the Eastern Townships, initially supposed to be reserved for English settlement.

The historical geographers' interest in this area is threefold:

1) The first question is whether the neighbourhood of French and English settled areas has provoked different aspects of the cultural landscapes and to what extent could there be mutual influences from one group on the other and vice versa.
2) The second question is, how, in the historical dimension, the two ethnic groups concerned have intermixed and whether there has been social and spatial segregation within the area.
3) The third question arises more from a modern social-geographical view-point: how do these neighbourhoods continue to be a conflict, and how could one define social areas within a given geographical unit. This last question is mainly considered by M. Schulte in this volume and will thus not be treated here.

If we concentrate on the first question, the answer seems, at first glance, to be trivial: there is, as Fritz Bartz (1955) pointed out, a very typical "French" landscape in the Lowlands of the St. Lawrence River, characterized by a long lot field pattern and strip settlements with houses recalling the French origin of the early settlers, mainly Britanny and Normandy. Strikingly opposed to these patterns is the layout of the townships east of the Lowlands reaching into the Appalachian area, characterized by its rectangular or even square patterns of units of more or less similar size (Fig. 1). Within these townships, however, the division into 12 rangs subdivided into 28 lots recalls the seigneurial strip pattern, although the dimensions are noticeably different. The same strip subdivision system is also observed in the so-called Western Townships (Ontario), thus in an dominantly English settled area.

This strip subdivision within a township is undoubtedly the most surprising fact, since the general pattern all over Canada and the United States is the square subdivision. In almost all cases of strip subdivision there seems to be a direct or indirect French influence. We must therefore look at the historical development and the events in the second half of the 18th century to make the phenomenon explicable.

After the Treaty of Paris (1763), when the Township-System was introduced to former Nouvelle France by the English conquerers, the common pattern for land subdivision in New England was already the Square-Section-System and strip patterns were almost non-existent in townships created at that time.

If we have a look at Carl Schott's work on "Landnahme und Kolonisation in Kanada am Beispiel Südontarios" we find that almost all the subdivision systems (Single Front System, Double Front System, 2.400 Acre-Section System and others) have a strip pattern. This means, we do have a French subdividing system in English settled areas. The differences in the subdivision practises between the United States and Canada only become explicable if we look at the jurisdiction in use in New France between 1763 and the constitutional foundation of Canada in 1791.

As a logical consequence of the conquest, the English conquerers abolished French jurisdiction in former Nouvelle France and introduced in 1764 the "Law of England", which became th. general rule and applicable to all people, French, English or others, settling in the new colony. But, except for the French, almost nobody was settling in this new land, either because there were no settlers coming from England, or these preferred not to be placed in the immediate neighbourhood of

Similarities of Land Survey Patterns in French and English settled Areas of Central Canada
Ähnlichkeiten der Landvermessung in französisch und englisch besiedelten Gebieten Zentralkanadas

Rang Settlement Pattern in Québec (Hypothetical Model)
Rang-Siedlungsmuster in Quebec (Hypothetisches Modell)

a)

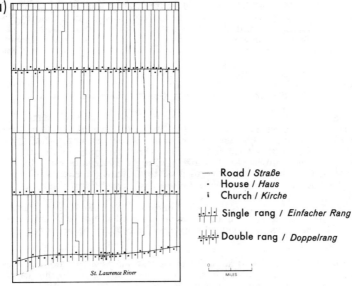

— Road / *Straße*
· House / *Haus*
i Church / *Kirche*

Single rang / *Einfacher Rang*

Double rang / *Doppelrang*

Source /*Quelle:* R.C. HARRIS and J. WARKENTIN, 1974: 74

Single Front System in Ontario (Hypothetical Model)
Single Front System in Ontario (Hypothetisches Modell)

b)

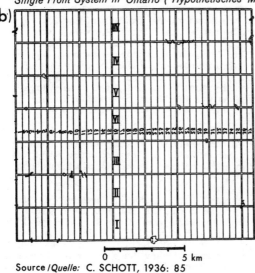

Source /*Quelle:* C. SCHOTT, 1936: 85

Fig. 2

167

the revolting New England colonies. We must note that the first townships were only created 20 years after the conquest, and that during this period the political situation in North America had radically changed. As we all know, the first non-French settlers coming to Canada were not people from England, but United Empire Loyalists - very often of German origin - who crossed the borderline after 1783.

The consequence of this situation was that after 1763 English law was applied to a large majority of people of French descent and to an almost non-existent English minority, consisting of administrative and military staff and a few settlers, living as unorganized squatters. It is logical that discontent among the people of French origin increased in this situation, and that they asked for the reestablishment of French jurisdiction. The English administration apparently did consider the French arguments very seriously, most probably because they could not risk being confronted by an increasingly revolutionary population in the New England colonies on the one hand and to an increasingly opposed population of French origin in the newly conquered colony, on the other. Already in 1767, in a proposal for an ordinance sent to Secretary of State Shelbourne, Governor General Carleton argues:

"... the said French Laws and Customs shall be deemed and taken to have continued without Interruption from the Time of the Conquest of this Country by the British Arms to the present Time; (...) And further this Oridinance shall extend not only to all Lands in this Province held immediately of the Crown by Grants made by the French King before the Conquest of this Country, and to all Lands held under these immediate of the Crown, who are commonly called Seigneurs, by Grants made by the said Seigneurs to inferior Tenants or Vassals, before the said Conquest, but likewise tu such Lands as have been granted (...) since the said Conquest, and likewise to all such Lands as shall be granted hereafter" (Can. Arch. Sess. Pap. Nr. 18, 1906/07: 205).

The frequent petitions and attempts to reestablish French Laws and Customs were finally fulfilled by King George in 1771, three years prior to the famous Québec-Act, by the following instruction to the Governor General:

"(...) being desirous to promote as far as in Us lies, the Welfare and Prosperity of Our said Province, have thought fit to revoke & do hereby revoke and annul all such parts of our Instructions to you; & every Clause, Matter and Thing therein, which contain any Powers or Directions in respect to the granting of Lands within Our said Province. And it is Our Will and Pleasure & you are hereby authorized and empowered to grant (...) the Lands which remain subject to Our disposal, in Fief or Seigneurie, as hath been practised heretofore antecedent to the Conquest thereof. And it is Our further Will and Pleasure that all Grants in Fief and Seigneurie, so to be passed by you, be made subject to Our Royal Ratification, in like manner as was Practised in regard to Grants held in Fief and Seigneurie under the French Gouvernment"
(Can. Arch. Sess. Papers, 18. 1906/07: 295).

These instructions reversed completely the existing system of land grants and land tenure, and they not only reestablished the legal situation which existed prior to the Treaty of Paris, but also applied these customs to all other people, including the British.

The geographical consequences of this decision are clearly to be detected in the early townships, which were surveyed during the last two decades of the 18th century. This survey comprised almost the whole area of the St. Lawrence Lowlands as far as not yet settled by the French and thus subdivided in Seigneuries, as well as the adjacent areas like the Appalachians in SE Québec, the later Eastern Townships. The Québec Act of 1774 was in this respect very decisive for the French settlement area, which became restricted to the limits of the seigneurial lands granted before 1763. The rest of former Nouvelle France was reserved for English settlement.

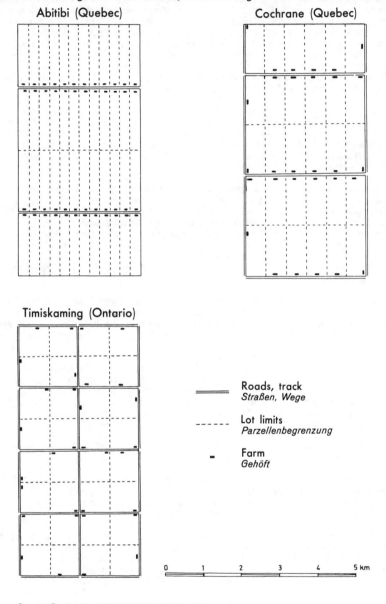

Fig. 3

Under these French rules the settlement process started with the creation of the so called Western Townships in the later Province of Ontario, a process which was described in great detail by Carl Schott in 1936. One of the characteristics in this land survey is, as mentioned before, the existence of different division patterns, recalling the French long lot system. Similarities are especially evident in the comparison of the so called "Single Front System" with the seigneurial "rotures". Relatively small lots are surveyed along a river or a road, with the result that the farms form a continued line of settlements very similar to the "rang" of a classical seigneurie (Fig. 2). It went so far, that the first lands given to English settlers were even granted as "fief" (lease), and the townships themselves were called "Seigneurie", because these terms were known by and common to everybody.

But the English settlers did not voluntarily accept French jurisdiction, and even less French terminology. They vigourously opposed the rigid and severe French laws, and the settlement of the Western Townships seemed, at least in the beginning to have suffered from this legislation. According to a report, signed by J. De Lery, S. Holland and J. Johnson in 1787, United Empire Loyalists were very reluctant to settle under these conditions.

> "The Loyalists, who have settled themselves above Montreal have transmitted to us certain Papers marked N° 13^c and 14^d, in which they intimate their wishes and Desires, that the Lands on which they are settled, should be granted under a different Tenure from that Signified in His Majestys Instructions*. But we are of opinion, that the terms and Conditions specified in the Instructions are fit to be adopted" (Can. Arch. Sess. Pap. 18, 1906/07: 640).
> * The mentioned instructions are those to Carleton from 1771, reestablishing French jurisdiction.

The number of petitions for reestablishment of the British law increased considerably in the late 1780's. A few examples might serve as documentation. On December 22, 1786 in a letter from the Magistrates at Cataraqui (later Kingston) to Sir Johnson, Baronet, the tenure of land is considered to be the object of most importance:

> "The Conditions on which they (the lands) have been granted to the Loyalists in this Province are so different from what they have been used to, that they are universally disagreable. Nothing in our opinion would conduce so much to the prosperity of these Settlements as the putting the grants on Lands on the same footing they are on in the Rest of British America. This would at once give the most universal satisfaction" (Can. Arch.; Sess. Pap. 18, 1906/07: 642/43).

On December 18th of the same year the Magistrates at New Oswegatchee (later Ogdensburg) had equally sent a letter to John Johnson, saying:

> "We must earnestly pray for ourselves and in behalf of the inhabitants of New Oswegatchee, that we may have our Lands by Grants free from any Seigneurial Claims or any other incumbrance whatever" (Can. Arch. Sess. Pap. 18, 1906/07: 645).

In almost all these petitions the common arguments are that the French legislation discourages settlers from settling, that many of them have left the land for this reason, and that, on the other hand, the introduction of British law would considerably encourage settlement and increase the prosperity of the Province. With this permanent support and demand from the settlers, Superintendant Sir William Jones in 1791 accepted the establishment of a settlement district near Cataraqui, where on demand of the settlers "British law and practice alone should prevail". When in 1791 the Constitutional Act was passed, British jurisdiction was reinstalled in Upper Canada, whereas in Lower Canada the application of French or British Law was made optional. Article XVIII of the Constitutional Act of 1791 defines:

"That all Lands which shall be hereafter granted within the said Province of Upper Canada shall be granted in Free and Commun Soccage; and that in every Case where Lands shall be hereafter granted within the said Province of Lower Canada, and where the Grantee thereof shall desire the same to be granted in Free and Commun Soccage, the same shall be so granted; but subject nevertheless to such Alterations (...) as may be established by any Law or Laws which may be made by His Majesty (...) by and with the Advice and Consent of the Legislative Council and Assembly of the Province" (Can. Arch., Sess., Pap. 18, 1906/07: 706).

The differences in land tenure were thus constitutionally legalized, and the Province of Lower Canada was able to take advantage of the possibilities offered by this paragraph in the Constitution to preserve the French influence.

In the following years, the newly surveyed townships in Upper Canada were almost all characterized by a very distinct square grid pattern, much like that given by the survey in use in the United States. In Lower Canada however, the strip system was maintained and in practice as well in the Eastern Townships, situated between the Seigneurial Lands and the US border, as well as in the Clay Belt region where settlement first took place in the late 19th and early 20th century. Investigating the settlement process of the 1920's/30's in the Clay Belt of Ontario and Québec, Hottenroth (1968) found that two very distinct and different patterns were used during the same time period, but according to different customs and laws. On the Ontarian side, the classical township layout with square grid pattern developed, whereas on the Québec side within the new townships of Abitibi and Temiscaming the old "rang"-system, similar to that of the seigneurial lands, prevailed (Fig. 3).

From these considerations the answer to the first question follows: The maintenance of French jurisdiction in Upper Canada between 1771 and 1791 and in Lower Canada even after the Constitution Act distinctively influenced land survey practices, conserving the very typical French strip division even in those parts where English settlement was initially supposed to have taken place. The most convincing example of this influence is the Eastern Townships of Québec, where in the time following 1791 the settlement process became a battlefield between French and British people.

This leads to the second question about a possible intermixture of these two groups. Again some historical facts must be remembered in order to recognize the whole dimension of the process, starting shortly after the Constitutional Act. The region known as the Eastern Townships was initially called County Buckinghamshire and was supposed to become an English settled area after 1763. By the Québec Act, French settlements were rigourosly limited to the lands occupied prior to 1763. Within County Buckinghamshire, the Catholic church was not allowed to establish parishes, which was probably the most severe obstacle for French people intending to settle in that area.

However, English settlement did not noticably start after 1791, even though within a few years a great number of townships was surveyed, especially near the US border. The reasons for the very slow settlement process seem to be twofold.

The very isolated geographical situation of the area surrounded by French settled lands in the West and the United States in the East was, in addition to the harsh topographical and climatical conditions, certainly a psychological obstacle for settlers intending to occupy this area. As mentioned before, the first people coming to this area were mainly United Empire Loyalists who had squatted even before the land-survey, but the very closeness to the United States might have been, for them, a constant danger. Most of them consequently moved on to the Western Townships in the later Province of Ontario.

The second reason, and probably even more discouraging to settlers, was speculation. The fact is well known that people like Asa Porter, Nicolas Austin, Thomas Dunn and others owned huge areas (see Table 1), not to speak of the

Table 1: Land Speculation in the Eastern Townships of Québec

Townships	Grantees	Date of grant		Extent of grants (acres)
Dunham	Thomas Dunn	1796	2 February	40,825
Brome	Asa Porter	1797	18 August	41,758
Bolton	Nicholas Austin	1797	18 August	62,621
Potton	Laughlan McLean	1797	31 October	6,000
Farnham	Samuel Gale	1798	22 October	23,000
Dorset	John Black	1799	30 December	53,000
Stoneham	Kenelm Chandler	1800	14 May	23,800
Tewkesbury	Denis Létourneau	1800	14 May	24,000
Broughton	Henry Juncken and W. Hall	1800	28 October	23,100
Stanstead	Isaac Ogden	1800	27 September	27,720
Upton	D. A. Grant	1800	21 May	25,200
Grantham	W. Grant	1800	14 May	27,000
Hunterstown	John Jones	1800	29 August	24,620
Stukeley	Samuel Willard	1800	3 November	23,625
Eaton	Josiah Sawyer	1801	4 December	25,620
Barnston	Robert Lester	1801	11 April	23,100
Shefford	John Savage	1801	10 February	35,490
Orford	Luke Knowlton	1801	5 May	13,600
Newport	Edmond Heard	1801	4 July	12,200
Stanbridge	John Catling	1801	1 September	38,600
Brompton	William Barnard	1801	27 November	40,200
Shipton	Elmer Cushing	1801	4 December	58,692
Stoke	James Cowan	1802	13 February	43,620
Barford	I. W. Clarke	1802	15 April	27,720
Chester	Simon McTavish	1802	17 July	11,550
Sutton	P. Conroy and Herman Best	1802	31 August	39,900
Halifax	Benjamin Jobert	1802	7 August	11,550
Inverness	Wm. McGillivray	1802	9 August	11,550
Wolfestown	Nicolas Mantour	1802	14 August	11,550
Leeds	Isaac Todd	1802	14 August	11,760
Ireland	Joseph Frobisher	1802	20 August	11,550
Durham	Thomas Scott	1802	30 August	21,991
Compton	Jesse Pennoyer	1802	31 August	26,460
Wickham	William Lindsay	1802	31 August	23,753
Arthabaska	John Gregory	1802	30 September	11,550
Thetford	John Mervin Nooth	1802	10 November	23,100
Ely	Amos Lay, junior	1802	13 November	11,550
Roxton	E. Ruiter	1803	8 January	16,400
Granby	Thomas Ainslie	1803	8 January	4,600
Buckingham	David Beach	1803	26 January	13,000
Clifton	Charles Blake	1803	5 March	22,000
Ascott	Gilbert Hyatt	1803	5 March	20,188
Burry	Calvin May	1803	15 March	11,550
Hatley	Henry Cull	1803	25 March	23,493
Ditton	Minard H. Yeomans	1803	13 May	11,550
Clinton	J. F. Holland	1803	24 May	12,400
Bulstrode	Patrick Langan	1803	27 May	24,463
Kingsey	George Longmore	1803	7 June	11,478
Kildare	P.P. de la Valtrie	1803	24 June	11,486
Clifton	Daniel Cameron	1803	23 July	5,800
Potton	Henry Ruiter	1803	27 July	27,580
Newport	Nathaniel Taylor	1803	4 August	12,000
Tingwick	S. E. Fernuson	1804	23 January	23,730
Warwick	Abraham Steel	1804	23 January	23,940
Westbury	Henry Caldwell	1804	13 March	12,262
Eaton	Isaac Ogden	1804	14 March	6,000
Somerset	C. de Lanaudière	1804	21 April	8,300

Table 1 continued:

Townships	Grantees	Date of grant	Extent of grants
Tring	Hugh McKay	1804 20 July	7,600
Kingsey	Major Holland's family	1805 14 January	1,400
Newton	J. E. Lemoine de Longueuil	1805 6 March	12,961
Melbourne	Henry Caldwell	1805 3 April	26,153
Chester	Samuel Philipps	1805 11 April	6,200
Dudswell	John Bishop	1805 30 May	11,632
Wendover	Thomas Cook	1805 24 June	3,400
Halifax	W. F. Scott	1805 25 June	11,700
Farnham	Jane Cuyler	1805 9 September	4,800
Hull	Philemon Wright	1806 3 January	13,701
Acton	James Caldwell	1806 17 February	17,500
Auckland	Elizabeth Gould	1806 3 April	23,100
Frampton	P. E. Desbarats	1806 10 July	11,569
Acton	Geo W. Allsopp	1806 22 July	24,004
Eardley	E. Sanford	1806 22 August	5,000
Chatham	D. Robertson	1806 31 December	5,000
Lingwick	W. Vondenvelden	1807 7 March	13,650
Lochaber	A. McMillan	1807 26 March	13,161
Templeton	A. McMillan	1807 26 March	8,949
Stanfold	Jenkin Williams	1807 8 July	26,810
Ham	Nancy Allen	1807 29 July	9,200
Frampton	R. A. de Boucherville	1808 9 September	4,100
Onslow	Henry Walcot	1808 12 November	10.950
Maddington	G. W. Allsopp	1808 1 December	10,400
Farnham	John Allsopp	1809 11 February	9,800
Sherrington	F. Baby and Bishop Mountain	1809 29 May	19,100
Wentworth	Jane de Montmolin	1809 3 June	11,880
Sherrington	Suzan and Margaret Finlay	1809 29 May	8,300
Stanstead	Sir R. S. Milnes	1810 2 March	21,406
Barnston	Sir R. S. Milnes	1810 2 March	13,546
Compton	Sir R. S. Milnes	1810 2 March	13,110

Source: J. C. Langelier 1891: 8-10

British American Land Company, undoubtedly the biggest landowner of all. Logically the consequence was that but a very few settlers became installed during the first half of the 19th century, and that especially the number of British people did not increase noticably.

Until 1851, persons of Anglo Saxon descent numbered in total only 63.000 in the Eastern Townships, the number of French Canadians was about half that high. Despite the restrictions of the Québec Act, the latter ones had started around 1840 to move into the Eastern Townships, mainly because overpopulation within the Lowlands became so dramatic that hundreds of thousands of French Canadians emigrated, mainly to the United States (see E. Waddell's contribution in this volume).

A significant change took place in 1849, when the Eastern Townships were opened to French Canadian settlers. The alteration of Article 9 of the Quebec Act, which had restricted the catholic church's influence to the old seigneurial lands, was the most decisive step in the opening of the area. Once the Church was allowed to exercise its influence in the Eastern Townships, it took an active part in the colonization process, encouraging French Canadians from the Lowlands to settle in the Appalachians, and also trying to repatriate those who had emigrated to the United States, probably almost half a million people. The consequence of this initiative was that within 20 years the number of French Canadians increased from 32.000 in 1851 to 71.000 in 1871,

Table 2: First Settlers in the Townships of Ditton and Emberton between 1869 and 1874

Name	Persons	Year	Lot	Rang	Origin
L. H. Weston	4	1863	40	VI	Cookshire P.Q.
Hans A. Osen	4	1868	22	V	Norwegen/Norway
Christian Hansen	8	1868	18	V	Norwegen/Norway
Christian Osen	5	1868	19	V	Norwegen/Norway
Ole Johnsen	5	1868	21	v	Norwegen/Norway
Gundner Larsen	5	1868	20	V	Norwegen/Norway
Ewen Mc Kalsen	5	1868	25, 26	V	Norwegen/Norway
Hans Hansen	4	1868	18	V	Norwegen/Norway
Holver Sutter	7	1868	26	VI	Norwegen/Norway
Juliana Harwood	8	1869	36, 37	VIII	England
Arthur Hearn	6	1870	22	III	England
John Daniels	9	1870	22	III	England
Benjamin Lintot	8	1870	34	VII	England
Thomas Painter	5	1870	34	VIII	England
James Smith	5	1870	34	VIII	England
Henry Shell	3	1870	35	VIII	England
Thomas Craig	7	1870	35	VII	England
Henry Rawdon	2	1870	38, 39	VIII	England
Thomas Dawes	5	1870	16	IV	England
James Williams	8	1870	4	II	Capelton, P.Q.
Archibald Irving	8	1870	9	III	Schottland/Scotland
Etienne Gobeille	7	1870	12	V	Chesnut-Hill Connecticut
Pierre Lacasse	8	1870	14	V	Fall River Connecticut
Francois Lamothe	11	1870	12	III	Williamsville Connecticut
Francis Bell	4	1871	23	III	Schottland/Scotland
Edward Price	3	1871	36, 37	VII	England
Philias Gendreau	2	1871	28	IV	Cookshire P.Q.
William Smith	11	1871	24, 25	IV	Cookshire P.Q.
Etienne Pelchat	5	1871	17	V	Cookshire P.Q.
Joseph Robidoux	9	1871	7	III	Baltic, Connecticut
François Poulin	8	1871	51	V	St. Liboire P.Q.
J. B. Brousseau	11	1871	45	V	St. Simon P.Q.
Joseph Dubreuil	9	1872	49	V	Ste. Rosalie P.Q.
Jean Carrière	8	1872	23	III	Cookshire P.Q.
R. Renaud Dumoulin	2	1872	29	IV	St. Valérien P.Q.
L. Alfred Gendreau	5	1872	part 28	IV	Waterloo P.Q.
Damase Brault	6	1872	part 28	IV	Westbury P.Q.
Josef Gendez	3	1873	23	IV	All Event P.Q.
Francois Hennuset	3	1873	38	V	Namur, Belgien/Belgium
Josef Roy	6	1873	19	IV	Lambton P.Q.
Léon Rancourt	2	1873	27	V	Cookshire P.Q.
Félix Goudreau	8	1873	59	V	Manchester P.Q.
Georges Labonne, père	7	1873	8	II	Taftville P.Q.
Eugène Brégier	2	1873	62	IV	Veselay P.Q.
David Bolduc	1	1873	62	V	Manchester P.Q.
Georges Labonne, jr.	6	1874	6	II	Bazrahville P.Q.
Salomon Labonne	4	1874	14	II	Baltic P.Q.
Joseph Bréard	7	1874	8	III	Baltic P.Q.
Achille Fortier	4	1874	47	VI	Shenley P.Q.
Napoléon Boulay	1	1874	48	VII	Shenley P.Q.
Joseph de La Fontaine	3	1874	49	VI	Shenley P.Q.
Jacques Roy	6	1874	20	IV	Taftville P.Q.
Nil Gobeille	9	1874	5	IV	St. Alphonse P.Q.
Iram Sunderby	6	1874	42, 43	VIII	Cookshire P.Q.

Source: Centenaire de La Patrie, 1975

whereas the number of Anglo Canadians increased only slightly during those 20 years. By 1900, almost all counties had a French Canadian majority, even those that had developed as centers of British settlement like Brome, Missisquoi or Stanstead. These changes in the ethnic structure were occurring so quickly that the metaphor chosen by R. Blanchard in his description of "Le Canada Français" is appropriate - "raz de marée française" the "French Tide".

For a geographer, it is exiting to look at the details which characterize these population changes. The analysis is especially interesting in those townships where during the first half of the 19th century the Anglo Canadian population was mainly concentrated, that is the southern part of the Eastern Townships. Three brief examples might be given to clarify, how these changes identify simultaneously with a spatial and a social segregation process. The first example is Ditton Township at the far end of the Eastern Townships next to the American border. It is the less typical case, because the survey only took place between 1863 and 1870, which means an anglophone population was not present when the "French Tide" was already on its way. Nevertheless, the first settlers coming to Ditton were either of Norwegian or British descent, the Norwegians settling in the fifth rang, the British mainly in the eighth rang which they called, patriotically, Little England. After 1871 however, when the catholic church took the initiative and intended to occupy this area with repatriated French Canadians from the United States, almost all settlers were definitely of French descent and occupied other rangs (Table 2). These settlers too emphasized patriotic feelings by calling their rangs Petit Canada, Petit Québec; the main village was called "La Patrie", the "Fatherland". Discouraged by the constantly increasing number of French Canadians, the Anglophones and also the Norwegians moved away before the end of the century, leaving behind just a name on the topographical map: Little England (Fig. 4).

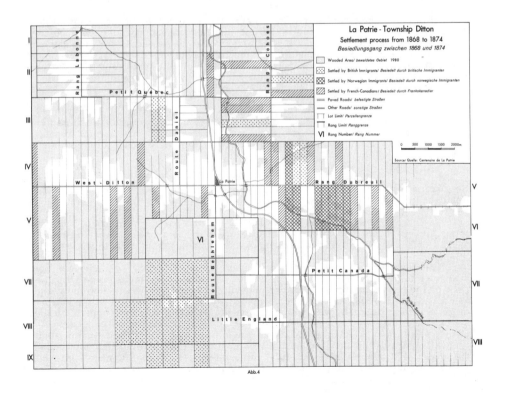

Abb. 4

Another example is Compton Township, one of the centers of British settlement during the 19th century, where all lands had been granted to people of Anglo-Saxon descent. The concentration of anglophone population in this area was without doubt a major reason for the late beginning of the "French Invasion". The inversion of the ethnic structure in favour of the French Canadians took place only after the turn of the century, as Table 3 shows clearly.

Table 3: Comparative French and English Canadian Population Trends in Compton

	1871	1881	1901	1911	1921
English	2.059	2.014	2.113	1.878	1.291
French	687	733	1.194	1.815	2.492
Total	2.746	2.747	3.307	3.693	3.783

Source: M. Bellavance 1982: 25

The reversal of the ethnic structure assumes the proportions of a genuine revolution. In the village of Compton, in 1901, 67.1% of the inhabitants were English speaking whereas only one third was French speaking. Ten years later, their respective positions were proportionally reversed, and in 1921 85,5% of the village's population was composed of French Canadians. Marcel Bellavance has described these changes as follows:

"Compton's English speaking inhabitants left so quickly that one could almost say they fled; however, the suddenness of this phenomenon does not obscure the complexity of the exodus, signs of which could already be seen a few decades earlier. This is confirmed by reports submitted by the Reverends C. H. Parker and J. S. Brewer, who were successively the ministers of St. James Anglican Church between 1875 and World War I. Awareness of the insidious demise of the English community in the village and the township runs through their reports like a leitmotiv.

- 1885: Like every other parish and mission throughout the townships we are suffering from the diminution of members. During the year we have had several losses, and some of the oldest and warmest supporters of the church have dropped out of our number.

- 1896: We are reminded of the gradually diminishing numbers, and slowly dying. Newcomers, as well as many of our own people, are moving to the overestimated North-West.

- 1903: The numbers of deaths in the Parish and the passing of many of our best farms into the hands of another nationality press the fact upon us that we are a rapidly decreasing congregation, making our future a matter of serious anxiety."

The departure of English speaking inhabitants of Compton Township was paralleled by an equally massive influx of French Canadians. On the average until the turn of the century, only one French speaking family arrived in Compton per year (Table 3). In 1900 and 1902, respectively 28 and 29 families of French Canadian origin settled in Compton, with an average in the following years of about 20 families. A most surprising fact is that the exodus of English speaking inhabitants from Compton Township affected all people of Anglo-Saxon descent, regardless of their religion, which means that the Irish Catholics too left the area. This contradicts the thesis of Robert Sellar (1916/1974), who interpreted French Canada's inroads into the Eastern Townships as a Catholic onslaught against Non-catholics.

Fig.5: Anglo Canadian and French Canadian Land Ownership (or Tenantship) in Brome Township (Quebec) 1892
   Anglokanadische und Frankokanadische Landeigentümer (oder Pächter) in Township Brome (Quebec) 1892

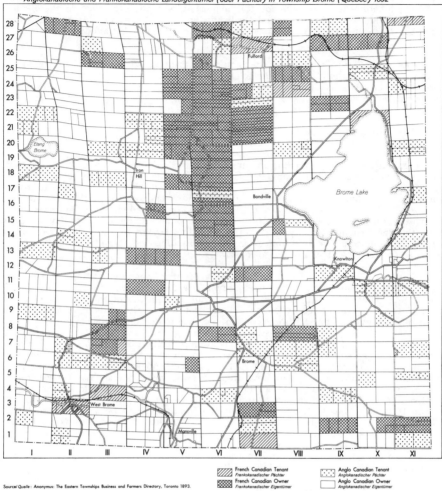

Source/Quelle: Anonymus: The Eastern Townships Business and Farmers Directory, Toronto 1893.

French Canadian Tenant / Frankokanadischer Pächter
French Canadian Owner / Frankokanadischer Eigentümer
Anglo Canadian Tenant / Anglokanadischer Pächter
Anglo Canadian Owner / Anglokanadischer Eigentümer

Unlike the situation in Ditton Township, where the submersion of the English settlers occurred through the settlement of virgin land and vacant lots by the arriving French Canadians, one could call the observed reversal of the ethnic structure in Compton a replacement of one ethnic group by the other. In fact, all land lots of Compton Township, according to the study of the "Terriers" in Québec, had been owned by Anglo-Saxons at the middle of the 19th century. By the end of the century, the French Canadians started taking over the lands sold by the departing English speaking inhabitants. The number of French Canadians being owner or tenant within Compton Township was however still very limited by the end of the 19th century, according to the Farmers register of 1892. Figure 5 reveals, that the

177

French started obviously to settle in nuclei, thus concentrating in different parts of the township, trying to avoid wherever possible isolated settlement amongst English speaking inhabitants. Evidence for this argument is especially given in the SE part of the township along the so called Cochrane Rang, and also in the rangs I and II from Lot 14 to 20, where a pre-1900 concentration of French Canadians is documented.

The same Figure also shows that, starting from these early nuclei, the French invasion spread spatially during the following decades. Looking at the different time periods, it is recognizable that the French occupation continued in waves finally to cover the whole township, where but very few English speaking "Islands" are left today.

The information necessary to establish this map was compiled from the archives of the Registry Offices, where all transactions of real estate were examined back to 1880, when the first changes in favour of the French Canadians took place. The classification was made according to the first occurring transaction from non-French towards a French speaking proprietor (or tenant), without looking at further changes except if a French Canadian reverted to Anglo Canadian. But in the whole township there was not found a single case where, once the French Canadians had occupied a land lot, it had been resold to an English speaking individual, even in those cases where the owner changed frequently. There was undoubtedly an insignificant demand from the non-French, leaving the land rather than trying to stay by all means, but another reason could be that the French are less disposed to sell the land to the rivaling group once they are the owners.

The last example seems to confirm this French Canadian attitude. Brome Township is the most interesting case, given the fact that the anglophone population outnumbered the French until 1971. Thus it is an absolutely singular case within the whole Province of Quebec. This, however, only holds true looking at the mothertongue criteria, whereas by ethnic origin French predominates.

Historically, the situation in Brome Township is much like the previous example. The first settlers in the region were Loyalists who came from the United States in the 1780's. They were, in fact, squatters and attempts were made by the government of Lower Canada to move them to other areas of Loyalist settlements, especially in Upper Canada. As a whole, the role of the Loyalists in the settlement of Brome Township, as of the Eastern Townships in general, was negligible. According to D. Booth (1966), the principal wave of settlement in the area started after 1791 and lasted up to approximately 1830, an immigration of great dimension. Between 1791 and 1812, almost 20.000 Americans, mostly footloose New Englanders seeking new land, crossed the border to Lower Canada, and most of those staying in the area settled around Missisquoi Bay and in the townships next to the American border, with an especially important nucleus in Brome Township.

A second source of settlers in the area was the British Isles. The English and Irish formed the largest portions of this group, but the numbers of Scots emigrating to Canada were far from insignificant. This immigration started mainly in the mid-1830's and continued to about 1870, although decreasing after 1850 with the beginning of the last principal wave of settlement, the French Canadian infiltration. Brome Township and Brome County were, at that early stage, less affected by this wave than the rest of the Eastern Townships.

Nevertheless, the French Canadian population was constantly increasing even in the main bastion of the British, already in 1871 reaching 694 inhabitants as opposed to 1590 of British or other origin. Ten years later, the number of the French Canadians had increased to 970 souls, while the British had declined to 1.475 inhabitants. If we look at the situation in the 1981 census, we find 7.900 people of English descent opposed to 8.860 of French origin.

Today, the proportions are rather even, and the question about spatial and social segregation becomes exciting because the conflict, if there is one, has not only a historical dimension. Based on the study of the registrar's archives, the following

Fig.6: The Substitution of Anglo Canadian by French Canadians Land Owners (or Tenants) in Compton Township during the 20 th Century
Die Verdrängung anglokanadischer durch frankokanadische Landbesitzer (oder Pächter) in Compton Township während des 20. Jahrhunderts

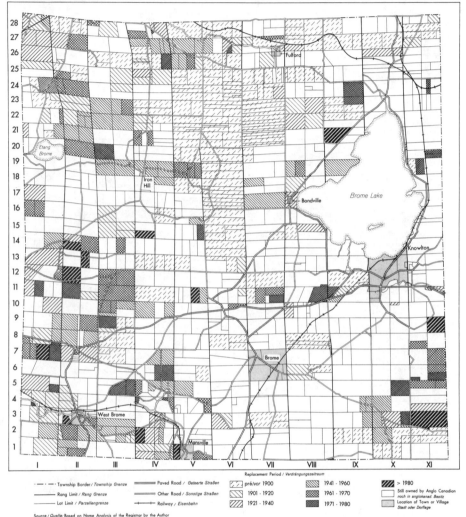

maps have been elaborated (Fig. 6 and 7). The map of 1892 shows the expected fact of a spatial segregation of French Canadian settlers, which took place during the last two decades of the 19th century. There is a distinct concentration of lands owned by French Canadians in the sixth rang between lot 14 and 25, more or less including the adjacent rangs. Only a very few lots were owned or leased by French Canadians in the rest of the township.

The Substitution of Anglo Canadian by French Canadian Land Owners (or Tenants) in Brome Township during the 20th Century

Die Verdrängung anglokanadischer durch frankokanadische Landbesitzer (oder Pächter) in Township Brome während des 20. Jh.

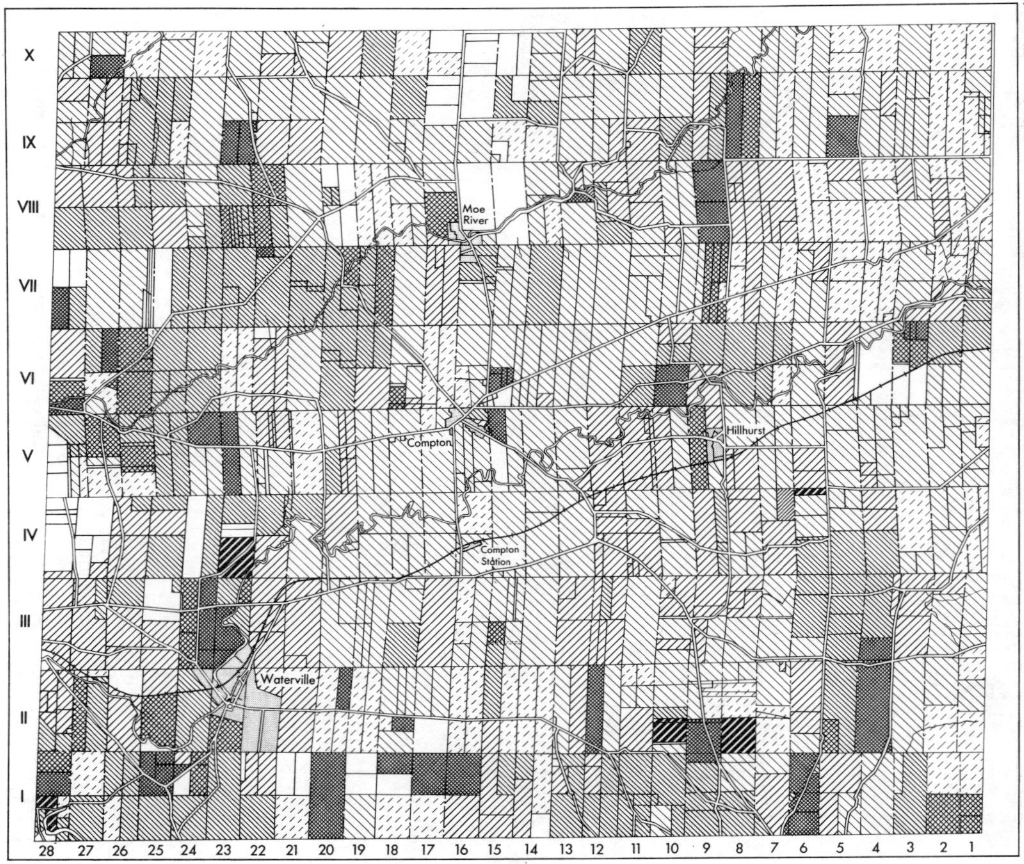

Replacement Period / Verdrängungszeitraum
- pré/vor 1900
- 1901 - 1920
- 1921 - 1940
- 1941 - 1960
- 1961 - 1970
- 1971 - 1980
- >1980
- Anglo Canadian Owner / Anglokanadische Eigentümer
- Location of town or village / Ortslage

Source/Quelle: Based on Name Analysis of the Registrar by the Author
Zusammengestellt aufgrund von Namensanalysen im Liegenschaftsamt durch den Autor

Fig. 7

But a comparison of the 1892 map with the following transactions confirms distinctly the tendencies already observed in Compton. The heavy francophone nucleus in the sixth rang obviously served as a starting point for the French Canadian expansion during the following decades. Like a puzzle lot by lot was acquired by people of French descent, with the result that Anglo Canadian property became rather sporadic in the north-western part of the township.

An even more convincing example of this systematic occupancy of the Francophones once they had put down roots, are the south-western and the south-eastern parts of Brome Township, where 100 years ago the French Canadian presence had only been as rare squatters. But it is evident that these squatters, too, served as vehicles for an expansion in the following years, a tendency which is still going on today.

On the other hand, the Anglo Canadians have preserved their claims more or less intact around Brome Corner and Knowlton, both well known as the purest Anglo-Saxon citadelles within the Eastern Townships and in all the rural parts of the province. Whether these bastions will survive in the future cannot be predicted in all consequences, but the French Canadian invasion, even though it is certainly not a "spring tide" any more, seems to be a peaceful but steady conquest of the former battlefield. The French Canadians, in all respects, seem to have the trump in their hands. The anglophone population is very clearly overaged with very low birth rates, new immigrants have not been noticed for decades, and emigration is frequent. The very British facade still found in Knowlton represents a situation that could be compared to a hollow tree that is bound to die within the next generation or two. Thus, the French Canadian conquest will be accomplished and geographers will certainly continue to observe, whether or not this conquest will wipe out and extinguish those aspects of the cultural landscape recalling the British presence lasting more than two centuries in this area. May be only the next generation of geographers will be able to give the final answer to this question, but it is already obvious that ethnic structures have been most decisive for the shaping of the landscape in this area, thus creating a very interesting geographical case.

References

Adair, E. R., 1954: "The French Canadian Seigneury". Canadian Historical Review, Vol. 35, pp. 187-207.

Anonymus, 1883: The Eastern Townships Business and Farmers Directory, 1882, Toronto.

Barrette, G., 1952: "Contribution de l'arpenteur-géomètre à la géographie du Québec". The Canadian Geographer, No. 1.

Bartz, F., 1955: "Französische Einflüsse im Bilde der Kulturlandschaft Nordamerikas". Erdkunde, 9. Jg., S. 286-305.

Bellavance, M., 1982. A Village in Transition: Compton, Québec, 1880-1920, Hull.

Blanchard, R., 1947: Le centre du Canada français, province de Québec, Montréal.

—   1960: La Canada Français, Paris, Montréal.

Bloch, M., 1960: "Seigneurie française et manoir anglais". Cahiers des Annales, No. 16, Paris.

Booth, J. D., 1966: Historical Geography of Brome County 1800-1911. Thesis, Lennoxville.

Canada Archives, 1901 and foll: Sessional Papers.

Deffontaines, P., 1953: "Le rang, type de peuplement rural du Canada français". Publications de l'Institut d'Histoire et de Géographie, No. 5, Paris.

Denecke, D., 1976: "Tradition und Anpassung der agraren Raumorganisation und Siedlungsgestaltung im Landnahmeprozeß des östlichen Nordamerika im 17. und 18. Jahrhundert". Verhdlg. des 40. Dt. Geogr. Tages Innsbruck, Wiesbaden, S. 228-255.

Derruau, M., 1956: "A l'origine du 'rang' canadien". Cahiers de Géographie de Québec, No. 1, pp. 39-47.

Harris, R. C., 1966: The Seigneurial System in early Canada: A Geographical Study. Madison, Wisc.

—   and J. Warkentin, 1974: Canada before Confederation. A Study in Historical Geography. New York, London, Toronto.

Hottenroth, H., 1968: The Great Clay Belts in Ontario und Quebec. Marburger Geogr. Schriften, Heft 39, Marburg.

Hunter, J., 1939: The French Invasion of the Eastern Townships; a regional Study. Thesis (MA Sociology) Mc Gill, Montreal.

Lavoie, Y., 1972: L'émigration des Canadiens aux Etats-Unis avant 1930: mesure du phénomène. Montréal 1972.

Lighthall, W. D., 1914: "English Settlement in Québec". In Canada and its Provinces: A History of the Canadian People and their Institutions by One Hundred Associates. Ed. Adam Shortt and Arthur G. Doughty. Toronto, Vol. 15, Pt. 1, pp. 121-126.

Little, J. I., 1976: The peacable conquest, French Canadian Colonization in the Eastern Townships during the 19th Century. Thesis PhD, Ottawa.

Lovell, J. (ed.), 1909: Lovell's Farmer's Register of the Garden of the Eastern Townships. Montreal.

McGuigan, G. F., 1962: Land policy and land disposal under tenure of free and common soccage, Quebec and Lower Canada, 1763-1809. Thèse PhD Laval, Québec.

Mercier, J., 1956: L'Estrie, Coll. Histoire de l'Estrie No. 1, Sherbrooke.

Miner, H., 1939: St. Denis; A French Canadian Parish. Chicago.

Müller-Wille, L. und A. Pletsch, 1981: "Ethnizitätskonflikt, sozioökonomischer Wandel und Territorialentwicklung in Quebec/Kanada". Die Erde, 112. Jg., S. 61-89.

Nitz, H.-J., 1972: "Zur Entstehung und Ausbreitung schachbrettartiger Grundrißformen ländlicher Siedlungen und Fluren. Ein Beitrag zum Problem Konvergenz und Übertragung". In: Hans Poser Festschrift. Göttinger Geogr. Abhlg. Heft 60, Göttingen, S. 72-93.

—   1976: "Konvergenz und Evolution in der Entstehung ländlicher Siedlungsformen". Verhdlg. des 40. Dt. Geogr. Tages Innsbruck, Wiesbaden, S. 208-227.

Pletsch, A., 1980: "Kolonisationsphasen und Kulturlandschaftswandel im Südosten der Provinz Quebec (Kanada)". Erdkunde, 34. Bd., Bonn, S. 61-73.

—   1982, "Les Cantons de l'est canadien, colonisation et abandon d'une région marginale". Norois, No. 114, Poitiers, p. 185-204.

Pletsch, A., "Township and Rang - some deliberations on their origin, mutual influence and on land tenure in Quebec and Ontario before Constitution", in: F. Helleiner, ed.: Cultural Dimensions of Canada's Geography. = Occasional Paper 10, Dept. of Geography, Trent Univ. Peterborough Ont., pp. 347-357. Trent Univ. Occ. Papers Nr. 10, Peterborough, Ont.

Poisson, J.-A., 1888: "Mouvement de la population française dans les Cantons de l'Est". La Canada français, Vol. 1 Québec, pp. 182-204.

Ross, A. D., 1943: "The Cultural Effect of Population Change in the Eastern Townships". Canadian Journal of Economics and Political Science, Vol. 9 No. 1, Toronto, pp. 447-463.

—   1954: "French and English Canadian Contacts and Institutional Change". Canadian Journal of Economics and Political Science, Vol. 20, No. 3, Toronto, pp. 281-295.

Saint-Amant, J. Ch., 1932: Un coin des Cantons de l'Est: histoire de l'envahissement pacifique mais irrésistible d'une race. La Parole, Drummondville.

Address of the author:
Prof. Dr. Alfred Pletsch
Fachbereich Geographie
der Philipps-Universität Marburg
Deutschhausstraße 10
3550 Marburg/Lahn

L'espace social des francophones et des anglophones dans une communauté rurale des Cantons de l'Est (Québec)

Martin Schulte

Abstract: In many rural communities of the Eastern Townships (Cantons de l'Est) of Québec French- and English-speaking populations have lived together for several generations. Here too interethnic relations have been affected by the recent changes within the society of Québec initiated by its urban centres since the "Silent Revolution" of the sixties. They have accelerated the process of francisation that has been going on in the area for a long time already. Using the example of Sawyerville (Compton county) and its evolution since the 1940s this article focuses on the spatial structure of the social relations - both inter- and intraethnic - of the two groups present there, which increasingly go beyond the limits of their community, region or even province. Work relations and family relations have been chosen to illustrate to what extend the two ethnic groups, although sharing the territory of the same rural community, "live" in two different social spaces.

Résumé: Dans de nombreuses communautés rurales de la région des Cantons de l'Est (Eastern Townships), située au sud-est du Québec, des francophones et des anglophones habitent ensemble depuis plusieurs générations. Aussi dans ce milieu rural, les changements récents dans la société québecoise depuis la "Révolution tranquille" des années soixante, produits du monde urbain, ont eu des effets sur les relations interethniques; ils y ont accéléré le processus de francisation qui a lieu dans la région depuis déjà longtemps. Le cas de la communauté de Sawyerville (comté de Compton) et son évolution depuis les années quarante servant d'example, l'exposé porte sur la structure spatiale des relations sociales - tant en constellation interethnique qu'intraethnique - chez les deux groupes présents, celles-ci dépassant de plus en plus les limites de la communauté, de la région et même de la province. L'analyse des relations de travail et des relations de famille permet d'illustrer à quel point les deux groupes ethniques, tout en étant voisins sur le territoire de la même communauté rurale, "habitent" pourtant des espaces sociaux différents, caractéristiques de chaque groupe.

Zusammenfassung: In vielen ländlichen Gemeinden der Cantons de l'Est (Eastern Townships), im Südosten Québecs, leben französisch- und englischsprachige Bevölkerung seit mehreren Generationen gemeinsam. Auch hier haben die seit der "Leisen Revolution" der 60er Jahre durch die städtischen Zentren ausgelösten Veränderungen in der Gesellschaft Québecs Auswirkungen auf die interethnischen Beziehungen gehabt und dabei den in diesem Gebiet stattfindenden Französisierungsprozeß beschleunigt. Am Beispiel der Gemeinde Sawyerville (comté de Compton), einer von drei untersuchten Gemeinden, und ihrer Entwicklung seit den 40er Jahren beschäftigt sich dieser Artikel vor allem mit der räumlichen Struktur der sozialen Beziehungen - sei es in inter- oder intraethnischer Konstellation - der beiden dort ansässigen Gruppen, die zunehmend über die Grenzen der Gemeinde, der Region oder selbst der Provinz Québec hinausgehen. Anhand ihrer Arbeits- und Familienbeziehungen kann illustriert werden, in welchem Ausmaß die beiden ethnischen Gruppen, obgleich sie sich beide auf dem Territorium ein und derselben Gemeinde befinden, unterschiedliche, ihnen je eigentümliche, Sozialräume herausbilden.

∞∞∞∞∞∞∞∞∞∞∞∞

Dans la région des Cantons de l'Est (Eastern Townships) située au sud-est du Québec (voir fig. 1), des francophones et des anglophones habitent ensemble en milieu rural depuis quelques générations (1). A cause de cette particularité, la région a attiré à plusieurs moments de son histoire des chercheurs en sciences sociales, qui se sont penchés sur le problème des relations interethniques dans ce contexte (2) qui contraste avec celui du milieu urbain de Montréal, mieux connu. Les transformations de la société québecoise depuis la "Révolution tranquille" des années soixante (3), les conflits sociaux qui les accompagnaient, les nouveaux modes de relations interethniques qui en résultaient, notamment la révalorisation de la langue française et son usage accru dans tous les domaines (4), ont été le produit du monde urbain. Or, le milieu rural aussi en a été atteint. Ces transformations y ont eu des impactes divers et parfois contradictoires sur les relations interethniques; ainsi le déclin du pouvoir des institutions religieuses a facilité les contacts entre individus, permettant des mariages mixtes entre francophones catholiques et anglophones protestants; par contre la politique linguistique récente du Québec a entrainé chez les anglophones souvent unilingues de nouveaux conflits avec l'Etat provincial et ses institutions.

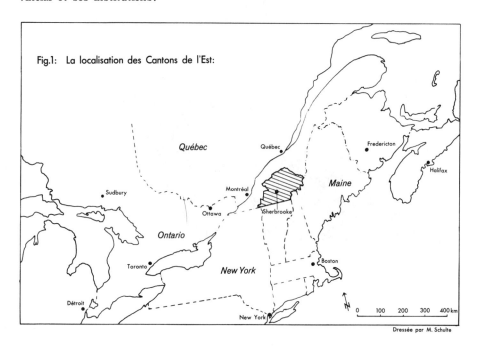

Fig.1: La localisation des Cantons de l'Est:

Dressée par M. Schulte

La majorité de la population des Cantons de l'Est (5) (569.294 habitants) est aujourd'hui francophone (86,4%). La population anglophone minoritaire (8,5%), descendante des premiers colons de la région, se trouve concentrée dans sa partie méridionale, proche de la frontière avec les Etats-Unis. La ville de Sherbrooke avec ses 74.075 habitants (92,2% de francophones) est le centre administratif, commercial et industriel de la région (6). Dans de nombreuses communautés rurales des Cantons de l'Est les deux groupes ethniques (7) coexistent en proportions différentes. J'en avais choisi trois (voir fig. 2) pour y faire une étude sur l'aspect spatial de leurs relations sociales partiellement interethniques. Il s'agit de Sawyerville (comté de Compton), Durham-Sud (comté de Drummond) et Stanbridge East (comté de Missisquoi) (8). Dans cet article l'interêt portera surtout sur la communauté de Sawyerville qui a une population de 1307 habitants en 1982 (9), village et campagne environnante comprise (voir Fig. 3). Elle est à peu près à moitié francophone (48,2%), à moitié anglophone (46,7%) (10); la population anglophone y est en baisse (voir fig. 4) comme c'est généralement le cas dans la région. Sawyerville et les villages voisins ont déjà été l'objet d'une thèse de doctorat en sociologie faite par Aileen D. Ross pendant les années quarante (11) ce qui permet de voir l'évolution du milieu étudié au cours de la dernière génération.

Les membres des deux groupes ethniques et leurs institutions locales occupent en commun le territoire de la communauté; ils y impriment les marques de leur présence et de leur mode de relations. Néanmoins, on peut constater qu'au delà de

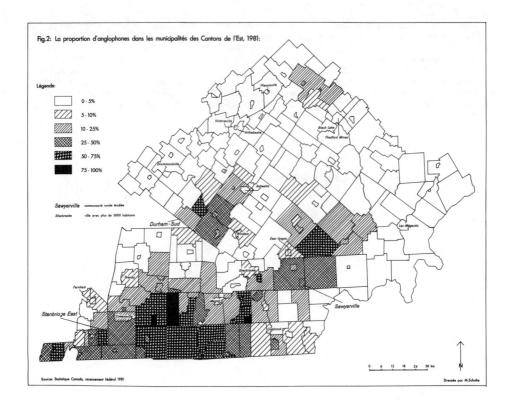

Fig.2: La proportion d'anglophones dans les municipalités des Cantons de l'Est, 1981:

leur voisinage au village et à la campagne environnante une autre dimension spatiale rend les deux groupes bien différents l'un de l'autre, c'est la structure spatiale de leurs relations sociales, c'est à dire leurs espaces sociaux (12). Les habitants francophones et anglophones de Sawyerville, étant résidents du même endroit dans les Cantons de l'Est, n'habitent pourtant pas le même espace social. Ces espaces sociaux ethnospecifiques ont chacun subi une mutation notable au cours de la dernière génération.

Les relations diverses qu'entretiennent les habitants de Sawyerville, soit avec l'Etat et ses institutions, soit dans le contexte de l'économie ou de la famille, dépassent en grande partie et de plus en plus les limites de leur village, de leur région et même souvent de leur province. Il n'y a guère que les relations de voisinage, de la vie associative, une partie réduite des relations économiques et celles qui ont lieu dans quelques institutions locales, telles les Eglises et le conseil municipal, qui encore de nos jours se restreignent à Sawyerville même et qui par là maintiennent la cohérence sociale propre aux communautés rurales de la région. Pour considérer la problématique interethnique dans ce milieu et les conflits sociaux divers qui la soutiennent, il faut tenir compte du fait qu'ils sont alimentés par la societé extérieure, car les relations sociales entretenues au sein de la communauté même de Sawyerville ne représentent qu'une fraction de l'espace social de ses habitants francophones et anglophones. Ce sont ces espaces sociaux dont je voudrais décrire certains éléments caractéristiques.

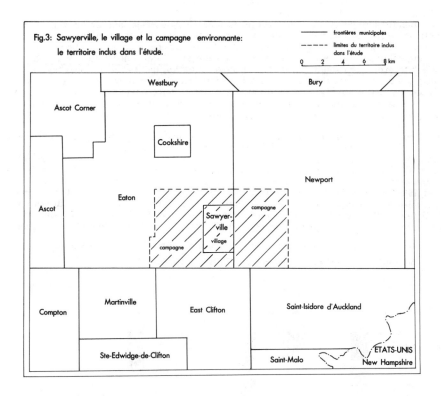

Fig.3: Sawyerville, le village et la campagne environnante: le territoire inclus dans l'étude.

Fig.: 4 L'évolution de la population francophone et anglophone de Sawyerville (village), 1941 - 1981:

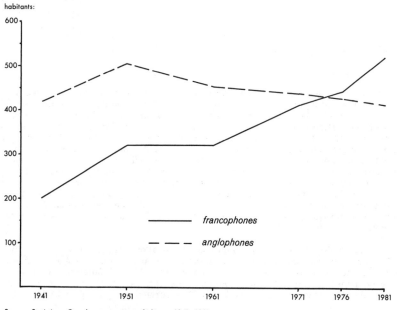

Source: Statistique Canada, recensements fédéraux 1941 - 1981

Quelques regards sur les structures spatiales des relations de travail et des relations de famille, tant en constellation interethnique qu'intraethnique, permettront de donner un aperçu de la différence entre l'espace social des francophones et celui des anglophones. Ces structures spatiales reflètent l'occurence plutôt rare de relations interethniques dans ces deux domaines chez les habitants de Sawyerville. Aujourd'hui on y travaille la plupart du temps pour un employeur de sa propre langue; les mariages s'y font habituellement entre deux partenaires qui se parlent dans une langue maternelle commune. Pourtant il y a eu des changements notables dans ces deux domaines depuis quelques années.

Pour faire l'analyse des relations de travail des deux groupes ethniques sous l'aspect de leurs structures spatiales respectives, il faut d'abord observer la constitution de ces relations, qui se fait sur le marché de travail. La distribution actuelle (en 1983) des résidences d'anciens élèves de Sawyerville qui sont sortis des écoles secondaires protestantes et catholiques à la fin des années scolaires 1970/71, 1975/76 et 1980/81 (voir fig. 5 et 6) va nous servir d'indice (13). La plupart d'entre eux s'est mise à la recherche d'un emloi depuis le départ de l'école. Les résultats sont révélateurs. Un tiers des anglophones s'est orienté vers l'extérieur du Québec, deux tiers même si l'on ne regarde que ceux de 1970/71. Ils se sont installé surtout en

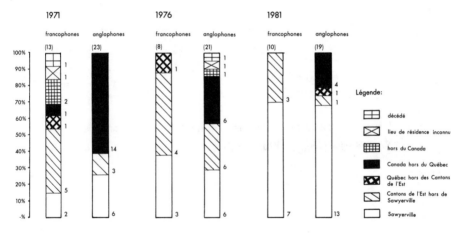

Fig.5: La distribution des lieux de résidence d'anciens élèves francophones (31) et anglophones (63) de Sawyerville sortis des écoles secondaires en 1971, 1976 et 1981; avril 1983:

Source: commissions scolaires et informateurs, avril 1983

Ontario, dans les zones urbaines de Toronto, Hamilton, London ou Belleville y travaillant pour des employeurs de leur langue. Les jeunes francophones du meme âge par contre sont restés dans les Cantons de l'Est, surtout dans la métropole régionale de Sherbrooke. Bien que ni le niveau de scolarité, ni la fréquence d'études post-secondaires ne soient différents chez les deux groupes, les villes de l'Ontario prennent pour les anglophones la place qu'occupe Sherbrooke pour les francophones lors de la constitution de leurs premières relations de travail, la région de Montréal ne jouant presque aucun rôle ni pour l'un ni pour l'autre des deux groupes. Beaucoup de ceux sortis de l'école en 1981 se trouvent encore dans leurs familles à Sawyerville en 1983; il faut y voir l'effet non seulement de leur jeunesse relative et de la poursuite d'études post-secondaires, mais aussi du chômage des jeunes dans la crise économique actuelle qui a fait revenir quelques uns de ceux déjà partis en Ontario sans y avoir trouvé un emploi.

Pour faire le deuxième pas de l'analyse, nous allons regarder les relations de travail déjà constituées des salariés francophones et anglophones toujours résidents de Sawyerville et ayant un emploi en novembre 1982 (14). Il faut annoter que depuis les recherches d'Aileen D. Ross pendant les années quarante, l'économie de Sawyerville est de moins en moins basée sur ses fermes et que même l'industrie du

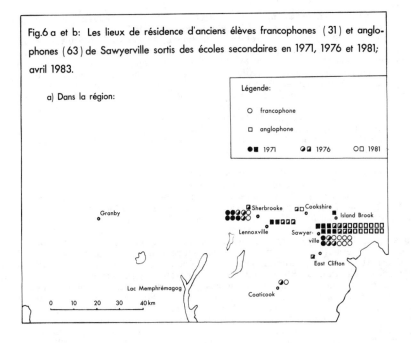

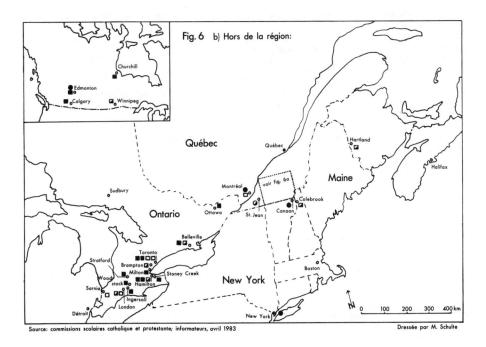

Fig.6 a et b: Les lieux de résidence d'anciens élèves francophones (31) et anglophones (63) de Sawyerville sortis des écoles secondaires en 1971, 1976 et 1981; avril 1983.

bois traditionelle y a perdu de son poids relatif. Avec les moyens de transport modernes, on est entré de plus en plus dans la zone d'influence de Sherbrooke et de son économie. A Sawyerville les relations de travail en constellation interethnique (15) sont plus rares de nos jours qu'autrefois chez les francophones. C'est le cas de 11 personnes seulement (7,8%) parmi les 139 salariés de langue française. La grande industrie forestière américaine n'a plus besoin de leur travail saisonnier; les petites entreprises de l'industrie et du commerce à Sawyerville et ses alentours ont aujourd'hui des patrons de leur langue. Chez les 90 salariés anglophones la situation est inverse. 14 d'entre eux (15,6%) travaillent maintenant pour un employeur francophone, phénomène très récent, qui résulte de la fermeture d'une scierie américaine en 1975, dernière entreprise anglophone importante à Sawyerville, et de la vente d'une usine de matières plastiques à Cookshire, petite ville voisine, par ses anciens propriétaires americains à des Québecois français en 1982.

Dépendant des types de relations traditionels avec le patronat des divers secteurs de l'économie régionale, qui a le pouvoir de favoriser l'un ou l'autre groupe lors de l'embauche et de la promotion de son personnel, la distribution des lieux de travail n'est pas la même chez les francophones et les anglophones de Sawyerville; la direction de leurs migrations quotidiennes diffère (voir fig. 7 et 8). Ainsi les anglophones s'orientent de façon concentrée vers les deux créneaux de l'économie régionale contrôlés par des entreprises ou institutions anglophones qui subsistent à une distance permettant le voyage tous les jours à partir de leur communauté; c'est premièrement la grande industrie manufacturière américaine ou anglo-canadienne dans la métropole régionale de Sherbrooke et ses alentours, deuxièmement le complexe des institutions anglophones, surtout scolaires et universitaires, à Lennoxville, dernier centre urbain de la région avec une population à majorité anglophone. Les salariés francophones par contre, lorsqu'ils travaillent dans l'industrie privée, le font dans de petites et moyennes entreprises appartenant aujourd'hui presque toutes à des propriétaires de langue française et qui se trouvent plus dispersées dans l'arrière-pays de Sherbrooke, autour de Sawyerville ou à Sawyerville même. S'il y en a qui travaillent à Sherbrooke, c'est parce qu'ils ont trouvé un emploi dans le secteur tertiaire, en croissance accélérée depuis les années soixante, souvent dans les institutions scolaires ou hospitalières sous le contrôle francophone de l'Etat provincial.

En résumé on peut constater les traits suivants qui caractérisent les structures spatiales des relations de travail partiellement interethniques chez les francophones et les anglophones de Sawyerville ainsi que leur évolution au cours de la dernière génération. Dans le cas des francophones on peut retenir

- une baisse considérable de leurs relations interethniques autrefois fréquentes avec des employeurs anglophones à Sawyerville même et dans ses environs immédiats,
- une importance accrue de leurs relations de travail intraethniques avec des employeurs francophones surtout à Sawyerville même et ses environs, mais de plus en plus à Sherbrooke, la métropole régionale, et dans d'autres villes plus petites de la région,
- une extension très faible, plus réduite qu'autrefois, de leurs relations de travail saisonnières ou permanentes hors du Québec avec des employeurs américains ou anglo-canadiens.

Chez les anglophones par contre, on observe

- l'apparition récente et une augmentation modeste mais continue de leurs relations de travail interethniques avec des employeurs francophones surtout à Sawyerville et dans ses environs immédiats,
- une tendance sensible à concentrer leurs relations de travail intraethniques de plus en plus sur quelques créneaux, de moins en moins nombreux à l'interieur de la région, où subsistent des employeurs anglophones, notamment à Sherbrooke et à Lennoxville
- l'extension accrue de leurs relations de travail avec des employeurs au Canada anglais, c'est à dire une forte tendance à se détourner de la région et du Québec.

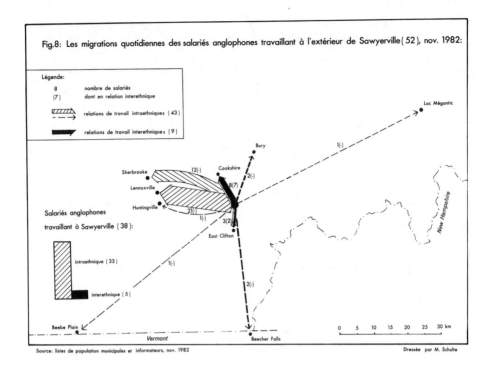

Fig.8: Les migrations quotidiennes des salariés anglophones travaillant à l'extérieur de Sawyerville (52), nov. 1982:

Source: listes de population municipales et informateurs, nov. 1982 Dressée par M. Schulte

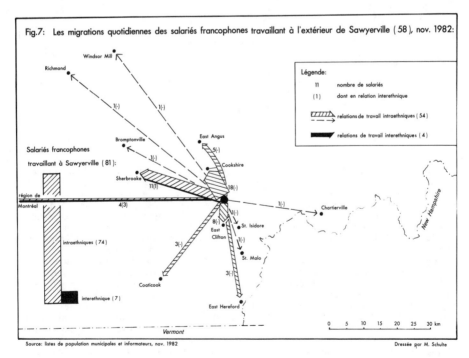

Fig.7: Les migrations quotidiennes des salariés francophones travaillant à l'extérieur de Sawyerville (58), nov. 1982:

Source: listes de population municipales et informateurs, nov. 1982 Dressée par M. Schulte

Les structures spatiales des relations sociales dans le contexte de la famille, l'autre thème de cet exposé, sont souvent en étroite liaison avec celles des relations de travail qu'on vient d'analyser. Elles aussi vont être regardées sous deux aspects, d'abord la constitution des familles à Sawyerville au cours des années soixante-dix, et ensuite les relations dans les familles constituées et établies dans la communauté en 1982. Pour l'analyse de la constitution des familles je me réfère aux mariages qui ont eu lieu dans les quatre Eglises de Sawyerville (catholique, unie, anglicane et baptiste) au cours de la dernière décennie, de 1971 à 1980 (16). Les mariages interethniques en constellation francophone-anglophone ont été exceptionnels à Sawyerville avant les années soixante-dix, fait dû en partie à l'influence de l'Eglise catholique et à la politique de ses curés, qui ne toléraient pas encore de mariages entre francophones catholiques et anglophones protestants, mais dû également au clivage entre classes sociales autrefois prononcé à Sawyerville entre une population anglophone établie de vieille date et plus aisée et leurs voisins francophones arrivés plus récemment (17). C'est seulement depuis quelques années qu'il y a eu un changement presque spectaculaire avec l'apparition de nombreux mariages mixtes entre francophones et anglophones, la plupart du temps d'appartenances religieuses différentes. Mais la majorité des mariages à Sawyerville continue à se faire en couples confessionellement et religieusement homogènes (voir fig. 9).

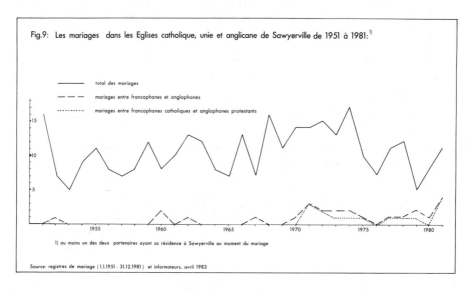

La structure spatiale de la constitution des familles correspond à deux phases de ce processus (voir fig. 10 à 12). Il y a d'abord l'espace d'où est recruté le deuxième partenaire avec lequel les jeunes de Sawyerville se sont mariés; il y a ensuite l'espace de leur établissement commun en tant que couple marié. Dans le cas des mariages mixtes, le deuxième partenaire vient toujours des environs immédiats de Sawyerville ou de la communauté même. C'est différent dans le cas des couples linguistiquement homogènes; leur rayon de recrutement est plus étendu, mais ne dépasse que rarement les limites des Cantons de l'Est chez les deux groupes. Au moment de l'établissement commun du couple marié, les différences quant au choix de leur lieu de résidence s'accentuent. Comme on l'a vu chez les jeunes sortants de l'école secondaire, les couples anglophones, bienque mariés à Sawyerville et ayant parfois passé une certaine periode après le mariage dans la région, ont egalement tendance à s'installer hors du Québec, avant tout en Ontario. Parmi ceux qui restent dans leur région d'origine, beaucoup se sont établie à Sawyerville même. Les couples francophones par contre ne quittent que rarement les Cantons de l'Est; ils se répartissent plutôt sur les villes de leur région. Les couples mixtes - fait remarquable - sont restés au Québec, souvent dans les environs de Sawyerville.

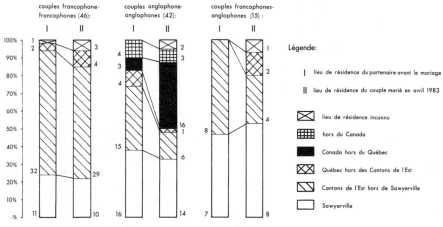

Fig. 10: La structure spatiale de la constitution des familles chez les francophones et les anglophones qui étaient résidents de Sawyerville au moment de leur mariage dans une des quatre Eglises du village (1.1.1971 - 31.12.1980):

Source: registres de mariage des Eglises catholique, unie, anglicane et baptiste; informateurs, avril 1983

Il faut encore jeter un coup d'œil sur les relations sociales déjà constituées dans les familles de Sawyerville en 1982. On n'y trouve guère de personnes au-dessus de l'âge de cinquante ans dans un couple mixte francophone-anglophone, ceci malgré l'âge moyen très élevé de la population. Sur les 320 couples habitant ensemble dans les ménages au village et à la campagne, seulement 18 sont mixtes en constellation francophone-anglophone (18). Quant aux relations de parenté, fruit de la constitution des familles, elles aussi finissent par dépasser le ménage, permettant ainsi d'en étudier les structures spatiales; elles aussi se révèlent structurées différemment dans l'espace chez les deux groupes ethniques. Les départs fréquents de jeunes anglophones ont provoqué inévitablement une extension des réseaux de parenté des autres membres de leurs familles qui sont restés dans la communauté; vu l'espace de leurs relations sociales parfois plus orientées vers l'Ontario que vers les Cantons de l'Est, on pourrait dire que ces derniers aussi - surtout quand ils sont âgés - "n'habitent plus" tout à fait dans leur région. Le fait que leur parenté réside souvent plus loin que celle de leurs voisins francophones ajoute à l'isolement relatif du groupe anglophone majoritairement unilingue. Ce sont les couples mixtes restés près de Sawyerville ou dans la communauté même qui sont en train de construire des réseaux de parenté interethniques d'une certaine envergure pour la première fois dans l'histoire de Sawyerville.

En résumant les traits caractéristiques des structures spatiales dans le domaine des relations de famille, elles aussi partiellement interethniques, et de leur évolution au cours de la dernière génération, tels qu'on a pu les dégager chez les deux groupes ethniques de Sawyerville, on peut observer la situation suivante. En ce qui concerne les relations interethniques il y a eu

- une augmentation considérable des mariages mixtes depuis quelques années entre francophones et anglophones, les deux partenaires venant de Sawyerville et de ses environs immédiats, et les couples mariés s'établissant au Québec.

Quant aux relations de familles intraethniques, elles sont plus étendues dans l'espace chez les deux groupes; or,

- chez les francophones l'espace de leurs relations (lieux de recrutement du deuxième partenaire, réseaux de parenté) se limite à la région des Cantons de l'Est,
- chez les anglophones il y a recrutement du deuxième partenaire dans la région, mais fréquemment établissement du couple marié hors du Québec, leurs

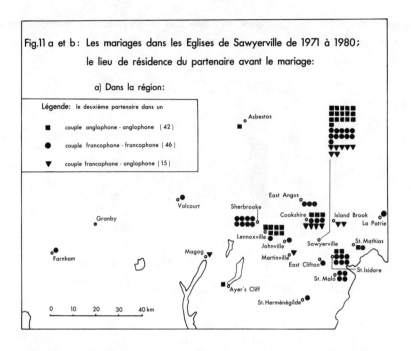
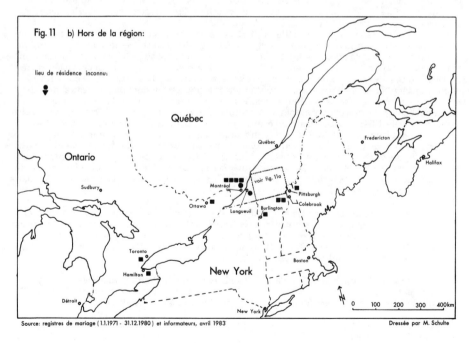

Fig.11 a et b: Les mariages dans les Eglises de Sawyerville de 1971 à 1980; le lieu de résidence du partenaire avant le mariage:

Source: registres de mariage (1.1.1971 - 31.12.1980) et informateurs, avril 1983   Dressée par M. Schulte

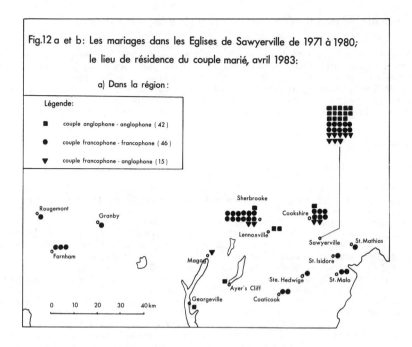

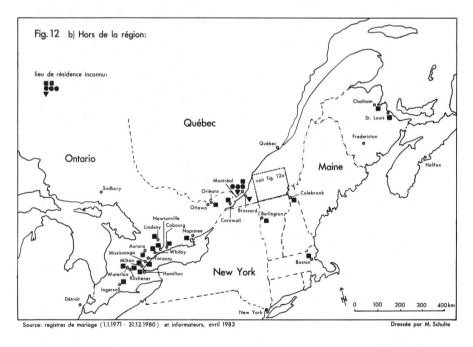

réseaux de parenté s'étendant de plus en plus vers l'Ontario.

Le contraste entre l'espace social des francophones de la communauté rurale de Sawyerville et celui de leurs voisins anglophones, dont je viens de présenter quelques éléments caractéristiques, montre à quel point les deux groupes ethniques habitant sur un territoire commun n'ont pourtant pas la même identité spatiale. Cette différence s'est prononcée au cours de la dernière génération, ce qui est dû à la mobilité accrue des habitants du monde rural, mais aussi au changement du statut des deux groupes ethniques dans la société québecoise contemporaine.

Annotations

(1) pour l'histoire des Cantons de l'Est voir Gravel (1938).
(2) notamment Hughes (1943), Ross (1950), Handricks (1982).
(3) voir Rioux et Martin (1971).
(4) dont la dernière manifestation spectaculaire a été la loi 101 sur la "Charte de la langue française" en 1977.
(5) Il s'agit ici de la région des Cantons de l'Est dans le sens historique qui dépasse la région administrative actuelle de "l'Estrie". Elle comprend les douze comtés de Missisquoi, Brome, Stanstead, Compton, Shefford, Sherbrooke, Wolfe, Frontenac, Richmond, Drummond, Arthabaska et Mégantic.
(6) chiffres sur la population du recensement du Canada 1981. Sur l'évolution démographique de la population anglophone hors de Montréal voir Caldwell (1980).
(7) L'appartenance à un groupe ethnique est basée ici sur le critère linguistique, la "langue maternelle" etant aujourd'hui dans le milieu etudié un meilleur indice de l'identité ethnique actuelle que "l'origine ethnique" du recensement fédéral ou l'appartenance religieuse. Toujours est-il qu'à quelques exceptions près, les francophones y sont d'origine française et catholiques - pratiquants ou non-pratiquants -, les anglophones y sont d'origine britannique et protestants.
(8) Dans le cadre de mes recherches j'ai eu l'occasion de passer de nombreuses semaines dans chacune des trois communautés entre septembre 1982 et août 1983.
(9) Le territoire de la communauté de Sawyerville (dans le sens sociologique) dépasse celui de la municipalité de Sawyerville (qui égale une subdivision du recensement fédéral); pour cette raison l'étude est basée sur les listes de population de trois municipalités voisines, celle de Sawyerville (village) et partiellement de celles d'Eaton et de Newport (campagne) en 1982; elles recouvrent un territoire correspondant mieux à la zone d'influence du village.
(10) Les renseignements sur la langue maternelle des habitants viennent d'informateurs connaissant bien le milieu; en cas de doute les personnes en question ont été consultés eux mêmes. Les enfants de mariages mixtes ont été mis a part dans une tierce catégorie provisoire de "francophone-anglophones"; il y en a a 32 (2,4%) en 1982.
(11) voir Ross (1950). En même temps un de ses étudiants a fait sa maîtrise en sociologie également sur Sawyerville ("Belleville"); voir Gauthier (1948).
(12) L'espace social particulier à un groupe social donné comprend l'ensemble des structures spatiales des relations sociales entretenues par les sujets composant le groupe.
(13) Les renseignements sur les anciens élèves, dont les listes ont été établies dans les archives des commissions scolaires catholiques (East Angus) et protestantes (Lennoxville) viennent d'anciens camarades de classe toujours résidents de la région.
(14) L'analyse des relations de travail de la population active de Sawyerville se base sur des renseignements recueillis à partir de listes de population municipales chez plusieurs informateurs de chaque groupe, bons connaisseurs de la population de ce milieu rural de par leurs positions dans la communauté. En cas de doute ou de contradictions entre informateurs les personnes en question ont été consultées elles-même.
(Les fils de cultivateurs travaillant sur les fermes de leur pères sont inclus dans l'analyse.)
(15) c'est à dire salarié et employeur appartenant à des groupes ethniques différents (sans tenir compte ici du problème de l'usage des langues au lieu de

travail). Les institutions de l'Etat provincial sont considerées comme francophones, sauf si elles sont traditionellement contrôlees par le groupe anglophone (p.e. le système scolaire protestant); celles de l'Etat fédéral et de la municipalité (juridiquement provinciale) sont considerées comme "mixtes", anglophone-francophones.
(16) Les couples entrés dans les registres paroissiaux des quatre Eglises ont été retenus seulement lorsqu'au moins un des deux partenaires avait indiqué Sawyerville (Eaton Corner et Randboro inclu) comme résidence avant le mariage. Pour connaître la langue maternelle des partenaires et leurs résidences actuelles il fallait avoir recours à des informateurs.
(17) voir Ross (1950).
(18) Les listes de population municipales utilisées pour cette étude groupent la population par ménages, ce qui permet d'en analyser la structure ethnique, une fois l'identité linguistique des individus connue.

Bibliographie

Blanchard, Raoul, 1960: Le centre du Canada français, province de Québec. Montréal.

Caldwell, Gary, 1980: Le Québec anglophone hors de la région de Montréal dans les années soixante-dix, évolution sociodémographique. Dossiers du Conseil de la langue française, études et recherches No 4, Québec.

— 1983: Les études ethniques au Québec. IQRC, collection: instruments de travail No 8, Québec.

— et Waddell, Eric, 1982: The English of Quebec, from Majority to Minority Status. Québec.

Channell, L. S., 1896: History of Compton County and Scetches of the Eastern Townships, District of St. Francis, and Sherbrooke County. Cookshire (Québec).

Gauthier, Claude, 1948: "Belleville", communauté rurale des Cantons de l'Est. Thèse de maîtrise en sociologie, Univ. Laval à Québec.

Gravel, Albert, 1938: Les Cantons de l'Est. Sherbrooke.

— 1973: Josiah Sawyer au Township d'Eaton, Notre-Dame-du-Saint-Rosaire de Sawyerville, Messire A. E. Dufresne et les anglo-protestants. Dans: Gravel, Albert. Mélanges historiques dans et autour des Cantons de l'Est II. Sherbrooke, pp. 1-24.

Handrick, Philip J., 1981: Institutions, Ideology and Power, Social Change in the Eastern Townships of Quebec. Thèse de doctorat en anthropologie sociale, Michigan State Univ.

Hughes, Everitt C., 1943: French Canada in Transition. Chicago.

Hunter, Jean, 1939: The French Invasion of the Eastern Townships, a Regional study. Thèse de maîtrise en sociologie, Univ. McGill à Montréal.

Laberee, Waymer S., 1980: The Early Days of Eaton. Sherbrooke.

Little, J. I., 1976: The Peacable Conquest, French Canadian Colonization in the Eastern Townships during the 19th Century. Thèse de doctorat en histoire, Univ. d'Ottawa.

Office de planification et de développement du Québec, 1977: L'espace rural de l'Estrie, région 05. Dossier d'inventaire et d'analyse, Québec.

Pletsch, Alfred, 1980: Kolonisationsphasen und Kulturlandschaftswandel im Südosten der Provinz Québec, Kanada. Erdkunde No 3, pp. 61-73.

Rioux, Marcel et Martin, Yves (editeurs), 1971: Le société canadienne-française. Montréal (première édition en anglais à Toronto en 1964).

Ross, Aileen D., 1943: The Cultural Effects of population Changes in the Eastern Townships. Canadian Journal of Economics and Political Science, Vol. IX No 4, pp. 447-462.

– 1950: Ethnic Relations and Social Structure, a Study of the Invasion of French-speaking Canadians into an English Canadian District. Thèse de doctorat en sociologie, Univ. de Chicago.

– 1954: Ethnic Group Contacts and Status Dilemma. Phylon No 3, pp. 267-275.

Adresse de l'auteur:
Martin Schulte
Wilhelm-Busch-Straße 3
3550 Marburg/Lahn

Ethnic Groups as Charter Groups in Ontario, Canada*

Alfred Hecht

Abstract: Canada's charter or ruling elite segment of society has, over time, changed its nature and composition. Before the conquest, colonial Canada was ruled by the Paris-designated French colonial administration. It determined the socio-economic life norms in Canada. After the takeover of Canada by the British and in the early years of Confederation, people of British Isle descent constituted the major power group in Canada. But with the opening of Canada to immigrants from all of the world in the late 19th century, the basis was set for an eventual modification of the ethnic background of Canada's charter or core group of people. Much of this change has occurred in recent years after the descendants of the immigrants had adopted the behavioural norms of the traditional British Isle charter group. This has meant that in large part ethnicity is no longer a variable that designates a second class standing in overall Canadian society. This paper examines the 1971 to 1981 trend of ethnic groups in Ontario to adopt and accept the socio-economic characteristics and its implied behaviour of the traditional British Isle charter group. It is hypothesized that this process of identification with the old charter group was strongest in this time period by people of northwest European (eg Germans) origin, followed by those of eastern European (eg Poles), Mediterranian (eg Italians) and lastly by those of Native Indian origin. Secondly, it is hypothesized that this process of identification with the old charter group is strongest in the economic and political core of Ontario, namely southern Ontario, and weakest in the northern periphery. The data source for the testing of these hypotheses consists of two special runs of Statistics Canada for Ontario, linking ethnicity by census divisions with socio-economic characteristics of the ethnic groups for 1971 and 1981.

Résumé: Au Canada, les couches sociales qui ont été muni du pouvoir public ont bien changé au cours de l'histoire. Avant la conquête britannique le Canada était gouverné par l'administration française instaurée par Paris. Ceci a déterminé les normes de la vie canadienne à cette époque. Après la prise du Canada par les anglais, et également au début de la Confédération, les descendants des Iles britanniques ont constitué le groupe qui a tenu le pouvoir. Mais au fur et à mesure que le Canada s'est ouvert, à la fin du 19 e siècle, à d'autres immigrants venant d'à travers le monde entier, la base de ces structures du pouvoir fut modifiée. Des changements dans ces structures peuvent particulièrement être décelés au cours des années récentes une fois les descendants des immigrants avaient adopté les normes de comportement du groupe au pouvoir et venant traditionnellement des Iles britanniques. Ceci veut dire que les structures ethniques ne sont plus les variables décisives pour une hiérarchisation de la société canadienne. L'article examine, pour la période entre 1971 et 1981, la question dans quelle mesure les groupes ethniques, en Ontario, adoptent et acceptent les caractéristiques socio-économiques ainsi que le comportement de ce groupe au pouvoir et venant des Iles britanniques. Une première hypothèse de l'article part de l'idée que le processus d'identification avec ce groupe traditionnel est particulièrement prononcé parmi les immigrants venant de la partie nord-ouest de l'Europe (p.e. les allemands), suivi par ceux de l'Europe de l'est (p.e. les polonais), de l'Europe méridional (p.e. les italiens) et en dernier lieu par la population autochtone. Une deuxième hypothèse établi l'idée que le processus d'identification est plus dynamique au centre du pouvoir économique et politique, donc particulièrement au sud de l'Ontario, tandis qu'il est le moins prononcé à la périphérie septentrionale de cette province. Les données pour pouvoir examiner

---

* I would like to express my sincere appreciation to my colleagues Prof. A. Pletsch and Dr. L. Müller-Wille members of the larger research project 'Ethnicity in Central Canada' for their encouragement and for their critical suggestion. A hearty thank you also goes to the Volkswagen Foundation for supporting this research financially. Mr. Robert Elsworth of WLU computer center helped in making the data retrieval system operational. My appreciation also goes out to my research assistants Kimberly Naqvi and Robert Nolk. For some financial help by SSHRC, Ottawa, I am grateful.

ces hypothèses on été établis par Statistiques Canada pour la province de l'Ontario, correlant les structures ethniques et socio-économiques des deux recensements de 1971 et 1981.

Zusammenfassung: Die machtausübenden Teile der kanadischen Gesellschaft haben im Laufe der Zeit immer wieder gewechselt. Vor der englischen Eroberung war das koloniale Kanada durch von Paris aus eingesetzte Verwaltungsinstitutionen gesteuert. Sie bestimmten die sozio-ökonomischen Lebensnormen in Kanada. Nachdem Kanada durch die Briten erobert worden war, und auch in den ersten Jahren der Konföderation, stellten diese die bedeutendste Machtgruppe in Kanada dar. Aber mit der Öffnung Kanadas für Immigranten aus der ganzen Welt im späten 19. Jahrhundert wurde die Grundlage geschaffen für potentielle Veränderungen der ethnischen Zusammensetzung in der machtausübenden Schicht des Landes. In jüngerer Zeit hat sich dieser Wandel verstärkt vollzogen, nachdem die Nachkommen dieser Immigranten die Verhaltensnormen der traditionellen britischen Entscheidungsgruppe angenommen haben. Dies bedeutet, daß im allgemeinen Ethnizität nicht länger als ein determinierender Faktor bei der Hierarchisierung der kanadischen Gesellschaft gesehen werden kann. Der Beitrag untersucht, inwieweit im Zeitraum von 1971 bis 1981 ethnische Gruppen in Ontario sozio-ökonomische Charakteristika und die entsprechenden Verhaltensnormen der traditionellen britischen Entscheidungsgruppe annehmen. Dabei wird als erste Hypothese formuliert, daß der Identifikationsprozeß mit dieser Gruppe während dieses Zeitraums am stärksten von Immigranten aus nordwesteuropäischen Ländern (z.B. Deutschen) vollzogen wurde, gefolgt von den Osteuropäern (z.B. Polen), den Südeuropäern (z.B. Italienern) und an letzter Stelle von der Urbevölkerung. Die zweite Hypothese ist, daß sich der Identifikationsprozeß räumlich in den wirtschaftlichen und politischen Entscheidungszentren, besonders in Süd-Ontario, am stärksten vollzieht, während er an der nördlichen Peripherie am schwächsten ist. Das Datenmaterial zur Überprüfung der beiden Hypothesen wurde durch zwei spezielle Datenbänke geliefert, die Statistics Canada für die Provinz Ontario bereitstellte, und in denen auf der Grundlage von Zensuseinheiten Ethnizitätsmerkmale und sozio-ökonomische Charakteristika der verschiedenen ethnischen Gruppen für die Jahre 1971 und 1981 miteinander korreliert wurden.

Introduction

One of the distinguishing features of Canadian Society is that it is made up of many different ethnic groups that have come from different parts of the world. Of Canada's 24-odd million people as recorded in the 1981 census, some 16 per cent are first generation immigrants (Statistics Canada, Canada's Immigrants, 1984, Table 1). But even more are second or third generation who still retain their ethnic identity. Despite the fact that Canada has only two official languages, nearly three million people in 1981 had a language other than English or French as their mother tongue. The most important of these languages were Italian, German, Ukrainian and Chinese (Statistics Canada, Canada at a Glance, 1983).

From where did these immigrants come? Although over time the importance of some countries as sources of immigrants has varied, figures show that a substantial number have consistently come from countries with Caucasian populations. Only in more recent years have third world countries contributed a substantial number of immigrants to Canada. Many of these have come in as political refugees. A high proportion of them are what one may term visible minorities once they are in Canada. Between 1970 and 1981 approximately 55 per cent came from Asia, the Caribbean, Central and South America, and Africa alone. A possible implication of this third world origin is that the newer immigrants will probably have to adopt a different strategy of associating with Canadian society than what their previous immigrant counterparts had to do. Most of the immigrants before 1970 came from European countries which in many respects had similar behavioural norms and attitudes as well as similar physical characteristics to the two founding nations of Canada, the British and the French. But this essay is not to address these newly arrived visible immigrants, as this is done in another paper, but rather this paper will focus upon the old immigrants, those that came mainly from northern Europe to see what their socio-economic status is in Canada's largest province, Ontario.

But to what extent do the immigrant groups arriving in Canada through the years participate in Canadian culture as well as share in its wealth and benefits? That first generation immigrants have language problems, and social and adjustment problems goes without saying. One would expect that their descendents however would have an easier time to adjust provided the general Canadian society is an open one and allows this integration process to take place. Within Canadian society and certainly within the Ontario society this adjustment process has traditionally been one of modelling themselves after the initial charter group that settled Ontario, namely the people of British Isle descent. In Quebec it was the French people that first settled the province of Quebec and formed the initial charter group. These two groups together formed the two founding nations but each with its own area of rule and dominance at least until 1763. That this overall dominance has not disappeared at the upper level of Canadian society is still normally accepted without much controversy. Ramcharan in 1982, for instance, still claimed that "white non-British and non-French ethnic groups comprise 1/3 of the population (but) are hard-put to (have) one per cent membership in the economic elite of Canada" (p. 69).

Although they may not have reached the complete upper echelon of the economic hierarchy in Canada many of the earlier immigrants from northern Europe are in fact participating fully in its economic, political and social life. One may in fact hypothesize that they, together with the old British charter group now form the new Ontario charter group. If any ethnic group has gone through the adjustment process, these groups should have since their backgrounds were not that different and no major visible distinguishable features separated them from the people of British Isle descent. It is the aim of this paper to explore this hypothesis by examining the socio-economic similarities of people with northern European background and those of British Isle background. The ethnic groups examined will be the French, Germans, Jewish and Ukrainians. The Native Indians will be used as an ethnic group which is visible and one which was forced to locate in rather remote areas of the province and hence was not able to participate fully in the socio-economic life of the province.

As indicated before, at the time of confederation, the people of British Isle descent were the main settlers in Ontario and constituted 82% of the total population (Schott, 1936: 79). Much of the remainder of the population was of German, Native Indian or French Canadian descent. Through time however this dominance of people of British Isle descent decreased. By 1981 the percentage with British Isle ethnic roots in Ontario was down to 52.6 per cent single ethnic origin (those that claimed only one ethnic ancestry), and 59.3 per cent with single and multiple ethnic combined origin (Statistics Canada, Advance information by selected ethnic origins, 1983: 3). The decline of people of British Isle descent over time leads to the hypothesis that the initial charter group subsequently integrated immigrants with similar value structures and appearances into itself and together they now form the new charter society of Ontario (Fig. 1). In 1981 the number of people of British Isle and Northwest European descent was close to 80 per cent. The remaining 20 per cent in Ontario is made up of visible minorities and Native people. Such a development is naturally of mutual benefit. It forms a broad mutual support base against the inflow of the new visible minorities from all over the world. Should the hypothesis regarding the new charter society be true, then Ontario and maybe Canada is entering a new phase in its ethnic group relations. The hypothesis also suggests that for a charter group to remain or retain its dominance in a society by pure number of people and not by force, as is the case in South Africa, it may have to absorb similar smaller ethnic groups in order to protect its position against culturally and physically dissimilar ethnic groups. Where this critical number lies is debatable but a rough indication of Figure 1 would indicate it may be around the 80 per cent mark.

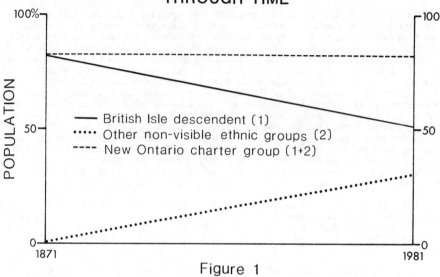

Figure 1

Theoretical Perspective

Like many empirical evaluations, this paper relies on a theoretical framework in which to place its findings. The concept of how ethnic groups can become members of the charter group is derived from Gordon's (1978) study of American assimilation, Anderson and Frideres' (1981) study of Canadian ethnic behaviour and Hecht, Sharpe and Wong's study (1983) of ethnic group relations within the core-periphery framework. In Figure 2 these three concepts are brought together in one diagram. In this figure it is hypothesised that at the beginning of the settlement process a region is settled first by a group of people called the charter group and secondly, by ethnic minorities. The charter group because of its early arrival captures political, economic and social power early and consequently determines and sets the norms and regulations of society. It occupies the so called core position within socio-economic space. It also occupies the more favourable position and frequently the charter group, because of its early lead in settlement, also occupies the best geographic space. Ethnic minorities on the other hand correspondingly occupy the peripheral areas in the socio-economic space of society as well as in the geographic space. A clear hierarchical relationship exists between these groups of society. Given this starting point, Gordon (1978) in his discussion of the North American assimilation process, believes that the charter group as well as the ethnic minority groups will with time disperse on the socio-economic dimension of society to the point where they are equally representative on the extreme spectrum of the core-periphery dimension. According to Gordon this homogenising process, as suggested earlier, follows one of the following three assimilation paths: (1) ethnic conforming to the charter group norm, in North America meaning English conformity, (2) both charter and ethnic groups "melting" into a new society as is sometimes hypothesized for the U.S.A. or (3) the establishment of equality between the ethnic groups in which case the result is a society with cultural plurality. In Canada the latter is supported by the government and is called multiculturalism.

The process that takes place in the socio-economic sphere is also hypothesized to take place in geographic space. Whereas at the beginning of the process ethnic groups tend to be located on the peripheries of the charter settlement hearth, by the end of the assimilation or integration process these groups should be proportionally equally represented in various regions of the geographic space. This hypothesis naturally assumes a country or region where regional mobility is feasible and is practiced. Although the diagram does not differentiate between regional

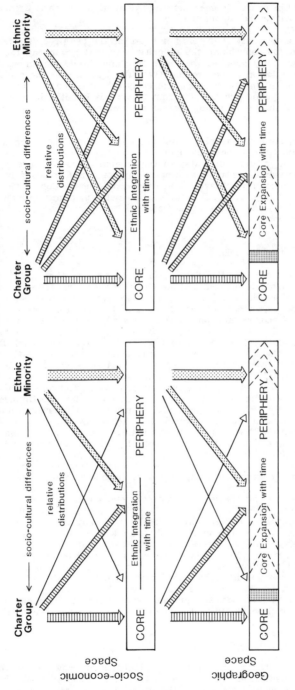

Figure 2

space or metropolitan space, it goes without saying that the same process of diffusion is feasible within metropolitan space.

If the diagram correctly represents or captures the two processes taking place between ethnic groups, one being the majority (charter) group and the other one being the ethnic minority groups, then with time one should expect similar socio-economic characteristics in these groups. Over the last decade one could expect a strong convergence in Ontario between the early ethnic minority groups and the early Anglo-Saxon charter group. This convergence is hypothesized because of the threat of the large number of visible minorities people which have entered Canada recently.

That the process of geographic integration may not be occurring as rapidly as in socio-economic space is not surprising. Once settled in a region, people would tend to put roots down and hence stay in that region. Also, because of limited opportunities the process of assimilation/integration should not be going on as rapidly in the peripheral regions of Ontario as in the Toronto core. Consequently one can hypothesize that although geographic integration between ethnic groups will take place over time, the socio-economic integration in the peripheries will be lagging behind that of the core.

Historical Settlement of Ontario

As previously indicated, the first agricultural settlers that occupied Ontario were people of British Isle descent. Although French fur traders and trappers lived in Ontario before the English arrived at the end of the eighteenth century, their impact on the permanent settlement scene of Ontario was minimal. They had attached themselves economically and partially socially to the Native Indians and when these were pushed to the periphery so were the French. For Ontario then, the first major agricultural settlers were the Loyalists who came north from the United States after the end of the War of Independence (Moore, 1984). In all, some ten thousand arrived in Upper Canada by 1784, of which it has been estimated by Schott (1936: 71) that some one thousand were troops that had fought on the British side but had originally come from Hessen, Germany. This anomaly notwithstanding, the influx of people with British Isle roots into Ontario continued for some 90 years. By 1871, five years after Canadian Confederation and at the time of the first Canadian Census, Ontario had 82% of its population of British Isle descent. Homogeneity within this group was however far from the norm since strong differences did exist between the Scottish, Irish and British subjects. By this time also the Native Indian population was securely placed on the reserves and for all intents and purposes was completely pushed into both the socio-economic as well as the geographical periphery of Ontario's mainstay society.

By the end of the nineteenth century however, a number of Ontarians started to move west to the prairies to settle new lands. In part, as a result of this westward expansion, Canadian immigration increased and many came to Ontario. Some of these were the French from Quebec, Jewish and Ukrainians from eastern Europe and Germans from central Europe. By 1910 the settlement pattern of Ontario was fairly well set (Hecht, Sharpe, Wong, 1983). Germans continued to trickle in, but their numbers decreased drastically after the Nazi's took over in Germany and only reappeared for a short time with substantial numbers in the 1950's and early 60's. On the whole, however, by the 1980's most European ethnic groups were fairly well settled within Ontario's general societies and as hypothesized earlier now together with those of British Isle descent, formed part of the new Ontario charter society.

Data Source and Methodology

To see if those ethnic minority groups identified are now part of the Ontario charter group, a close examination will be made of their socio-economic characteristics in relation to those people that formed the initial charter group, namely those of British Isle descent. Two basic data sources were used for this purpose. Both were bought in part with the financial help of the Volkswagen grant. The first data source describes the socio-economic characteristics of ethnic groups of Ontario as recorded in the 1971 Census. A special run by Statistics Canada extracted for each ethnic individual by census divisions, his socio-economic characteristics such as mother tongue, education attained, income received and marriage ties. A similar set of data was purchased from Statistics Canada in 1984 based upon the 1981 Census. Again membership in an ethnic group was selected and the socio-economic conditions of that individual were recorded. At this time it should be pointed out however, that unfortunately between 1971 and 1981 the definition of ethnicity in the Canadian Census changed. In 1971 and earlier, ethnic background on the father's side determined the ethnicity of an individual. In 1981 the ethnic affiliation decision was left to the individual to decide. Consequently the two sets of Census data are not quite comparable. In the 1981 Census, individuals could for the first time also give a multiple ethnic response, indicating an ethnic duality in parents. In 1981 nearly eight per cent of all Canadians claimed a dual or more ethnic background (Statistics Canada, Population by Selected Ethnic Origins, advanced data, 1983). Therefore, comparisons made in this essay should be viewed with this difference in data in mind.

Empirical Analysis

The assimilation process of ethnic groups into the cultural majority and consequently forming part of the charter group itself, is one that is explored empirically here. What is done is to examine the condition of the ethnic groups mentioned earlier in relation to the British group. A comparison will be made in four major areas. These major areas are language adaptability, educational and income achievements and inter-ethnic marriages. In either of the intergrative processes in North America, the Anglo-Saxon-conformity theory or the melting pot theory, these are the major sequential steps through which ethnic groups have to go in order to become part of the charter group.

As indicated earlier the six ethnic groups will be compared using 1971 and 1981 Census data. The regions in which they will be compared are Ontario as a whole, Metropolitan Toronto and some of the peripheral areas such as the Bruce Peninsula, Cochrane, Rainy River and Kenora Census divisions of northwestern Ontario (Fig. 3).

Language

In Table 1 the number of ethnic people in Ontario that had adopted the English language as their mother tongue in 1971 and 1981 is compared. That the percentage for those of British Isle descent is nearly 100% is not surprising. In 1971 for Ontario as a whole the group with the highest percentage of English as the mother tongue was the Jewish. Nearly 72% of its people in Ontario had English as the mother tongue. The Germans on the other hand had 65%, the Native Indians 53%, the Ukrainians 49% and lowest were the French with 38%. The small French proportion can probably be attributed to the high concentration of French in northern Ontario (e.g. Cochrane) where they make up a high proportion of the total population in some communities. A second reason may be that the French in Ontario also consider themselves as one half of the Canadian founding nation. This may be a reason why more retain their mother language than other ethnic groups. Except for the Native Indians and the Jewish people the ethnic groups in Toronto adopt the English language as the mother tongue less so than do the groups in the peripheries. This is certainly the case for the Germans, the French and the Ukrainians. One reason is certainly the large number of recent immigrants that have come to the metropolitan area. For the Germans and the French this may be the case but not for the Ukrainians. One can also hypothesize however, that in the big metropolitan areas the ethnic groups are big enough so that they can support each other through cultural events, and family and friend ties, all of which help to retain the ethnic language. Such support is not present in the rural peripheral regions where ethnic groups are small and dispersed. But if the above observation

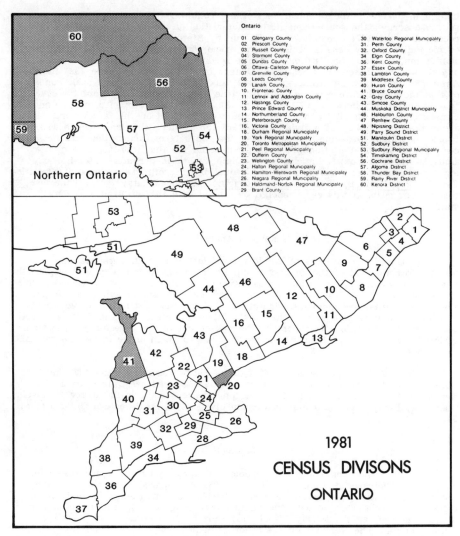

Figure 3

is true for all ethnic groups, then the model as hypothesized in Fig. 2 is false.

By 1981 the language retention situation had changed for all five ethnic groups in Ontario as a whole. Although the calculations are not quite comparable, the proportion that had English as a mother tongue decreased for the Germans by 10% and the Ukrainians by 6%, but increased for the Jewish by 13% and for the Native Indian by 18%. The French also decreased their proportion from 38 to 33%. They seem to resist the changeover to English as the mother tongue the most. It may be the result of the bilingual policy of the federal government and the movement of many Ontario school boards to offer French as a second language in earlier grades now. Or it may be the result of offering immersion French in some schools. With such institutional support families with French Canadian background are certainly more able to retain their language ability than other groups. Furthermore as suggested earlier

Table 1: Proportion of English as Mother Tongue by Various Ethnic Groups 1971*

	British	French	German	Jewish	Native Indians	Ukrainian
Ontario	.988	.383	.647	.725	.537	.488
Toronto	.987	.575	.471	.706	.792	.374
Bruce	.994	.678	.870	1.000	.464	.786
Cochrane	.939	.086	.667	.683	.181	.549
Rainy River	.988	.637	.657	.000	.442	.549
Kenora	.984	.578	.669	.727	.070	.589
1981**						
Ontario	.99	.326	.54	.86	.723	.432
Toronto	.99	.45	.29	.85	.79	.29

* Source: Special run, Statistics Canada, 1971.
** Special run, Statistics Canada, 1981, Calculated in the following method: 1 - Ethnic mother tongue/ethnic group size: Only single responses were used.

the high rural concentration of the French in the north may also allow them to retain their language more.

The larger number of Germans and Ukrainians using English as the mother tongue in Ontario as a whole when compared to Toronto again points to the fact that language retention may be stronger in metropolitan areas than in rural areas.

A cursory examiniation of data on multiple ethnic responses for Ontario, but not documented in this paper, shows that 97% have English as the mother tongue. This compares to 86% for single ethnic responses. Of other ethnic mother tongues in multiple ethnic backgrounds, French was the most important outdistancing Italian by a ratio of 9 to 1. In Ontario society, families or individuals with ethnic background other than English certainly have accepted the Anglo-Saxon language trait.

Education and Income

In the past one of the fastest ways ethnic groups could move up the socio-economic scale in Canadian society was by means of education.

One of the interesting features of recent immigrants to Canada has been their high level of education even before entry. This has not always been the case. Before the mid 1960's a large number of immigrants were sponsored by families. Since the change in policy in the mid 60's immigrants have been allowed to come in on the basis of qualifications, and education has been an important one. Table 2 shows that immigrants who have arrived since 1960, have had a substantially higher education level that non-immigrants. Nearly twice as many men have university degrees than is the case for the overall Canadian population. It is nearly the same for women. In contrast, male immigrants who arrived before 1961 had approximately equal university degree achievements to their Canadian counterparts while the immigrant woman was less educated than her Canadian counterpart.

But education in Canadian society is usually taken for the purpose of achieving a better economic standard of living. In Table 2 we can see that the immigrants who arrived between 1971 and 1979, although they were highly educated, did receive a slightly lower income than the Canadian non-immigrant population. Immigrants who had arrived before 1971 however had a higher income than non-immi-

Table 2: a) Percentage of Immigrant and Non-immigrant Populations 15 Years and Over Not Attending School Full-Time with University Degrees, by Sex and Period of Immigration, Canada 1981

	Arrived before 1961	Arrived 1961-1970	Arrived 1971-1981	Total immigrants	Non-immigrants
Men	9.	17.5	19.	13.	9.
Women	4.	9.0	12.	7.5	6.

b) Average[1] 1980 income of the Immigrant and Non-immigrant Populations 15 Years and Over, by Period of Immigration and Sex, Canada 1981

Period of immigration	Total	Men	Women
Arrived before 1971	14,500	19,100	9,000
Arrived 1971-1979	12,600	16,300	8,400
Total immigrants[2]	14,100	18,500	8,900
Non-immigrants	12,800	16,600	8,300

1) For persons with income
2) Excludes immigrants who arrived in 1980 and 1981

Source: Statistics Canada: Canada's Immigrants, 1984 after Tables 10 and 6

grants. The data presents a positive economic picture for immigrants. Part of their favorable economic well-being however may be due to the fact that in 1980 proportionally they probably had more people in their high income earning years than Canada as a whole.

But let us now take a closer look at the ethnic groups under consideration in this essay. In Table 3 we see the income of the six ethnic groups for Ontario in 1971 broken down by age group as well as by income groups. For each age group the proportion of people earning one of the seven income categories is presented. By summing these proportions and comparing the proportion to those of the British, one can test whether both groups could have come from the same underlying economic population distribution. The test is known as the Kolmornov-Smirnov test (Norcliffe, 1982: 102).

On examining Table 3 we find the following. The French in Ontario have a significant different income distribution than the British for each of the six age categories. In most other ethnic groups the proportion of people with no income is higher than those of the British. Although the fit between the German and the British is closer than between French and British, the German ethnic group as a whole also has a different income distribution for any given age category, except for the 15-25 age category. The ethnic group that differs from the rest is the Jewish. For each age category the proportion of people with no income is less than the British except for those in retirement. On the other hand the proportion earning more than $ 15,000 a year is higher than the British. Again for each category the Native Indian population shows extreme deviation from the British. Its population is more highly represented in the low income categories. In the high income categories their proportion is as low as 25 per cent of the British. The Ukrainians have a surprisingly strong income distribution in comparison to the British. Except in the 55-64 age category, the Ukrainians have proportionally less people in no income categories than the British charter group. But, on the other hand, they also do not have as many represented in the upper income echelon as the British do.

Table 3: Income by Ethnic and Age Groups - Province 1971
(Total Income Level / Total Income)

	British	French*	German*	Jewish*	Canadian* Indian	Ukrainian*
A 1	.193	.252	.199	.170	.327	.189
A 2	.251	.220	.232	.250	.310	.241
A 3	.195	.190	.191	.171	.198	.196
A 4	.172	.176	.178	.146	.110	.187
A 5	.078	.079	.088	.062	.028	.087
A 6	.076	.064	.081	.088	.022	.074
A 7	.036	.020	.032	.113	.005	.026
B 1	.316	.365	.308	.274	.506	.312
B 2	.343	.278	.349	.450	.296	.359
B 3	.200	.202	.202	.168	.132	.193
B 4	.116	.124	.116	.082	.058	.109
B 5	.018	.023	.019	.013	.005	.018
B 6	.005	.008	.006	.010	.002	.007
B 7	.001	.001	.001	.004	.001	.001
C 1	.188	.228	.199	.178	.278	.180
C 2	.139	.128	.133	.138	.228	.132
C 3	.167	.172	.161	.154	.236	.152
C 4	.230	.231	.219	.168	.168	.223
C 5	.125	.120	.132	.091	.047	.144
C 6	.116	.097	.122	.134	.038	.130
C 7	.035	.023	.034	.137	.005	.040
D 1	.180	.230	.182	.151	.259	.170
D 2	.151	.138	.143	.137	.264	.128
D 3	.169	.176	.174	.150	.240	.186
D 4	.190	.196	.200	.162	.142	.240
D 5	.111	.114	.120	.078	.044	.124
D 6	.128	.106	.121	.127	.042	.110
D 7	.071	.039	.059	.195	.011	.042
E 1	.175	.237	.194	.150	.244	.187
E 2	.190	.193	.190	.137	.361	.170
E 3	.192	.200	.207	.186	.236	.226
E 4	.203	.195	.207	.191	.094	.236
E 5	.092	.082	.089	.084	.044	.086
E 6	.093	.065	.073	.107	.017	.070
E 7	.055	.028	.040	.145	.005	.024
F 1	.011	.014	.018	.024	.014	.019
F 2	.517	.609	.528	.418	.723	.580
F 3	.283	.243	.278	.226	.196	.272
F 4	.105	.082	.104	.140	.046	.084
F 5	.031	.022	.029	.049	.008	.023
F 6	.030	.021	.026	.060	.005	.014
F 7	.021	.009	.017	.082	.005	.008

* significantly different from the British

Age Group:
A = 5-14
B = 15-25
C = 25-39
D = 40-54
E = 55-64
F = +64

Income-Level:
1 = No Income
2 = Less than $ 1999
3 = $ 2000-4999
4 = $ 5000-7999
5 = $ 8000-9999
6 = $ 10000-14999
7 = $ 15000

Table 4: Income by Ethnic and Age Groups - Kenora 1971
(Total Income Level / Total Income)

	British	French	German	Jewish	Canadian* Indian	Ukrainian
A 1	.227	.235	.258	.125	.394	.195
A 2	.240	.205	.200	.125	.376	.237
A 3	.180	.198	.178	.125	.176	.171
A 4	.166	.191	.151	.250	.043	.193
A 5	.091	.103	.096	.000	.006	.116
A 6	.077	.053	.096	.000	.003	.072
A 7	.018	.012	.022	.125	.001	.014
B 1	.333	.356	.357	.500	.584	.318
B 2	.333	.309	.341	.500	.313	.356
B 3	.184	.181	.163	.000	.082	.174
B 4	.122	.112	.093	.000	.024	.106
B 5	.022	.032	.023	.000	.000	.038
B 6	.005	.011	.008	.000	.000	.000
B 7	.001	.005	.000	.000	.000	.000
C 1	.226	.226	.250	.333	.362	.189*
C 2	.137	.118	.128	.333	.323	.131
C 3	.136	.190	.147	.333	.233	.107
C 4	.223	.210	.199	.000	.071	.254
C 5	.149	.154	.135	.000	.008	.172
C 6	.114	.072	.122	.000	.005	.115
C 7	.016	.021	.013	.000	.000	.025
D 1	.217	.208	.214	.000	.317	.161
D 2	.147	.101	.115	.000	.361	.140
D 3	.167	.181	.176	.000	.250	.175
D 4	.174	.255	.168	1.000	.053	.210
D 5	.123	.148	.122	.000	.010	.182
D 6	.134	.087	.160	.000	.010	.105
D 7	.035	.020	.046	.000	.000	.028
E 1	.192	.145	.224	.000	.281	.148*
E 2	.168	.217	.122	.000	.494	.093
E 3	.179	.203	.245	.000	.191	.241
E 4	.201	.261	.143	.500	.022	.315
E 5	.126	.101	.122	.000	.011	.130
E 6	.107	.087	.122	.000	.000	.074
E 7	.030	.014	.041	.000	.000	.019
F 1	.017	.000	.042	.000	.011	.019
F 2	.538	.488	.542	.000	.783	.596
F 3	.304	.366	.292	.000	.185	.231
F 4	.086	.122	.042	.000	.011	.115
F 5	.023	.024	.042	.000	.011	.019
F 6	.020	.000	.042	.000	.000	.038
F 7	.017	.000	.000	.000	.000	.000

* significantly different from the British

Age Group
A = 5-14
B = 15-25
C = 25-39
D = 40-54
E = 55-64
F = +64

Income Level
1 = No Income
2 = Less than $ 1999
3 = $ 2000- 4999
4 = $ 5000- 7999
5 = $ 8000- 9999
6 = $ 10000-14999
7 = $ +15000

In summary one could say that in 1971 all ethnic groups, except for the Jewish, had a higher proportion of their people in the lower income categories holding constant age. These differences were statistically significant. The Jewish group was statistically significant above the British. The Native Indians were by far the poorest group.

In Table 4 the income distribution by ethnic groups by age is shown for a peripheral region of Ontario, namely Kenora. It shows some very interesting income distribution by age groups. In this area of Ontario only one group is statistically different from the British and that is the native Canadians, namely the Indians. They are overrepresented in the poor income distribution and underrepresented in the high income. The Jewish distribution because of their low numbers cannot be used to test for their difference from the British. On the other hand the French, German and Ukrainian groups are only slightly different from the British. The Ukrainians in the 25 to 39 age category and in the 55 to 64 age category are statistically different from the British but they are different in the positive sense since their income proportion is distributed more towards high income categories than the British. It seems that in the Kenora region the British, French, Germans and to a large extent the Ukrainians have become one similar kind of so-

Table 5: Education by Ethnic and Age Groups - Province 1971
(Total Education Level / Total Education)

	British	French	German	Jewish	Canadian Indian	Ukrainian
A 1	.030	.030	.034	.023	.051*	.027
A 2	.730	.739	.730	.682	.781	.689
A 3	.239	.231	.236	.294	.168	.284
A 4	.000	.000	.000	.000	.000	.000
B 1	.004	.007	.004	.004*	.018*	.007
B 2	.013	.024	.013	.008	.095	.010
B 3	.757	.797	.746	.561	.790	.714
B 4	.225	.172	.238	.427	.096	.269
C 1	.004	.006	.003	.005*	.072*	.005
C 2	.022	.075	.022	.014	.199	.024
C 3	.655	.705	.626	.403	.620	.624
C 4	.319	.215	.349	.578	.110	.347
D 1	.004	.013*	.003	.008*	.148*	.012*
D 2	.037	.165	.047	.043	.258	.141
D 3	.725	.687	.705	.648	.534	.694
D 4	.235	.134	.244	.301	.062	.143
E 1	.006	.031	.009	.042*	.250*	.069*
E 2	.067	.243	.115	.092	.303	.323
E 3	.733	.618	.709	.686	.417	.508
E 4	.194	.108	.167	.181	.032	.100
F 1	.015	.071*	.024*	.215*	.309*	.202*
F 2	.151	.338	.229	.185	.334	.453
F 3	.709	.526	.651	.513	.328	.306
F 4	.125	.060	.097	.087	.029	.039

* significantly different from the British

Age Group:
A = 5-14
B = 15-24
C = 25-39
D = 40-54
E = 55-64
F = +64

Education Level:
1 = No Education
2 = Les than Gr. 7
3 = Gr. 7 - Gr. 13
4 = Some University or College

cio-economic ethnic group. If one considers that the Native Indians form the visible minority in Kenora, the data may support the hypothesis advanced at the beginning of the paper that a new charter group has been formed in this area of Ontario.

If one examines the education achievement level of the original charter group and compares it to that of the other ethnic groups (Table 5) one can see that in 1971 in Ontario as a whole nearly every ethnic group was statistically significantly different from that of the British. In nearly all instances they were substantially less well-educated than the British. For Kenora however (Table 6) the situation is quite different. Here the Germans are equally educated in the different age classes with the exception of the 55 and over, age group. Ukrainians are proportionally less educated in the 40 and up age categories. It is also surprising that the French, except for the 5 to 14 age category are also statistically significantly less educated than the British. As expected, the Native Indians do differ from the British in all the age categories even in the lowest age category of 5 to 14 years. Thus even though at the income level the French, British, Germans and Ukrainians in Kenora were very similar to each other in 1971, when one looks at their educational background, statistically different situations emerge.

Table 6: Education by Ethnic and Age Groups - Kenora
(Total Education Level / Total Education)

	British	French	German	Jewish**	Canadian Indian	Ukrainian
A 1	.046	.033	.034	.000	.087*	.022
A 2	.715	.736	.730	.500	.815	.710
A 3	.239	.226	.236	.000	.098	.269
A 4	.000	.000	.000	.000	.000	.000
B 1	.004	.005*	.008	.000	.055*	.000
B 2	.015	.016	.008	.000	.318	.015
B 3	.799	.894	.845	1.000	.592	.824
B 4	.184	.909	.140	.000	.034	.168
C 1	.003	.010*	.000	.000	.270	.000
C 2	.031	.077	.039	.000	.476	.041
C 3	.735	.785	.716	.333	.225	.730
C 4	.231	.128	.258	.667	.024	.238*
D 1	.009	.027*	.008	.000	.572*	.007*
D 2	.046	.208	.084	.000	.269	.161
D 3	.780	.698	.771	1.000	.144	.755
D 4	.165	.067	.153	.000	.014	.084
E 1	.011	.014*	.020*	.000	.700*	.074*
E 2	.099	.304	.204	.500	.233	.370
E 3	.747	.623	.694	.500	.056	.500
E 4	.143	.043	.102	.500	.000	.056
F 1	.017	.071*	.083	-	.802	.269
F 2	.215	.286	.333	-	.165	.519
F 3	.693	.571	.542	-	.033	.231
F 4	.076	.048	.083	-	.000	.000

* significantly different from the British
** not sufficient data

Age Group:
A = 5-14
B = 15-24
C = 25-39
D = 40-54
E = 55-64
F = +64

Education Level:
1 = No Education
2 = Less than Gr. 7
3 = Gr. 7 - Gr. 13
4 = Some University or College

But what was the situation in 1981 during the last full Canadian census? In Table 7 the average employment income by age and by education for the ethnic groups under consideration is given for the province of Ontario as a whole. As can be seen, average income for the 15 to 24 age group irrespective of education has the following rank. Ukrainians are first, second are the French, third are the Germans, fourth the British, fifth the Jewish and sixth the native Indians. For the 25 to 30 age category however, the order has changed substantially. Now the Jewish population is far ahead of all the other groups, some 25% above the next nearest group, the Ukrainians. British, French, Germans and Ukrainians have very similar average incomes. The Native Indian single response group earns only about 75% of what these four groups earn. Even the Native Indian multiple response group has an average income of only $ 13,000, substantially less than the $ 15,500 earned by the British. In the prime working years of 40 to 54, the average income in 1981 was $ 31,000 for the Jewish, $ 18,600 for the Ukrainians, $ 18,300 for the British and $ 18,100 for the Germans. The values were somewhat lower for the French, $ 16,000, and substantially lower, $ 10,000, for the Native Indians. The Native Indian multiple response group had an average income of $ 15,000, still a good thousand or so below

Table 7: Average Income by Education for Ontario 1980, by Ethnic Groups by Age

| Age Group | Education | British | proportion of British | | | | Native* Indians (single response) | Native* Indians (multiple response) |
			French	German	Jewish**	Ukrainian**		
15-24	Total	6162	1.11	1.05	.91	1.12	.79	.90
	no ed.	4825	1.25	1.08	-	-	1.92	-
	1-7 yrs	4932	1.36	.94	-	-	.72	-
	7-13 yrs	5681	1.14	1.04	.72	1.09	.79	.83
	some U	7119	1.08	1.04	.84	1.09	.87	1.03
	U compl.	7139	1.10	.98	1.13	1.11	1.14	1.39
25-39	Total	15536	.97	1.00	1.34	1.08	.67	.83
	no ed.	8032	1.27	.81	.46	1.42	.87	-
	1-7 yrs	9679	1.33	1.04	.80	1.06	.70	1.35
	7-13 yrs	13416	1.02	1.01	1.14	1.05	.72	.87
	some U	15561	.98	1.03	1.06	1.03	.75	.81
	U. compl.	21746	.97	.93	1.14	1.02	.75	.87
40-54	Total	18373	.89	.99	1.70	1.02	.57	.80
	no ed.	9787	1.26	1.22	1.70	.94	.61	.40
	1-7 yrs	12210	1.13	1.16	1.50	1.22	.64	.98
	7-13 yrs	15539	.97	.98	1.50	1.05	.70	.85
	some U	18407	.93	1.05	1.38	1.03	.68	.78
	U. compl.	35368	.88	.92	1.32	.93	.72	.84
55-64	Total	16046	.81	.95	1.62	.93	.52	.76
	no ed.	8922	1.04	.90	2.86	1.30	.65	-
	1-7 yrs	10348	1.00	1.04	1.66	1.15	.55	.15
	7-13 yrs	13369	.91	.99	1.63	1.05	.71	1.06
	some U	17332	.91	.98	1.52	1.08	.66	.77
	U. compl.	36256	.83	.90	1.27	.82	.87	.81

* significantly below British group using α = .05 and the binominal distribution test
** significantly above British group using α = .05 and the binominal distribution test

Source: Special Run, Statistics Canada, 1984

that of the French.

It is frequently hypothesized that by the time people reach their 55 birthday they have reached their upper limit of earnings. From this table this certainly seems to be the case. Income is down for each ethnic group. However the rank order does not seem to have changed. The Jewish population still earns substantially more than any other category. On the other hand the Native Indians only earn half as much as the British in this age category. On the whole, Table 7 shows that statistically there is no difference between the British and the French and the Germans.

Table 7 also shows some very consistent relationships between average income, age, and education. People with no education earn only 1/3 the amount university educated people earn. Also as age increases income increases for each education level up to age 55, after which it decreases somewhat.

The situation for Toronto for these ethnic groups is not much different than for Ontario as a whole (Table 8). The major difference is that the Ukrainians do not vary statistically from the British. Average income for nearly every age and

Table 8:   Average Income by Education for the Metro Toronto Census Division 1980, by Ethnic Groups by Age

Age Group	Education	British	French	German	Jewish**	Ukrainian	Native* Indians (single response)	Native Indians (multiple response)
15-24	Total	6700	1.07	1.06	.80	.97	.91	.95
	no ed.	5570	-	-	-	-	-	-
	1-7 yrs	5299	1.38	-	-	-	-	-
	7-13 yrs	6174	1.09	1.02	.70	.89	.88	.88
	some U	7467	1.07	1.07	.79	.99	1.03	1.14
	U. compl.	7830	.93	.95	1.01	.96	.71	-
25-39	Total	16315	.96	1.03	1.29	1.04	.72	.85
	no ed.	9583	-	-	.37	-	1.13	-
	1-7 yrs	10060	1.09	.86	.72	1.25	-	.94
	7-13 yrs	13674	1.01	1.04	1.13	1.05	.74	.83
	some U	15926	.97	1.05	1.02	.98	.82	.81
	U. compl.	21495	.95	.92	1.16	.98	.66	1.03
40-54	Total	20288	.83	1.01	1.54	.91	.52	.67
	no ed.	9987	.90	1.21	1.29	.76	.52	-
	1-7 yrs	12035	1.06	1.23	1.40	.97	.80	.95
	7-13 yrs	16328	.88	.95	1.43	.99	.62	.77
	some U	19877	.91	1.06	1.28	.91	.64	.60
	U. compl.	38720	.81	1.02	1.22	.82	.32	.62
55-64	Total	18426	.81	.92	1.38	.86	.52	.69
	no ed.	9692	.70	-	2.99	1.05	1.43	-
	1-7 yrs	11739	.74	1.03	1.48	1.02	.18	-
	7-13 yrs	14851	.92	.93	1.48	1.01	.58	.79
	some U	19185	.83	.92	1.35	1.00	.73	-
	U. compl.	40209	.90	.80	1.13	.65	-	-

* Significantly lower from the British group using α = .05 and the binomial distribution test
** Significantly above British group using α = .05 and the binomial distribution test

Source: Special Run Statistics Canada, 1984

education group is about $ 2,000 higher than for Ontario.

For the periphery, Kenora, the statistical differerence between ethnic groups is removed except for the Native Indians (Table 9). They have significantly less income for each age as well as education level. It is even lower than for the province as a whole or Toronto. Their relatively large number in Kenora certainly does not help them to get a larger share of the economic benefits of the region.

Table 9: Average Income by Education for the Kenora Census Division 1980, by Ethnic Groups by Age

Age Group	Education	British	French	German	Jewish	Ukrainian	Native* Indians (single response)	Native Indians (multiple response)
15-24	Total	7501	1.08	.86	–	1.20	.52	.82
	no ed.	0	–	–	–	–	–	–
	1-7 yrs	0	–	–	–	–	–	–
	7-13 yrs	6969	1.09	.88	–	1.23	.51	.88
	some U	9032	1.21	.80	–	1.08	.70	–
	U. compl.	6249	–	–	–	–	–	–
25-39	Total	16947	.91	1.05	–	1.05	.43	.90
	no ed.	0	–	–	–	–	–	–
	1-7 yrs	0	–	–	–	–	–	–
	7-13 yrs	15675	.97	1.00	–	1.01	.49	.94
	some U	16842	.90	1.07	–	1.06	.54	1.02
	U. compl.	21143	.90	1.34	–	1.23	.79	–
40-54	Total	18443	1.04	.98	–	.93	.40	.67
	no ed.	0	–	–	–	–	–	–
	1-7 yrs	16281	1.34	–	–	–	.38	–
	7-13 yrs	17261	1.10	.91	–	.93	.53	–
	some U	16994	1.09	1.08	–	1.11	.98	–
	U. compl.	33292	.58	.71	–	.93	–	–
55-64	Total	14446	1.02	1.18	–	1.03	.38	–
	no ed.	0	–	–	–	–	–	–
	1-7 yrs	10584	1.33	–	–	.82	.54	–
	7-13 yrs	13628	1.09	1.22	–	1.08	.50	–
	some U	14665	–	1.08	–	1.59	.48	–
	U. compl.	33758	–	–	–	–	–	–

* Significantly lower from the British group using $\alpha = .05$ and the binomial distribution test

Source: Special Run Statistics Canada, 1984

Inter-ethnic marriages

Milton Gordon (1978) as well as other sociologists believe that the integrating and assimilating process of ethnic groups is complete when intermarriages between members of the two ethnic groups are the norm rather than the exception. To what extent this has taken place between the ethnic groups discussed here in 1971 and 1981 can be seen by examining Table 10 and 11.

An interesting picture emerges from the inter-ethnic marriage rates in 1971. Intermarriage within the British ethnic group is highest in the core of Ontario,

Table 10:   Ethnic Origin of Spouse (Ethnic Origin / Total Ethnic Origin)

Region		British	French	German	Jewish	Canadian Indian	Ukrainian
Province	B	.845	.322	.389	.054	.217	.446
	F	.049	.585	.046	.006	.048	.049
	S	.000	.000	.477	.910	.638	.352
	O	.105	.092	.088	.029	.096	.151
Toronto	B	.873	.495	.332	.034	.426	.444
	F	.033	.372	.029	.003	.051	.043
	S	.000	.000	.528	.938	.364	.376
	O	.094	.132	.111	.025	.153	.128
Bruce	B	.873	.473	.415	1.000	.077	.333
	F	.015	.345	.025	.000	.000	.333
	S	.000	.000	.551	1.000	.923	.333
	O	.112	.182	.009	.000	.000	.333
Rainy River	B	.696	.352	.303	.000	.080	.000
	F	.080	.305	.079	.000	.020	1.000
	S	.000	.000	.382	1.000	.760	.000
	O	.223	.343	.224	.000	.120	.000
Kenora	B	.700	.344	.333	.000	.019	.667
	F	.069	.391	.071	.000	.000	.000
	S	.000	.000	.417	.500	.940	.000
	O	.231	.265	.179	.000	.038	.333

B - British, F - French, S - same as ethnic group, O - other

Source: Special Run, Statistics Canada, 1971 Census

Toronto and lowest in the peripheral regions. But even in the latter at no time is their rate below 70%. Since they made up only about 55 per cent of the population in 1971 this still shows strong cohesion. For the French, marriages within their own group are highest for the province of Ontario as a whole (58.5%), while in Toronto they are about 20 percentage points lower. By far most inter-éthnic marriages take place with people of British Isle descent.

The Germans and to a large extent the Ukrainians, also exhibit this same kind of marriage behaviour. The intermarriages of the latter two ethnic groups with their own kind is 47.7% and 35.2% respectively in Ontario. With the English, the rate is only about 10% below that. Jewish people on the other hand, are very strongly knit together in their social structures and their intermarriage rates reflect this. Over 90% of all Jewish marriages are to Jewish partners. With the Jewish group ethnicity and religion combine to form this strong bond. Native Indians also show a strong tendency to marry within the group. Only in Toronto where their numbers are not great, is the intermarriage rate with people of British Isle descent higher than with other Native Indians. In general then the figures point out that marriage within an ethnic group tends to be higher for the Toronto metropolitan core than in the peripheries, the exception being the French and the Native Indians. This is probably due to one of two reasons: the large number of ethnic people present in Toronto and the high proportion of recent immigrants in Toronto compared to the rural areas, many of whom brought their spouses with them when they came to Canada.

Unfortunately for 1981 we do not have comparable data for intermarriage rates to 1971. In Table 11 is given the intermarriage rates of ethnic groups within themselves and with other groups but only for immigrants, that is, people that were born abroad. These figures therefore do not capture the marriage behaviour of people of different ethnic backgrounds but born in Canada as the 1971 data does.

The above problem not withstanding, one can see an interesting pattern. For the province as a whole, again, intermarriage between immigrants of British Isle descent is highest, some 90%. Next in order are people of Jewish background followed by Native Indians, Germans, Ukrainians, French and Native Indians (multiple response). The under 50% rate of the French is substantially lower than the others. In their case some 26% have already married people of British Isle descent.

The situation for the city of Toronto is not much different than for all of Ontario. Except for the French and the multiple response Native Indian group all marriage rates are above 75%. Because of the relatively small number of immigrants in Kenora, the number of coefficient values for this region is somewhat sparse. Where given however, they are of the same magnitude as those for Ontario as a whole.

Table 11: Intermarriage Ratios Between Ontario's Ethnic Immigrant Groups (single response), 1981

Husband	Wife British	French	German	Jewish	Ukrainian	Native Indian (single response)	Native Indian (multiple response)
Ontario							
British	.9						
French	.26	.45					
German	.07		.81				
Jewish	.03			.89			
Ukrainian	.05				.75		
Native Indian (single)	.06					.82	
Native Indian (multiple)	.12						.33
Toronto							
British	.88						
French	.26	.41					
German	.08		.76				
Jewish	.03			.91			
Ukrainian	.04				.79		
Native Indian (single)	.04					.86	
Native Indian (multiple)	.11						.32
Kenora							
British	.85						
French	–	.67					
German	–		.84				
Jewish	–			–			
Ukrainian	–				.85		
Native Indian (single)	–					–	
Native Indian (multiple)	–						–

Source: Statistics Canada, Special Run, 1984

Since the data in Table 11 only reflects the first generation immigrant marriages, one cannot really expect many marriages between people of different ethnic backgrounds. Many immigrants came as families and hence the marriage relationship was set in the old country. It is true that the children of these parents could intermarry with other ethnic groups. If one takes a conservative estimate that each couple had at least two children, then one can hypothesize that about half the marriage rates is Table 11 were formed before coming to Canada.

But what is clear from the 1981 data is that people of British Isle descent proportionately marry more within their group than the remaining ethnic groups. This is again what one would expect from an initial charter group. Only the Jews have such a high intermarriage rate.

Conclusion

This essay has analyzed the socio-economic conditions of some ethnic groups in the Ontario society. The hypothesis was raised that European ethnic groups would with time join with those of British Isle descent to form a new Canadian charter group in Ontario. Evidence that was examined to evaluate this hypothesis related to similarities in language, similarity in education, similarity in income and inter-ethnic marriage rates. The evidence from the first three empirical analyses points in the direction that the hypothesis is, in part at least, true. The intermarriage rates between the different ethnic groups however is not so strong that one can conclude that the selection of an ethnic partner is independent of the ethnic background of the chooser. Surprisingly the evidence points to the fact that ethnicity seems to be able to retain its nature better in large centers than in the peripheries. This evidence is contrary to what was hypothesized in the model presented and needs further analysis.

Bibliography

Anderson, A. B. and J. S. Frideres, 1981: Ethnicity in Canada, Theoretical Perspectives. Toronto: Butterworth.

Block, W. E. and M. A. Walker (eds.), 1982: Discrimination, Affirmative Action, and Equal Opportunity. Vancouver: The Fraser Institute.

Brookfield, H. C., 1975: Interdependent Development. Toronto: Methuen.

Clark, C., D. Ley and C. Peach, 1984: Geography and Ethnic Pluralism. Winchester, Massachusetts: Allen and Unwin.

Clement, W., 1975: The Canadian Corporate Elite: A Study of Economic Power. Toronto: McClelland and Stewart.

Froeschle, H., 1981: "German Immigration into Canada: A Survey", in H. Froeschle (ed.), German-Canadian Yearbook. Toronto: Historical Society of Mecklenburg Upper Canada Inc., pp. 16-27.

Gordon, M. M., 1978: Human Nature, Class and Ethnicity. New York: Oxford University Press.

Hecht, A., R. Sharpe and A. Wong, 1983: Ethnic Well-being in Central Canada: The Case of Ontario and Toronto. Marburg: Marburger Geographische Schriften.

Hecht, A., 1983: "The Germans in the Anglo-Saxon Milieu in Central Canada", in M. S. Batts, W. Riedel and R. Symington (eds.), German-Canadian Studies in the 1980s, Vancouver: CAUTG Publication #9, pp. 110-142.

Hecht, A., C. Wesol and R. Sharpe, 1982: "Peripheral location of Indian People in Ontario", in A. Hecht (ed.), Regional Developments in the Peripheries of Canada and Europe. Winnipeg: Manitoba Geographical Studies 8, Department of Geography, University of Manitoba, pp. 52-80.

Hechter, M., 1975: Internal Colonialism: The Celtic France in British National Development, 1536-1966. Berkeley: University of California Press.

Koch, A., A. Pletsch and I. Vestweber, 1984: "Deutsche in Kanada - eine verschwindende Minorität?" Zeitschrift der Gesellschaft für Kanada-Studien. 4. Jahrgang / Nr. 1, Band 6, pp. 123-132.

Kramarich, M. A., 1983: "Southern Europeans in Ontario's Periphery and Core: A Socio-economic Analysis Based on the Core-Periphery Model", unpublished B. A. Honours Thesis, Department of Geography, Wilfrid Laurier University.

Lehmann, H., 1931: Zur Geschichte des Deutschtums in Kanada, Band 1, Stuttgart: Ausland und Heimat Verlag - Aktiengesellschaft.

Lenz, K., 1978: "Das regionale Problem Kanadas in seiner ethnischen und sprachlichen Ausprägung". Wirtschafts-Geographische Studien, Heft 4, pp. 92-112.

Lescott-Leszczynski, J., 1984: The History of U.S. Ethnic Policy and Its Impact on European Ethnics. Boulder, Colorado: Westview Press.

Moore, C., 1984: The Loyalists: Revolution, Exile, Settlement. Toronto: Macmillan of Canada.

Norcliffe, G. B., 1977: Inferential Statistics for Geographers, London: Hutchinson.

Pletsch, A. and I. Vestweber, 1983: "Die Deutschen in Quebec - Aspekte der sozialen und wirtschaftlichen Integration", in M. S. Batts, W. Riedel and, R. Symington (eds.), German-Canadian Studies in the 80s. Vancouver: CAUTG Publication #9, pp. 42-72.

Ramcharan, S., 1982: Racism: Nonwhites in Canada, Toronto: Butterworth.

Schott, C., 1936: Landnahme und Kolonisation in Canada am Beispiel Südontarios. Schriften des Geogr. Instituts der Universität Kiel, Bd. VI, Kiel.

Statistics Canada, 1981: Canada at a glance, Ottawa: Federal and Media Relations Division, Statistics Canada based on 1981 census data.

— 1984: Canada's Immigrants, Ottawa: Ministry of Supply and Services (99-936).

— 1984: Canada's Native People, Ottawa: Minister of Supply and Services (99-937).

— 1984: Special 1981 Census Runs for 26 Ethnic Groups for Ontario and Quebec and Greater Toronto and Montreal, 13 tables.

— 1981: Special 1971 Census Run for 43 Ethnic Groups by Census Division for Ontario, Quebec, Toronto and Montreal, 19 tables.

Address of the author:
Alfred Hecht, Professor
Dept. of Geography
Wilfrid Laurier University
Waterloo/Ont.
Canada N2L 3C5

Germans on the Great Plains:
Environment and Acculturation

Bradley H. Baltensperger

Abstract: German immigrants who settled on the North American Great Plains in the late nineteenth century encountered an alien cultural system and an alien environment. In order to thrive in the new setting, they needed to modify their social and economic behavior. But the acculturation process on the Great Plains was affected by characteristics of the physical environment - specifically, a subhumid climate in which humid-land agricultural practices were unsuitable, and where low population densities were common. Furthermore, the process of organized colonization led to the spatial concentration of most immigrant groups in ethnic enclaves and to minimal contact between immigrant communities and the larger culture. The result was a high degree of retention of cultural traits by those immigrant groups who settled in sizeable numbers and in sufficiently exclusive neighborhoods. With the onset of World War I, however, the cultural isolation of German Americans on the plains vanished. The qualities of the plains environment which had slowed acculturation were overwhelmed by irresistible political and social pressures for Americanization. Within a decade, widespread use of the German language, numerous German American social organizations, a vigorous national press, and German American visibility and identity had disappeared. Pride in cultural heritage was destroyed. Even so, persons of German ancestry have not been totally assimilated. Analysis of the 1980 Census of Population reveals that German Americans remain distinctive in such attributes as educational attainment, income, occupation, and place of residence. In spite of a century of acculturative forces and in spite of the low visibility of German Americans, ethnicity appears to remain a powerful force on the Great Plains.

Résumé: Les immigrants allemands qui se sont installés dans les Grandes Plaines de l'Amérique du Nord à la fin du 19 e siècle se trouvaient confrontés à une culture et à un environnement inconnus. Afin de survivre dans ces conditions ils devaient modifier leurs comportements social et économique. Mais ce processus d'acculturation dans les Grandes Plaines était influencé par des charactéristiques de l'environnement physique, où regnait particulièrement un climat semi-humid qui ne se prêtait pas aux pratiques préalablement appliquées dans un climat humid, et où la densité de la population était très faible. En plus, le processus d'une colonisation organisée menait à une concentration spatiale et la plupart des immigrants vivait dans des enclaves ethniques avec très peu de contacts avec la société. La conséquence en était une forte retention des traits culturaux chez les immigrants du moment où ils vivaient en assez grand nombre et dans un voisinage exclu. Pourtant, cet isolement culturel des germano-américains dans les Plaines disparu après la première guerre mondiale. Les conditions de l'environnement dans ces Plaines furent refoulées par des pouvoirs irresistibles sur les plans social et politique envers une américanisation. Au bout de dix ans disparurent l'usage fréquent de la langue allemande, de nombreuses organisations germano-américaines sur le plan social, une influente presse dite nationale tout autant que la visibilité et l'identité germano-américaine. La fiérté du passé culturel fut annéanti. Mais, les descendents des immigrants allemands n'ont pas été totalement assimilés. L'analyse du récensement de 1980 démontre que les germano-américains se distinguent nettement du reste de la société, par exemple sur le plan de l'éducation, du revenu, de l'occupation ou du lieu de résidence. En dépit des forces d'acculturation pendants presqu'un siècle, en dépit aussi du fait d'une faible visibilité des germano-américains, l'ethnicité semble encore être une force efficace dans les Grandes Plaines.

Zusammenfassung: Deutsche Immigranten, die in den Great Plains von Nordamerika im späten 19. Jahrhundert gesiedelt haben, waren mit einem fremden Kulturraum und Naturraum konfrontiert. Um in dieser Umgebung überleben zu können, mußten sie ihr gesellschaftliches und wirtschaftliches Verhalten ändern. Doch dieser Akkulturationsprozeß war beeinträchtigt durch die Eigenschaften der physischen Umwelt, speziell durch das semi-humide Klima, in die Agrartechniken der humiden Breiten nicht übertragen werden konnten, und durch die dünne Besiedlung. Darüber hinaus führte der gelenkte Kolonisationsprozeß zu einer räumlichen Konzentration der meisten Immigrantengruppen in ethnischen Enklaven und zu einem geringen Kontakt zwischen der Gemeinschaft der Immigranten mit der Gesellschaft. Das Ergebnis war eine weitgehende Persistenz eigener kultureller Werte bei den Gruppen, die in einer bestimmten Anzahl und in entsprechender räumlicher Isolierung lebten. Nach dem Ersten Weltkrieg jedoch begann diese kulturelle Isolation für die Deutsch-Amerikaner zu schwinden. Die Eigenschaften des Naturraumes, die den Akkulturationsprozeß gehemmt hatten, traten zurück hinter den ständigen politischen und sozialen Druck zur Amerikanisation. Innerhalb eines Jahrzehnts verschwanden der verbreitete Gebrauch der deutschen Sprache, zahlreiche deutsch-amerikanische Sozialeinrichtungen, eine einflußreiche deutsch-nationale Presse sowie deutsch-amerikanische Identität und Erkennbarkeit. Der Stolz auf das kulturelle Erbe war zerstört. Dennoch ist die deutsche Abstammung nicht völlig verwischt. Die Analyse der Volkszählung von 1980 ergibt, daß Eigenschaften wie Ausbildungsniveau, Einkommens- und Beschäftigungsverhältnisse und Wohnverhalten noch deutlich von den Durchschnittsverhältnissen abweichen. Trotz eines fast einhundertjährigen Akkulturationsprozesses und trotz der geringen physischen Unterschiedlichkeit der Deutsch-Amerikaner scheint sich die Ethnizität als eine starke Kraft in den Great Plains zu behaupten.

In the middle of the nineteenth century, the settlement frontier in the United States emerged from the humid Midwest onto the subhumid Great Plains. Agricultural settlers, facing an unfamiliar environment, initially sought to replicate humid-land agricultural systems. For much of the nineteenth century, plains farmers utilized agricultural practices which took little account of the climatic realities of the region. Eventually recognizing the need for adjustments to the subhumid conditions of the plains, they modified cropping systems, adopted irrigation, experimented with new techniques and crops, or left the region (Webb, 1931; Malin, 1944; 1947; Bowden, 1975; Baltensperger, 1979).

For immigrant farmers entering the same environment the adjustment process was two-fold: they needed an agricultural and settlement system for the subhumid environment and they needed a social, economic, and cultural system which would function in an alien cultural environment. For immigrants, adjustment necessitated both adaptation and acculturation.

The interaction between these two processes was unique in the westward expansion of the United States. Almost inevitably, the acculturation of immigrants was affected by the process of adaptation. The subhumid nature of the plains and the low population densities which accompanied extensive agriculture had considerable bearing on immigrant settlement, agricultural practices, and contact with American culture.

From the earliest years of settlement, German farmers were on the vanguard of the plains frontier (Johnson, 1951). In county after county, Germans settled on virgin prairie in advance of rail lines and surveyors. Some of those newly established counties were nearly 100 per cent German in 1870 and 1880.

This clustering was largely due to the prevalence of organized colonization, particularly after 1870. State governments and railroad companies flooded Europe with pamphlets extolling the plains, and established offices in major European ports. Agents arranged for colonies of settlers to travel together and select land in one locale; entire villages often relocated to North America and gained effective and exclusive control of entire communities. The result was a patchwork of immigrant enclaves scattered across the plains states (Luebke, 1977).

The rate and degree of acculturation of an immigrant group are affected by characteristics of the group prior to migration and by the nature of the group's contacts with the host culture. Peoples with experience as a minority group within a larger culture often have developed a tradition of resistance to acculturation. Cohesive groups, particularly those focused upon religious beliefs, have also been better prepared to survive without being overwhelmed by the host culture. Those immigrant groups which were most unlike the host culture in religion, values, and outlook on life, were likewise more resistant to acculturation.

Settlement in large enclaves, particularly in rural areas where little interaction with the dominant culture was necessary or even possible, slowed the rate of acculturation. When physical isolation was accompanied by religious and social isolation, acculturative forces were further weakened. Groups which were able to support social institutions, such as newspapers, music societies, and fraternal orders, were more likely to survive without drastic cultural change. Finally, those groups which have not been perceived as threatening, either because of their numbers, behavior, or values, have not had to contend with overt pressures to conform (Kloss, 1966; Luebke, 1969; Conzen, 1980).

Given the numbers of Germans who settled on the plains and the opportunities for establishing exclusive national communities, it would seem that German cultural characteristics would be more likely to persist than would be the case of Germans in other parts the U.S. or of other immigrants on the plains. However, the diversity of German immigrants worked against cultural stability and retentiveness.

Germans came from a wide range of source areas - the Volga region of Russia, the southern Ukraine and Bessarabia, the Rhineland and Oldenburg, the Crimea and Wisconsin. Some were Swiss, others were from the Austrian empire. Before unification immigrants from the various German states thought of themselves less as Germans than as Prussians, Hessians, or Wurtembergers (Luebke, 1974).

Most importantly, they were religiously heterogeneous - Lutherans, Catholics, Mennonites, Reformed, Hutterites, Methodists. Germans in the United States did not exhibit the uniformity or unity of other groups, nor did they behave as one cohesive immigrant community. Instead, they found their identities as, for example, Volga Catholics or Swiss Mennonites or Darmstadt Lutherans.

German immigrants to the Great Plains encountered nearly irresistible institutional pressures for acculturation, particularly in economic matters. Few European agricultural practices were preserved for long on the Great Plains. In spite of extensive experience in the cultivation of small grains, German farmers adopted maize in Kansas and Nebraska, where it was the dominant crop of the Anglo-American majority (Baltensperger, 1980; 1983). Where wheat was the principal crop, Germans did not stand out as distinctive.

Although they often maintained a preference for certain items of domestic consumption, such as potatoes and rye, Germans were commercial farmers. They raised crops and livestock for which there was a market. Furthermore, immigrants often preferred to defer to the apparent experience and practices of native-born farmers, who presumably knew how best to deal with the plains environment. The result was that, almost from the beginning, German agricultural practices on the Great Plains did not differ significantly from Anglo-American practices (Jordan, 1966; Baltensperger, 1980; Swierenga, 1981).

Only in the diversity of cropping systems did German operations contrast markedly with Anglo-American practices. Germans from Russia were especially likely to maintain diverse operations, an adjustment to subhumid conditions they had developed on the steppe. But even they quickly adopted most Midwestern agricultural traits and thereby subordinated their adaptive system to their need for economic acculturation (Baltensperger, 1983).

Replication of the agricultural village system was not impossible within the constraints of a land division system which favored individual ownership of dispersed unit-block landholdings, but it was unlikely. Most attempts to preserve agglomerated settlement were abandoned within a few years. There were a few exceptions. Volga Catholic settlements in Ellis County, Kansas, included some land held in common for grazing, as had been the case in Russia, but most land was divided into narrow strips which were distributed to individuals in proportion to their contribution to the purchase price of the land. Some villages had garden strips which were still visible as late as late as the 1960s (Petersen, 1970; Stucky, 1956). Mennonites in Jefferson County, Nebraska, claimed 80 acre (32 ha) homesteads laid out in strips one mile (1.6 km) long by one-eighth mile (200 m) wide. The result was a street village which remained apparent into the 1950s (Miller, 1954).

Traditional European housing forms were slightly more resistant to change. German construction styles were common in settlements in central Texas. Russian German settlers utilized materials and designs similar to those used in Russia (Jordan, 1966; Petersen, 1970). A large number of rammed earth and puddled clay houses still stand on the northern Great Plains; many are still occupied (Sherman, 1974).

The evidence for greater persistence of German farmers relative to American-born settlers is mixed. Some scholars have found little difference in rates of population turnover among cultural groups in the Midwest (Bogue, 1963; Curti, 1959). However, extremely low farm turnover rates characterized Ellis County, even during the early twentieth century (Petersen, 1970). Mennonites in Kansas had low farm turnover rates which resulted in the progressive consolidation of Mennonite territory - a factor likely to enhance the survival of other cultural traits (McQuillan, 1978; Conzen, 1980). On the other hand, Volga German tenant farmers who settled in Clay County, Nebraska, remained for only a few years before moving to other rural areas which offered greater opportunities for landownership (Baltensperger, 1983).

By the end of the nineteenth century, German American economic behavior was little different from that of their Anglo-American counterparts. They had been well acculturated into the Midwestern agricultural system, which was only marginally adapted to subhumid conditions. However, because of low densities, physical isolation, and ethnic clustering - characteristics unique to the Great Plains region - they retained a considerable degree of "Germanness", expressed in politics, language, and social institutions and behavior.

In 1910, 8.6 million German immigrants and their children constituted nearly 10 per cent of the U.S. population. Another 1.1 million were Germans born in other countries (Kloss, 1966). This potential political force was most effectively mobilized on issues such as prohibition and woman suffrage. When these ethnocultural issues were unimportant, the German vote was splintered along religious lines. The importance of the German vote was acknowledged by direct, but often unsuccessful, political appeals for their support (Luebke, 1969; Petersen, 1968).

The German language was probably spoken by approximately 9 million American residents in 1910 (Kloss, 1966). These German-speakers - immigrants, their children, and some third and fourth generation German-Americans - used their native tongue extensively at home, to some degree in business and trade, and often in school and church. In numerous public and parochial schools on the Great Plains, instruction was exclusively in German. Missouri Synod Lutheran congregations, typically found in rural areas where the social isolation of German communities was almost complete, were especially likely to support parochial schools with instruction in German. Roman Catholic schools were more likely to promote assimilation and provide instruction in English because they more frequently served polyglot communities (Luebke, 1969).

German-Americans were also accustomed to worshipping in German. German Evangelicals, the German Reformed Church, Mennonites, and most Lutherans continued to use German in the early twentieth century. Catholic parishes in predominantly German rural areas utilized the German language, as well. For Lutherans and Mennonites, language preservation was not an end in itself, but rather a central issue of doctrine. Both denominations were strong forces of continued cultural isolation because their members were almost solely of German extraction. They slowed acculturation through opposition to marriage outside the faith, which would have meant marriage to non-Germans. German Baptists, Presbyterians, and Methodists, on the other hand, were theologically indistinguishable from Anglo-American congregations and therefore more easily adopted English in worship (Luebke, 1969; 1974).

In their formal organizations and informal social contacts, Germans in the United States remained distinctive well into the twentieth century. German banks, insurance companies, cultural centers, Turnverein, fraternal orders, and singing societies thrived throughout the nation (Luebke, 1969). The German-language press, especially strong on the plains, helped foster a sense of cultural heritage and group consciousness (Wittke, 1957).

The German-language press had much to do with the development of feelings of German nationality among German-Americans in the United States. The maintenance of German identity was valuable for the press and other occupations and institutions - German merchants, clergy, teachers, restaurateurs, insurance companies, and social organization. The relatively slow assimilation of Germans prior to World War I was a product of the large numbers of German-Americans along with the plethora of German-American associations and institutions which stressed "Germanness" (Luebke, 1974).

Rippley has contended that, prior to World War I, "Germans did not easily shed the customs of their Fatherland, even after several generations had lived and died in America (Rippley, 1976: 99)". Germans on the Great Plains had been outwardly acculturated in many ways; but inwardly they remained Germans. They spoke German at home and church, they read German newspapers and associated with other German-Americans in ethnic-based organizations (Luebke, 1969). Not all German-Americans fit this mold. Some rebeled against their ethnic background and attempted to anglicize their behavior, their outlook, and their names. Germans in the U.S. argued with one another about the value of assimilation and whether to cut their ties with Europe or to stress language retention and ethnic idenfitication. But for most German-Americans assimilation and acculturation were individual choices, not requirements dictated by the larger society. Most could remain as German as they wished.

Germans on the Great Plains - especially those with previous experience as a minority group, particularly Russian Germans - were able to retain their "Germanness" because of their predominantly rural character, their concentrations in ethnic enclaves, the prevalence of German-language chools, adherence to religious denominations which promoted cultural isolation, and low population densities which minimized their contacts with Anglo-American culture (Luebke, 1969; Rein, 1980). The characteristics of the Great Plains assisted in the maintenance of German cultural identity.

With the entry of the United States into World War I, the tolerance and support for cultural diversity afforded by the plains was suddenly subordinated to a national climate of anti-German hysteria. Superpatriotism called into suspicion everything German, including churches, schools, organizations, and newspapers. State councils of defense - voluntary, extra-legal organizations designed to monitor loyalty - vigorously attacked the German language. The use of German in schools, in religious services, and in public conversation was routinely forbidden. German-Americans were threatened, harrassed, tarred-and-feathered, and whipped. Students in Yankton, South Dakota, dumped German-language textbooks into the Missouri River and German language books were burned in several Nebraska communities. At one South Dakota Hutterite colony, which refused to purchase war bonds, a mob drove off and sold all the livestock and then used the proceeds to purchase bonds (Luebke, 1980, 1974; Rippley, 1976).

The size of the German element in the United States, the prevalence of German-American institutions, and widespread retention of the German language all contributed to German visibility. Their cohesiveness, even if only within religious bounds, was interpreted as conspiratorial.

The most extreme reaction on the part of German-Americans was emigration. Nearly all the Hutterite colonies relocated from South Dakota to Manitoba. Many Russian German Mennonites in Oklahoma and South Dakota also fled (Hostetler,

1974; Luebke, 1974).

Antagonism between immigrants and their children intensified - parents would speak in German, their children would respond in English. Like many Anglo-Americans, the second generation came to see inferiority in everything German. Under pressure to appear patriotic and American and not to be distinctive, they discarded as much of their German heritage as possible (Sallet, 1974).

The hostility and contempt encountered by German-Americans were instrumental in the rapid acculturation which occurred in the ensuing decade. In order to defend themselves against charges of disloyalty, German communities obliterated the outward manifestations of their cultural background. Germantown and Berlin, Nebraska, became Garland and Otoe. Families changed their surnames or the spelling or pronunciation of those names. German-American organizations disbanded.

Churches and schools precipitously adopted the English language. As late as 1919, 62 per cent of all Missouri Synod Lutheran services were in German. By 1926 that figure was down to 46 per cent; only one-fourth of the congregations did not have at least one service in English each month (Rippley, 1976; Luebke, 1974). Over one-half of the Mennonite conferences in Kansas introduced English during the war. Most parochial schools in the plains states switched to English. Even after the most strident anti-foreign-language laws had been declared unconstitutional, English remained the principal mode of instruction (Kloss, 1966).

The German-language press was devastated by this dramatic change in the rate of acculturation. Seventy daily newspapers were published in German in the United States in 1910; by 1920 only 29 remained. The number of weeklies dropped from 433 to 172, as Americans of German descent decided to accept more complete assimilation into American society (Fishman, Hayden, and Warshauer, 1966).

Long after the overt harrassment and humiliation of the war era had subsided, ethnic pride and identification of German-Americans remained low. Even during the 1960s ethnic revival, when Czechs, Swedes, Danes, and Poles on the Great Plains began holding festivals celebrating their traditions, Germans remained out of public view.

Today, only 13,000 German immigrants reside in the Great Plains states. Slightly more than 100,000 claim to speak German - this repesents about 2 per cent of the population and 10 per cent of those who claim German ancestry (Table 1).

Table 1: German Ancestry Population in 1980

	No. Dak.	So. Dak.	Nebraska	Kansas
Total Population	652,717	690,768	1,569,825	2,363,679
German Ancestry	170,007	179,186	352,873	356,453
% German Ancestry	26.0	25.9	22.5	15.1
German & Other Ancestry	136,739	144,293	371,292	472,450
% German & Other	20.9	20.9	23.7	20.0
Speak German at Home	37,134	21,956	17,894	26,212
% German Who Speak German	21.8	12.3	5.1	7.4

Source: 1980 U.S. Census of Population.

Very few congregations on the plains use the German language in worship (Kloss, 1966). German influence on English usage by German-Americans remains significant in some areas and has been thoroughly examined for central Texas, where pronunciation, grammatical constructions, and vocabulary often reflect German styles (Wilson, 1980).

In spite of the small number of immigrants and declining use of the language, more plains states residents claim German ancestry than any other background. In Kansas, Nebraska, South Dakota and North Dakota, 1,058,519 persons indicated German ancestry in 1980 and an additional 1,124,774 designated themselves as having a German background, along with some other group. These 2.2 million persons account for 41.4 per cent of the 5.3 million people in the four states.

The pattern of persons of German ancestry closely mirrors that of German pioneer settlement in the late nineteenth and early twentieth centuries. The largest and most completely German population cluster is in central North Dakota and north-central South Dakota (Figure 1). Four of these counties report over 60 per cent German ancestry, not including those of mixed background. A second concentration is in southeastern South Dakota and northeastern Nebraska; a third cluster is in west-central Kansas.

Figure 1: Percent German Ancestry, 1980

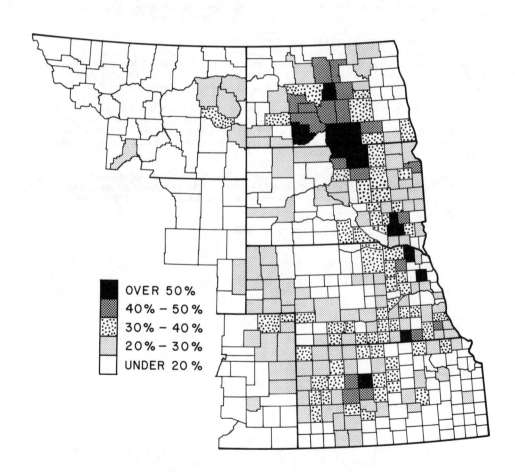

Germans are conspicuous by their absence in western South Dakota, the Sandhills region of Nebraska, and on the high plains of Wyoming, Montana, and southeastern Colorado. In most of southeastern Kansas persons of German ancestry are not numerous. Many areas with low German concentrations specialize in livestock ranching and were settled after the last major wave of German immigration had subsided in the 1890s. Southeastern Kansas was settled mainly from neighboring southern states, rather than by colonization.

In spite of high ancestral identification, Germans appear less attached to their heritage than are many other ethnic groups. Whereas 44.6 per cent of the Germans in Nebraska consider their ethnicity important, ethnic background is important to 69.7 per cent of the Czechs, 68.0 per cent of the Italians, and 61.4 per cent of the Swedes (Whitt, 1977). The differences may be ascribed in part to the earlier arrival of most German immigrants and to the lack of overt symbols of ethnicity which characterize the other groups.

Aside from their labels, are Germans an identifiable ethnic group in the plains states? German farmers in the Missouri Ozarks practice a somewhat more intensive form of agriculture and possess a deeper committment to an agrarian way of life than do their Anglo-American neighbors, but they are not distinctive in farm size, crop selection, cropt yield, or tenancy rate (Gerlach, 1976). Germans in central Texas retain some attachment to German social organizations and to the spoken language, but agriculturally they are indistinguishable from non-Germans (Jordan, 1966). In the central plains Volga Germans became clearly associated with the production of sugar beets. By 1930 they operated over half the sugar beet farms on the plains and today remain numerous in areas of sugar beet production (Kloberdanz, 1980; Sallet, 1974).

Impressionistic evidence suggests that most German-Americans differ little from the "average American" in social, economic, or political behavior. Citizens of German ancestry are as likely as Anglo-Americans to participate fully in political activities. They have contributed their share of legislators and governors and if they are more disposed toward one political party over the other, that can be explained primarily on the basis of other factors such as rural or urban residence and socio-economic status.

The cultural landscape of German areas is not noticeably different from that of Anglo-American areas. Intermarriage of Germans and non-Germans seldom elicits notice, except when an inter-denominational union is involved. Germans continue to be, predominantly, Lutherans, Roman Catholics, or Mennonites. They are more likely to be associated, particularly through the Missouri Synod-Lutheran church, with rural, open-country congregations.

The most heavily German counties are rural, not urban. In general, the larger the town or city, the lower the percentage of German ancestry, particularly in Kansas and Nebraska (Table 2). German Americans are found in greatest proportions on farms.

Table 2: Per cent of Population Claiming German Ancestry, by Place of Residence

	Kans	Nebr	SDak	NDak
State	15.1	22.5	25.9	26.0
Urban (places over 2500)	12.7	18.5	24.3	25.7
Urbanized Areas	10.3	14.0	20.3	24.1
Cities, 10,000-50,000	15.2	27.9	30.2	29.6
Cities, 2,500-10,000	16.2	24.8	21.9	25.2
Rural Places, 1,000-2,500	19.0	26.4	27.4	26.1
Other Rural	20.1	30.1	27.4	26.5
Rural Farm	26.7	34.9	32.8	29.8

Other traits may still characterize German-Americans on the plains. The 1980 census tabulated ancestry group responses across a number of social and economic variables, many of which indicate continuing German-American distinctiveness. The data must be used with caution, however, as the designation of German ancestry is made by respondents on the basis of individual perception, not on the basis of some objective measure.

Furthermore, other variables - particularly age and place of residence - may account for differences among ethnic groups.

The German population of the Great Plains states is somewhat older than the white population and considerably older than persons having German and other ancestry (here termed "mixed Germans"). The median age of Germans was approximately 32.5, compared to white median age of 30 and median age of mixed Germans of about 22. Age differences among groups were less pronounced for Kansas than for the other three states.

Noticeable differences are found in demographic characteristics, education measures, and income and occupation factors. German birth and fertility rates were similar to those of all whites. However, in the three northern states the fertility rate of women aged 15-24 is about 10 per cent higher among Germans (about 320/1000) than among whites (approximately 290/1000). The figures for mixed Germans in the same age group are substantially lower - about 240/1000. Germans appear more likely to begin their families at an early age. The divorce rate among Germans is about 20 per cent lower than for the white population. Some of this difference can be explained by the higher rate of rural residence among Germans - the German divorce rate was roughly comparable to the rate for rural whites - yet half of all plains Germans are urban (Table 3).

Table 3: Per cent of Population Groups Reporting Urban Residence

	Germans	Whites	Mixed Germans
Kansas	56.1	64.5	65.6
Nebraska	51.7	61.6	65.1
South Dakota	43.4	47.6	49.4
North Dakota	48.1	49.3	48.7
Total	51.2	59.5	61.3

Education levels are generally lower for Germans than for whites. The difference in high school graduation rates was most pronounced among those over age 25 in the Dakotas. Among 18-24 year olds, Germans and whites in the Dakotas reported comparable high school completion rates; but in Nebraska and Kansas, Germans report higher graduation rates. In Kansas, Germans are more likely than whites to be enrolled in college. Elsewhere, German enrollment rates are lower than the white population - the contrast is most evident in North Dakota, where 34 per cent of the white 20 and 21 year olds are enrolled in school, compared to only 25 per cent of the Germans. Likewise, the proportion of 18-24 year-olds who have graduated from college is higher among Germans than whites in Kansas, but lower in the other three states. Mixed Germans resemble the white population in educational attainment and are more likely than whites to be enrolled in college in all four states.

German distinctiveness is quite noticeable in occupation. Germans are more numerous in manual labor and agriculture than in professional or managerial positions (Table 4). They are especially overrepresented in farming in Nebraska and Kansas, where nearly twice as many Germans are farmers as would be expected if the ethnic group were fully assimilated. In Nebraska, 56 per cent of all farmers claim German or mixed German ancestry. The tradition of German preference for landownership and agriculture appears to have survived.

German occupation characteristics are evident in economic status. Although the median income of Germans in Kansas was virtually identical to that of whites, in the other three states Germans recorded substantially lower incomes. Persons of mixed German ancestry invariably reported highest median incomes.

Table 4:   German Americans as a Per cent of Persons in Occupation Categories

	Kans	Nebr	SDak	NDak
Employed Persons over age 16	17.1	24.8	29.0	28.7
Executive, Administrative, and Managerial Occupations	16.7	22.5	26.3	26.6
Engineers; Scientists	15.9	19.3	23.5	21.6
Teachers, Elementary/Secondary	18.1	23.5	25.5	23.5
Service Occupations	15.5	22.7	28.0	29.9
Operators, Laborers	15.2	24.2	30.4	31.1
Farm Workers	23.2	32.5	34.7	32.5
Farm Operators and Managers	30.5	40.5	36.5	34.1

Even when age cohorts are compared, the higher income of mixed Germans and the lower income of Germans persist. Table 5 indicates the income differences among the three groups for South Dakota. Similar patterns characterize Nebraska and North Dakota. In most instances, the incidence of poverty is higher among Germans than whites, but lower among mixed Germans (Table 6).

It is worth noting that Germans are NOT significantly different from the white population one some variables. There is no consistent relationship between ancestry and the proportion of males over 65 in the labor force, the proportion of women, 55-64, in the labor force, number of persons per household, percentage of children living with both parents, or high school dropout rate.

Differences remain between persons of German ancestry and the white population of the Great Plains states, particularly in the areas of education, occupation, and income. Some differences may be related to age and place of residence. Without controlling for these important variables, it is impossible to attribute contrasts among population groups to ethnic heritage. German Americans remain distinctive, but for reasons that cannot be clearly discerned.

Table 5: Median Family Income by Age Cohort, South Dakota, 1980

Age	White	German	Mixed German
15-24	12,091	12,231	12,158
25-34	16,793	16,693	17,169
35-44	20,364	19,337	21,095
45-54	21,091	19,300	21,640
55-64	17,395	16,327	18,683
65 & Over	9,958	9,200	10,983
Total	16,321	15,535	17,448

Table 6: Per cent of Families Below Poverty Level

	White	German	Mixed German
Kansas	6.4	6.3	5.2
Nebraska	7.3	8.1	6.6
South Dakota	11.5	13.3	10.3
North Dakota	9.1	9.7	9.6

American culture has been highly conducive to assimilation. Factors such as rapid industrialization and urbanization, public education, a high degree of social mobility, geographic mobility, and American nationalism worked against the maintenance of cultural tradition among immigrant groups. As a result, millions of people were rapidly "de-ethnicized" (Fishman, 1966).

Yet, ethnic consciousness remains, even among the descendants of German immigrants. It may well be that, in spite of outward appearances, ethnicity is still a powerful, but unrecognized, force in American society. It is the task of scholars of ethnicity to attempt to identify the persistent manifestations of cultural heritage within a landscape of assimilation.

References

Baltensperger, B. H., 1979: Agricultural adjustments to Great Plains drought: the Republican valley, 1870-1900. In The Great Plains: Environment and Culture, eds. B. W. Blouet and F. C. Luebke, pp. 43-50. Lincoln: University of Nebraska Press.

— 1980: Agricultural change among Nebraska immigrants, 1880-1900. In Ethnicity on the Great Plains, ed. F. C. Luebke, pp. 170-189. Lincoln: University of Nebraska Press.

— 1983: Agricultural change among Great Plains Russian Germans. Annals of the Association of American Geographers 73: 75-88.

Bogue, A. G., 1963: From Prairie to Corn Belt. Chicago: University of Chicago Press.

Bowden, M. J., 1975: Desert Wheat Belt, plains Corn Belt: environmental cognition and behavior of settlers in the plains margin, 1850-1899. In Images of the Plains: The Role of Human Nature in Settlement, eds. B. W. Blouet and M. P. Lawson, pp. 189-201. Lincoln: University of Nebraska Press.

Conzen, K. N., 1980: Historical approaches to the study of rural ethnic communities. In Ethnicity on the Great Plains, ed. F. C. Luebke. Lincoln: University of Nebraska Press, pp. 1-18.

Curti, M., et al., 1959: The Making of an American Community. Stanford, Calif.: Stanford University Press.

Fishman, J. A., 1966: The Historical and Social Concepts of an Inquiry into Language Maintenance Efforts. In Language Loyalty in the United States, ed. J. A. Fishman. The Hague: Mouton & Co., pp. 21-33.

—   Hayden, R. G. and Warshauer, M. E., 1966: The non-English and the ethnic group press, 1910-1960. In Language Loyalty in the United States.

Gerlach, R. L., 1976: Immigrants in the Ozarks. Columbia: University of Missouri Press.

Hostetler, J. A., 1974: Hutterite Society. Baltimore: The Johns Hopkins University Press.

Johnson, H. B., 1951: The location of German Immigrants in the Middle West. Annals of the Association of American Geographers 41: 1-41.

Jordan, T. G., 1966: German Seed in Texas Soil. Austin: University of Texas Press.

Kloberdanz, T. J., 1980: Plainsmen of three continents: Volga German adaptation to steppe, prairie, and pampa. In Ethnicity on the Great Plains, ed. F. C. Luebke, pp. 54-72. Lincoln: University of Nebraska Press.

Kloss, H., 1966: German-American Language Maintenance Efforts. In Language Loyalty in the U.S., ed. J. A. Fishman. The Hague: Mouton & Co., pp. 206-252.

Luebke, F. C., 1969: Immigrants and Politics: The Germans of Nebraska, 1880-1900. Lincoln: University of Nebraska Press.

—   1974: Bonds of Loyalty: German-Americans and World War I. DeKalb: Northern Illinois University Press.

—   1977: Ethnic group settlement on the Great Plains. Western Historical Quarterly 8: 405-30.

—   1980: Legal Restrictions on Foreign Languages in the Great Plains States, 1917-1923 in Languages in Conflict: Linguistic Acculturation on the Great Plains, ed. P. Schach. Lincoln: University of Nebraska Press.

Malin, J. C., 1944: Winter Wheat in the Golden Belt of Kansas. Lawrence: University of Kansas Press.

—   1947: The Grassland of North America: Prolegomena to its History. Lawrence: James C. Malin.

McQuillan, D. A., 1978: Territory and ethnic identity: some new measures of an old theme in the cultural geography of the United States. In European Settlement and Development in North America: Essays on Geographical Change in Honour and Memory of Andrew Hill Clark, ed. J. R. Gibson, pp. 136-69. Toronto: University of Toronto Press.

Miller, D. P., 1954: Jansen, Nebraska, a story of community adjustment. Nebraska History 35: 127-36.

Petersen, A. J., 1968: The German Russian Settlement Pattern in Ellis County, Kansas. Rocky Mountain Social Science Journal 5: 52-62.

Petersen, A. J., 1970: German-Russian Catholic colonization in western Kansas: a settlement geography. Ph.D. dissertation, Louisiana State University.

Rein, K., 1980: German Dialects in Anabaptist Colonies on the Great Plains. In Languages in Conflict: Linguistic Acculturation on the Great Plains, ed. P. Schach. Lincoln: University of Nebraska Press, pp. 94-110.

Rippley, L. J., 1976: The German-Americans. Boston: G. K. Hall & Co.

Sallet, R., 1974: Russian German Settlements in the United States, trans. by L. J. Rippley and A. Bauer. Fargo: North Dakota Institute for Regional Studies.

Sherman, W. C., 1974: Prairie architecture of the Russian-German Settlers. In R. Sallet, Russian German Settlements in the United States, trans. by L. J. Rippley and A. Bauer. Fargo: North Dakota Institute for Regional Studies, pp. 185-95.

Stucky, H. J., 1956: The German Element in Kansas. In Kansas: The First Century, 4 vols., ed. J. D. Bright. New York: Lewis Historical Publishing Company, pp. 329-354.

Swierenga, R. P., 1981: The new rural history: defining the paramaters. Great Plains Quarterly 1: 211-23.

Whitt, H. P., 1977. Ethnic Identification in Nebraska. Nebraska Annual Social Indicators Survey Rept. #10. Lincoln: University of Nebraska-Lincoln: University of Nebraska-Lincoln; Bureau of Sociological Reserarch.

Wilson, J. B., 1980: The English Spoken by German-Americans in Central Texas. In Languages in Conflict: Linguistic Acculturation on the Great Plains, ed. P. Schach. Lincoln: University of Nebraska Press, pp. 157-173.

Wittke, C., 1957: The German-Language Press in America. Lexington: University of Kentucky Press.

Address of the author:
Bradley H. Baltensperger
College of Sciences and Arts
Departement of Social Sciences
Michigan Technological University
Houghton, Michigan 49931
USA

Les Allemands à Montréal -
intégration ou ségrégation d'une minorité ethnique

Inge Vestweber

Abstract: The Germans in Montréal form a group that does not reveal its presence within the reality and the society of Montréal. From this point of view, it seems that they are well integrated in their host-society. From this arise the following questions: What are the orientations and the grounds of their integration? What are their reactions to the Quebec frenchifying policy? This article deals with the above mentionned questions emphasizing first on the constitution and the geographic distribution of the Germans in Montréal, second on their socio-linguistic orientation and their economic situation, and third on their relations with the other ethnic groups and within their own.

Résumé: Les allemands à Montréal constituent un groupe qui ne se manifeste pas visiblement dans la réalité et dans la société montréalaise. En conséquence leur intégration dans la société d'accueil semble être bien réussie. Ceci amène aux questions suivantes: Quels sont les fondements et les orientations de leur intégration? Quels sont leurs réactions face à la politique de francisation au Québec? Cet article aborde les questions soulevées ci-déssus en mettant l'accent, premièrement, sur la constitution et la repartition géographique des allemands à Montréal, deuxièmement, sur leur situation socio-linguistique et économique et, troisièmement, sur leurs relations intra- et interethniques.

Zusammenfassung: Bezeichnend für die Deutschen in Montréal ist, daß sie eine Gruppe darstellen, die in der Öffentlichkeit und im öffentlichen Bewußtsein der Stadt und ihrer Bewohner nahezu "unsichtbar" scheint. Ihre Integration - im Sinne von Anpassung - ist demzufolge vollzogen. Aus dieser Feststellung ergeben sich folgende Fragen: Was ist das Bestimmende und welches sind die Orientierungspunkte der Integration der Deutschen? Wie reagieren sie auf die Politik der Französisierung in Québec? Der Beitrag geht folgendermaßen auf die oben gestellten Fragen ein. Erstens, indem er sich mit der Zusammensetzung und der räumlichen Verteilung der Deutschen in Montréal beschäftigt, zweitens, indem er ihre sozio-linguistische Orientierung und ihre ökonomischen Verhältnisse erörtert und drittens, indem er auf ihre intra- und interethnischen Beziehungen eingeht.

L'objet du texte suivant est l'étude du mode d'insertion des allemands à Montréal (1). Une telle étude trouve son intérêt suite aux aspects suivants.

D'abord, à titre socio-culturel, il importe de cerner l'attitude adaptive des allemands dans la réalité montréalaise; une attitude qui leur fait attribuer le caractère d'invisibilité de la part des québécois. Ainsi, dans une brochure publiée par le Conseil Scolaire de l'Ile de Montréal, nous trouvons l'introduction suivante:

"On signale la présence parmi nous d'un mystérieux phénomène: on l'appelle le groupe ethnique invisible. Il est là, on ne le voit pas, et pourtant, il ne se cache pas. Ce n'est pas un groupe extra-terrestre, il vient d'un pays pas si lointain, situé de l'autre côté de l'Atlantique et appelé Allemagne" (J. MESSIER, 1981: 3).

Les questions se posent, qu'est-ce qui fait qu'on parle des allemands en termes de 'mystérieux phénomène'; pourquoi le mode d'insertion des allemands semble être différent que celui des autres minorités ethniques à Montréal.

De plus, il importe d'évaluer les changements dans le comportement de l'intégration des allemands face aux changements socio-politiques dans les années '70 au Québec. Sans vouloir entrer dans les détails, il reste à souligner que cette période a demandé aux groupes ethniques minoritaires de s'adapter à une société québécoise en voie de francisation. La mise en place de la Charte de la langue française (loi 101) en 1977, c'est à dire d'une loi qui fait du français la première langue du travail et de l'enseignement, a affecté les groupes ethniques minoritaires. Plutôt orientés vers l'adoption de la langue anglaise comme langue d'usage, c'est à dire de la langue dominante dans le domaine économique au Québec et la langue principale sur tout le continent nord-américain, les minorités ethniques étaient alors forcées de se ranger du côté francophone. Comme on va voir, les allemands constituent un des groupes le plus orienté vers les anglophones du Québec. Dans ce sens, une étude de leur réaction permet de mieux cerner l'impact possible de l'intervention linguistique gouvernementale sur des groupes ethniques, concernés par cette intervention.

Pour discuter ces deux problématiques soulevées ci-dessus, nous traiterons trois volets de la réalité germano-québecoise.

Le premier concerne la distribution spatiale, c'est à dire la question de ségrégation ou de dispersion des allemands à Montréal. Le deuxième est une mise en perspective de la situation socio-économique des allemands et le troisième volet porte sur la dimension socio-psychologique de leur intégration à Montréal.

Comme informations de base pour les deux premières parties de ce texte, nous avons utilisé les données des recensements de 1971 et 1981. Cependant, dans la partie qui porte sur l'aspect socio-psychologique, les informations sur les relations intra-et interethniques sont le fruit des connaissances acquises au cours des recherches faites sur le terrain, telles: les entrevues personnelles avec les représentants des différentes organisations allemandes à Montréal, l'étude des bulletins communautaires allemandes et des deux rapports sur le groupe allemand, mandatés par le Ministère de l'Immigration du Québec.

Avant d'aborder le champ d'étude comme tel, il reste quelques termes de base à préciser. Le terme 'groupe ethnique' est, dans les deux premières parties de ce texte, défini selon les critères imposés par Statistique Canada. Ceux-ci portent sur l'aspect généalogique, c'est à dire sur l'appartenance ethnique des ancêtres. En 1971, l'origine ethnique s'est uniquement référée à l'ancêtre paternel, tandis que, lors du recensement de 1981, la question sur l'origine ethnique permettait aux répondants d'indiquer leur appartenance en fonction de l'origine ethnique des ancêtres masculins et feminins. Ainsi, nous trouvons la distinction entre les allemands d'origine allemande simple, dont les deux parents sont allemands, et d'origine allemande mixte, dont un parent est d'origine allemande et l'autre d'une autre origine différente. Nous tenterons dans la troisième partie de ce texte à opposer l'origine ethnique telle que définie par Statistique Canada à l'identification ethnique au niveau subjectif et collectif.

Le concept de 'l'intégration', utilisé ici comme point de repère dans l'étude de l'insertion des allemands à Montréal, s'applique dans un sens large et purement descriptif. Celui-ci est caractérisé par la distribution spatiale, la position socio-économique et les relations intra- et interethniques des allemands.

I. Le groupe ethnique allemand, sa composition et sa repartition géographique à Montréal

Le tableau No. 1 nous indique que, lors du recensement de 1981, seulement 0.8%, c'est à dire 22285 personnes, de l'ensemble de la population de la région métropolitaine de Montréal se sont déclarés comme appartenant au groupe ethnique allemand d'origine simple. A ce chiffre, nous devons ajouter le nombre d'allemands d'origine multiple, dont: allemand-anglais, allemand-français et allemand-autre. Ainsi, nous arrivons à un total de 32610 personnes d'origine allemande simple et multiple, qui forment 1.2% de l'ensemble de la population montréalaise.

Il est à noter que les allemands d'origine allemande-française ne sont pas si nombreux que ceux d'origine allemande-anglaise et allemande-autre. Aspect surprenant, vu le fait que la majorité de la population montréalaise est composée de francophones; aspect moins surprenant, si on regarde l'attraction que le groupe anglophone - comme détenteur d'un fort pouvoir économique - exerce sur les allemands. Quant au grand nombre d'allemands d'origine allemande-autre, il faudrait avoir des informations supplémentaires pour qu'on puisse interpréter la nature de telles relations interethniques.

Tableau 1: Population allemande à Montréal (RMR), 1981

	nombre	%
Pop. allemande totale	32615	100.0
Pop. allemande d'origine simple	22285	68.3
Pop. allemande d'origine multiple	10330	31.7

	nombre	% multiple
Pop. allemande-anglaise	3680	35.6
Pop. allemande française	1680	16.3
Pop. allemande-autre	4970	48.1

Source: Statistique Canada, Recensement de 1981

    En comparant le nombre d'allemands en 1981 avec les données du recensement de 1971, où les allemands étaient encore au nombre de 38440, nous constatons une baisse de la population d'environ 15%. Ce déclin démographique durant la décennie 1971 à 1981 tient son origine d'une part dans la possibilité de la ré-définition en ce qui concerne l'appartenance ethnique et d'autre part, avant tout, dans une migration accentuée des allemands du Québec vers d'autres provinces du Canada. En plus, l'immigration de l'Allemagne est en stagnation suite aux restrictions imposées par la législation sur l'immigration au Canada.

    Regardons de près la structure démographique du groupe allemand en 1981. La représentation de la pyramide des âges du groupe allemand d'origine simple et celle d'origine multiple en comparaison avec celle de la population montréalaise, nous révèle la différente structure des allemands d'origine simple et ceux d'origine multiple (Fig. 1).

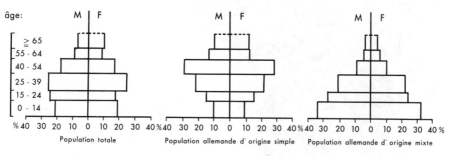

Fig. 1

Source: Statistique Canada, Recensement de 1981

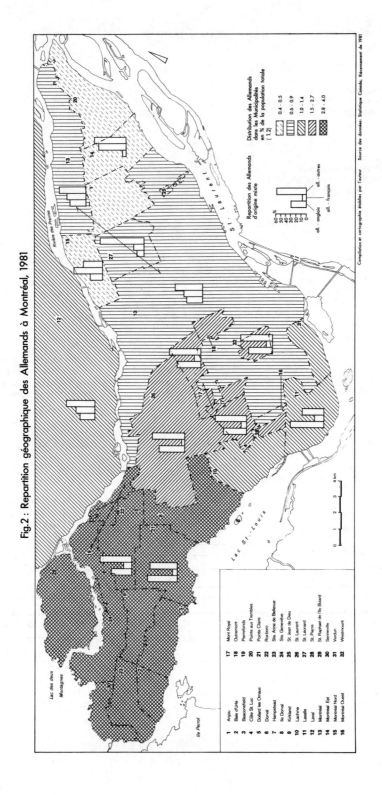

Fig.2 : Repartition géographique des Allemands à Montréal, 1981

Il est évident que les allemands d'origine simple constituent un groupe en vieillissement. Ils sont surreprésentés dans les catégories d'âges les plus élévées et nettement sousreprésentés dans les catégories des jeunes de 0 à 14 et de 15 à 24 ans. La forte proportion d'allemands de l'âge entre 40 à 54 ans tient son origine dans la vague d'immigration dans les années '50 et '60.

En ce qui concerne la structure d'âge des allemands d'origine mixte, nous observons la forte proportion des jeunes entre 0 à 24 ans. Dans tous les autres groupes d'âge, les allemands d'origine multiple sont sousreprésentés en comparaison avec la population totale et le groupe d'allemands d'origine simple. Alors, étant donné que les allemands d'origine multiple forment un tiers de la population allemande à Montréal et qu'ils sont majoritairement en-dessous de 25 ans, nous constatons que le taux de reproduction est actuellement beaucoup plus élévé dans les relations interethniques. Autrement dit: les allemands ont une forte tendance à chercher leurs contacts affectifs à l'extérieur de leur groupe ethnique.

Maintenant nous allons nous pencher sur la repartition géographique des allemands à Montréal. Cette repartition doit être vue en fonction de la structure résidentielle générale à Montréal. Arrivés à Montréal, les allemands font face à la presence de deux grands groupes linguistiques et culturels qui dominent la société, c'est à dire les francophones et les anglophones. Cette co-éxistance est cependant caractérisée, non par une co-habitation, mais par une division spatiale. Le groupe anglophone est surtout concentré dans l'ouest de l'île de Montréal, tandis que le groupe francophone vit davantage dans les quartiers de l'est de l'île.

La Fig. No. 2 porte sur la distribution des allemands d'origine simple et multiple sur l'île de Montréal et à Laval. En plus, elle fait ressortir les proportions des allemands d'origine allemande-anglaise, allemande-française et allemande-autre.

Quant à la repartition de l'ensemble du groupe allemand, nous observons que les allemands habitent tous les quartiers de la région étudiée - mais dans des proportions différentes. Le pourcentage supérieur à 2.8 dans les quartiers dans l'ouest de l'île, un pourcentage qui est fort au-dessus du pourcentage moyen de 1.2 pour l'ensemble de la région métropolitaine de Montréal, nous indique une plus forte concentration d'allemands dans des quartiers anglophones que dans les quartiers francophones. Malgré cette différence proportionelle, on ne peut pas parler d'une ségrégation résidentielle des allemands. Leur mode d'habitation ne se distingue pas de façon considérable en comparaison avec l'ensemble de la population montréalaise. En effet, des études comparatives ont fait ressortir que les allemands constituent un des groupes ethniques le plus dispersé sur l'île de Montréal (M. POLÈSE, 1971).

Quant à la proportion d'allemands d'origine multiple dans des parties différentes de l'île, une correlation entre le lieu d'habitat et l'origine allemande-anglaise et allemande-française est à noter. Ainsi, dans les quartiers anglophones, nous trouvons plus d'allemands d'origine allemande-anglaise que dans les quartiers francophones et vice versa.

II. Quelques caractéristiques linguistiques et socio-économiques du groupe ethnique allemand à Montréal

Le tableau No. 2 nous indique qu'en 1971 - c'est à dire avant la mise en place de la Charte de la langue française - presque la moitié des allemands possédaient l'allemand comme langue maternelle. La plupart de ces gens faisaient partie de la première génération d'immigrants. Dans les générations suivantes, les allemands adoptent surtout l'anglais comme langue maternelle.

Ceci est appuyé par le fait que plus de la moitié des allemands de langue maternelle allemande abandonnent leur propre langue en faveur de l'anglais comme langue d'usage et transmettent ainsi cette dernière langue à leurs enfants, nés au Canada. La tendance des allemands de s'orienter linguistiquement vers l'anglais et d'abandonner vite la langue ethnique se dégage encore de façon plus accentuée si on regarde le groupe allemand en général. 56.6% des allemands favorisent l'anglais comme langue

Tableau 2: Langue maternelle et langue d'usage des allemands, Montréal (RMR) 1971 (en %)

	total	langue d'usage: anglais	français	allemand	autre
origine ethnique:					
allemand	100.0	56.6	19.1	22.6	1.7
dont langue maternelle:					
anglais	32.5	94.6	3.0	-	2.4
français	17.6	8.3	90.5	-	1.2
allemand	48.4	49.0	4.3	45.8	0.9
autre	1.5	49.2	5.9	24.6	20.3

Source: Statistique Canada, Recensement de 1971

Tableau 3: Langue maternelle et langue d'usage des allemands d'origine simple, Montréal (RMR) 1981 (en %)

	total	langue d'usage: anglais	français	allemand	autre
origine ethnique:					
allemand	100.0	60.5	17.9	20.7	0.9
dont langue maternelle:					
anglais	26.7	93.3	4.4	2.0	0.3
français	14.9	7.2	91.9	0.6	0.3
allemand	56.7	59.4	5.3	35.0	0.3
autre	1.7	50.0	1.3	14.1	34.6

Source: Statistique Canada, Recensement de 1981

d'usage contre seulement 19.1% qui adoptent la langue de la majorité à Montréal, le français, et 22.6% qui gardent l'allemand comme langue d'usage. Le fait que plus de 75% des personnes d'origine allemande utilisent quotidiennement une langue différente que l'allemand traduit alors un faible intérêt linguistique du côté allemand par rapport à leur origine ethnique.

Ensuite, il importe d'analyser les changements linguistiques à l'intérieur du groupe allemand pendant la période entre les deux derniers recensements (2). Nous posons l'hypothèse que ces changements sont susceptibles d'indiquer partiellement l'impact de la politique de francisation sur le groupe allemand.

Ainsi, la comparaison des chiffres des recensements de 1971 et 1981 fait généralement ressortir que les allemands n'ont pas changé quant à leur intégration linguistique (cf. Tab. 2 et Tab. 3). Au contraire, le pourcentage de l'utilisation de l'anglais comme langue d'usage pour le groupe ethnique allemand a augmenté d'environ 4% entre 1971 et 1981, tandis que l'utilisation du français a baissé de 1.2% durant cette même période. Pour les allemands de langue maternelle allemande, l'attraction de l'anglais comme langue d'usage est encore plus évidente. Ainsi, en 1981, 59.4% des allemands ont choisi l'anglais comme langue d'usage contre 49.0% en 1971. Comme le taux d'utilisation du français a augmenté de façon minime, soit 1%, une grande partie du transfert linguistique allemand - anglais s'est fait au détriment de l'allemand comme langue d'usage. Les considérations précédentes sur le choix linguistique des allemands ne réflètent cependant qu'une partie de la réalité allemande en se référant uniquement aux allemands d'origine simple. Quant aux allemands d'origine mixte, en 1981, 74.8% ont adopté l'anglais comme langue maternelle et 79.0% comme langue d'usage (cf. Tab. 4). L'usage du français n'a pas atteint 20%. La force d'attraction de l'anglais se révèle surtout, si on regarde le groupe d'origine allemande-autre qui constitue presque la moitié des allemands d'origine multiple et dont environ 3/4 ont adopté l'anglais comme langue principale.

Tableau 4: Langue maternelle et langue d'usage des allemands d'origine multiple, Montréal (RMR) 1981 (en %)

	\multicolumn{5}{c}{langue maternelle et langue d'usage:}
origine ethnique:	total	anglais	français	allemand	autre
allemand-multiple (total)					
- langue maternelle	100.0	74.8	18.0	5.7	1.5
- langue d'usage	100.0	79.0	18.1	1.9	1.0
allemand-anglais					
- langue maternelle	100.0	92.7	4.5	2.7	0.1
- langue d'usage	100.0	93.3	4.9	1.7	0.1
allemand-français					
- langue maternelle	100.0	35.3	60.8	3.6	0.3
- langue d'usage	100.0	41.1	58.0	0.9	-
allemand-autre					
- langue maternelle	100.0	74.5	13.8	8.4	3.3
- langue d'usage	100.0	81.3	14.4	2.4	1.9

Source: Statistique Canada, Recensement de 1981

Il en découle que les jeunes allemands n'ont pas encore effectué une réorientation linguistique vers la langue française - et ça, malgré l'intégration des enfants dans les écoles françaises, imposée par la Charte de la langue française.

Dans une autre idée, il nous apparaît fondamental de décrire brièvement la situation socio-économique des allemands afin de bien saisir leur position dans la structure socio-économique de la société québecoise.

Soulignons que les membres du groupe ethnique allemand - et surtout ceux d'origine mixte - sont très bien scolarisés. Ainsi, le recensement de 1981 fait apparaître qu'à l'intérieur du groupe allemand, le pourcentage de ceux ayant commencés ou accomplis des études universitaires est plus élevé en comparaison avec l'ensemble de la population. Ce niveau de scolarisation élévé peut alors être considéré comme un facteur qui joue en faveur des allemands quant au succès économique.

En effet, selon le recensement de 1981, les allemands sont surreprésentés dans les catégories de revenu plus élevé (cf. Tab. 5). Ainsi, 21.9% des allemands gagnent plus que $ 21670 par année en comparaison avec 14.7% de toute la population, 14.2% des francophones et 18% des anglophones. Cependant, dans les catégories de revenu faible en bas de $ 10834, les allemands se dégagent comme le groupe le moins représenté face aux autres groupes, nommés ci-haut.

Au niveau des professions, les allemands sont surreprésentés dans les emplois qualifiés, tels que dans les domaines de la gestion et de l'administration, des sciences naturelles, de l'enseignement et de la main d'oeuvre qualifiée.

Tableau 5: Revenu annuel par catégories de revenu, Montréal (RMR) 1981 (en %)

origine ethnique:	total	sans revenu	revenu ($ can) 1- 4333	4334- 10834	10835- 17335	17336- 21669	>21670
total	100.0	16.5	18.1	24.5	17.6	8.6	14.7
anglais	100.0	14.7	17.8	24.2	17.1	8.2	18.0
français	100.0	16.5	18.4	24.4	17.6	8.9	14.2
allemand	100.0	14.6	15.9	21.4	16.8	9.4	21.9

Source: Statistique Canada, Recensement de 1981

La bonne position économique des allemands est d'ailleurs confirmée par leur taux de chômage faible. En 1981, ce taux s'est élevé à 4% contre 7.9% pour toute la population montréalaise.

Signalons en résumé que sur le plan spatial, linguistique et socio-économique, les allemands ne se trouvent point en marge de la société québecoise; bien au contraire, ils se dégagent comme groupe intégré à la société.

III. Le groupe allemand, son organisation interne et ses relations interethniques

Outre les aspects spatiaux et socio-économiques, il faut tenir compte de la dimension psycho-sociale du groupe allemand afin de saisir son mode d'intégration. Cette dimension porte premièrement sur l'identification ethnique et l'organisation interne et, deuxièmement, sur les relations interethniques et sur la représentation allemande dans la réalité montréalaise.

Commençons à étudier de plus près la problématique de l'identification ethnique des allemands. Le concept de 'l'identité' en général revêt plusieurs dimensions. L'identité d'une personne est alors composée des différentes façettes, comme par exemple l'identité sociale, personnelle, professionnelle, nationale, ethnique etc. En fonction des diverses circonstances de vie et selon des différentes personnes, les façettes peuvent prendre un poids différent. Dans ce sens, l'identité ethnique, contrairement à la définition de l'origine ethnique adoptée par Statistique Canada, ne repose par sur les données biologiques, mais sur les conditions sociales. En d'autres termes: l'identité ethnique d'une personne ou d'un groupe se façonne en fonction des relations intra- et interethniques.

Nous posons l'hypothèse qu'une forte identité ethnique se traduit par un réseau institutionnel ethnique plus ou moins complèt. Un réseau qui est capable de satisfaire les besoins des membres du groupe ethnique à l'intérieur du groupe, comme par exemple le travail, l'éducation, la consommation, l'assistance sociale et médicale, et qui, le cas échéant, peut jouer comme une force socio-politique à l'intérieur de la société d'accueil.

En ce qui concerne les allemands à Montréal, nous nous sommes demandés, quels sont les choix collectifs et le réseau institutionnel, susceptibles de symboliser une cohérence ethnique et l'ampleur de l'identité ethnique allemande.

Lors des entretiens avec les réprésentants des différentes organisations allemandes à Montréal, l'inexistance d'une identité collective a nettement ressorti. Selon les observations des personnes interrogées, les allemands - je cite en traduction libre - "ne sont ni organisés, ni coordonnés comme groupe", "ils sont dispersés sur le plan résidentiel et sur le plan d'action collective", "il n'existe pas de sens communautaire parmi les allemands", "ils se privent de défendre leurs intérêts ethniques au sein de la société québecoise" et "ils s'assimilent facilement dans le seul but de réussir sur le plan économique" (3).

Les énoncés ci-dessus sont assez représentatifs de la perception générale des allemands rencontrés à l'égard de leur groupe ethnique. Ce qui en découle, c'est la prédominance des identités individuelles - identités qui portent plutôt sur la famille, la profession ou la classe sociale en général - au détriment d'un fort sens d'appartenance ethnique allemand. Au lieu de maintenir les contacts à l'intérieur du groupe ethnique, les allemands préfèrent une orientation socio-culturelle vers les autres groupes existant dans la société québecoise.

Pourtant, cette orientation socio-culturelle ne signifie pas l'absence totale des organisations ethniques allemandes à Montréal. En 1983, on comptait trois paroisses réligieuses (dont une a été fermée dernièrement), une école allemande, quatre écoles de langue allemande du samedi, un théâtre allemand, deux organisations dites bénévoles d'aide, sept organisations de loisir avec plusieurs sous-groupes d'activités, comme la section de 'bowling', de danse folklorique etc., et la représentation de l'association trans-canadienne des canadiens-allemands.

Comme média d'information, deux bulletins de club, un journal allemand publié à Montréal, un journal allemand trans-canadien et des émissions allemandes hebdomadaires, transmises par la Télévision et par la Radio, sont disponibles. De plus, l'Allemagne est représentée par le Consulat, par l'Institut Goethe et par la Chambre de Commerce allemande-canadienne.

Ces organisations ne forment cependant pas de véritable réseau institutionnel. Par exemple, les clubs de loisir ne font que promouvoir l'aspect folklorique, tout en fêtant l'Oktoberfest, le Karnaval etc. En plus, le nombre d'allemands regroupés dans de telles organisations est minime. A cause du faible taux de participation, 'das Deutsche Haus' (la maison allemande), c'est à dire un bâtiment de réunion réservé aux organisations allemandes, a fait faillite dernièrement.

Quant aux institutions éducatives, les écoles de langue allemande du samedi sont de plus en plus fréquentées, non par les gens allemands ayant l'intention d'améliorer leurs connaissances en allemand, mais par des personnes intéressées à apprendre l'allemand comme langue étrangère. Ainsi, la plupart de la clientèle des écoles allemandes du samedi est d'origine francophone.

Suite à la mise en place de la Charte de la langue française, la seule école allemande qui enseigne toutes les matières en allemand est réservée aux enfants, dont les parents ne restent que temporairement à Montréal. Selon les informations obtenues par la directrice de cette école, certains allemands qui ne remplissent pas la condition d'accueil tentent d'envoyer leurs enfants dans cette école afain qu'ils ne recoivent pas l'enseignement en français.

Au point de vue réligieux, les curés allemands ont avoué que l'attraction des paroisses allemandes est assez faible. Le service se fait en allemand et en anglais parce que les connaissances de l'allemand diminuent et ne permettent plus de célébrer la messe de façon uniquement allemand.

Tout compte fait, on ne peut pas parler d'intérêt commun parmi les différentes institutions allemandes - au contraire, au cours des recherches éffectuées sur le terrain, des fortes tensions entre plusieurs organisations se sont dégagées; tensions qui trouvent souvent leur origine dans des questions financières, par exemple à l'égard des subventions à obtenir de la part du consulat allemand. Ce manque de consensus se traduit dans une négligeance complète de la dimension politique dans la réalité du groupe ethnique allemand.

Lors des discussions autour du projet de loi de la Charte de la langue française, les allemands étaient les seuls des groupes ethniques comparables qui ne se sont pas prononcés officiellement. Pourtant, comme nous l'avons démontré, ils y étaient très touchés suite à leur orientation antécédante vers l'adoption de la langue anglaise. Leur opposition était surtout à caractère discrèt et silencieux: soit ils ont quitté la province, soit, comme démontrent les données du recensement de 1981, ils n'ont pas changé leur mode d'intégration.

En résumé, l'identification des allemands à leur groupe ethnique est d'un niveau faible. Ils ont enclin à un repli sur eux-mêmes, refusant de se mêler de politique et ne voulant surtout pas élever la voix pour reclamer leurs intérêts ethniques.

Ensuite, il faut se pencher sur les relations interethniques; relations qui, dans une grande partie, sont déterminées par l'image que donnent les allemands dans la réalité montréalaise.

Au début de ce texte, nous avons déjà cité la notion d'invisibilité à l'égard de la perception des allemands de la part des québecois. L'exemple suivant va démontrer dans quel dégré les allemands essaient de rester invisibles et de s'adapter à leur environnement.

Au sujet de la maison allemande, son identification porte sur un des aspects folkloriques des allemands: la bière. La façade de la maison allemande est alors décorée par un verre de bière et le mot 'Biergarten'. Cependant, dans le journal allemand 'Echo' (Das Echo, avril 1983: 3), nous avons trouvé une annonce, où la maison allemande figure sans aucun nom imprimé, tandis que, dans le journal quotidien de langue anglaise 'The Gazette' (The Gazette, 20/3/1982: 8), la représentation de la même maison se fait en anglais. On y trouve le nom 'Bavarian Garden" au lieu de la désignation en allemand. Nous pensons que les annonces publicitaires ont été créées par les allemands, ce qui met en évidence leurs tendances à se conformer à l'autrui.

Dans un mémoire, commandé par le Ministère de l'Immigration du Québec, on fait alors allusion à l'interdépendance entre l'image publique des allemands et leurs relations intergroupes. L'auteur dit au sujet des allemands: "Leur discrétion et leur mimétisme ... sont d'autres éléments qui jouent pour les allemands, on fait plus confiance à des immigrants qui paraissent si bien intégrés ou désireux de s'intégrer, qui n'affichent pas trop les signes de leur différence" (J. P. GOSSELIN, 1983: 34). Dans ce sens, le concept de 'présence discrète' des allemands leur crée un préjugé favorable d'intégration, malgré l'existence de l'image négative des allemands au Québec; l'image liée aux souvenirs de deux guerres mondiales.

En outre, ce qui joue dans les relations interethniques, c'est le fait que les allemands ont du succès au niveau économique. Ce succès facillite l'intégration socio-culturelle.

Le choix linguistique et résidentiel des allemands nous a montré que cette intégration se fait traditionellement surtout au profit de la communauté anglophone. Donc, on peut en conclure, que la distance psycho-sociale entre les allemands et les anglophones est moins grande qu'entre les allemands est les francophones. Les raisons sont multiples: il y a d'abord le fait qu'il y a une parenté de langue entre les allemands et les anglophones; ensuite, la langue du travail et de la promotion économique a longtemps été l'anglais, de même que le capital. En outre, les allemands trouvent plus de tolérance chez les anglophones à leur égard que chez les francophones. Ainsi, lors des entrevues, les allemands ont révélé que les écoles françaises n'étaient pas accessibles aux enfants de religion non-catholique. Toutefois, du côté anglophone, il n'y avait pas d'obstacles vis-à-vis une intégration des enfants allemands.

Quant à la communauté franco-québecoise, les sentiments des allemands sont plutôt ambigus. L'analyse socio-spatiale a fait ressortir que les allemands ne sont pas nécessairement orientés vers la majorité francophone à Montréal. Ceci trouve son fondement - comme nous l'avons déjà dit - dans des raisons économiques et dans une certaine xénophobie des francophones à l'égard des autres groupes ethniques. En plus, les allemands prennent une position très réservée en ce qui concerne le côté nationaliste dans la politique et la conscience québecoise. Un allemand s'y exprime comme suit: "Jusqu'à un certain degré les allemands sympathisent avec la population de langue française, mais ils détestent beaucoup les tendances nationalistes - ils en ont même peur" (4).

Selon les dires de plusieurs personnes allemandes, cette peur trouve son origine dans les mauvaises expériences d'un nationalisme éxagéré, vécu à l'époque de la Troisième Reich en Allemagne.

En guise de conclusion, à l'égard de la question de 'non-visibilité' des allemands à Montréal, nous constatons que celle-ci est due à leurs tendances de se disperser spatialement, à adapter facilement une des langues de la société d'accueil et à bien réussir sur le plan économique. Ces tendances vont de pair avec un faible niveau d'identification ethnique.

Parler des fondements de tels comportements, ce serait toucher des domaines non-suffisamment explorés. Quand même, on pourrait formuler trois hypothèses à verifier. D'abord, on peut expliquer le manque d'identification et d'action collective des allemands en termes historiques. Les allemands ne cherchent pas à manifester leur appartenance ethnique dans des questions d'intérêt politique et publique afin de ne pas évoquer les stéréotypes, liés à l'image militariste des allemands. Ils préfèrent s'intégrer 'en silence' dans la société québecoise.

Une autre tentative d'explication trouve son origine dans le même sens, c'est à dire dans l'histoire après-guerre. Beaucoup d'allemands ont quitté l'Allemagne dans les années '50, c'est à dire dans une époque, où l'Allemagne était en état de reconstruction et où le niveau de vie était encore relativement bas. Les immigrants cherchaient avant tout à l'étranger le succès économique et l'oubli de la guerre. Cette volonté d'oublier s'est traduit dans des options en faveur des relations interethniques - au détriment des liens intraethniques.

Une troisième explication renvoit cependant la non-identification des allemands comme communauté ethnique à un autre contexte. Dans cet ordre, l'accent est plutôt mis sur l'analogie que sur la spécificité du mode d'intégration des allemands. Dans ce sens, les allemands montrent une attitude d'insertion semblable à d'autres groupes d'immigrants de l'Europe du Nord et du Centre, comme les scandinaves, les hollandais, les suisses et les autrichiens. Tous ces groupes d'immigrants ont généralement un bon niveau d'éducation et ils valorisent la réussite matérielle au désavantage des valeurs communautaires.

A l'égard de la question des réactions des allemands face aux changements socio-politiques dans les années '70 au Québec, nous soulignons en conclusion que les allemands tentent à échapper à la politique de francisation en quittant la province ou en continuant à favoriser l'anglais comme langue d'adoption. Donc, même si les allemands n'ont fait aucune reclamation publique à l'époque de la mise en place de la Charte de la langue française, ça ne veut pas dire qu'ils en étaient d'accord. Au contraire, les allemands interviewés manifestaient carrément leur appréhensions à l'égard de la politique linguistique de francisation au Québec. Ils optaient plutôt pour la politique fédérale, celle du 'bilinguisme'; option alors fort divergente de celle des québecois francophones.

Tout compte fait, parler des allemands en termes de groupe intégré à la société montréalaise, ça n'implique pas un accord fondamental entre la minorité ethnique allemande et le groupe majoritaire, les francophones.

Annotations

1   Le texte présent s'inscrit dans le cadre d'une thèse de doctorat commencée en septembre 1984. Les résultats présentés ici sont alors d'ordre fort préliminaire.
2   Malgré que la définition de l'origine ethnique ne soit pas la même aux deux recensements, nous avons pris l'initiative de faire une comparaison à titre indicatif.
3   Entrevues personnelles avec les représentants des organisations allemandes à Montréal, effectuées par l'auteure du texte présent en mars 1983.
4   Entrevue personnelle, mars 1983 (traduction libre).

Bibliographie

Amyot, M., 1980: La situation démo-linguistique au Québec, Québec: Editeur officiel.

Anderson, A. B., Frideres, J. S., 1981: Ethnicity in Canada, Theoretical Perspectives, Toronto: Butterworth.

Balakrishnan, T. R., 1982: Changing Patterns of Ethnic Residential Segregation in the Metropolitan Areas of Canada, Revue Canadienne de Sociologie et Anthropologie, 19 (1), p. 92-110.

Breton, R., 1983: La communauté ethnique, communauté politique, Sociologie et Sociétés, vol. XV, no. 2, oct. 1983, p. 23-38.

Caldwell, G., 1983: Les études ethniques au Québec: bilan et perspectives, Québec: Institut Québecois de Recherche sur la Culture.

Cappon, P., 1974: Conflit entre les néo-québecois et les francophones de Montréal, Québec: Centre International de Recherche sur le Bilinguisme.

Ciaccia, J., 1979: Les communautés ethniques au Québec, Montréal (non-publié).

Cohen, A. (ed.), 1974: Urban Ethnicity, London: Tavistock.

Dahlie, J., Fernando, T., (eds.), 1981: Ethnicity, Power and Politics in Canada, Toronto: Methuen.

Debor, H. W., 1964: Die Deutschen in der Provinz Quebec 1664-1964, Quebec: Come.

Driedger, L., Church, G., 1974: Residential Segregation and Institutional Completeness: a Comparaison of Ethnic Minorities, Revue de Sociologie et Anthropologie, vol. 11, no. 1.

Froeschle, H., 1975: Deutschkanadische Studien, Aufgaben und Möglichkeiten, Deutschkanadisches Jahrbuch, 2, p. 6-23.

Giguere, G. E., 1974: Les groupes ethniques du Canada: les Allemands, Video Press, vol. 3, Montreal 1974.

Glazer, N., Moynihan, D., 1975: Ethnicity: Theorý and Experience, Cambridge: Harvard Univ. Press.

Gosselin, J. P., 1983: Rapport de recherche sur les allemands, Montreal, Ministère de Communications Culturelles et de l'Immigration, Mai (non-publié).

Gürttler, K., 1980: Deutsch-kanadische Beziehungen als akademisches Forschungsfeld, Deutsche Gesellschaft zu Montreal.

Hardt-Dhatt, K., 1976: Etude socio-linguistique sur l'intégration de l'immigrant allemand au milieu québecois, Québec: Centre International de Recherche sur le Bilinguisme.

Hecht, A., 1983: The Germans in the Anglo-Saxon Milieu in Central Canada, CAUTG Publication Series Nr. 9, Vancouver, p. 110-142.

Helling, R., 1962: A Comparison of the Acculturation of Immigrants in Toronto, Ontario and Detroit, Michigan, Michigan: Wayne State Univ. Press.

Isajiw, W. (ed.), 1973: Identities, The Impact of Ethnicity on Canadian Society, Canadian Ethnic Studies, Toronto: P. Martin.

Kliem, O., 1970: Deutsche in Kanada, Diss. Erlangen.

Kloss, H., 1977: Zahlen zur Einwanderung nach Kanada aus ganz oder überwiegend deutschsprachigen Ländern seit 1946, Deutsch als Muttersprache in Kanada, Deutsche Sprache in Europa und Übersee, Bd. 1, Wiesbaden.

Koch, A., Pletsch, A., Vestweber, I., 1984: Deutsche in Kanada - eine verschwindende Minorität? Bericht zur Forschungslage, Zeitschrift der Gesellschaft für Kanada-Studien, 4. Jg., Nr. 1, Bd. 6, p. 123-132.

Koch-Hillebrecht, U., 1977: Das Deutschenbild, München: Beck.

Kovacs, M. L., 1978: Ethnic Canadians, Culture and Education, Regina: Canadian Plains Research Center.

Labudde, H. J., 1952: Die deutsche Auswanderung nach Kanada, Diss. Hamburg.

Lehmann, H., 1931: Zur Geschichte des Deutschtums in Kanada, Bd. 1: Das Deutschtum in Ostkanada, Schriften des deutschen Auslands-Instituts Stuttgart, A. Kulturhistorische Reihe, Bd. 31, Stuttgart.

Liddell, P. (ed.), 1983: German Canadian Studies, Vertical Approaches, CAUTG (Canadian Association of University Teachers of German) - Publication Nr. 8, Vancouver.

Lorrain, L., 1969: Dossier du groupe ethnique allemand et germanophone, Gouvernement du Québec, Ministère de l'Immigration, Montréal.

Malycky, A., 1973: University-Research in German Canadians. Supplement: Canadian Ethnic Studies, 5, p. 63-65.

Marbach, N., 1973: Zur Lage der Deutsch-Kanadier, dans: Sudholt, G. (ed.): Deutsche Annalen, Leoni, p. 179-193.

Marx, H., 1983: Deutsche in der Neuen Welt, Braunschweig.

McGahan, P., 1982: Urban Sociology in Canada, Toronto: Butterworth.

Messier, J., 1981: Profil d'une communauté ethnique de Montréal, Lès allemands à Montréal, Conseil Scolaire de l'Ile de Montréal.

Möllmann, A., 1937: Das Deutschtum in Montreal, Schriften des Instituts für Grenz- und Auslandsdeutschtum an der Universität Marburg, H. 11, Marburg.

Pletsch, A., Vestweber, I., 1983: Die Deutschen in Québec - Aspekte der sozialen und wirtschaftlichen Integration, CAUTG Publication Series Nr. 9, Vancouver, p. 42-72.

— 1984: The Germans in Montréal - Aspects of Social and Economic Integration, Trent University Occasional Papers Nr. 10, Peterborough.

Polèse, M. u.a., 1978: La géographie résidentielle des immigrants et des groupes ethniques: Montréal 1971, INRS-Urbanisation, Etudes et Documents no. 12, Montréal.

Schermerhorn, R. A., 1978: Comperative Ethnic Relations. A Framework for Theory and Research, Chicago: The University of Chicago Press.

Stadler, B., 1983: Language Maintenance and Assimilation, The Case of selected German-Speaking Immigrants, CAUTG Publication Nr. 7, Vancouver.

Vestweber, I., 1984: Die Deutschen in Montreal - Aspekte ihrer räumlichen, sozialen und ökonomischen Integration (Staatsarbeit), Marburg.

Weissenborn, G. W., 1982: L'allemand au Canada: Ses chances de survie: Langue et Société, no. 9, p. 16-19.

Adresse de l'auteur :
Inge Vestweber
Raiffeisenstr. 6
3540 Korbach
Tel. 05631/8094

Gypsies as a Visible Minority in Finland.
The Proactive Policing of an Ethnic Minority

Martti Grönfors

Abstract: In this paper I will attempt to establish how an ethnic minority, such as the highly visible gypsies in Finland, through certain stereotypical notions about their culture and social organisation face control policies and tactics which do not react to illegal actions but are active and proactive lawenforcement. In this the beliefs of the majority about the minority are reflected in the beliefs and actions of the legal agents, especially the police. The views of the minority on their part about the majority reinforce and aid their own marginality, which means that excessive control is directed to the deviantly-perceived minority. In order to understand the situation of gypsies in Finland some background material on their history and situation in Finland is given. The police, on the other hand represent the Finnish majority. However there are certain uniformities in their background which establish their views on the gypsies on the more conservative side than those of the general population. I will also give some details of the background, and training of police and how these manifest in practice in the type of hierarchical organisation as is the police force.

Résumé: L'auteur de l'article discute la question, comment une minorité ethnique, ici particulièrement les tsiganes au Finlande, réagit sur les mesures de contrôl exercées par la police, mesures qui d'une part sont justifiées par des stéréotypes ethniques et culturaux et qui ne constituent pas, d'autre part, des réactions contre des actes criminels, étant plutôt des mesures d'ordres préventives et effectives. Ces mesures reflètent l'opinion majoritaire envers la minorité. Elles renforcent le processus de marginalisation, ce qui entraîne de noveaux mechanismes de contrôl. L'auteur examine sous cet aspect les relations entre tsiganes et police dans un context historique. La police représentant la majorité finlandaise se revèle d'être plus conservateur que l'opinion général, ce qui amène à une étude sur la situation socio-culturelle de ce groupe, examinant des questions telles que l'origine des policiers, leurs niveaux d'éducation, leurs positions dans la hiérarchie professionelle etc., aspects qui, entre autres, déterminent aussi le comportement des policiers envers la minorité visible des tsiganes.

Zusammenfassung: Der Autor befaßt sich mit der Frage, wie eine ethnische Minderheit, hier die äußerlich auffallenden Zigeuner in Finnland, auf Kontrollmaßnahmen der Polizei reagiert, die einerseits auf gewisse ethnische und kulturelle Stereotypen zurückzuführen, aber andererseits nicht als Reaktion auf Verstöße gegen das Gesetz, sondern als wirksame und vorbeugende Ordnungsmaßnahmen zu verstehen sind. In den Maßnahmen der Polizei spiegelt sich die Einstellung der Mehrheit gegenüber der Minderheit wider. Dadurch wird die Stellung der Minderheit als Randgruppe bestärkt und somit eine ausufernde Kontrolle ausgelöst. Dies zeigt sich in den Beziehungen zwischen Zigeunern und Polizei, wie ein historischer Abriß erläutert. Die Polizei vertritt dabei die allgemeine Einstellung der finnischen Gesellschaft, obwohl die Polizei weitaus konservativere Auffassungen äußert als der einfache Finne. Diese Feststellung wird durch Angaben über Herkunft und Ausbildung sowie über Stellung der Polizisten in der Polizeihierarchie ergänzt und belegt.

※※※※※※※※※※※※

Gypsies in Finland; from an unhappy coexistance to assimilation and control

Gypsies have been in Finland since the late middle-ages, forming today the numerically largest ethnically distinct and visible minority, numbering between 6.000 and 8.000 people. Until the latter half of this century they were very much a rural folk, who operated an unhappy but a workable symbiosis with the Finnish peasant. The gypsies traded mainly horses with them, and the peasants provided gypsies with shelter, food, and money. In the latter half of this century the gypsy population, together with the Finnish rural population, has been moving rapidly into cities, and today it can be said that most Finnish gypsies live in cities and towns. An estimated quarter of the total are living in and around the capital city of Helsinki.

Physically the gypsies stand out in the basically very homogenious Finnish culture. They are on average very much darker in complexion than are the Finns. The dress of the Finnish gypsy woman is probably the most colourful and elaborate of the gypsy attire anywhere in the world. Their physical visibility is aided by the visibility of certain features of their culture.

I lived with the Finnish gypsies between 1976 and 1978 a total of one and half to two years as a full participant observer, a privilege which is not easily granted to outside researchers. During that time I studied their culture and social organisation, and made a study of their blood feuding institution (GRÜNFORS, 1977), and a separate study of their somewhat unhappy relationship with the police (GRÜNFORS, 1979, 1981).

In addition to my knowledge about the gypsies, obtained through participant observation, 45 police officers were interviewed informally but thoroughly in the two largest cities in Finland, Helsinki (35 officers) and Tampere (10 officers). During my participant observation study of the gypsies I had not only witnessed some police tactics, but also collected systematically some case studies of the ways in which the gypsies had been treated by the police. Through interviewing the police about their ideas of gypsies, their culture and social organisation and police-stated practices in the case of the gypsies, the picture about this relationship became clearer. By getting the police to state their views on gypsies, it was assumed that those views represent something of the reality of the police-gypsy interaction in the streets.

Gypsies have always interested the legal authorities, and when the special laws affecting gypsies and their movement in Finland were ended in the latter part of the last century, the laws about vagrancy became the main weapon in attempts to curtail their activities and in an effort to assimilate the gypsies into the mainstream Finnish society. However, as earlier there was at least a degree of mutual dependency between the country folk and the gypsies, the arm of the law was employed only spasmodically on gypsies, usually trickered of by a specific event, such as a fight during the market in towns. Also, being primarily located in the remote country areas, the vigilance by the police was not easy to effect, even when it was desired.

With the post-war improvements in economic conditions and social welfare provisions in Finland, the gypsies started moving into towns en masse in the 1960s. Where the assimilative attempts by the legal authorities had failed over the centuries, the social welfare authorities were succeeding in a couple of decades. Today three quarters of the gypsy households receive all or most of their income in various social welfare payments. This has made gypsies a relatively easy target for control policies, and now gypsies are more dependant on the majority population than ever before in their lives. At the same time their indigenous culture is disappearing at a very fast rate with the consequent social problems of alcoholism, mental illnesses, criminality, and the like.

The concentration of gypsies into urban centres has also meant that they are now very much more exposed to the practices of the law enforcement agents, who according to my research seem to focus their attention with undue vigour and harshness on the gypsies. The special police tactics are fuelled by often very erroneous beliefs about the nature of gypsy culture and social organisation, and from their part add to the criminalisation of Finland's gypsy population. This paper will examine the difficulties which gypsies have, when they have been brought under the surveillance of the professional city cops, by examining some of the attitudes which each group has from the other.

My sample of police officers is not particularly large, and cannot be called anything resembling a representative one. Apart from the smallness of the sample, another fact which ascewed the representativeness of the police sample was the fact that it was not possible to exercise any control over the selection of the interviewed officers. In granting the research permission, the police wanted to retain the control of who is and who is not to be interviewed. However, from a number of various indicators something about the nature of the sample can be said. It is evident that the heads of the various police sections selected the officers for interviews by using at least two different criteria: firstly, it was evident that the known racists were kept hidden from the researchers and only "reasonable" cops selected to be studied. Secondly, in some police stations there were officers who were known to have "good" relationship with the local gypsies, or were known as "gypsy experts", and those were pushed forward to be interviewed. Therefore it is possible to say with some degree of certainty that the hostility and negative sentiments towards gypsies expressed in this study quite likely underestimate those feelings in the police force as a whole.

The Finnish police and their views about gypsies

The Finnish police does not differ a great deal in the recruitment practices, training, internal organisation, and in the structure of the forces from its other Western counterparts (BOWDEN 1978: 32, McNAMARA 1967, CHAPPELL & WILSON 1969: 4). The recruitment is from the ranks of the Finnish majority, often from the farming sections or other conservative sections of the community. The forces are usually joined at a young age, and the job is often the only one for the officer. Training takes place in boarding schools under a strict army-type regime, which continues all through the working life of the officer. In the forces there is a clear hierarchy with little room for individual initiative. It is not therefore surprising that the police officers are somewhat alienated from the reality of everyday life, and that they tend to regard the world in simple black and white terms of normal or abnormal, acceptable or unacceptable, lawful or illegal. Also it is not surprising to hear that the police officers tend to spend much of their free time with other police officers.

It can therefore be said that in general the conservative outlook which is already in the home background of the officers becomes amplified in their daily work, and the company of those thinking alike reinforces these attitudes. The police tend to oppose social change, have a suspicious attitude towards cultural and behavioural differences, and stress the law and order very strongly. For the police the "normal" citizen is one who fulfills his or her societal obligations as a taxpayer, is not on welfare, is married, has children and operates within a nuclear family, does not protest but accepts the societal norms as given. Against that background I shall explore some of the attitudes which the police pretty well unanimously have about the Finnish gypsies as a cultural group.

"Gypsies exist only for the moment, seeking immediate gratification"

The morality of gypsy men is thought to be very questionable, although the high moral of the gypsy women gets praise from the police. However, the morality of women is not the property of women but they are forced to be moral by their men. Also some officers thought that althought they do not have any evidence of the immorality of gypsy women, it is because immoral acts are contained within the gypsy society. According to the police the gypsies as a group are guilty of regular incest as they "live together and breed together". When the gypsies do not formalise their marriage-type liaisons, that is seen by the police as a serious flouting of the moral norms of the Finnish society.

The could-not-care attitude of gypsies is also "evidenced" by the fact that they are not seen to pay taxes, which the police officers see as an insurance against bad luck, illness, unemployment and old age. The gypsies are thought not to be willing to put anything into the system, but are seen only interested in what they might get out of the system. The police see the gypsies as being an unwarranted burden and drain on Finland's social welfare system.

Above all the police believes that all gypsies are involved in criminal activity, and most police officers believe that the majority of the gypsy population gets most of its income from that source. The gypsies are thought to attempt to get as much out of the surrounding Finnish society with as little effort as possible. Criminality is thought to be institutionalised and a cultural feature of gypsies, and the police believe that the gypsies socialise their children into systematic criminal activity from early on. The gypsy women are thought to get most of their income from selling black market booze and from shop-lifting, whereas this kind of small-time criminality is thought to be beyond gypsy man's dignity. The men are believed to be the brains behind the criminal activities of women and children, as well as pulling off the bigger jobs themselves.

"Gypsies are spontaneous and do not want any external limitations to their behaviour"

People who are spontaneous throw themselves into activity without thinking of the possible consequences. Spontaneous activity, according to the police, if it is practiced in a large scale, will lead to a societal chaos. The gypsy "desire for freedom" the police explains as spontaneity which is not acceptable. Many police officers think of this type of behaviour as typical of children. The gypsies do not pay enough attention to the demands of the majority society to settle down. Many police officers also believe that this "desire for freedom" is biological, "in their blood". In order to build predictability into the affairs of the society - one of the prime requirements for effective control - the members of a society must be able to be reached, or at least their mobility should follow some rules and have some clearly discernible ends, says the police. The mobility of the gypsies in the officers' opinion is without any aim and therefore it is not possible to predict their likely movements, and hence it is against the ordered society and its norms.

To restrict the mobility of gypsies in one way or another, is believed to lead to a quick and violent reaction from them. To resort to physical violence in situations of conflict is another characteristic which the police believes to be typical of gypsies. "Normal" people are believed to be able to control their violent tendecies, or to limit them to appropriate situations, such as the wars or sport. If violence is limited to appropriate situations it can be controlled. According to the police, the spontaneous violence of gypsies is a threat to the ordered society, as it can erupt in any situation or in any form. The violence of gypsies is lacking predictability, and that makes it a cultural feature, which is against the ordered society, believes the police.

"Gypsies are anarchists"

To obey bureaucratic rules is thought by the police to be a necessary condition of any ordered society. It is purposeful and furthers order and continuity in society. Its opposite, anarchy, is seen to threaten the order. To deviate from the dominant culture, the Finnish one, and to uphold differing forms of social organisation, the police experiences as anarchy which threatens the ordered society. The more the individuals and groups deviate in their values and behaviour from the norms of the majority, the more anarchistic are these people and the less useful they are from the point of view of society. "Decent people" alter their values to correspond those of the majority. To persist in deviant values is against society and therefore to be condemned.

The police see the entire indigenous culture of gypsies as anarchy against the ordered society. Even such characteristics as the extended families of gypsies are thought as being against the norms in that they make the activities of the authorities more difficult. Excessive familiy affection, for example, means such things that when a gypsy is arrested the police station is filled with concerned relatives, and that is seen significantly to hamper the effective work of the police. In all, the mere fact that the gypsies value their own culture in preference to that of the majority, is considered against the ordered society. A decent citizen does not differ significantly from others.

Of the individual cultural features the police draws attention to the gypsy ways of dress, which is seen as a serious deviation from the norms of a decent society. Above all it is seen as a serious external sign of their deviation, a deliberate tease to the police and other "decent" citizens. In addition to cultural features, some officers believe that the deviant biological characteristics, such as dark, foreign physical features are an added problem, in that they make all gypsies look alike, which hampers the identification of the individual gypsies. That, in turn, makes the effective working of the police difficult, as it is often impossible to find culprits from among them. Also it is thought to give rise to special forms of criminality, in that this physical similarity allegedly allows the gypsies to share the same identity papers and driver's licences, without too much fear from detection. Also the police believes that gypsies know that the police are unable to identify them, and therefore the names of the gypsies who are not in police books are used by those who are wanted by the police.

"Gypsies want new experiences and excitement in their lives"

To search for experiences and excitement for their own sake is not desirable from the point of view of ordered society, believes the police. Routine is necessary for predictability, and everything which differs from routine, is an obstacle to ordered society and at the same time to the work of the police. The work of the police depends greatly on the predictability of certain series of events, and any deviation from normal draws the attention of the police. It is for example acceptable to express one's feelings if there is a clearly discernible reason for it. Then it is possible to relate to it with the attention which is appropriate. However, it is suspect to express emotions for which there does not seem to be any acceptable or understandable reason, and to which one cannot relate appropriately. The police believes that the emotionalism of gypsies is of the latter kind. The police also believes that the gypsies require in their everyday life a certain amount of excitement which is usually achieved through illegal methods and in activities which are against the norms of the "decent" society. In fact, some police officers think that gypsy criminality is activity for seeking excitement and emotional experiences rather than material gains.

The deviant emotional life of gypsies is also evidenced in some pseudo-psychological fears, which the police thinks gypsies show when they have been caught by the police. The most common such fears listed by the police are the fear of being left alone (for example in a cell), a greater than normal fear of pain, fear of dogs and darkness. Normal people, believes the police, also experience such fears but are able to overcome them, and only deviant individuals let themselves go. In their work on the beat the police acknowledges that it has been useful to utilise these special gypsy fears, for example on occasions when a confession to a crime is required: "If they are kept long enough alone in the cell, they confess anything"?

"Gypsies are workshy: their activities are without purpose"

The police attitude towards work emphasises the value of work in pursuit of goals. Work is seen as opposite of leisure and pleasure, not something one should enjoy or get satisfaction from. If work-like activities in themselves are thought to bring about pleasure, and are not only utilised as a means to an end, the police believe it to be deviant and therefore suspicious. People who enjoy their work, according to the police mix two concepts, work and pleasure, and therefore such activity does not deserve to be called work.

The gypsies who work in their traditional occupations, mainly connected with house-to-house trade, are not working in the real sense of the word, because they are not bound by regular working times nor by routine. Even more so, they cannot be working, officers insist, as work does not separate gypsies from their normal social milieus, from their families and family-life. According to the police, responsible attitude towards work is one of the corner stones of ordered society, and they are unanimous that gypsies fall far short in their attitudes towards work.

"Gypsies flout the social signs which are appropriate for their social status"

To understand one's appropriate social status and to stick to it, the police consider as one of the responsibilities of a decent citizen. Different social classes carry certain signs, indicators which are considered appropriate for their class. These could be a particular type of house in a particular neighbourhood, appropriate car, and so on. To deviate from these appropriate class labels in one direction or another is viewed with suspicion.

The gypsies to the police represent the lowest of the low in the Finnish social structure, and their external indicators should point to that place. If their class labels differ from those expected, the suspicions of the police are roused. Therefore the gypsies receive heavy criticism from the police about matters such as having new and tidy cars, instead of beaten-up wrecks as they should: "Even Mercedes!" Suspicion is also created by the fact that some gypsies may have sums of money in the bank, as their social situation would not warrant savings piling up. The gypsies are criticised by the police about having the nerve to sit in the best seats in horse races, as those are "reserved" for the better classes.

Police act on their beliefs

In all the gypsy culture and social organisation differ from everything which the police consider acceptable and worthy in our society. Therefore it is not particularly surprising that the police equate gypsy culture with criminal culture and gypsy social organisation with social organisation which has grown around and serves the needs of their criminal activities. The gypsies are the group of people in our Finnish society which above all "must be controlled", and in their everyday work the police have an armoury of special tactics how this is achieved. The often absurdly erroneous picture which the police have about gypsy culture and social organisation governs the police-gypsy interaction.

In their everyday work the police, according to their own statements (but more than amply confirmed by gypsy accounts of the same), utilise many tactics through which they are attempting to make their control of gypsies more effective. Most police officers acknowledge that the gypsy cars are stopped much more often than other cars: "We always stop the car if we see a gypsy driving". Also the licence plates come off more easily, for lesser traffic violations, than happens in the case of other Finns: "Sometimes we make a sport out of it." Also the police admit that the movements and gatherings of gypsies are being watched more closely than other people's: "When we see them together we are always wondering what they might be up to". The police believes that there is a good reason for their suspicion: "If they are not already doing something illegal, then they are at least planning to". In attending a gypsy matter the police admit that they use many more officers than they would in an equivalent non-gypsy one. In brief, the police believe that because the gypsies deviate so much from the norms of the host society, the majority Finnish one, the gypsies are not entitled to be treated equally with other citizens.

Although the police has always been the practical arm of the state which has been called to administer the prejudices of the state towards the gypsies, never before has the situation between the gypsies and the police been quite as problematic as it is today. Like the gypsies, the police in the earlier times - especially in the countryside - was part of the community, not loved by the gypsies but not hated either. With the rapid urbanisation and industrialisation the nature of the police forces and policing has changed, alongside industrial expansion and efficiency the police forces in Finland became a force of efficient and detached professionals (cf. WALSH 1977: 150). The local cop became the thing of the past and the bicycles became black cars, the gap between "ordinary" people and the police grew.

At the same time there was a great improvement in the level of education of the police officers, and the police officer with only the minimum primary education became the station museum piece. It may be that the better educational standards of the police improved their efficiency, but my investigation showed that it most certainly did not broaden their minds to accept other cultures alongside the Finnish one. One young, well-educated constable put it succintly when he was enquired whether he had had any education about gypsies at the police training school: "We had to read one book about them. I cannot remember anything else about it except that it was full of sentimental stuff, and that the gypsies should be understood."

An analysis of the responses by police officers about their attitudes towards the gypsies showed unequivocally that the best indicators of a thoroughly racist cop were young age and good education, the least hostile being those who were the oldest and had the least education (see GRÖNFORS 1981). With that in mind I shall lastly examine briefly the attitudes of the gypsies towards today's police officers, keeping in mind that most of those whom the gypsies are likely to meet in the streets are young newly-trained constables.

Gypsy attitudes towards the police

The gypsies have their own ideas about the Finnish society as a whole. The Finnish society represents all that which the gypsy society is not; it is dirty, immoral, unjust and violent. The police represent to the gypsies the culmination of those attitudes. The gypsies believe that their worst fears about the nature of the Finnish society are personified in the police force. The gypsies see the police as an occupational group whose main task is to disturb the otherwise reasonably peaceful existence of Finland's gypsies.

"The police does not think gypsies as human beings"

Most gypsies state their opinions about the police in rather strong words. The gypsies feel that the police does not treat them as equal with other people, and consider that in their attitudes and behaviour the police express an extreme loathing of gypsies. The police does not separate "good" or "bad" gypsies from each other on the basis of what they may have or may not have done. The gypsies are treated in their own opinion, en masse, the lowest of the low in this society.

Most gypsies have some very personal experiences to relate about the police, and usually those experiences are coloured with felt injustice. They include things like having been arrested without reason, being kept in the cells unnecessarily long, isolation, and so on. Many complain that the police does not allow gypsies to explain, nor are gypsies told the reason for their arrest. Gypsies also feel that when the trouble for which they have been arrested involves both Finns and gypsies, the police always automatically believes the Finns' version of the events, and never the gypsy one. Many gypsies have experienced unlawful acts of discrimination, for example when being refused entry to a restaurant. When the police is called the gypsies have been arrested for having caused a disturbance. The gypsies believe that the legal guarantees for the equality of treatment mean little in practice, and also that the way in which the police treats them is demeaning gypsies as human beings.

"The police is violent towards gypsies"

The gypsies expect the police act violently. However, the gypsies are not overly critical about the police violence as such, but criticise the police for using more violence towards gypsies than other people. All gypsies have examples to offer about police violence, either towards them or their kin. The violence which is directed towards women, old people and children is particularly condemned by the gypsies.

"The police creates situations where they can arrest gypsies"

The general experience of gypsies is that any contact with the police could potentially lead to an arrest, although no crime necessarily has been committed. Gypsies feel that their chances of defending themselves at the police stations and in the court are negligible. Also, gypsies feel that the police often provoke gypsies into situations, where they can be arrested. The gypsies cannot understand how their peaceful journey, according to their own definition, can be interrupted by the police, and the travellers be taken into the police station for fingerprints and photographs. Offering resistance in those situations leads to an offence of resisting the police. Any protests or appeal to equality and rights has been experienced to lead to further charges. Gypsies feel also that the police uses threateningly large numbers of police officers when they attend gypsy cases, creating situations where out of fright the gypsies could act violently. Being threatened by arms is felt to be something particularly distasteful and frightening to gypsies.

"The police is biased"

One of the most common complaints which the gypsies level at the police is the accusation of bias. The gypsies feel that they are targets of police action much more easily than other Finns. All tell experiences about police harassment on the roads, and some tell that they have been stopped four-five times during the course of one journey. The stopped cars are inspected more thoroughly than other people's cars, often stripped, and when they gather to chat at markets or in the streets the police usually comes and disperses the group. If there is a crime which has been commited in the neighbourhood where there are gypsies living, the police come first to the gypsies. The unequal treatment continues at the police station, where many gypsies have felt that their treatment is much worse than other people's. The relatives of those arrested complain that they are not notified about the arrest of their relative, but always hear from it from sources other than the police. Even in the case of the gypsy minors, when the law requires the guardians to be notified, the gypsies feel that the police do not carry out their legal obligations.

"However, not all the police are the same"

The gypsies do make a distinction between one police officer and the next. Most feel that the older constables are softer in their attitudes and behaviour than the young ones, although a few think the opposite too. Most have examples of individual polise officers whose behaviour actually receives praise from the gypsies. Some geographical areas are better than others, and so on.

A conclusion

Some of the problems which the Finnish gypsies especially in the urban areas have are experienced by some other people and groups also. However, the intensity of negative feelings directed at the gypsies is unsurpassed. They stand in opposition to all the values the Finnish society wants to uphold and defend. Of course there are other groups whose life-styles are condemned, such as the members of certain political and religious groups, or some youth subcultures. What then makes the gypsies a special group? One concrete demonstration of the displeasure of the dominant society is the organisation social control of perceived deviance. In order to be able to direct social control activities upon people, there must be a recognition which makes it possible to attach certain deviant acts or characteristics to a person. When the official control machinery uses its capacity to identify deviants from among the non-deviants, it resorts to institutional suspicion. The "normal" behaviour or people do not attract attention. The (often) stereotypical bases for suspicion are made official by the politics and legal processes of the country. The concrete practice of institutional suspicion is a mixture of official attitudes and individual justifications of the officials who have a power of labelling.

What I have attempted to show here is that the individual attitudes and stated behaviour of the police officers follows the more general attitudes of the majority Finnish people towards the gypsies. In addition, those are interpreted and realised by the officers themselves through their backgrounds and individual beliefs in their everyday policing practices. When there is a certain uniformity in the backgrounds, training and political views of the officers, individual attitudes and actions have certain collectivity in real life situations.

The gypsies, from their part, form an ideal group to whom the displeasure of the Finnish society and its law-enforcement agents can be channelled in that they are really the only "deviant" group which can readily be identified. By their physical features, their clothing and their visible expression of their culture they are on permant view in Finland. Their generally low and marginal position in the Finnish society means that whatever injustices there are in their treatment, those go without any or little public attention. This visibility has a number of consequences, both to the gypsies themselves and to the agents of social control.

Consequences to the gypsies

The gypsies are viewed as a group, related to as a group, acted upon as a group. Whatever individual variations there are in behaviour, those are not noticed. The gypsies are perceived to have a collective existence, they are collectively a criminal group. From the point of view of the majority society and its law enforcement, when gypsies are seen as a group, it in practice means that establishing the guilt of the individual gypsy is not particularly important as long as somebody from the group is brought to meet the charges. Hence all gypsies are potential suspects. The justice is frequently not done, but more often it is seen to have done.

The gypsy visibility enables control tactics, which in practice means that the gypsies are controlled more than are other Finnish people. In terms of equality this means that the gypsies have measures applied to them which are not applied to other people. They are more registered than other people, and so on. This would also make possible some mis-carriage of justice in that a presumed guilt in an unequal situation could predistine the definition of some situations against the gypsies. They are judged to be guilty before they are even tried. There are numerous examples of the gypsies being the only people arrested in a situation of conflict with the white population, although the gypsies may have only defended themselves (MÄKINEN, 1984). Similar situations have occurred when gypsies have attempted to defend their rights under the Race Relation Act of 1971 and have themselves become the guilty party, being accussed of causing a disturbance. Their everyday pursuits are hampered, when they are for example stopped after being identified as gypsies (not as criminals or road code violators) on the roads, when they are picked to be searched by the customs officers, and so on. They have fewer chances of escaping official attention than other Finns even when a crime has been committed.

Through action, prompted by beliefs about gypsies and their culture, the agents of control continuously receive confirmation for their beliefs about the deviant nature of the gypsy culture. This leads to a sort of self-fulfilling prophecy, where prejudiced and erronious beliefs become confirmed and reinforced at the everyday level of social control.

Consequences to the police

While attention is directed to those elements of the society which seem the furthest away from the ideas of normality of the police officers themselves, the police get into the pattern of operations which focusses attention primarily at only certain sections of the society. Those sections, such as the gypsies, tend to be the sections which are the least able to defend themselves. The idea of what is and what is not a crime, who is and who is not a criminal, become institutionalised, they become typifications. Society and its police do not react so much to actions, but become proactive and coercive. There is only a short step from excessive policing of gypsies into politically-motivated policing.

References

Bowden, Tom., 1978. Beyond the limits of the law. A comparative study of the police in crisis politics. Harmondsworth, Penguin.

Chappell, D. and Wilson, P. R., 1969: The police and the public in Australia and New Zealand. University of Queensland Press.

Grönfors, Martti, 1977: Blood feuding among Finnish gypsies. University of Helsinki Dept. of Sociology Research Reports, No. 213.

—   1979: Ethnic minorities and deviance: The relationship between Finnish gypsies and the police. University of Helsinki, Sociology of Law Series, No. 1.

—   1981: "Police perception of social problems and clients". International Journal of the Sociology of Law, 9.

Mäkinen, Tuija, 1984: Mustalaisten kohtelusta (The treatment of gypsies). Oikeuspoliittinen tutkimuslaitos, Helsinki.

Address of the Author:
Martti Grönfors
Lastenkodinkatu 2F3
00180 Helsinki, Finland

Visible Ethnic Minorities in Ontario and Toronto

Robert G. Sharpe

Abstract: Immigration into Canada between 1971 and 1981 has had a profound impact on the ethnic composition of Ontario and Metropolitan Toronto. To examine the recent influx of visible ethnic minorities requires an approach different from traditional models of assimilation and spatial integration intended to explain the situation of European ethnic minorities. An alternate view is that the spatial distribution and socio-economic conditions of visible ethnic minorities are related to their subordinate positions in a segmented or dual labour market. Using the 1981 Census of Canada, this paper examines the position of Chinese, Indo-Chinese, Indo-Pakistani, West Indian, and Native Peoples in the labour market of Metropolitan Toronto. In comparison to the British majority, only the most recent immigrant group, the Indo-Chinese, are distinctly over-represented in low-paying occupations and concentrated in the city centre. In contrast the Chinese are found in two separate labour markets: a majority who remain concentrated in low-paying occupations in the city centre; and a smaller group of more recent immigrants with managerial, well-paying occupations in the suburbs. The Indo-Pakistani, West Indian, and Native People groups exhibit higher concentrations in the suburbs but are over-represented in low-paying occupations. In general terms the position of visible ethnic minorities in Toronto reflects their status on entering the labour market.

Résumé: L'immigration au Canada entre 1971 et 1981 a eu un impact considérable sur la composition ethnique de l'Ontario et du Toronto métropolitain. L'étude de la récente affluence de ces minorités ethniques visibles requiert une approche différente des modèles traditionnels d'assimilation et d'intégration spatiale européens. Un modèle alternatif explique la distribution spatiale et les conditions socio-économiques des minorités ethniques visibles soient reliées à leurs emplois de subordonnés à l'intérieur d'un marché du travail segmenté et dédoublé (dual). Utilisant les données du recensement canadien de 1981, cet article examine la situation socio-économique des chinois, indochinois, indopakistanais, indiens de l'ouest et autochtones sur le marché du travail de la région métropolitaine de Toronto. Par rapport à la majorité britannique, seul le plus récent groupe d'immigrants, les indochinois, sont distinctement sur-représentés dans les emplois peu rémunérés et concentrés au centre-ville. Les chinois, quant à eux, se retrouvent dans 2 segments distincts du marché du travail: la majorité est concentrée dans des emplois peu rémunérés et vit au centre-ville; et un petit groupe récemment immigré, occupe des fonctions de cadres et habite en banlieue. Les indopakistanais, les indiens de l'ouest et les autochtones pour leur part, sont concentrés dans les banlieues mais sont toutefois sur-représentés dans des emplois peu rémunérés. De façon générale, la situation matérielle des minorités ethniques visibles à Toronto reflète leur statut à leur entrée sur le marché du travail.

Zusammenfassung: Die Einwanderungen nach Kanada zwischen 1971 und 1981 haben einen tiefgehenden Einfluß auf die ethnischen Strukturen Ontarios und Torontos gehabt. Die jüngsten Zuwanderungen von sog. "sichtbaren Minderheiten" verlangen einen anderen Arbeitsansatz im Vergleich zu traditionellen Modellvorstellungen über Assimilation und räumliche Integration, die für die Erklärung der Stellung ethnischer Minderheiten europäischer Herkunft verwendet wurden. Eine alternative Sichtweise ist, daß die räumliche Verteilung und die sozio-ökonomischen Bedingungen sichtbarer ethnischer Minderheiten im Zusammenhang stehen mit ihren untergeordneten Stellungen in einem differenzierten Arbeitsmarkt. Unter diesen Gesichtspunkten werden, auf der Basis der Volkszählung von 1981, Chinesen, Indo-Chinesen, Indo-Pakistani, West-Inder und die Urbevölkerung in ihrer Arbeitswelt im Großraum Toronto beleuchtet. Im Vergleich zu der britischen Mehrheit ist lediglich die jüngste Immigrantengruppe, die Indo-Chinesen, deutlich in den niedrigen Einkommensgruppen überrepräsentiert und räumlich im Stadtzentrum konzentriert. Die Chinesen finden sich demgegenüber in zwei unterschiedlichen Positionen des Arbeitsmarktes: eine Mehrheit verbleibt ebenfalls in niedrigen Einkommensgruppen und im Stadtzentrum, gegenüber einer kleinen Gruppe, die in gut bezahlten Führungspositionen am Rande der Stadt lebt. Indo-Pakistani, West Inder und Urbevölkerung sind jeweils stärker in den Stadtrandbezirken vertreten und gehören überwiegend zu den niedrigeren Einkommensgruppen. Die Stellung der sichtbaren Minderheiten Torontos kann, ganz allgemein, am Grad ihrer Integration in den Arbeitsmarkt bewertet werden.

Introduction*

Immigration during the decade 1971-81 has had a profound impact on the ethnic composition of the population in Ontario and Toronto. One consequence of the increasing visibility of non-white minorities has been a growing awareness of racial inequalities in the Canadian labour market. The purpose of this paper is to describe the spatial pattern of inequalities between Toronto's visible minority and British populations in terms of several labour force characteristics. First, a theoretical perspective is outlined which links a group's distribution to the structure of the urban labour market. Second, the spatial distribution and associated socio-economic conditions of visible ethnic minorities in the Metropolitan Toronto labour market are described through an exploratory analysis of the 1981 Census of Canada.

Theoretical Background

Canadian studies of ethnic minorities have been dominated by an assimilationist perspective. This perspective is based on the human ecological model of ethnic integration (Park, 1950) which hypothesizes a race relations cycle of "contact, competition, accomodation and eventual assimilation" (150). In geographic terms, according to the Burgess model of urban growth, immigrants are expected to diffuse outwards from their initial reception areas as they become socio-economically integrated into the larger social structure (Burgess, 1967). The extent to which non-white minorities have become spatially integrated into the British ethnic majority of Canada is not clear from past studies. Although both Asian and Black populations have tended to expand outwards toward the suburbs there remain distinct patterns of residential concentration and segregation (Balakrishnan, 1976, 1982; Kalbach, 1980). Where patterns of spatial integration do occur they are often only weakly associated with an improvement in socio-economic conditions (Hecht, Sharpe, Wong, 1983). Nevertheless, the assimilation of non-white minorities into the mainstream, assumed to be inevitable, is understood to be somewhat slower than among the European ethnic minorities.

A growing literature by non-white academics questions the relevance of assimilation models to the situation of non-white minorities in Canada (Basran, 1983; Bolaria, 1983). They argue that assimilation perspectives may be accurate in explaining the integration of European ethnic minorities into North American society but do not account for the disadvantages experienced by non-white minorities. European ethnic minorities face fewer constraints to integration because the boundaries between minority and majority are 'soft' and negotiable, whereas the boundaries between visibly distinct groups (such as those defined by skin colour) are more rigid and permanent over time. Consequently, some theorists hypothesize that "racial cleavages tend to merge into class differences ..." (Grove, 1984: 320-321). In other words that non-white immigrants become trapped in subordinate positions in a labour market segmented by socio-economic class.

According to models of labour market segmentation (including for example the concept of dual labour markets) the occupational mobility of racial minorities is constrained by discrimination which forces them to concentrate in a 'secondary' sector characterized by low pay, short-term employment, poor working conditions, and above all little chance for advancement. In contrast the 'primary' sector, which

* The data on which this paper is based was collected under the research project "Ethnicity in Central Canada" supported by the Volkswagen Foundation. I would like to express my thanks to Dr. Alfred Hecht for his encouragement and suggestions.

offers jobs with high wages, good working conditions, employment stability, and chances for advancement, is restricted to the dominant racial group (Cooke, 1983; Gordon, Edwards & Reich, 1982).

In a geographic context, the occupation structure of a split labour force is linked to the spatial structure of the urban labour market. Job openings in the secondary sector are filled from a highly localized labour market, whereas the primary sector draws on a more spatially extensive population who are highly mobile. As a result there is a general association between the secondary labour market and the deteriorating inner-city areas of large cities. This is particularly evident in the United States where the secondary sector accurately portrays the condition of the black urban ghetto labour markets (Piore, 1971). In contrast workers in the primary sector have greater mobility and tend to disperse across the more desirable suburbs (Bramley, 1971).

Initially the dual labour market model was proposed to explain the persistently low status of blacks in the United States. In Canada there has been much less tendency to apply models based on inter-racial competition to a society thought of as multicultural. Until recently it was generally understood that Canadian society did not have a history of institutional racism so that attitudes of racial discrimination were not entrenched. Furthermore, the initial evidence of socio-economic stratification suggested that most non-white immigrants were highly selected in terms of education and other skills and therefore more likely to achieve high status.

Models of the segmented labour market have become more attractive in light of recent evidence of racial discrimination and inequality in Canada. Mounting evidence confirms that non-white immigrant groups earn less than expected given their education and skills. Moreover recent studies of racial discrimination in Canada (Canada, 1984) and Metropolitan Toronto (Henry & Ginzberg, 1985) have shown that Blacks and Asians suffer considerable discrimination in the labour market. Therefore it is now instructive to examine the socio-economic conditions of visible minority groups in the Toronto labour market and to speculate on how these conditions are linked to the spatial structure of that labour market.

Unfortunately the Census of Canada does not provide sufficiently detailed data for a rigourous test of the model of segmented and spatially differentiated labour markets in Canada. Nevertheless, the concepts suggest a tentative framework for the empirical analysis in the next section.

II. Visible Minorities in Ontario

The analysis now proceeds to an aggregate statistical study of the distribution of visible minorities in Ontario, and in the core labour market of the Census Metropolitan Area of Toronto. Five non-white groups are examined in this paper: Chinese, Indo-Chinese, Indo-Pakistanis, West Indians, and for comparative purposes the Native Peoples. It is important to note that these categories are census aggregations of single responses to the question on ethnic origin and hence do not portray socially cohesive ethnic collectivities. In fact, within these categories there are considerable differences in birthplace, language, and religion. Despite these differences individuals within a category generally share similar physical features and consequently share a similar ascription from the dominant society. Together the five categories constitute the large majority of peoples known as visible minorities in Canada. In this paper the terms 'non-white' and 'visible ethnic' are used interchangeably.

In 1981, Canada's highest concentrations of each of the five visible minorities were located in Ontario, with the exception of the Indo-Chinese who were more prevalent in Quebec. Table 1 illustrates the extraordinary growth of the visible minority population in Ontario between 1971 and 1981. Such rapid expansion of non-traditional immigrant groups is a direct result of relaxation in federal immigration policy in 1967 combined with the introduction of a selection procedure designed to meet the needs of an expanding labour force. Although the total provincial population expanded by close to 11%, the British declined by almost 2% for the first time in Ontario's history. In total the five visible minority groups constitute 4.4% of the provincial population compared to about 2.4% in 1971.

Table 1:   Population Changes Among Ontario's Visible Minority Groups, 1971-81

COUNTY		TOTAL	BRITISH	CHINESE	INDO-CHINESE *	INDO-PAKISTANI	WEST INDIAN	NATIVE PEOPLES
ONTARIO	1971	7703105	4576010	39320		30920	19560	62420
	1981	8534260	4487800	118635	12815	93995	65140	83855
% of 1981 Total			52.6%	1.4%	0.2%	1.1%	0.8%	1.0%
	% CHANGE	10.8%	-1.9%	201.7%		204.0%	233.0%	34.3%
TORONTO - METRO	1971	1800315	1111620	25055		18175	14520	5995
	1981	2120245	912765	77705	4445	52390	43715	9060
	% CHANGE	17.8%	-17.9%	210.1%		188.3%	201.1%	51.1%
OTTAWA-CARELTON	1971	471930	264950	2910		2060	665	1030
	1981	542095	263850	8065	1940	5755	1775	1640
	% CHANGE	14.9%	-0.4%	177.2%		179.4%	166.9%	59.2%
WATERLOO	1971	254035	125385	570		885	505	395
	1981	302700	136655	1735	775	3090	1440	735
	% CHANGE	19.2%	9.0%	204.4%		249.2%	185.2%	86.1%
KENORA	1971	53230	20765	95		45	20	11180
	1981	59030	20275	215	20	60	5	15415
	% CHANGE	10.9%	-2.4%	126.3%		33.3%	-75.0%	37.9%
COCHRANE	1971	95835	27470	415		105	0	3500
	1981	96105	23730	300	40	170	5	5845
	% CHANGE	0.3%	-13.6%	-27.7%		61.9%		67.0%

*   1971 data not available for this category

Source: 1971 and 1981 Census of Canada, custom tabulations

When the spatial distribution of the visible minority population is examined it is clear that the greatest growth has occurred in the expanding labour markets of the southern Ontario core (for example, Metropolitan Toronto, Ottawa-Carleton, Waterloo). In contrast the more remote, peripheral counties of northern Ontario exhibit a much smaller growth, or even a loss of visible minorities (for example, Kenora, Cochrane).

III. Visible Ethnic Minorities in the Toronto Labour Market

In order to study the distribution of visible minorities throughout the local labour market of Toronto it is necessary to include the suburbs outside the Metropolitan boundaries. Unlike previous studies of ethnic integration in Metropolitan Toronto which use census tract data, it is appropoiate at this expanded geographic scale to use larger spatial units, namely census subdivisions. Figure 1 shows the

Figure 1: Toronto Census Metropolitan Area

Figure 2: Toronto Census Metropolitan Area Labour market zones

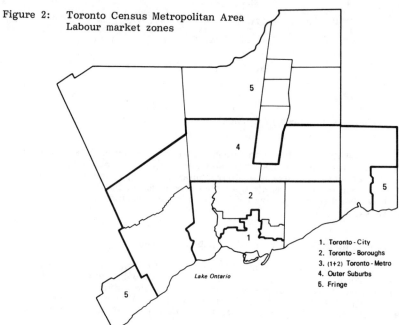

1. Toronto - City
2. Toronto - Boroughs
3. (1+2) Toronto - Metro
4. Outer Suburbs
5. Fringe

twenty census subdivisions that make up the Census Metropolitan Area (CMA), the main labour market area or commutershed of Metropolitan Toronto.

Visible minorities make up almost 8% of the Toronto CMA total population, the largest group being the Chinese followed by the Indo-Pakistani, West Indian, Native People, and Indo-Chinese groups. Although at least 75% of each group reside within the metropolitan boundaries, the surrounding outer suburbs and fringe include a notable proportion of Toronto's non-white labour force. Each visible minority group tends to cluster or concentrate within particular census subdivisions. Notable concentrations of the Chinese are located in the City of Toronto, and in suburban areas of Scarborough and Markham. The Indo-Pakistani group also exhibits two concentrations: the suburbs of Scarborough, East York, and North York; and the outer suburbs of Mississauga and Brampton. Heavy concentrations of the Indo-Chinese are found in the City of Toronto and in York, although there is a notable outlying cluster in Whitchurch-Stouffville. West Indians are located primarily in York and Scarborough whereas the Native Peoples are concentrated in the City of Toronto and York.

Rather than further analyzing these patterns in terms of residential segregation, the intention here is to link group distributions to a more generalized spatial structure within the labour market delimited by the Toronto CMA. For descriptive purposes the Toronto CMA can be divided into three broad zones arranged in concentric tiers around the City of Toronto. These zones, illustrated in Figure 2, correspond roughly to variations in the levels and types of employment opportunities and the intensity and type of residential development. Also, they closely resemble variations in average industrial earnings documented in a study of the Toronto labour market in 1971 (Scott, 1981).

Although such labour market zones lack internal homogeneity, each poses a different set of opportunities and constraints for the non-white immigrant. The City of Toronto has historically attracted most new immigrants because it has met their needs for low cost, primarily rental housing, and proximity to entrance status employment opportunities. More recently employment opportunities in the city have declined overall while the type of labour in demand requires more skills and training. The continuing decentralization of industry and intensive suburban development have increased opportunities for new immigrants and minorities in the zone of metropolitan boroughs. It is the burgeoning outer suburbs and to a lesser extent the smaller dormitory communities and rural estates of the fringe which remain the privilege of those with higher status occupations and greater mobility.

Visible minority groups occupy a variety of positions across all four zones of the labour market area. Table 2 indicates that half of the British reference group is concentrated in the metropolitan boroughs. This distribution has been shifting outwards as their numbers declined between 1971 and 1981 in every zone except the outer suburbs. Half of the Chinese group is also concentrated in the metropolitan boroughs, although a notable 36% is located in the City of Toronto. A large component of the Chinese population, almost 12%, has been growing outside Metropolitan Toronto in the most desirable outer suburbs. Of all the visible minority groups the Indo-Chinese are the most heavily concentrated in the City of Toronto with their numbers dropping dramatically towards the outer zones. The distributions of Indo-Pakistanis and West Indians are similar to one another with relatively small concentrations in the City of Toronto and over 62% in the metropolitan boroughs. In addition both groups have substantial and growing populations in the outer suburbs. Over 25% in the Native Peoples are located in the City of Toronto, another 52% reside in the surrounding metropolitan boroughs, while the remainder constitute a growing group in the outer suburbs. Overall there is considerable variation both within and between the distributions of the five visible minority groups.

Table 2: Distribution and Changes Among Toronto's Visible Minority Groups, 1971-81

AREA		TOTAL	BRITISH	CHINESE*	INDO-CHINESE*	INDO-PAKISTANI*	WEST INDIAN*	NATIVE PEOPLES
ONTARIO	1981	8534260	4487800	118635	12815	93995	65140	83855
	% change 1971-81	10.8%	-1.9%	201.7%		204.0%	233.0%	34.3%
TORONTO - CMA	1981	2966260	1383545	89520	5270	69700	54875	11375
	% change 1971-81	14.2%	-6.0%	238.1%		242.4%	249.0%	64.1%
TORONTO - METRO	1981	2120245	912765	77705	4445	52390	43715	9060
	% of group	71.5%	66.0%	86.8%	84.4%	75.2%	79.7%	79.7%
	% change 1971-81	17.8%	-17.9%	210.1%		188.3%	201.1%	51.1%
TORONTO - CITY	1981	592625	233635	32390	2915	8635	8145	3145
	% of group	20.0%	16.9%	36.2%	55.3%	12.4%	14.8%	27.7%
	% change 1971-81	-18.4%	-29.7%					-0.8%
METRO - BOROUGHS	1981	1527615	679120	45310	1535	43755	35580	5920
	% of group	51.5%	49.1%	50.6%	29.1%	62.8%	64.8%	52.0%
	% change 1971-81	42.2%	-12.9%					109.6%
OUTER SUBURBS	1981	605695	317480	10500	580	16110	10240	1990
	% of group	20.4%	23.0%	11.7%	11.0%	23.1%	18.7%	17.5%
	% change 1971-81	-2.1%	37.5%					272.0%
FRINGE	1981	164990	107770	565	155	535	685	255
	% of group	5.6%	7.8%	0.6%	2.9%	0.8%	1.3%	2.4%
	% change 1971-81	-7.2%	-16.7%					-36.3%

Source: 1971 and 1981 Census of Canada, custom tabulations

IV. Labour Force Characteristics

This paper's primary contention is that the location of a visible minority group depends a great deal on the opportunities and constraints faced by individuals in the labour market. A comparison is now made of 1981 labour force characteristics across the four zones of the Toronto labour market.

Table 3 summarizes two characteristics of labour force activity: a) rates of unemployment; and b) the percentage of individuals not participating in the labour force. Overall unemployment is higher among the visible minorities than the dominant British group. Having the highest unemployment rates, Indo-Chinese, West Indians and Indo-Pakistanis seem to be the most disadvantaged in the labour force. For the majority, unemployment rates decline in outer zones except in the Indo-Chinese and Native People groups. This may reflect that employment opportunities for these two groups are localized in the City and not the suburbs.

Table 3: Distribution of Visible Minority Groups Across Toronto CMA, 1981 by Labour Force Activity

a) % UNEMPLOYED

AREA	TOTAL	BRITISH	CHINESE	INDO-CHINESE	INDO-PAKISTANI	WEST INDIAN	NATIVE PEOPLES
TORONTO - CMA	3.6%	3.2%	3.6%	6.6%	5.0%	5.2%	4.4%
TORONTO - CITY	4.0%	3.7%	4.4%	6.1%	5.9%	7.2%	2.3%
METRO - BOROUGHS	3.6%	3.4%	3.4%	7.5%	4.9%	5.1%	4.3%
OUTER SUBURBS	3.0%	2.6%	3.2%	7.4%	4.7%	3.9%	6.6%
FRINGE	2.5%	3.1%	0.0%	-	0.0%	0.0%	-

b) % NOT IN LABOUR FORCE

AREA	TOTAL	BRITISH	CHINESE	INDO-CHINESE	INDO-PAKISTANI	WEST INDIAN	NATIVE PEOPLES
TORONTO - CMA	29.7%	32.4%	30.2%	26.2%	23.3%	21.7%	24.0%
TORONTO - CITY	32.5%	34.3%	33.9%	28.5%	22.4%	24.8%	22.8%
METRO - BOROUGHS	30.3%	34.7%	28.1%	18.3%	23.4%	21.2%	26.0%
OUTER SUBURBS	24.3%	25.9%	27.1%	20.0%	22.8%	20.6%	16.5%
FRINGE	28.3%	29.9%	28.6%	100.0%	31.8%	93.6%	-

\- very small population in this category

Source: 1981 Census of Canada, custom tabulations

A group's participation in the labour force gives some indication of their dependency on the labour market for earning an income. The British reference group has the lowest participation rates suggesting that a larger proportion of this group is not dependent on incomes from employment. In contrast the five visible minority groups have a higher proportion of individuals who are dependent on labour force activity.

The concept of a segmented labour force in the Toronto CMA is illustrated most vividly by the distribution of visible minority groups across selected occupation categories. Table 4 shows that the British reference group is the most highly concentrated in managerial occupations and the least concentrated in service and product fabricating occupations. In contrast all the visible minority groups show the converse, being heavily over-represented in service and product fabricating occupations. It is also evident that some visible minority groups are specialized within particular occupations which reflect their entrance status as immigrants. For example most of the Indo-Pakistanis entering Canada have been highly educated with professional skills suited to managerial occupations. In contrast the majority of Indo-Chinese entered Canada as refugees and brought skills less closely matched to

Table 4: Distribution of Visible Minority Groups Across Toronto CMA, 1981 by Selected Occupation Groups

AREA	TOTAL	BRITISH	CHINESE	INDO-CHINESE	INDO-PAKISTANI	WEST INDIAN	NATIVE PEOPLES
TORONTO - CMA							
% managerial	11.7%	13.8%	9.2%	0.0%	9.2%	4.8%	5.1%
% service	9.9%	8.3%	15.7%	10.7%	6.3%	12.1%	10.3%
% product fabric.	9.1%	6.5%	13.5%	28.7%	14.9%	13.5%	12.0%
TORONTO - CITY							
% managerial	11.4%	15.3%	5.6%	0.0%	7.7%	5.0%	7.7%
% service	13.5%	9.7%	24.8%	14.5%	10.0%	20.1%	17.2%
% product fabric.	8.0%	3.6%	18.8%	33.1%	15.2%	11.0%	11.9%
METRO - BOROUGHS							
% managerial	10.7%	12.6%	10.5%	0.0%	9.4%	4.4%	4.9%
% service	9.5%	8.2%	11.8%	0.0%	6.4%	11.6%	8.3%
% product fabric.	9.4%	6.6%	11.3%	25.8%	14.4%	14.0%	11.9%
OUTER SUBURBS							
% managerial	13.5%	15.0%	14.4%	0.0%	9.4%	6.7%	3.0%
% service	7.7%	7.2%	6.4%	17.0%	4.1%	8.1%	8.0%
% product fabric.	9.6%	7.8%	9.0%	17.0%	16.7%	15.2%	13.6%
FRINGE							
% managerial	12.5%	12.7%	0.0%	–	0.0%	–	0.0%
% service	9.2%	9.1%	0.0%	–	0.0%	–	0.0%
% product fabric.	8.7%	8.3%	0.0%	–	0.0%	–	0.0%

– very small population in this category

Source: 1981 Census of Canada, custom tabulations

the demands of the labour market. As a result this group has been less competitive in the labour market and thus become concentrated in lower status occupations.

The structure of occupation segmentation is accentuated over space. In the City of Toronto over 15% of the British labour force is found in managerial occupations while all visible minority groups are heavily concentrated in the secondary labour market. Furthermore the occupation breakdown within visible minority groups varies considerably outside the City of Toronto. This variation is most striking in the Chinese group where the population can be divided into two distinct labour forces: a concentration of those in the secondary occupations of the City of Toronto; and a second concentration of those in managerial occupations residing in the outer suburbs.

Indicators of socio-economic well-being also substantiate the notion of a segmented labour market in the Toronto CMA. Table 5 portrays the general pattern of spatial variation in levels of socio-economic well-being using two indicators: a) the ratio of high employment income to low employment income; and b) the percentage of a group owning their place residence.

Table 5: Distribution of Visible Minority Groups Across Toronto CMA, 1981 by Employment Income and Home Ownership

a) Ratio of High Income/Low Income

AREA	TOTAL	BRITISH	CHINESE	INDO-CHINESE	INDO-PAKISTANI	WEST INDIAN	NATIVE PEOPLES
TORONTO - CMA	1.22	1.44	0.79	0.04	1.02	0.61	0.41
TORONTO - CITY	1.01	1.42	0.29	0.07	0.47	0.23	0.36
METRO - BOROUGHS	1.13	1.33	1.00	LOW	0.93	0.56	0.29
OUTER SUBURBS	1.59	1.63	2.37	LOW	1.57	1.24	0.85
FRINGE	1.42	1.54	1.13	0.00	4.40	HIGH	0.00

high inc. = employment income $21,670 and over.   LOW = all in low income category
low inc. = employment income 0 - $4,333   HIGH = all in high income category

b) % of Households Owning Homes

AREA	TOTAL	BRITISH	CHINESE	INDO-CHINESE	INDO-PAKISTANI	WEST INDIAN	NATIVE PEOPLES
TORONTO - CMA	56.4%	52.6%	63.7%	10.8%	49.5%	35.9%	22.1%
TORONTO - CITY	40.7%	35.0%	45.6%	3.7%	31.4%	23.2%	13.2%
METRO - BOROUGHS	55.6%	50.2%	71.4%	18.1%	45.9%	29.6%	20.1%
OUTER SUBURBS	71.1%	66.9%	86.4%	25.9%	72.8%	74.5%	48.0%
FRINGE	78.4%	76.7%	76.9%	25.0%	78.8%	88.2%	25.0%

Source: 1981 Census of Canada, custom tabulations

As expected in the British reference population there are more individuals earning high incomes than low incomes. In contrast low income earners dominate the visible minority population except amongst the Indo-Pakistanis. Spatial variations in the income ratios reveal that all visible minority groups have a much higher proportion of low income earners in the City of Toronto than do the British. These income ratios rise dramatically in the zones surrounding the City, whereas income ratios in the British population remain relatively constant across the Toronto CMA.

Home ownership provides a different measure of socio-economic well-being reflecting the accumulation of wealth, and constraints faced within the housing market. A higher percentage of Chinese own homes than all other groups including the British. This may reflect an adjustment strategy of the Chinese to counteract barriers to occupation and income mobility through property ownership. In comparison to the British a similar percentage of Indo-Pakistanis own homes, while home ownership is less common in the West Indian, Native Peoples, and Indo-Chinese groups. In every group the spatial pattern of home ownership closely resembles the residential structure of the Toronto CMA with the percentage of owned homes increasing in zones that are more distant from the City of Toronto. Hence, a majority of those residing in the outer suburbs and fringe own their homes with the exception of the Indo-Chinese and Native Peoples groups.

Together the indicators of income and home ownership reveal several important associations. First, most Chinese, Indo-Pakistanis, and West Indians in the outer suburbs have high levels of home ownership and exhibit very high employment income ratios. Second, where relatively high levels of home ownership coincide with low incomes it is probable that the homes purchased are of lower value. This is evident in the large concentration of Chinese in the City of Toronto and in the majority of West Indians who are concentrated in the metropolitan boroughs.

V. Conclusions

The limited evidence analyzed in this paper supports the contention that the labour market of the Toronto CMA is stratified and spatially differentiated. Overall, visible minority groups in this labour market are characterized by a socio-economic and occupational status which is much lower than that of the dominant British population. However, there is great variation within the visible minority population as each group has a characteristic spatial distribution that reflects its particular mix of occupational skills.

In comparison to the British, all visible minority groups have a larger percentage of individuals with low-status occupations and low incomes who are concentrated in the City of Toronto and the metropolitan boroughs. It might be argued, using more appropriate data, that these populations are constrained to a secondary labour market which is spatially limited. However the concept of labour market segmentation is less relevant to the visible minority population as a whole. A small but notable percentage of the visible minority population has high-status occupations, earns good incomes, and owns homes in the desirable suburbs outside of the boundaries of Metropolitan Toronto. This does not imply an absence of socio-economic inequality nor an absence of discrimination, but reflects that the members of visible minority groups face different constraints in the Toronto labour market.

Bibliography

Balakrishnan, T. R., 1976: "Ethnic Residential Segregation in Metropolitan Areas of Canada". Canadian Journal of Sociology, vol. 1 no. 4, pp. 481-510.

— 1982: "Changing Patterns of Ethnic Residential Segregation in Metropolitan Areas of Canada". Canadian Review of Sociology and Anthropology, vol. 19, no. 1, pp. 92-110.

Basran, Gurcharn, S., 1983: "Canadian Immigration Policy and Theories of Racism". In Racial Minorities in Multicultural Canada, pp. 3-14. Edited by Peter S. Li and B. Singh Bolaria. Toronto: Garamond Press.

Bolaria, B. Singh, 1983: "Dominant Perspectives and Non-White Minorities". In Racial Minorities in Multicultural Canada, pp. 157-169. Edited by Peter S. Li and B. Singh Bolaria. Toronto: Garamond Press.

Bramley, Glen, 1979: "The Inner City Labour Market". In Urban Deprivation and the Inner City, pp. 63-91. Edited by C. Jones. London: Croom Helm.

Burgess, Ernest, 1967: "The Growth of the City: An Introduction to a Research Report". In The City, pp. 47-62. Edited by Robert Park and Ernest Burgess. Chicago: University of Chicago Press.

Canada. Parliament, 1984: Equality Now. Report of the Special Committee on Visible Minorities in Canadian Society. Ottawa: Queen's Printer.

Cohn, Elchanan, C. Glyn Williams, and Richard M. Wallace with Janet C. Hunt, 1978: "Urban Labour Markets and Labour Force". In Selected Readings in Quantitative Urban Analysis, pp. 37-61. Edited by Samuel J. Bernstein and W. Giles Mellon. Toronto: Pergamon Press.

Cooke, Philip, 1983: "Labour Market Discontinuity and Spatial Development". Progress in Human Geography, vol. 7, no. 4, pp. 543-565.

Gordon, D. M., R. C. Edwards and M. Reich, 1982: Segmented Work, Divided Workers. Cambridge: Cambridge University Press.

Grove, John, 1974: "Differential Political and Economic Patterns of Ethnic and Race Relations: A Cross National Analysis". Race, vol. 5, no. 3, pp. 303-329.

Hecht, Alfred, Robert Sharpe and Amy C. Y. Wong, 1983: Ethnicity and Well-Being in Central Canada: The Case of Ontario and Toronto. Marburger Geographische Schriften, vol. 93.

Henry, Francis and Effie Ginzberg, 1985: Who Gets the Work: A Test of Racial Discrimination and Employment. Urban Alliance on Race Relations, Social Planning Council of Metropolitan Toronto. Toronto.

Jackson, Peter, and Susan J. Smith, eds., 1981: Social Interaction and Ethnic Segregation. Institute of British Geographers Special Publication, No. 12. Toronto: Academic Press.

Kalbach, Warren, E., 1980: Historical and Concentrational Perspectives of Ethnic Residential Segregation in Toronto, Canada. Research Paper No. 118, University of Toronto Press.

Park, Robert E., 1950: Race and Culture. Glencoe, Illinois: Free Press.

Piore, M. J., 1971: "The Dual Labor Market: Theory and Implications". In Problems in Political Economy: An Urban Perspective. Edited by D. M. Gordon. Lexington, Mass.: D. C. Heath & Co.

Ramcharan, Subhas, 1982: Racism: Nonwhites in Canada. Toronto: Butterworths.

Scott, Allen J., 1981: "The Spatial Structure of Metropolitan Labor Markets and the Theory of Intra-Urban Plant Location". Urban Geography, vol. 2, pp. 1-30.

Ujimoto, K. Victor, and Gordon Hirabayashi, eds., 1980: Visible Minorities and Multiculturalism: Asians in Canada. Toronto: Butterworths.

Address of the author:
Robert G. Sharpe
Dept. of Geography
York University
4700 Keele Street
Downsview Ontario
Canada M3J1P3

Visible Minorities in Canada:
Problems in the Investigation and Analysis of Non-White Immigrants

Roland Vogelsang

Abstract: This paper attemps to explain some of the main aspects of 'visible minorities' in Canada which have generated considerable attention as a result of recent immigration. First, the term 'visible minorities' is briefly discussed and it is pointed out that the term is a more and more used but nevertheless unsatisfactory description of what could more exactly be called 'nonwhite immigrants'. Second, specific problems in analysing this category of people are set forth. Difficulties arise because many distinguishable groups are often summarized as a residual category ('other', or n.o.s.') in statistics and comparable sources. It is demonstrated that the category 'other' is numerically growing in particular. On the other hand historical and current facts show that the numerical strength of a specific 'visible' ethnic group is only a rough clue but not as important a factor for its situation in Canadian society as is generally assumed. Third, similarities and differences of some non-white immigrant groups are worked out. In a comparative analysis the Chinese, the Japanese, the heterogenous East Indians, and the Philippinos in Canada are investigated as to their historical experiences, their present occupational and demographic characteristics, as well as their distribution and settlement patterns.

Résumé: Le phénomène des 'minorités visibles' suscite un intérêt accru en raison des récents mouvements d'immigration. Le présent exposé voudrait apporter des éclaircissements sur quelques uns des problèmes fondamentaux relatifs à ces groupes ethniques en prenant le Canada comme exemple. Le premier chapitre analyse le terme 'minorités visibles' et propose, malgré l'usage fréquent qui en est fait dans les ouvrages scientifiques, de le remplacer par un terme plus exact, celui d'immigrants non-blancs'. Le deuxième chapitre se penche sur quelques uns des problèmes spécifiques soulevés par l'étude de ces groupes. Une des principales difficultés vient du fait que plusieurs groupes différents n'apparaissent dans les statistiques que sous la rubrique commune: "autres". Or c'est cette catégorie d'immigrés qui s'est développée le plus rapidement au cours des 20 dernières années. D'ailleurs l'histoire et la situation actuelle nous enseignent que l'influence réelle d'un groupe donné ne se mesure pas à son importance numérique: celle-ci peut tout au plus servir d'indice et est loin de jouer le rôle d'un facteur aussi déterminant qu'on le croit généralement. Le troisième chapitre relève les ressemblances et les différences qu'il y a entre quelques uns des groupes d'immigrants non-blancs. Il se livre à une étude comparée de quelques groupes particuliers (Chinois, Japonais, Philippins, groupe hétérogène des immigrants venus de l'Inde) en esquissant leur histoire, leur situation sur le plan professionnel, leur structure démographique et leur répartition géographique.

Zusammenfassung: Die 'Visible Minorities' in Kanada verdienen aufgrund der jüngeren Einwanderung verstärkt Beachtung. Es wird versucht, zur Klärung einiger grundsätzlicher Probleme dieser Bevölkerungsgruppen beizutragen. Im ersten Abschnitt wird der Begriff 'Visible Minorities' diskutiert und herausgearbeitet, daß dieser Terminus in der Literatur häufig genutzt wird, aber dennoch unscharf und besser durch den Begriff 'nicht-weiße Einwanderer' zu ersetzen ist. Der zweite Abschnitt widmet sich spezifischen Problemen, die bei der Untersuchung dieser Gruppen auftauchen. Schwierigkeiten bestehen, da viele zu unterscheidende Gruppen nur zusammengefaßt als 'Sonstige' in statistischen Quellen erfaßt werden. Es wird dargelegt, daß diese irrelevante Kategorie in Kanada in den letzten zwanzig Jahren zahlenmäßig am stärksten gewachsen ist. Andererseits belegen die historische und die gegenwärtige Situation, daß die zahlenmäßige Größe einer speziellen, sichtbar unterscheidbaren ethnischen Gruppe lediglich ein grober Anhaltspunkt für deren Bedeutung ist und als Faktor für deren Beurteilung weniger wichtig ist als allgemein angenommen. Im dritten Abschnitt werden Ähnlichkeiten und Unterschiede einiger nicht-weißer Einwanderergruppen herausgestellt. Chinesen, Japaner, Philippinos und die heterogene Gruppe der Inder in Kanada werden kurz historisch, nach ihrer gegenwärtigen beruflichen und demographischen Struktur und ihrer räumlichen Verteilung analysiert.

INTRODUCTION

Over the last two decades, 'visible minorities' in Canada have attracted considerable attention, in public awareness and to some extent academic cirles. In general, this is not only a result of growing sensitivity toward problems of ethnic relations which were seen less problematic in the fifties, but is also a consequence of the increased number of 'visibles' which is by itself a result of a complex interaction of race-related policies, immigration strategies, and changes in the ethnic composition of Canada's population. Still in search for a unique Canadian Identity, the widely accepted idea of multiculturalism (although not without some criticism) raised specific questions regarding visible minorities. These minorities do not only have different cultural traditions but are as a visible group without choice because of racial aspects different from the majority. In this context, this paper attempts to discuss some selected problems of the 'visible minority'.

First, terminological problems are examined to promote a more accurate but nevertheless manegeable use applicable to the main ethnic categories. Second, specific methodological problems in analysing visible minority groups are set forth. It is argued that the frequently used residual category 'other' is dissatisfying. Third, as a consequence of this discussion, some differences and similarities of specific non-white immigrant groups are worked out to demonstrate the need for further differentation.

The Term 'visible minorities'

The meaning of the term seems to be clear. In connection with ethnic problems in Canada, North America, or in general, in countries with a society dominated by white people, the subordinated segment of a population with physical, or more precisely, selected phenotypical traits different from the majority may be called 'visible minority'. The term consistently refers to a racial unit but at the same time it implies an important sociological dimension since primarily not the biological or genetic differences, which may be identified by physical anthropologists, are essential but the perceived significance of a group and its potential implications as to prejudice and discrimination. In the last decade, the term under discussion has been used more frequently in North America and particularly in Canada. The reason for this seems to be that it does not show overtly the traditionally existing race-relationship. It is seemingly neutral and less emotionally incriminated. Therefore, it fits the officially proclaimed goal of conquering racism and ethnically motivated submission.

Inspite of its seemingly neutral connotation, the term 'visible minority' is not precise and therefore often misleading. In general use, of course, even white groups may be a subcategory of the 'visible minority', and thus in the North West Territories of Canada it seems logical to count all Non-Natives to the 'visible minority'. If we look at the socio-ethnic stratification of Canada, it is a question wether some ethnic groups from Southern or Eastern Europe, obviously different from the charter groups, should be included or not. In Canadian practice, however, there is a consensus that only non-whites belong to the visible minority group, but in reality it is not uniformly used as such. In the anthology on Visible Minorities, edited by UJIMOTO and HIRABAYASHI (1980), only papers on Asians in Canada are to be found. Similarly, in the chapter 'Visible Minorities' DAHLIES' and FERNANDO's 'Ethnicity, Power, and Policies in Canada' (1981) only problems of Asian groups are discussed. In other cases, however, e.g. Evelyn KALLEN (1982), ANDERSON and FRIDERES (1981) the term is used to denote all non-whites but excluding the Native Indians and Inuit who as aboriginals are considered as a special group. In contrast to this view, ADAIR and ROSENSTOCK (1979) in their study of adolescent dominant-group attitudes towards visible minorities, deal with Orientals, Asians, Blacks, and Native Peoples. Considering the ethnic situation we should shortly look at the currently used terminology and groupings of the Canadian population, as shown in Table 1. Many authors, directly or indirectly, use a concept that is based on four ethnic categories e.g. BERRY, KALIN and TAYLOR (1977), ELLIOTT (1983) or PINEO (1977) as well as PORTER (1965). These categories may be identified as:

1) Aboriginals or indigenous people
2) Anglo- and French Canadians or charter groups
3) Other European immigrants
4) Non-white immigrants

This paper will focus on the last category. Although and because the term 'non-white immigrant group' is definitely race-related in the original sens of the word and because it is historically adequate, it can be considered to be more precise than the term 'visible minorities' which is most often used instead.

Table 1:   Main Ethnic Categories as used for Canada

Author (Short Titel, Year of Publ.)		Main Ethnic Categories
ANDERSON/FRIDERES: Ethnicity Canada 1981		No Categorization
BERRY/KALIN/TAYLOR Multiculturalism, Ethn. Attitudes 1977	I II III IV	(indirect): charter groups Non-english/Non-french: elected Europeans Native People 'Others'
CLEMENT Canadian Corporate Elite 1975	I II III	Anglo-Canadien French-Canadien 'Third Ethnics'
DAHLIE/FERNANDO (Ed.s) Ethnicity, Power ... 1981	I II III IV	Pluralism and Power Protest and Radicalism Visible Minorities ... (Asians) Ethnic Origins, Prejudice ...
DRIEDGER (Ed.) Canadian Ethnic Mosaic 1978	I II III IV V	Ethnic Perspectives Ethnic Migration, Immigration Psychological Problems Identity: Native People Identity: Minorities (Mennonites, Jews, Italians)
ELLIOTT (Ed.) Minority Canadians (2 Vols.) 1971	A B I II III	Native People Immigrant Groups Religious Minorities Racial Minorities National Origin Minorities
ELLIOTT (Ed.) Two Nations, Many Cultures 1983 (2nd Ed.)	I II III IV	Native People French/(English) 'Others': a) European 'Others': b) Third World
KALBACH/MCVEY Demographic Basis Canad. Soc. 1979 (pp. 193 ff)	I II III IV	British French Other: a) Other European Other: b) Asiatic
KALLEN Ethnicity a. Human Right Canada 1982 (indirect: Chapter 3)	I II III	Charter Groups Aboriginal Peoples Others (Immigrants)

Table 1 continued:

KRAUTER/DAVIS
   Minority Canad. Ethn.
   Groups 1978
	I
	II
	III
	IV
	V
	VI
		European Immigrants (Excluding Brit. a. French)
		Canadian Indians
		Inuit
		Blacks
		Chinese and Japanese
		Other Asians

LENZ
   Region, Probleme I. Eth-
   nisch ... 1978
	I
	II
	III
	IV
	V
	VI
		British
		French
		Germans
		Other Europeans(
		Canadian Indian and Inuit
		Others

PINEO
   Social Standing Ethnic a.
   Racial Groupings 1977
	I
	II
	III
	IV
		Charter Groups
		Western and North European
		Mediterranean and Central Europe
		Non-Caucasian Groups

PORTER Vertical Mosaic 1965	I II III IV	Charter Groups Entrance Groups: North, Western Europe Entrance Groups: Later Immigrants: South, East Europe Aboriginals
UJIMOTO/HIRABAYASHI Visible Minorities ... 1980		Asians

STATISTICS CANADA
   Census 1961
   (Dominion Bureau of
   Statistics)
	I
	II
	III
	IV
	V
	VI
		British
		French
		Other European
		Asiatic (Chinese, Japanese, Other)
		Native Indians a. Eskimo
		Other a. n.s.

STATISTICS CANADA Census 1981	I II III IV V VI VII VIII IX X XI	British French German Italian Ukrainian Dutch Scandinavian Chinese Other Asiatics Native Peoples Other

Specific Problems

As a result of strong racial hostility and ever-increasing governmental restrictions on the entry of non-white groups, while encouraging whites at the same time, particularly those from Great Britain, the non-whites remained small minorities throughout the first half of this century. Only the Negroes, Chinese, and Japanese were counted separately at times. The policy of multiculturalism and the effort toward the legitimate acceptance of the individual ethnic groups are reflected in the more recent publications of Statistics Canada. The 1981 Census lists 83 different ethnic groups in corresponding publications. 41 of them are specified Europeans, including Byelorussians and Albanians with just more than 1,000 persons or those from Luxembourg with 730, whereas 104,700 are summarized as 'Other Indo-Pakistani'. The census is using subcategories of 'others', e.g. there are 5,500 'Other Europeans' but about 240,000 'Non-European others'. Quantitatively this indicates the enormous problems with which we are faced in analysing the non-white immigrants adequately.

Until recent years, however, most often the non-white immigrants have been categorized as 'others'. In practice, they are frequently included with the 'non stated' cases. This fact and the very small size of some groups which means that there have been many different ones, causes specific problems in analysing the non-white minorities. Though it is an extremely heterogenous category, more heterogenous than the Europeans, the ethnocentric view of the whites makes it obvious why they are seen in many cases as a residual category in official statistics and comparable Canadian sources.

Table 2: Total Population and Non-White Immigrants in Canada 1871-1981

Year	Total Population Number (1,000s)	Per Cent Increase	Non-White Immigrants[1] Number (1,000s)	Per Cent Increase	Per Cent of Total
1871[2]	3,522	–	30,957	–	0,87
1881	4,325	22.8	69,363	124.1	1.60
1901	5,371	24.2	72,852	5.0	0.09
1911	7,207	34.2	95,449	31.0	1.32
1921	8,788	21.9	105,641	10.7	1.20
1931	10,377	18.1	113,583	7.5	1.09
1941	11,507	10.9	138,266	21.7	1.20
1951	14,009	21.7	261,248	88,9	1,86
1961	18,238	30.2	364,262	39.4	1.99
1971	21,568	18.3	491,630	35.0	2.28
1981	24,083	11.7	1,057,660[3]	115.0	4.39

1) Other than European, Native and Inuit Origin
2) Includes British Columbia
3) Includes Caribbean and Haitian only of those from Latin America (single origin) as well as multiple origins other than European and Native

Sources: Dominion Bureau of Statistics/Statistics Canada: Census of Canada; WARD, 1978: 170

Table 2 demonstrates what has been, with the fore-mentioned exeptions, counted as 'others', and what could be called in our terminology 'non-white immigrants' (for supplementary figures cf. LACROIX'S paper in this volume). Until World War II they were a small group, still less than 2% of the total population in 1951. Since that time their number has grown considerably, much more than any other subgroup of our categories.

Today there are more than one million non-white immigrants in Canada or about 4.5% of the total population. Between 1961 and 1981 only, their number increased by 190%, and among the non-whites the different Asiatic groups are the most important numerically.

Whereas the 'Other Asiatics' together counted less than both the Chinese as well as the Japanese during earlier periods of Asiatic immigration to Canada, the proportions have changed since 1961. The considerable increase of Chinese is even surpassed by the 'Others' with a plus of about 95,000 or 276% between 1961 and 1971 and more than 235,000 or another 182% between 1971 and 1981.

Table 3: Population of Asiatic Origin in Canada 1951-1981

Year	Asiatic Total Number	Per Cent Increase	Chinese Number	Per Cent Increase	Japanese Number	Per Cent Increase	'Other Asiatic' Number	Per Cent Increase
1951	72,850	(-1.7)	32,550	(-6.1)	21,650	(-6.4)	18,650	(14.4)
1961	121,750	67	58,200	79	29,150	35	34,400	84
1971	285,550	135	118,800	104	37,250	28	129,450	276
1981	728,850[1]	155	289,250[2]	143	41,000[2]	10	398,600[1]	209

Numbers rounded;
1) Single and multiple origin, approximate
2) Single origin only

Source: Statistics Canada: Census 1951 to 1981

In this context it is worthwhile to point out two aspects. First, the absolute as well as the relative numbers of the non-whites as a whole or of specific ethnic groups in Canada are not as important for their specific situation in Canadian society as is generally assumed. If the size of an ethnic minority is not the single most important factor for the attention and the treatment they receive in the host society (even for white groups, as can be seen in the case of the Hutteries or Doukhobors) this fact holds true for the visible minorities in particular. This is to say that other factors such as racial or religious prejudices, degree of cohesion of the minority group, their cultural and ethnic distance towards the majority, attitudes of the dominant group towards the specific minority in the community, on the provincial or national level, the situation of the labour market, settlement patterns, and the frequency of actual contacts between the majority and the minority in question often are more consequential than the mere numerical strength, which is not more than a rough clue for their investigation.

The second aspect refers to time of immigration and length of stay in the country. Newcomers are often seen as strangers, and this applies in particular to 'visible strangers'. For that reason it is necessary to comment briefly on more recent immigration. Because there are no statistics on immigration by ethnic origin, the immigration by countries of last permanent residence have to be used instead as a makeshift source of information, though this is highly problematic. - As a result of the Immigration Acts of 1952 and 1966 and later amendments a remarkable shift in the immigration pattern has taken place (s. table 4).

In 1960 the leading source countries were all European and the United States, most of these immigrants being white. The new immigration of non-whites began to show in 1968, when Hong Kong placed fifth and moved to third place by 1973. In that year, three other countries which can be considered as non-white appeared in the list of the first nine: Jamaica, India and the Philippines. Most recently the people from South-Asian countries have been dominant. Only Britain and the United States hold an exceptional position, while the importance of Portugal has fallen off.

If we look at immigration by major world regions and compare the years 1968 and 1980, the summarized shift in the migration streams is impressive. (s. fig. 1). The European percentage decreased by more than half from 65% to roughly 30%, whereas immigration from Asia shows an increase from 9 to 50%. Actually, there are even more from the latter region, since about 1,200 persons born in South-Asia had their last residence in Britain and several hundred came through the United States; still others came by way of Africa, e.g. from Uganda.

The problem of some of the visible minority groups result from the relatively high percentage of foreign-born residents combined with the factor of 'strangeness' based on race.

Table 4: Immigration to Canada: Leading Countries of Last Permanent Residence

1960	1968	1973	1980
Italy	Britain	Britain	Vietnam
Britain	United St.	United St.	Britain
United St.	Italy	Hong Kong	United St.
Germany	Germany	Portugal	India
Netherlands	Hong Kong	Jamaica	Hong Kong
Portugal	France	India	Laos
Greece	Austria	Philippines	Philippines
France	Greece	Greece	China (P.R.)
Poland	Portugal	Italy	Portugal

_____ Non-white Countries

Source: Canada, Manpower a. Immigration, 1974; and Immigration Statistics: diff. Years

Figure 1: Canada: Landed Immigrants by World Regions, 1968, 1980

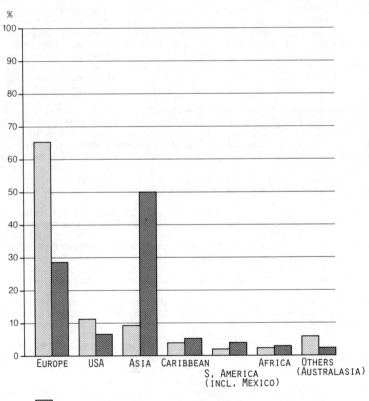

1968 TOTAL IMMIGRATION: 184,000
1980 TOTAL IMMIGRATION: 143,120

SOURCE: CANADA, EMPLOYMENT A. IMMIGRATION: IMMIGRATION STATISTICS

Similarities and Differences of Non-White Immigrants

In the third paragraph of this paper I want to illustrate some similarities and differences within the non-white immigrant group. In the setting of this conference this cannot be done systematically, and therefore I will only concentrate on selected groups and features.

Blacks in Canada were slaves until 1833, when all of them in the British Empire were officionally freed. Those Blacks who came during the Revolutionary War as free man considered themselves as Loyalists. Most of the about 60,000 Blacks in 1860 were fugitives from the United States of whom many returned later (POTTER a. HILL, 1966; WINKS, 1971). The Immigration Act of 1910 which incorporated all previous restrictions along racial lines strongly limited a movement of Blacks into Canada. - More recent immigrants from West India and some African regions particulary (e.g. Nigeria) are of a different cultural background and have (many of them are students) other intrests and goals than the earlier immigrants with which they share the same skin colour. - For the outsiders, the white majority, the visibility was dominant in the attendance and egalized these differences (DOYLEY, 1978).

Similar facts could be worked out for some Arab groups, but in the following I will concentrate on the Asians as one of the more prominent groups. It has attracted considerable attention, has caused social conflicts, and it illustrates best the remarkable chances in recent times.

It is a common assumption that Asians in Canada are a homogeneous group. The visible difference to white people is often typified by the phrase: "They all look alike" (KITANO, 1981:126). Moreover, this carelessness in regards to the physiognomy is transferred on to the cultures as well.

In reality, the term Asian-Canadians covers about 20 nationalities, each of them with their own history, traditions, economic and political changes in their homeland, cultures as expressed in their original languages or religions etc. Their social situation in Canada in the past and at present has been notably effected by conditions which my be described by an interdependent triangle of:

1. the political framework,
2. the ethnic background of the specific group and
3. attitudes of the host society.

The way how these factors interact and differentiat the Asians will be exemplified for the Chinese, Japanese, East Indians and Philippinos in the following discussion.

Military superiority of the British, as demonstrated during the Opium War, and the resulting unilateral treaties created favourable conditions for migration of Chinese to Canada at a time when a foreign labour force from China could be used under Canadian requirements. China suffered from economic, social and political troubles and emigration was not controlled by the government (SUNG, 1967: 10 f). Based on the dubious premise that Chinese were of an inferior race, the stereotype carried on that they were unassimilable. Moreover, since their wages were lower than those of their white counterparts, many whites believed that the Chinese threatened the economic status of the west coast labourers. Moulded by a debased civilization, the Chinese were accustomed to low pay and wretched living conditions and accepted their treatment in Canada apparently more patiently than other groups (WARD, 1978: 10, 17). Some pressure groups, such as the Workingman's Protective Association (1878) or the Anti-Chinese Union (1879) agitated against the Chinese and politicians used the popular sinophobia during the 1880s as an instrument to win municipal and provincial elections (LAWRIE, 1980). The Chinese were early excluded from enfranchisement. Other pressure groups, e.g. influential company-contractors and industrialists, were interested in cheap labourers. Possible solutions had to taken Sino-British treaties into consideration. These problems were handled between 1885 and 1903 by head taxes which were paid without strong protest by the weak government in China or the Chinese in B.C. In 1923 the federal government abandoned this policy and launched the infamous Chinese Exclusion act. - But many legislative attacks towards the Chinese in B.C. were declared void by the federal government.

In this respect Canada acted more diplomatic than the United States.

On the other hand, traditional customs in China required that a man working in a foreign country travel without his wife, and the return to his family and home-village was thus secured. Canadian immigration restrictions actually strengthened this custom in practice, thus lengthening the separation of husband and wife, and this in turn slowed down the build-up of a 'second generation' of Chinese in Canada. "Chinese lived abroad a lonely life of labor, dependent on kinsmen and compatriots for fellowship and on prostitutes and vice for outlet and recreation" (LYMAN, 1975: 292). These facts fitted the stereotype which the white people had built up.

As was the case with China, several treaties of friendship, trade and commerce agreements between Britain and Japan containing immigration clauses were signed since the middle of the 19th century (NAKAMURA 1975: 295). On the other hand, Japan restricted emigration effectively. But internal problems in connection with speedy industrialization and exploitation of peasants by landlords induced the government to allow more people to leave since 1886. Emigration was first directed to Hawaii, but later included the U.S. and Canada. At a time when head taxes on Chinese were first introduced, Japanese immigration began to rise. Almost immediately negative stereotyped attitudes toward the Chinese were applied toward the culturally almost totally different Japanese as well (ADACHI, 1978: 3).

At first, Chinese and Japanese had to accept very low wages. Because they worked hard and were content with a low standard of living, they were a threat to the white workingman in B.C. Some people distinguished the two Asian groups, e.g. the commissioners of the Royal Commission in 1902. In doing so they argued that the Japanese were even more aggressive competitors against the white workingman than the Chinese and therefore more dangerous (Canada: Report ... 1902: 337/9; 397). The racial stereotype and connected negative attitudes emerged quickly and through a tendency of self-perpetuation have stayed until today.

One of the sources of the undifferentiated anti-Oriental consensus was the ideal concept of a homogeneous white society in B.C. During the early 1890s provincial legislators tried to apply restrictive legislation aimed at the Chinese to the Japanese as well, e.g. an Alien Labor Act (1897) or the so-called Regulation Act (1898) which banned Chinese and Japanese employment on a wide variety of public projects conducted under the provincial government's charter. The federal government under Sir Wilfrid Laurier sympathized with the West coast opinion but under the pressure of Japanese officials and the British Colonial Secretary had to repeal B.C.'s acts. Japan, after its amazing victories over China and Russia, was a power that other nations respected and the British Government actively cultivated friendly relations which should not be threatened by the Canadians. Whereas Chinese entry taxes were increased from 100 Dollars in 1900 to 500 Dollars in 1903, Canada and Japan signed a gentleman's agreement limiting the number of Japanese immigrants, an agreement Japan interpreted freely in the future. B.C.'s whites continued to see the increasing number of Japanese as unassimilable, just like the Chinese, but the victory over Russia added a new dimension to the Japanese image. Japanese immigrants were viewed as aggressive and loyal to Japan and therefore seemingly disloyal to Canada. From 1905 to the eve of Pearl Habour this fear remained, and it has survived in the form of a Japanese economic threat until today.

But Japanese in fact settled early on a more permanent basis than the Chinese. Neither custom nor law stopped the Japanese from bringing their wives to Canada. By 1921 they had already brought along enough women to generate a substantial number of Canadian born Japanese and to establish a domestic life in the New World (PETERSEN, 1971: 44).

East Indian immigrants trickled into B.C. since about the turn of the century but in 1906 and 1907 4,700 arrived during a time, when migration of Chinese and Japanese reached one of its peaks. With a few exceptions, virtually all of the Indian immigrants were Sikhs. Racially as well as by their mode of dress and their lifestyle they were visually different from the Chinese and Japanese but, in the words of W.P. WARD (1978: 82) they "entered a community of heightened racial awareness, enduring racial cleavage, and recurring racial tension. Consequently white perceptions of East Indians were framed by the community's fixed assumptions about previous Asian immigrants". Protests against Indian immigration increased, but as British subjects they had a special claim to enter Canada. Moreover, these citizens of the Empire could argue that past military services entitled them to special considerations. In this case the 'Asian problem' was solved by a simple trick: only those immigrants were allowed to enter Canada who came from the country of birth or citizenship by a continuous journey and with tickets purchased in their home country (Report ... 1907-08, 1909: 100-101). Formally this regulation applied indiscriminately to all immigrants, but in reality it worked only against East Indians and against Japanese who lived in Hawaii. It virtually stopped further entrance of Indians to Canada.

The early immigration of Sikhs had been almost exclusively of adult males as was typical for many immigrants during that time. The Sikhs wanted to bring their wives to Canada as early as possible but the 'Continuous voyage' regulation stopped the immigration. Since 1919, however, a special Order-in-Council allowed Indians already in the country to bring their wives and children to Canada.

Immigration of Philippinos to Canada in any sizeable numbers did not begin until the 1950s. This was the result of special relations between the United States and the Philippines and the restrictive immigration policy of Canada against Asians. With the new immigration acts of 1962 and 1967 the number of immigrants from the Philippines increased very fast. Between 1968 and 1973 about 28,000, between 1975 and 1980 nearly 34,000 entered Canada from the Philippines (Canada, Employment and Immigration, 1974; Immigration Statistics).

Various push factors (not specifically dealt with in this paper), immigration regulations and attitudes of the host society thus have created a fairly complex differentiation among the seemingly homogeneous Asiatic group.

This is not the place to examine all changes in immigration regulations since World War II and their consequences for Asians today (cf. RICHMOND, 1978, BEAUJOT, 1982: 94-109, and LACROIX, this volume). Nevertheless, it seems instructive to look at the present structure of Asian immigrants as defined by immigration categories and intended occupations, the latter, however, is not identical with the entrance status (table 5).

Remarkable differences exist between the four selected groups. Moreover, it can be illustrated that the Chinese are a heterogeneous group since the same characteristics seldom apply to those from Taiwan, Hong Kong, or the People's Republic. - To give some examples: Most of the Indians are not destined to the labour force, whereas most Japanese are. About a quarter of the immigrants from the Philippines come as students, even more than from Hong Kong. The corresponding percentages for immigrants from Japan and from the People's Republic of China are relatively small. Within the labour force category the Indians show an exceptionally high rate of 'others' and most of them are unskilled and do not have defined occupations. The average of 20 per cent in service jobs is the result of relatively high percentages among the Chinese from the People's Republic and low percentages for those from Taiwan. A similar picture evolves with the farming category where the highest and lowest rates can be found in these two subgroups.

If the occupations from 'Enterpreneurs' down to 'Clerical', as listed in the table, are added up, it can be stated that those from Hong Kong, Taiwan, and Japan are dominant in these professions, those from the People's Republic of China and India dominate the residual occupations, and those from the Philippines are in between, relatively many in the processing etc. occupations.

It can be concluded that there are immigration regulations in Canada at present which influence the selection of individual immigrants and in turn the structure of immigrant groups. More often than is generally assumed Asian groups show differences which are caused at least to some extent by their history and specific circumstances in the individual homelands.

Table 5: Immigrants to Canada by Country of Last Permanent Residence and (Intended) Occupational Groups, 1980

	China, P.R.	Hong-Kong	Taiwan	China total	India	Japan	Philip-pinos
Total	4,936	6.309	827	12,072	8,483	737	6,051
Per Cent of Total							
Not Distined to							
the Labour Force	56.4	68.9	71.0	63.9	73.0	43.7	61.7
Spouse, Children	38.5	32.1	39.8	35.2	31.6	32.4	21.1
Students	8.8	21.8	12.5	15.9	11.1	8.1	25.5
Other	9.1	15.8	18.7	12.8	30.3	3.1	15.1
Destined to the Labour Force							
Total	2,153	1,964	240	4,357	2,287	415	2,319
Per Cent of Total	43,6	31.1	29.0	36.1	27.0	57.3	38.3
Per Cent of Dest. Labour Force	100	100	100	100	100	100	100
Entrepreneurs Managerial, Administrative	0.4	8.8	17.9	5.1	1.7	8.2	2.2
Science	3.9	16.2	17.1	10.1	4.4	19.8	4.7
Teaching	1.2	1.3	2.5	1.3	1.3	1.9	0.7
Medicine and Health	2.1	3.5	3.3	2.8	2.1	4.8	4.4
Performing Arts; Sport, Recreation	0.8	1.7	2.9	1.3	0.5	7.2	0.9
Clerical	5.1	19.0	17.9	12.0	4.9	9.9	15.3
Sales	3.9	5.3	10.4	4.9	1.6	5.3	3.4
Service	27.8	13.3	5.4	20.0	1.9	20.5	6.3
Farming	23.3	0.5	1.2	11.8	9.2	2.9	1.5
Processing, Machining, Fabricating, Repairing	14.9	16.2	6.7	15.0	7.0	13.7	29.7
Construction, Transp. Equipm, Operating	3.6	2.7	–	3.0	1.7	1.9	5.6
Material Handling	2.4	1.1	0.4	1.7	0.3	0.2	1.4
Others	10.8	14.4	14.2	12.6	63.4	3.6	23.7

Source: Canada, Employment and Immigration: 1980 Immigration Statistics, Table 13

If the age and sex structure is examined (Figure 2) it is useful to give comparative figures. Compared to the total population or the British, the non-white immigrants together show significant deviations in the 30-44 and the 65 plus age groups. But this is a statistical artefect which is composed of noticeable single structures. The age and sex pyramid of the Japanese demonstrate a symmetrical

Figure 2: Population by Selected Origins, Showing Age Groups and Sex, Canada 1981

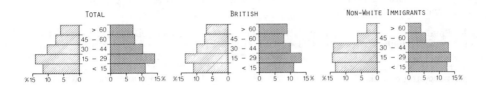

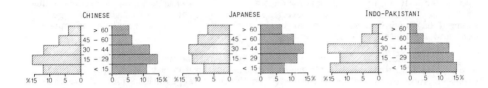

Table 6: Total Population, Charter Groups and Selected Non-White Immigrants, Canada and Regions (Provinces) 1981

Ethnic Origin[1]	Canada (Number)	Region/Provinces in Per Cent of Each Ethnic Group						
		B.C.	Alta.	Man.+ Sask.	Ont.	Queb.	Atl. Prov.	Territ.
Total	24,083,500	11.3	9.2	8.2	35.4	26.5	9.2	0.3
British	9,674,250	14.3	3.9	13.8	46.4	5.0	16.5	0.2
French	6,439,100	1.4	1.7	1.9	10.1	79.3	5.4	0.05
Non-White Immigrants[2]	1,057,700	22.0	11.5	5.8	45.3	12.4	3.0	0.1
Chinese	289,300	33.5	12.7	4.8	41.0	6.7	1.1	0.15
Japanese	41,000	39.1	12.8	3.7	40.7	3.4	0.2	0.1
Indo-Pakistani	196,400	28.6	10.9	3.7	47.9	7.2	1.7	0.1
Pacific Islanders	80,350	21.2	10.5	15.9	45.6	5.6	1.0	0.2

1) Single Origin
2) Other than European, Native, and Inuit Origin and see Footnote 3) Table 2

Source: Statistics Canada: 1981 Census (Cat. 92-911, Table 1)

picture with relatively old groups 45 and over occupying about 35%, whereas about 40% of the Indo-Pakistani and 51% of the Pacific Islanders are up to 25 years old and therefore characteristic young populations. The last two have extremes in the middle age group but with males dominating with the Indo-Pakistani and females with the Pacific Islanders. The Chinese, eventually possess a similar structure as the total but having still more males than females, little more in the middle age group and less in the oldest.

Finally, a glance at spatial distribution patterns reflects historical as well as more recent developments. First of all, non-white immigrants are more concentrated in two provinces than the total population or the British - the French in Quebec are the well-known exception. Early Asian immigrants still reside to an exceptionally high percentage in B.C. (33,5% and 39,1% compared to 11% of the total), although to a much lesser degree than before World War II when 54% of the Chinese and 95% of the Japanese lived there. - Most members of the non-white immigrant subgroups can be found in Ontario today, the younger immigrant groups to a higher degree than others. It might be surprising that the Pacific Islanders show to a certain degree lesser concentration. This pattern reflects the growing influence of the government on the initial settlement of immigrants which is more evident for independent and nominated than for sponsored immigrants.

Another table (7) illustrates the similarity among the non-white immigrant groups in comparison to differential settlement patterns of the majority. To a very high degree, all subgroups are urbanized and are living in large cities. This is the case for older as well as for younger Asian groups, though there are different reasons for it. Up to a point, the Japanese show a different pattern. 8.3% are rural and more of them than any other Asian group are living in smaller cities. This fact, as well as their concentration in B.C., can be considered to be an indication of Japanese resistance to discrimination since their early immigration. As much as possible they stayed in B.C. and in rural areas, and after their evacuation during 1942 to 1947 returned to this province. In contrast, the Chinese gave way to discrimination, spread earlier to other provinces and looked for protection in defensive Chinatowns. Corresponding settlements within North-American cities have been studied in more detail by VOGELSANG (1983, 1985, a; cf. also SHARPE, and WOLFF, this volume).

Table 7: Total Population, Charter Groups and Selected Non-White Immigrants, Showing Urban Size Groups, Rural Non-Farm and Rural Farm, Canada 1981

Ethnic Origin[1]	Canada Number	Urban Size Groups, Rural in Per Cent of each Ethnic Group				
		URBAN			RURAL	
		100,000 and over	10,000 -99,000	1,000 -9,999	Non-Farm	Farm
Total	24,083,500	51.8	14.6	9.3	20.0	4.3
British	9,674,250	47.5	16.6	10.5	21.2	4.3
French	6,439,100	47.7	15.5	10.1	23.3	3.4
Non-White Immigrants[2]	1,057,700	85.9	7.5	3.1	3.1	0.4
Chinese	289,300	89.2	6.0	2.8	1.8	0.2
Japanese	41,000	74.2	9.8	4.6	6.2	2.1
Indo-Pakistani	196,400	82.3	9.9	3.5	3.6	0.7
Pacific Islanders	80,350	91.3	4.8	1.8	1.9	0.1

1) Sigle Origin
2) Other than European, Native, and Inuit Origin and see Footnote 3) Table 2

Source: Statistics Canada: 1981 Census (Cat. 92-911, Table 1)

The aim of this paper has been to attract more attention to non-white immigrant groups in Canada, since research on questions and problems relating to these minorities has only just begun. The time has come to look at Canada as a multicultural and also as a multi-racial state including not only the first nations but also non-white immigrants.

References

Adachi, K., 1978: A History of the Japanese Canadians in B.C. 1877-1958. In: Daniels, R. (Ed.): Two Monographs of Japanese Canadians (repr.). New York.

Adair, D. a. J. Rosenstock, 1979: The Visible Minority in the Multicultural Society: A Study of Adolescent Attitudes. In: McLeod, K. A. (Ed.): Multiculturalism, Bilingualism and Canadian Institutions. Toronto, pp. 69-79.

Anderson, A. B. a. J. S. Frideres, 1981: Ethnicity in Canada. - Theoretical Perspectives. Scarborough, Ont.

Beaujot, R. a. K. McQuillan, 1982: Growth and Dualism: The Demographic Development of Canadian Society. Toronto.

Berry, J. W. a. R. Kalin a. D. M. Taylor, 1977: Multiculturalism and Ethnic Attitudes in Canada. Ottawa.

Buchignani, N., 1977: A Review of the Historical and Sociological Literature on East Indians in Canada. In: Canadian Ethnic Studies 9, 1, pp. 86-108.

Canada, Bureau of Statistics/Statistics Canada, 1886-1981: Canada Year Book. Ottawa.

— 1901-1981: Census of Canada. Ottawa.

— Manpower and Immigration, 1974: Immigration and Population Statistics. Ottawa.

— Citizenship and Immigration/Manpower and Immigration/Employment and Immigration, 1947-1981: Immigration Statistics. Ottawa.

— Manpower and Immigration and Information Canada (Ed.), 1974/75: Canadian Immigration and Population Study. Ottawa (4 Vol.s).

— Multiculturalism Directorate, 1979: The Canadian Family Tree. Ottawa.

— Report of the Dept. of Labour for the Fiscal Year 1907-1908, 1909: Ottawa.

Caron, F. A. (1958): The Chinese in Canada. In: Migration News 7, pp. 6-10.

Chan, A. B. (1981): Orientalism and Image Making: The Sojourner in Canadian History. In: Journal of Ethnic Studies 9, 3, pp. 37-46.

Chen-Tsu, W. (Ed.), 1972: Chink. A Documentary History of Anti-Chinese Predjudice in America. New York.

Clement, W. (1975): Access to the Canadian Corporate Elite. In: Canadian Review of Sociology and Anthropology 12,1, pp. 33-52.

Conroy, H. a. T. S. Miyakawa (Ed.), 1973: East Across the Pacific. Santa Barbara, Cal.

Dahlie, J. a. T. Fernando (Ed.), 1981: Ethnicity, Power and Politics in Canada. Toronto.

Daniels, R. (1977): The Japanese Experience in North America: An Essay in Comparative Racism. In: Canadian Ethnic Studies 9, 2, pp. 91 ff.

Davis, M. a. J. F. Krauter, 1978: Minority Canadians Ethnic Groups. Toronto.

Doyley, V. (Ed.), 1978: Black Presence in Multi-Ethnic Canada. Vancouver.

Driedger, L. (Ed.), 1978: The Canadian Ethnic Mosaik. A Quest for Identity. Toronto.

Elliot, J. L. (Ed.), 1983: Two Nations, Many Cultures. Ethnic Groups in Canada. Scarborough, Ont. (2. Ed.).

— (Ed.) 1971: Minority Canadians. 2 Vol., Vol. 1: Native Peoples. Vol. 2: Immigrant Groups. Scarborough, Ont.

Ferguson, T.A., 1975: A White Man's Country: an Exercise in Canadian Prejudice. Toronto.

Frances, H., 1973: Forgotten Canadians. The Blacks of Nova Scotia. Don Mills, Ont.

Ghosh, R. a. R. Kanungo, 1979: The Integration of South Asians in Canada. Montreal.

Hundley, N. (Ed.), 1976: The Asian Americans. Santa Barbara, Cal.

Iwaasa, D., 1972: Canadian Japanese in Southern Alberta. 1905-1945. Lethbridge, Can.

Jain, S., 1974: East Indians in Canada. The Hague.

Jensen, J. M., 1980: East Indians. In: Thernstrom, S. (Ed.): Harvard Encyclopedia of American Ethnic Groups. Cambridge, Mass., pp. 296-301.

Johnson, G. E., 1983: Chinese Canadians in the '70s: New Wine in New Bottles. In: Elliott, J. L. (Ed.): Two Nations, Many Cultures. 2. Vol. Scarborough, Ont., pp. 393-411.

Kalbach, W. E. a. W. McVey, 1979: The Cemographic Basis of Canadian Society. Toronto, 2. Vol.

Kallen, E., 1982: Ethnicity and Human Rights in Canada. Toronto.

Kitano, H. H. L., 1969: Japanese Americans: The Evolution of a Subculture. Englewood Cliffs, N. J.

— a. S. Sue (1973): The Model Minorities. In: Journ. of Social Issues 29, 2, pp. 1-9.

— 1980: Japanese. In: Thernstrom, S. (Ed.): Harvard Encyclopedia of American Ethnic Groups. Cambridge, Mass., pp. 561-571.

— 1981: Asian-Americans. The Chinese, Japanese, Koreans, Philipinos and Southeast Asiens. In: Gordon, M. (Ed.): America as Multicultural Society, pp. 125-138.

Lai, H. M., 1980: Chinese. In: Thernstrom, S. (Ed.): Harvard Encyclopedia of American Ethnic Groups. Cambridge, Mass., pp. 217-234.

Lawrie, B. R. (1980): Sinophobia in British Columbia. Anti-Chinese legislation, 1885-1923. In: Chinese Culture 21, pp. 79-89.

Lenz, K. (1978): Das regionale Problem Kanadas in seiner ethnischen und sprachlichen Ausprägung. In: Wirtschaftsgeogr. Studien. Österr. Ges. f. Wirtschaftsforschung 4, 2, S. 92-112.

Levine, G. N. a. D. M. Montero (1973): Socioeconomic Mobility Among Three Generations of Japanese Americans. In: Journal of Social Issues 29, 2, pp. 33-48.

—   a. C. Rhodes, 1981: The Japanese American Community. A Three-Generation Study. New York.

Li, P. S. (1979). A Historical Approach to Ethnic Stratification: The Case of the Chinese in Canada, 1858-1930. In: Canadian Review of Sociology and Anthropology 16, pp. 320-332.

Light, I. H., 1972: Ethnic Enterprise in America. Business and Welfare among Chinese, Japanese and Blacks. Berkeley, London.

Lyman, S. M., 1974: Chinese Americans. New York. (= Ethnic groups in comperative perspective, 7).

—   (1975): Contrasts in the Community Organization of Chinese and Japanese in North America. In: Yetman, N. R. a. C. H. Steele (Ed.): Majority and Minority. Boston, London, Sydney, pp. 285-296 (repr.).

Melendy, H. B., 1977: Asians in America: Filipinos, Koreans and East Indians. Boston.

—   1980: Filipinos. In: Thernstrom, S. (Ed.): Harvard Encyclopedia of American Ethnic Groups. Cambridge, Mass., pp. 354-362.

Montero, D., 1980: Japanese Americans. - Changing Patterns of Ethnic Affiliation over Three Generations. Boulder, Col.

Morton, J. W., 1974: In the Sea of Sterile Mountains. Vancouver.

Nakamura, M., 1975: The Japanese. In: Sheffe, N. (Ed.): Many Cultures - Many Heritages. Toronto etc., pp. 288-335.

Perrin, L., 1980: Coming to America. Immigrants from the Far East. New York.

Petersen, W., 1971: Japanese Americans: Oppression and Success. New York.

—   1978: Chinese Americans and Japanese Americans. In: Essays and Data on American Ethnic Groups. The Urban Institute. Washington D.C., pp. 65-106.

Pineo, P. C. (1977): The Social Standing of Ethnic and Racial Groupings. In: Canadian Review of Sociology and Anthropology 14, pp. 147-157.

Porter, J., 1965: The Vertical Mosaic. An Analysis of Social Class and Power in Canada. Toronto.

Potter, H. H. a. D. H. Hill, 1966: Negro Settlement in Canada, 1628-1965. Ottawa.

—   1982: Racism. Non whites in Canada. Toronto.

Report of the Royal Commission on Chinese Immigration, 1885: Ottawa.

Report of the Royal Commission on Chinese and Japanese Immigration, 1902: Ottawa.

Richmond, A. H. (1975/76): Black and Asian Immigrants in Britain and Canada: Some Comparisons. In: New Community (London) 4, 4, pp. 501-516.

- 1978: Canadian Immigration: Recent Developments and Future Prospects. In: Driedger, L. (Ed.): The Canadian Ethnic Mosaic. Toronto, pp. 105-123.

- a. W. E. Kalbach, 1980: Factors in the Adjustment of Immigrants and their Descendants. Ottawa.

Roy, P. E. (1979): White Canada Forever: Two Generations of Studies. In: Canadian Ethnic Studies, 11, 2, pp. 79-109.

- 1980: The Illusion of Toleration: White Oppinions of Asians in British Columbia, 1929-1937. In: Ujimoto/Hirabayashi (Ed.): Visible Minorities. Scarborough, pp. 81-91.

- (1980): British Columbias Fear of Asians, 1900-1950. In: Historie Soziale/Social History 13, pp. 161-172.

- 1981: Citizens Without Votes: East Asiens in British Columbia 1872-1947. In: Dahlie, J. a. R. Fernando (Ed.): Ethnicity, Power and Politics in Canada. Toronto, pp. 151-171.

Royal Commission on Bilingualism and Biculturalism, 1969: Report Book 4: The Cultural Contributions of the Other Ethnic Groups. Ottawa.

Simens, A. H. (1976): Ethnische Gruppen und der Gang der Besiedlung in Britisch-Columbien. In: Geogr. Rundschau 28, 2, S. 58-64.

Sung, B. L., 1967: Mountain of Gold. - The Chinese in America. New York.

Ujimoto, V. K. (1976): Contrasts in the Prewar and Postwar Japanese Community in British Columbia: Conflict and Change. In: Canadian Rev. of Sociol. and Anthrop. 13, 1, pp. 80-89.

- a. G. Hirabayashi (Ed.), 1980: Visible Minorities and Multiculturalism: Asians in Canada. Scarborough.

La Violette, F. E., 1948: The Canadian Japanese and World War II. Toronto.

Vogelsang, R. (1983): Chinatowns und die chinesische Minorität in Nordamerika. In: Erdkunde 37, pp. 212-226.

- (1984): Zur geographisch orientierten Untersuchung ethnischer Minoritäten, dargestellt am Beispiel der chinesischen Kanadier. In: Zeitschr. d. Gesellschaft f. Kanada-Studien 4, 1, S. 108-122.

- 1984: Probleme ethnischer Minoritäten in Kanada. In: Deutscher Geographentag: Tagungsbericht und wissenschaftliche Abhandlungen, Vol. 44, Stuttgart, S. 491-492.

- 1985 (a): Die chinesische und die japanische Minorität in den USA - Gegensätze und Gemeinsamkeiten in Geschichte und Gegenwart (i. Druck).

- 1985 (b): Ein Schema zur Untersuchung und Darstellung ethnischer Minoritäten - erläutert am Beispiel Kanadas. In: Geogr. Zeitschr. (i. Druck).

Ward, W. P., 1978: White Canada Forever. Popular Attitudes and Public Policy Toward Orientals in British Columbia. Montreal.

Winks, R., 1971: The Blacks in Canada. Montreal.

Wynne, R. E., 1978: Reaction to the Chinese in the Pacific Northwest and British Columbia, 1850-1910. New York.

Address of the author:
Prof. Dr. R. Vogelsang
Universität/Gesamthochschule
Warburger Straße 100
4790 Paderborn

Haitians and Anglophone West Indians in the Ethnic and Socio-Economic Structure of Montreal

Peter Wolff

Summary: Since the late sixties, when Canada changed her immigration policy the number of immigrants from Third World countries witnessed a sharp rise. Thus, Montreal, being Canada's second largest centre of immigration, saw the emergence of a number of sizeable visible minorities. The two most important groups amongst them, Haitians and Anglophone West Indians, are examined here, focussing on their size and residential distribution. Using results of the 1981 census, some important variables are compared in order to determine their socio-economic position. Despite the similarity of their racial or geographic origins the two groups have a strong tendency to concentrate in different sectors of the city. In doing so, they rather conform to the traditional ethno-linguistic division of Montreal established by the two charter groups. Although the two immigrant groups do not differ very much in terms of their educational background, the situation of the West Indians with respect to employment and income is disproportionately better. That raises the question whether the integration of an immigrant group into the anglophone sector of Montreal gives it an advantage when compared to an integration into the francophone sector.

Résumé: Avec le changement de la politique d'immigration du Canada à la fin des années soixantes le nombre d'immigrants en provenance du Tiers Monde a commencé à monter en flèche. C'est à partir de ce moment-là qu'à Montréal, le deuxième centre d'immigration du Canada, on observe l'émergence de plusieurs minorités visibles. Les Haitiens et les Antillais anglophones sont les deux groupes les plus importantes parmi eux. C'est leur nombre et leur distribution qui vont être analysés. En plus, on comparera quelques variables essentielles pour déterminer leur situation socio-économique. Malgré la similarité de leurs origines raciale et géographique, les deux groupes ont une forte tendance à se concentrer dans des secteurs différents de la ville. Ils se conforment plutôt à la division ethno-linguistique traditionnelle par les deux 'charter groups'. Bien que les deux groupes ne se distinguent pas beaucoup quant à leurs niveaux d'éducation, la situation des Antillais anglophones se revèle nettement meilleur en ce qui concerne leur situation d'emploi et la taille de leurs revenues. Donc la question se pose si l'intégration d'un groupe d'immigrants au secteur anglophone de la ville de Montréal lui donne un avantage par rapport à l'intégration au secteur francophone.

Zusammenfassung: Seit der Änderung der kanadischen Einwanderungspolitik Ende der sechziger Jahre nahm der Zustrom von Einwanderern aus Ländern der Dritten Welt stark zu. In Montreal, Kanadas zweitwichtigstem Einwandererzentrum, entwickelten sich damit auch mehrere sichtbare Minderheiten. Die beiden größten unter diesen Gruppen sind die Haitianer und anglophonen Westinder, deren Zahl und räumliche Verteilung untersucht wird. Daneben werden anhand von Zensusergebnissen von 1981 einige zentrale Größen zur Bestimmung der sozio-ökonomischen Lage beider Gruppen verglichen. Trotz der Ähnlichkeit in ihrer rassischen und geographischen Herkunft konzentrieren sich beide Gruppen weitgehend in verschiedenen Teilen der Stadt. Sie passen sich damit der durch die 'charter groups' vorgegebenen ethno-linguistischen Aufteilung der Stadt an. Obwohl sich beide in ihrem Bildungsstand nicht allzusehr unterscheiden, ist doch die Beschäftigungs- und Einkommenssituation der Westinder deutlich besser. Damit erhebt sich die Frage, ob die Integrierung einer Einwanderergruppe in den englischsprachigen Teil von Montreal ihr bessere Chancen eröffnet, als wenn sie sich dem französischsprachigen Teil der Stadt zuwendete.

◊◊◊◊◊◊◊◊◊◊◊◊◊◊

Montreal, being Canada's second largest centre of immigration, receives about 80% of all the immigrants coming to Quebec and almost all of the members of visible minorities. The largest one amongst Montreal's visible minorities is the Black community with its two most important segments, the Haitians and the Anglophone West Indians (1). What makes a comparison of these two groups so particularly interesting in Montreal is of course not only their size but also the unique ethnic framework in which they are placed here. Although these two groups have some important characteristics in common, or at least are quite similar (visibility, geographic region of origin, size, level of schooling) they integrate into the two ethnic sectors of Montreal according to their linguistic affinities. This eliminates to a large degree the language factor as a major barrier to communication and integration which often blurs the comparison of different groups. Thus, by comparing these two groups we should gain not only a better understanding of their position in Montreal but also have an indication about possible effects of the different environments of the city into which they integrate. Therefore, I would like to concentrate my attention on some important socio-economic variables in order to compare the position of the two groups with each other and with respect to some of the other major ethnic or immigrant groups. This should also help to fill part of the gap in the knowledge about both groups because the almost complete lack of hard data about their social and economic situation, particularly so for the West Indians, has been deplored by many authors (e.g. WARNER, 1983: 1, 18).

To speak about the size and distribution of the two groups brings me to the first problem which is statistics. The two major official sources available are immigration statistics and the census. The latter one will be the main source for this paper. - In Canadian census statistics a number of variables are used to describe the ethnic background of the population: ethnic origin, mother tongue, home language and place of birth. Obviously, the two language variables are of little use for the analysis of our two groups because you couldn't distinguish them from the charter groups. As far as the Black population is concerned, the ethnic origin categories in the Canadian census has always been a very unreliable one. The term 'Negro', in use since 1871, is a racial notion which lumps together people of very heterogenous backgrounds, like Canadian Blacks living in the country since generations, Americans from the U.S., West Indians of various origins and African Blacks of even more diverse origins. From its beginning, this concept was notorious for its undercoverage of the population aimed at (GREAVES, 1930: 44-52; WINKS, 1971: 488/9). The 1981 census brought a refinement of this concept. The category 'Negro' was broken down into Canadian Black, African Black and Other Black not elsewhere specified. The category 'West Indian', introduced in 1971, was further differentiated into Caribbean and Haitian in 1981. But still, the coverage of the potential population by the ethnic origin concept remained highly incomplete. This can be shown in table 1 where place of birth data are crosstabulated with ethnic origin.

The self-labeling of more than 40% of the population (15 years and over) that was born in Haiti as French and of almost 60% of those born in countries of the Anglophone West Indies as of British origin is a very interesting fact by itself. It may well suggest an interpretation that this behaviour represents an effort of these people 'to become invisible'.

In the following sections, the statistical material will be either straightforward place of birth data or a combination of ethnic origin (SR/MR) and two categories we asked Statistics Canada to create for the VW project. Those two categories included people born in Haiti (Anglophone West Indies) who were not of Haitian (Caribbean) ethnic origin (2). This still leaves us with the problem that an important part of the offspring of both groups that was born in Canada is not included in these categories. However, as the majority of these populations are recent immigrants this proportion should not be overly high. The percentage of people born in Canada in the ethnic origin groups may serve as a first approximation of the importance of that segment. For the Haitians (SR) it is 20.4% and for the Caribbean group it is 25.7% (BAILLARGEON/STE-MARIE, 1984: 48). Considering immigration since 1981 and natural increase, we can put the Haitian population of Quebec quite safely at about 40,000 of which about 95% live in Montreal (TARDIEU, 1979: 108/9; BENJAMIN, 1983: 13-19). As for the Anglophone West Indians, the much higher discrepancy between immigration statistics and census results for the 1971-81 period indicates a much higher rate of emigration for members of that group (see table 2). Given the

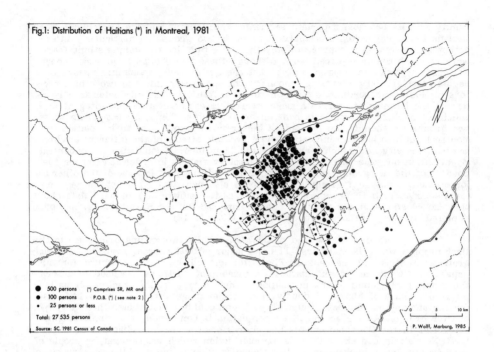

Fig.1: Distribution of Haitians (*) in Montreal, 1981

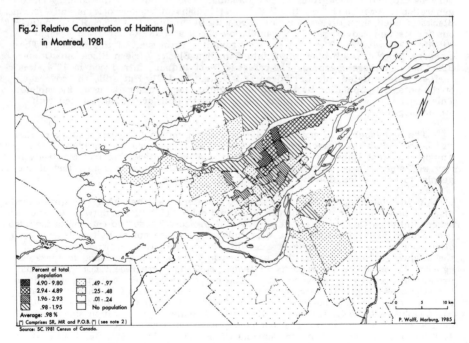

Fig.2: Relative Concentration of Haitians (*) in Montreal, 1981

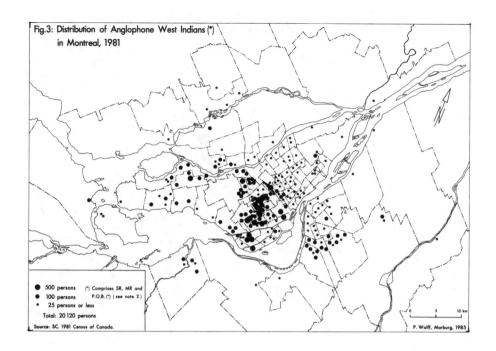

Fig.3: Distribution of Anglophone West Indians (*) in Montreal, 1981

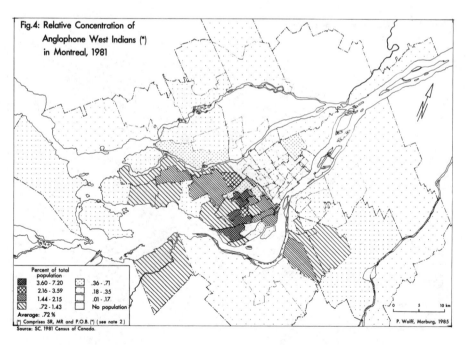

Fig.4: Relative Concentration of Anglophone West Indians (*) in Montreal, 1981

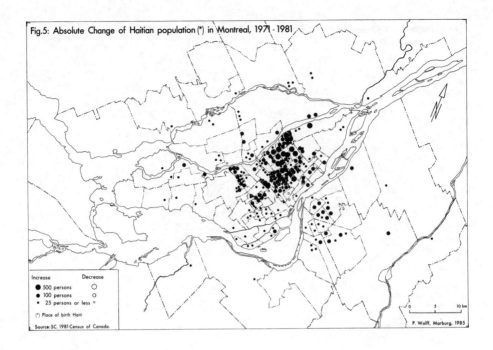

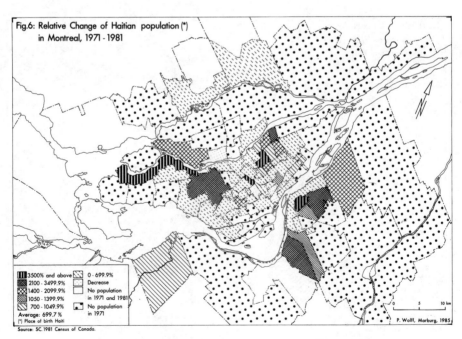

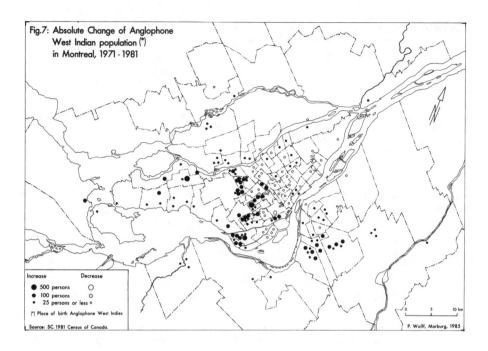

Fig.7: Absolute Change of Anglophone West Indian population (*) in Montreal, 1971 - 1981

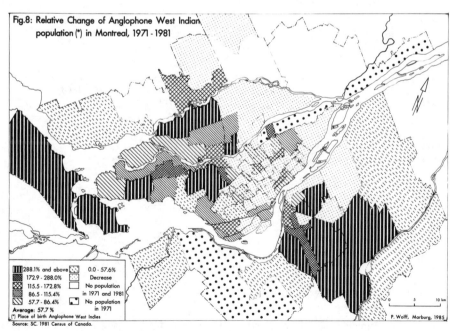

Fig.8: Relative Change of Anglophone West Indian population (*) in Montreal, 1971 - 1981

Table 1: Caribbean population, 15 years and over, by place of birth and ethnic origin, Montreal (C.M.A.), 1981 (2)

Place of Birth Anglophone West Indies	N	%	Place of Birth Haiti	N	%
Total Place of Birth	16,915	100.00	Total Place of Birth	21,475	100.00
SR British	9,840	58.20	SR Haitian	9,650	44.90
SR Caribbean	3,305	19.50	SR French	8,815	41.00
SR Indo-Pakistani	855	5.10	SR Native Peoples	300	1.40
SR Chinese	355	2.10	SR British	125	.50
SR Native Peoples	240	1.40	SR Caribbean	110	.50
SR French	200	1.20	All Other SR	1,325	6.20
SR Portuguese	95	.60	Total SR	20,325	94.60
SR Jewish	45	.30	MR Native Peoples	30	.10
All Other SR	1,525	9.00	All Other MR	1,105	5.20
Total SR	16,460	97.30	Total MR	1,155	5.40
MR Native Peoples	25	.10			
All Other MR	395	2.30			
Total MR	455	2.70			

Source: Statistics Canada. 1981 Census of Canada. Special tabulations.

Table 2: Retention rates for the major Caribbean immigrant groups, Quebec, 1971-81

Place of birth / Period of immigration	Immigration Statistics	1981 Census	Retention Rate (%)
Haiti			
1971-75	12,863	11,015	85.6
1976-81*	9,813	10,900	111.1 (3)
1971-81*	22,676	21,910	96.6
Jamaika			
1971-75	2,829	1,990	70.3
1976-81*	1.843	1.465	79.5
1971-81*	4.672	3.455	73.9
Trinidad & Tobago			
1971-75	2,916	1,705	58.5
1976-81*	1,027	805	78.5
Guyana			
1971-81*	2,374	1,255	52.9
Barbados			
1971-81*	1,509	1,110	73.6

* Includes the first five months of 1981, only.

Source: Ministère des Communautés Culturelles et de l'Immigration, Statistiques d'immigration, 1971-81. Statistics Canada. 1981 Census of Canada. Special tabulations.

rather modest immigration figures for this group since the late seventies, it is actually not unlikely that the increase due to immigration has been offset entirely by emigration out of the province. Therefore, the number of Anglophone West Indians is probably around 26,000 in the province of which more than live 98% in Montreal today.

When you add to this the old line Canadian Blacks of Montreal, the Black immigrants from Nova Scotia, Ontario and the U.S. and a small community of anglophone African Blacks you will find the total population of the anglophone Black community of Montreal somewhere in the same order of size than the Haitian group, that is around 40,000. This is dramatically less than figures advanced by community leaders over the past years. In its "Profile of the Black Community of Quebec" presented to the Ministery of Multiculturalism in 1982, the Black Community Council of Quebec (1982: 6/7) put the Black community of the province at 120,000 people of which 90,000 were supposed to the anglophones.

A look at the distribution of both groups clearly shows the concentration of the Haitian population in the predominantly French east of Montreal whereas the Anglophone West Indians are concentrated in the west which is earmarked by a high concentration of English speaking people. Thus, the similarity of their geographic and racial origins do not constitute a basis for a shared residential pattern. It is much rather the linguistic affinity with the two charter groups which shape the residential pattern of the immigrant groups. Côte-des-Neiges, the west of Ville St-Laurent with the adjoining neighborhood of Ahuntsic and Park Extension are the only areas where you find above average concentrations of both groups.

The two highest concentrations of Haitians (P.O.B.) reported in a census tract are 11.4 and 8.7% of the total population. For the West Indians the respective figures are 11.0 and 10.4%. Even when you consider the omission of the children born in Canada, the highest concentrations of both groups will at best reach 20% in a very few census tracts. This confirms common knowledge in Montreal that there are several concentrations of Blacks but nowhere is there something like a ghetto situation.

Quite different patterns are revealed by the four maps that show the relative and absolute change in population of the two immigrant groups between 1971 and 1981. First of all, the Anglophone West Indians show a much slower growth rate than the 700% increase of the Haitians. This is not a surprise because the great majority of the Haitians came during the seventies whereas about half of the West Indians had immigrated already before 1971. The Haitians show a remarkable trend towards the notheast of the city with major increases in Montréal-Nord, St-Michel and St-Léonard. Being a recent immigrant group, this movement has placed them unusually far from the downtown area. As this shift has continued after 1981, the concentration of Haitians now even extends into Rivière-des-Prairies. Only the beginning of this trend is visible on map 3. The residential pattern thus created resembles more that of the Italian than that of the French community. This is in fact confirmed by a segregation index of .38 between Haitians (SR + MR + P.O.B.*) and Italians (SR) as compared to .51 between Haitians and French (SR) (4).

The Anglophone West Indians show lower than average growth in their already established neighborhoods in the west of central Montreal (Côte-des-Neiges, Notre-Dame-des-Grâces, Park Extension). The greater increase in Little Burgundy appears to be the result of the return of former residents who had been driven out of this neighborhood by a massive demolition and urban redevelopment programme of the city. Almost all the other central and eastern parts of the city that had already low concentrations in 1971 showed even absolute losses. The areas of the highest absolute and relative increases are all peripheral with two major directions discernable. One goes north into Ville St-Laurent, Ahuntsic, Chomedey (Laval) and branches off to the northern municipalities of the West Island (Dollard-des-Ormeaux, Pierrefonds). The other move goes via LaSalle to the South Shore, with the greatest concentrations in Brossard and lesser ones in St-Hubert and Greenfield Park. All these areas are quite well-to-do with average or above average incomes. Obviously, this is a typically North American suburbanization process of an immigrant group whose economic situation has improved. It can be observed in every major growth area of the anglophone sector of Montreal. The movement of the Haitian population is much more en bloc and concentrated in areas with incomes below the average. For a recent immigrant group, the speed at which they have moved from a central to a peripheral location is without parallel in Montreal. This may suggest that something else than a regular suburbanization process is at work here.

For the examination of the socio-economic position of the two groups, I would like to start with a look at their level of schooling. It is one of the most important factors for the admission of immigrants and is paramount for their chances on the job market; though one may have certain reservations about the immediate comparability of this information for immigrants that come from practically all over the world. - One of the effects of the system of admission, introduced in Canada in the late sixties, was that immigrants from Third World countries have a high level of schooling, at least at an early stage of immigration. Once that group has reached a certain size, the sponsorship of family members increases the proportion of those who don't have to pass the filter of the point system and thereby lower the average educational level of that group.

Table 3: Level of schooling of Haitians and Anglophone West Indians immigrating to Quebec (workers only), Quebec, 1968-82

Level of Schooling	P.O.B. Haiti		P.O.B. Anglophone West Indies	
	N	%	N	%
0 years	218	1.3	47	.4
1- 7 years	2,838	16.3	2,097	18.0
8-11 years	7,226	41.4	6,015	51.6
12-13 years	3,988	22.9	2,260	19.4
14+ years	3,166	18.2	1,235	10.6
Total	17,436	100.0	11,654	100.0

Source: Compiled from immigration statistics of the Ministère des Communautés Culturelles et de l'Immigration.

From its beginning in the mid-sixties until about 1972, immigration from Haiti was characterized by a very high level of schooling which only in 1974 fell below the average of all the immigrants. Then the arrival of large numbers of unskilled and semi-skilled workers had changed from the white-collar immigration of doctors, teachers, technicians, nurses etc. of the early phase to a predominantly blue-collar immigration. This phenomenon of the two waves is well-known and has been described repeatedly (ROUSSEAU, 1978: 30; DEJEAN, 1978: 78-82).

On the West Indian side the situation is somewhat more difficult to assess because immigration statistics for Quebec only go back to 1968. As immigration from the Anglophone West Indies started already several years earlier, we don't know exactly what the educational level of these immigrants was. However, it is very likely that it was at least as high and probably higher than after 1968 when the average level of schooling was somewhat below the average of all newly arriving immigrants. From 1968 to 1975 it continued to decline gradually but persistently. After 1976, the educational level started to rise again and is now comparable to the situation in 1968.

In general immigration from Haiti is characterized by a comparatively high representation at the two extremes of the educational spectrum which means that people with a very high (14 years and more) and a very low level of schooling are overrepresented when compared to the West Indians.

This picture derived from immigration statistics is only partly confirmed by the results of the 1981 census (see table 4), even though the categories used do not exactly match those in the immigration statistics. They clearly show a higher concentration of Haitians in the two lower groups and a lower concentration in the intermediate group of grade 7 to 13. At the upper end of the scale, the category 'With some university or college' is equally important in both groups. The proportion of people who have completed university is higher in the West Indian community. Thus, the average level of schooling is lower in the Haitian community, mainly because of the proportion of people with a very low educational level.

Table 4: Population with 15 years and over by level of schooling for various ethnic groups, Montreal (C.M.A.), 1981

Level of Schooling		Total Population	Haitian (a)	Angl. W.I. (a)	French	British	Jewish
Total	N	2,237,550	21,080	16,815	1,467,255	265,815	74,490
Schooling	%	100	100	100	100	100	100
No Schooling	N	43,985	1,085	275	19,730	2,265	1,910
or Kindergart.	%	2.0	5.2	1.6	1.3	.9	2.6
Less Than	N	247,185	1,975	700	156,535	14,140	3,560
Grade 7	%	11.0	9.4	4.2	10.7	5.3	4.8
Grades	N	1,103,640	8,525	8,025	774,800	131,455	31,535
7 to 13	%	49.3	40.4	47.7	52.8	49.5	42.3
Some Univ.	N	618,620	7,740	6,135	397,105	83,135	21,165
or College	%	27.6	36.7	36.5	27.1	31.3	28.4
University	N	224,120	1,770	1,690	119,080	34,820	16,320
Completion	%	10.0	8.4	10.1	8.1	13.1	21.9

(a) Comprises SR and P.O.B.* (see note 2).
Special tabulations.

Source: Statistics Canada. 1981 Census of Canada. Special tabulations.

Two major causes may account for the discrepancy between immigration statistics and the 1981 census. Firstly, the aforementioned lack of data for the period prior to 1968 has most likely resulted in an underestimation of the educational level of the West Indian immigrants in table 3. Secondly, an unknown but probably considerable number of immigrants have upgraded their education in Canada.
Compared to the total population of Montreal, the position of the Anglophone West Indians is better than average. The Haitians have a slightly better position in the highly educated groups and do somewhat worse at the lower end of the spectrum. In total, their average educational level is somewhat below the standard of the total population of Montreal. When we now examine the distribution by industry division of the employed labour force the most striking difference between the two groups is the much higher proportion of Haitians working in the manufacturing industries (49%) which is almost twice as much as the 27.5% of the West Indians. Of all the major immigrant groups the Haitians have the highest proportion working in manufacturing. Comparatively lower is their representation in the service sector.

In a very interesting analysis of the sectoral distribution of the immigrant labour force in Quebec in 1971 PROULX (1979) classified the major industry divisions into weak and strong ones. This was done on the basis of wages and working hours. Unfortunately, the classification of the non-manufacturing sectors was altered so drastically for the 1981 census that it was only possible to use his categorization in 1981 for the manufacturing industries.

Table 5: Immigrant population 15 years and over, showing employed and active labour force by industry division, Montreal (C.M.A.), 1981

Industry Division		Place of Birth Total	Haiti	A.W.I.	USA	UK	France	Italy	Greece
Total	N	254,405	12,370	11,985	8,880	16,670	17,025	53,680	16,895
	%	100	100	100	100	100	100	100	100
Primary Sector (a)		.3	.2	.3	.2	.5	.5	.5	.1
Manufacturing		33.7	49.0	27.5	19.8	29.0	21.2	43.2	35.0
Construction		4.5	.7	1.5	2.9	2.3	3.3	11.8	3.3
Transportation, communication etc.		6.7	6.3	7.1	7.1	11.3	8.2	5.5	4.6
Trade		15.7	9.3	13.2	15.1	11.9	15.6	15.5	12.2
Finance, insurance and real estate		4.8	1.3	5.3	17.5	7.8	5.1	4.0	2.7
Education and related		6.7	4.5	5.7	8.7	10.3	13.0	2.9	1.8
Health and welfare services		7.3	12.6	21.6	2.7	8.1	6.9	3.1	4.2
Religious Institut.		.4	.1	.3	2.3	.7	.3	.4	.1
Amusement and recreation services		.8	.6	1.0	6.6	1.1	1.3	.4	.6
Services to business management		4.7	1.8	3.3	6.6	9.4	6.2	2.0	1.7
Personal services		2.2	3.3	4.0	1.4	.9	2.6	2.6	2.3
Accomodation and food services		7.5	5.7	6.0	4.8	2.2	7.8	4.4	26.3
Miscellaneous serv.		2.6	1.7	2.3	2.6	2.5	3.4	2.0	4.7
Public administration and defence		1.9	2.1	2.7	1.9	1.7	4.6	2.0	1.4

(a) Includes agriculture, forestry, fishing and trapping and mining.

Source: Statistics Canada. 1981 Census of Canada. Special tabulations.

Table 6: Immigrant population 15 years and over, showing employed and active labour force of selected immigrant groups, by strong and weak manufacturing industries, Montreal (C.M:A.), 1981

Weak Manufacturing Industries	Place of Birth Total Immigr.	Haiti	A.W.I.	USA	UK	France	Italy	Greece	Portug.
Wood	.2	.4	.1	.3	.0	.3	.2	.2	.7
Furniture	1.5	2.9	1.0	.5	.4	.9	2.5	1.5	2.9
Textile	1.6	3.4	1.4	1.3	.9	.4	2.4	.6	2.6
Knitting	1.8	18.7	5.4	.5	.4	.2	2.3	3.1	3.8
Clothing	10.2	5.2	1.0	1.9	1.0	1.9	18.3	20.4	18.7
Leather	.9	1.3	.8	.2	.1	.3	1.1	1.4	1.3
Miscellaneous	1.4	2.2	1.4	1.0	1.1	1.1	1.1	.9	.7
Total	17.6	34.1	10.1	5.7	3.9	5.9	27.9	28.1	31.7

The list of the seven weak branches of the manufacturing industries shows that about 70% of all the Haitians employed in manufacturing or 34% of the total labour force work in these weak sectors which is twice as much as the average of all the immigrants. Only the position of the Mediterranean groups is similar. Apparently, this is a consequence of the importance of the textile industries which employs about one quarter of the total labour force of these immigrant groups. The textile industry is the classic manufacturing branch in Montreal that has always employed large numbers of unskilled or semi-skilled immigrants, mostly women, and whose working conditions are known to be among the toughest of the entire labour market. - The percentage of the total labour force of the West Indians working in those weak branches is even much below the average of all the immigrants. This is not only the result of a far lower employment in the textile industries but also in each of the four remaining branches.

This trend of a better job situation of the West Indians holds as well when the situation for the six strong branches is compared. There, the proportion of the West Indians equals the average of all the immigrants whereas the percentage of the Haitians is lower despite their much higher proportion of people working in manufacturing.

Both Haitians and Anglophone West Indians are highly overrepresented in the health sector. More than 21% of the West Indian labour force or three times the average of all the immigrant groups are employed in that sector. This is an exact reflection of the great demand for medical personnel that had been created by the rapid expansion of the health services in Quebec during the sixties and early seventies. - Other sectors in which the Anglophone West Indians are overrepresented are personal services, amusement and recreation services and finance, insurance and real estate. Sectors of very low concentrations are public administration and defence and the construction industry. Besides the health services, the only other non-manufacturing sectors where Haitians are overrepresented are personal services and public administration and defence. Particularly low concentrations occur in the construction industry, in finance, insurance and real estate and in trade.

The general picture to be gained from this comparison is that Haitians are systematically overrepresented in weak sectors of the economy, particularly so in manufacturing. The West Indians, however, show a pattern which is much closer to the average of all the immigrant groups although they are overrepresented in the service sector.

An examination of the unemployment rates reveals the same pattern as found for the occupational distribution of the two groups, maybe, in an even more accentuated manner. With 20.6% of its active population unemployed the rate of the Haitian group (P.O.B.) is 237% that of the rate of the total population of Montreal and 268% that of its immigrant population. This is far more than the rate of any other immigrant group in Montreal. Compared with this, the 8.3% of the Anglophone West Indians is a surprisingly low figure. It places them about halfway between the averages of 7.7% for all the immigrants and 8.7% for the total population of the metropolitan area.

To a large degree the unemployment situation is determined by the period of immigration. Because of the recency of the Haitian immigration the average is pushed up further than for groups which arrived earlier. But even when you go back period by period, you will find an improvement but never does the rate get near the average of all the immigrants of that period. This finding is quite surprising when you consider the favourable educational and professional characteristics of the aforementioned first wave of Haitian immigrants. However, with unemployment rates of 9.1% (immigration period 1956-64) and 14.4% (immigration period 1965-71) the job situation of that group is not as good as generally assumed.

The breakdown of the unemployment situation by sex and age is shown in table 7. It reveals considerably higher rates for women than for men in every immigrant group. Another pattern which is very consistent for all groups is that the youngest segment of the labour force has to bear by far the highest unemployment rates. It is only in this age group (15-24 years) that the situation for the West Indians is considerably worse than the average of all the immigrants. Compared to this, the situation of the Haitians can only be described as desolate. In contrast to many other groups, for the Haitians unemployment is not only a problem of the youngest age group but it affects the entire community.

Table 7: Immigrant population 15 years and over, showing place of birth, age group, sex and unemployment rate, Montreal (C.M.A.), 1981

		Place of Birth								
		Total Imm.	Haiti	A.W.I.	UK	France	Germany	Italy	Greece	Vietnam
All Ages (a)	%	7.7	20.6	8.7	5.0	6.5	4.4	6.0	9.1	14.3
Female		10.6	23.9	10.0	6.5	8.9	8.2	9.2	14.3	16.3
Male		5.9	17.3	7.1	4.1	5.0	2.1	4.2	6.4	13.0
Ages 15-24		16.7	36.2	20.1	15.6	15.7	16.7	10.4	15.8	20.5
Female		17.2	38.8	22.7	13.7	14.0	17.5	9.9	20.2	21.3
Male		16.2	32.7	18.7	16.9	16.9	13.2	10.4	13.0	20.0
Ages 25-44		7.5	17.8	7.0	4.9	5.5	3.8	5.8	8.9	11.2
Female		10.2	20.8	8.4	7.0	8.5	8.6	8.2	14.4	14.9
Male		5.7	15.1	5.4	3.5	3.6	.7	4.5	5.8	8.5
Ages 45-64		5.6	19.1	6.0	3.1	5.4	4.0	5.5	8.4	17.3
Female		8.7	23.5	7.1	4.4	7.5	6.0	10.7	12.9	15.3
Male		3.9	15.2	4.8	2.3	4.3	2.5	3.2	6.1	18.9

(a) Includes the unemployed and active population of 65 years and over which is not significant, numerically.

Source: Statistics Canada. 1981 Census of Canada. Special tabulations.

After what has been said about the occupational distribution and the unemployment situation of our two groups it will not be surprising that the Haitians are placed at the lower end of the income distribution whereas the situation of the Anglophone West Indians is more favourable though it doesn't quite reach the level one might have expected from their occupational position and from their level of schooling.

When we further differentiate the income situation by the period of immigration we find a quite steady decrease in the relative position of both groups with respect to the average of all the immigrants as we go from early to recent immigrants. There seems as well to be some contradiction to the findings about the unemployment situation because Haitian immigrants who came during the fifties and sixties have a much higher income than the Anglophone West Indians who came during the same periods. A possible explanation may be a more polarized distribution of their population in terms of schooling (which couldn't show in our rather broad categories) which would be reflected in an income distribution and an unemployment situation as mentioned above.

Before I will end, let me just get back to the relation of the level of schooling and the income distribution. A breakdown of these variables by age shows that Anglophone West Indians have a higher income than Haitians at every level of schooling. This even holds for almost every age group.

This supports very strongly the findings from our examination of the other variables which brought us to the conclusion that despite a level of schooling of the Haitian population which was only somewhat below the average of the Montreal population and that of the West Indians their occupational and income situation is disproportionately worse.

Table 8: Immigrant population 15 years and over, showing average employment income by immigration period, Quebec, 1981

Place of Birth	Total Periods	Immigration Period Before 1946	1946–1960	1961–1970	1971–1981
All Immigrants $	14,643	17,487	16,575	14,984	11,380
%	100	100	100	100	100
United Kingdom	135.5	101.1	127.9	129.9	163.5
Germany	122.1	92.1	111.4	106.1	157.5
France	115.1	97.5	109.1	112.5	129.9
India	112.9	400.3	155.9	140.0	112.2
USA	107.0	97.2	93.9	95.4	135.5
Italy	90.9	112.3	86.2	80.6	95.0
China	84.3	41.7	95.3	88.0	76.2
Anglophone W.I.	83.7	142.2	101.1	89.2	79.2
Vietnam	75.8	-	153.4	157.0	83.4
Hongkong	74.8	-	115.4	83.6	80.6
Haiti	69.9	115.5	129.2	109.8	74.7

Source Statistics Canada. 1981 Census of Canada. Special tabulations.

Table 9: Population 15 years and over showing average total income (with income only) by place of birth*(2) by age by level of schooling, Montreal (C.M.A.), 1981

	Total Schooling	No School. or Kind.	Less Th. Grade 7	Grades 7-13	Some Univ. or College	Univ. Complet.
P.O.B.* Haiti (2)						
All Ages $	9,024	5,793	6,170	7,791	8,772	19,891
Ages 15-24	4,153	-	3,888	4,258	4,097	-
Ages 25-39	9,329	6,762	6,920	8,708	9,475	13,919
Ages 40-54	12,308	4,541	6,831	8,943	10,667	28,935
Ages 55-64	8,691	6,705	4,542	6,323	9,588	24,156
Ages 65 and over	7,932	4,604	3,687	4,717	-	35,679
P.O.B.* Anglophone West Indies (2)						
All Ages	12,021	8,054	8,517	9,700	11,811	23,732
Ages 15-24	5,356	-	-	5,586	5,321	3,288
Ages 25-39	11,658	12,339	10,536	9,992	11,975	16,817
Ages 40-54	15,945	6,287	9,926	11,762	15,280	31,402
Ages 55-64	13,334	-	-	10,827	11,898	31,068
Ages 65 and over	8,571	4,103	6,226	6,979	10,787	29,978

Source: Statistics Canada. 1981 Census of Canada. Special tabulations.

From that it seems to be obvious that the Haitians to a large extent have not been able to gain access to jobs that match their level of schooling. Instead they have been forced into low paying jobs particularly in manufacturing where they fill unskilled or semi-skilled positions. As for the Anglophone West Indians, they have found access to the more stable and better remunerated jobs in the service sector which gives them a comparatively better income position.

After this admittedly short overview, it is difficult to say whether it is better job opportunities in the anglophone sector of Montreal or a lesser degree of racial discrimination which is responsible for this discrepancy in the well-being of the two groups. As there is evidence for both arguments a combination of these factors appears to be likely.

Footnotes

1. For reasons of convenience, Anglophone West Indians (Indies) and West Indians (Indies) are used synonymously throughout this paper.
2. For the 1981 census, Statistics Canada for the first time offered the possibility to trace one's ancestry to more than one ethnic group. The resulting categories of 'single response/origin' and 'multiple response/origin' will be abbreviated SR and MR for the rest of this paper. The two categories which were created specifically for this project (Place of birth Haiti/Anglophone West Indies, ethnic origin not Haitian/Caribbean) will be abbreviated P.O.B.*, in contrast to P.O.B. which will mark a place of birth including all people born in that specific country.
3. Very interesting is the retention rate of 111.1% of the Haitian group. Most likely, it is the result of an enumeration of illegal immigrants. In 1981, a program for the regularization of illegal Haitian immigrants was started in Quebec which gave legal status to about 4,000 people by the end of 1982. Even though the program had barely begun on June 3, 1981, an apparently significant number of this group had been enumerated. Given the distrust and fear that prevail in such a situation, this result is remarkable. It can serve as an indication for the quality of the census.
4. The segregation indices were calculated on the basis of the 93 areas depicted on figure 1 to 8.

References

Baillargeon, Mireille/Gisèle Ste-Marie, 1984: Quelques caractéristiques ethno-culturelles de la population du Québec. Cahier No 2. Ministère des Communautés Culturelles et de l'Immigration. Diréction de la recherche. Montréal. Mimeographed.

Bayne, Clarence, n.d.: A sampling technique for the location of a very rare population. Montreal. Mimeographed.

Benjamin, Claire, 1983: Considérations sur l'évolution démographique de la population haitienne au Québec. Ministère des Communautés Culturelles et de l'Immigration. Diréction de la recherche. Montréal. Mimeographed.

Black Community Council of Quebec (BCCQ), 1982: Profile of the Black Community in Quebec. Report presented to the Ministery of Multiculturalism. Montreal.

Canada. House of Commons, 1984: Equality Now! Report of the Special Committee on Visible Minorities in Canadian Society. Chairman: Bob Daudlin, M.P. Ottawa.

Déjean, Paul, 1978: Les Haitiens au Québec. Montréal.

— 1981: La migration haitienne au Canada jusqu'en 1981. Communication à l'Instituto de Investigaciones Sociales de la Universidad Nacional Autónoma de México, 29 octobre. Mimeographed.

Giroux, Marie, 1984: La MEQ est a réviser la problématique du multiculturalisme a l'école. In: Le Devoir, August 24.

Greaves, Ida C., 1930: The Negro in Canada. National Problems of Canada. McGill University Economic Studies, No. 16. Orillia.

Groupe de Travail sur la Communauté Noire, 1978: Final Report on the Aspirations and Expectations of the Quebec Black Community with Regard to Education. Rapport presenté au Comité d'études sur les Affaires interconfessionelles et interculturelles du Conseil supérieur de l'Education. Montréal.

Proulx, Normand, 1979: La répartition sectorielle des travailleurs immigrants au Québec. Ministère de l'Immigration. Direction de la recherche. Études et documents, no 8. Montréal.

Rousseau, Philippe, 1978: Les Haitiens. Projet ETA. Recherches sur les groupes ethniques de la région métropolitaine de Montréal. Montréal. Mimeographed.

Tardieu, Camille, 1979: L'immigration haitienne au Québec de 1968 a 1977. Thèse de M.A. Université de Montréal, Département de Démographie. Montréal.

Warner, Louise, 1983. Profil de la communauté noire anglophone. Gouvernement du Québec. C.I.P.A.C.C. Comité pour l'Implantation du plan d'action à l'intention des communautés culturelles. Montréal.

Winks, Robin, 1971: The Blacks in Canada. A History. McGill-Queen's University Press - Yale University Press, New Haven and London.

Wolfe, Mitchell, 1973: The Black Community in Montreal. Cambridge, Mass., Harvard College. Mimeographed.

Address of the author:
Peter Wolff
Sebertsweg 2
D-6497 Steinau 3
Federal Republic of Germany